NEW JERSEY

NEW JERSEY

A History of the Garden State

EDITED BY

MAXINE N. LURIE AND RICHARD VEIT

RUTGERS UNIVERSITY PRESS
New Brunswick, New Jersey, and London

Second printing, 2012

Library of Congress Cataloging-in-Publication Data
New Jersey : a history of the Garden State / edited by Maxine N. Lurie and
Richard Veit.
    p.   cm.
Includes bibliographical references and index.
ISBN 978-0-8135-5409-9 (hardcover : alk. paper)
ISBN 978-0-8135-5410-5 (pbk. : alk. paper)
    1. New Jersey—History.   I. Lurie, Maxine, N., 1940–   II. Veit, Richard Francis,
1968–
F134.N49   2012
974.9—dc23   2012005542

A British Cataloging-in-Publication record for this book is available from the
British Library.

Rutgers University Press recieved a grant for this publication from the
New Jersey Historical Commission, an agency of the New Jersey Department
of State. In addition, this publication was made possible, in part, by a grant
from the New Jersey Council for the Humanities, a state partner of the National
Endowment for the Humanities. Other generous donors include Seton Hall
University, the Society for the Colonial Wars of New Jersey, the General Society
of Colonial Wars, Thomas Higgins, Barry Kramer, Robert E. Mortensen, and
Anne Moreau Thomas.

Visit our website: http://rutgerspress.rutgers.edu

Manufactured in the United States of America

CONTENTS

PREFACE

The two of us proposed this volume for several reasons. First, as teachers of New Jersey history, we perceived the need for a one-volume book on the state that could be used in our courses as well as in those taught by others in community colleges and universities. Second, it was clear that much had been written and that the interests of scholars had changed in the more than thirty-five years since the last brief history of the state appeared. Obviously, it was time for an update and a synthesis of the new material. Third, the citizens of New Jersey need an overview of the state's past so that they can understand where it has been and, perhaps, better conceive where it ought to go in the future. At the same time, another purpose has been to place the history of the state in a national context for New Jersey residents and those outside the state. Writing in 1978, John Cunningham described New Jersey as "A Mirror on America." We concur that through the study of our state we can better understand the history of the nation.

Of course, scholars have been studying and writing about New Jersey since Samuel Smith published *The History of the Colony of Nova Caesaria* in 1765. The nineteenth century saw the publication of several classic histories, such as Thomas Gordon's *A Gazetteer of the State of New Jersey* (1834) and William Barber and Henry Howe's *Historical Collections of the State of New Jersey* (1845 and later editions), with its large number of lithographs. Later in the nineteenth century substantial historical and genealogical volumes treated particular counties. It was also during this period that the New Jersey Historical Society began publishing its journal, originally titled *Proceedings* and much later simply *New Jersey History*. Many of the nineteenth-century histories were focused on famous individuals, the American Revolution, church and congregational histories, and, later, the Civil War experiences and service of New Jerseyans. Charles Conrad Abbott began writing about Native Americans, but many topics, most notably social history, women's history, and the history of minority groups, particularly African Americans, were largely overlooked. Authors were often journalists, jurists, and religious figures, as history was just beginning to professionalize as a field.

In the early twentieth century, several important regional and statewide histories were published, including *New Jersey: A Guide to Its Present and Past* (Federal Writers Project, 1932), A. M. Heston, *South Jersey* (1924), and Francis Bazley Lee, *New Jersey as a Colony and as a State* (1902). In the mid-twentieth century Richard P. McCormick and John Cunningham brought to the fore a more sophisticated and, in the case of Cunningham, popular view of New Jersey's history. Harold Wilson compiled an exceptional historical outline of the state (1950); in the 1960s, the state's Tercentenary Commission published numerous volumes reflecting the true diversity of New Jersey's history; and in 1975 Peter O. Wacker added his *Land and People*, now a classic work, to the literature on the state.

Among recent publications there are the collections of essays edited by Barbara Mitnick, *New Jersey and the American Revolution* (2005), Marc Mappen, *There Is More to New Jersey than the Sopranos* (2009), and Maxine N. Lurie, *New Jersey Anthology* (2010); Howard Green's collection of documents, *Words That Make New Jersey* (2006); and two reference works, the *Encyclopedia of New Jersey* (2004) and *Mapping New Jersey* (2009). But the most recent one-volume history of the state, Thomas Fleming's *New Jersey: A Bicentennial History*, was published in 1977, and the general works by John Cunningham, *You, New Jersey, and the World* (1998) and *New Jersey: A Mirror on America* (last updated in 2006), are aimed at a K–12 audience.

As editors of this volume, our intention is to provide a work that, in the tradition of Fleming and Cunningham, covers the scope of New Jersey's past from the earliest inhabitants to the twenty-first century, while incorporating recent scholarship, issues such as gender, race, and class, and social and cultural history as well as politics. We have been lucky in obtaining the help of excellent scholars who have contributed essays about their areas of expertise. The chapters that follow reflect their hard work, for which we thank them, and their endnotes document relevant recent scholarship on the state and the nation. We hope that this book is seen, as it is meant to be, as part of a long line of distinguished work on the state's history. We hope that it will catch the interest of our students and the public, and inspire other scholars to add to the body of work on the Garden State.

Maxine N. Lurie
Richard Veit
NOVEMBER 2011

ACKNOWLEDGMENTS

We would like to thank the following people for their generous assistance with this book.

For help with images: Gregory D. Lattanzi, New Jersey State Museum; William Sauts Bock; Joanne Nestor, New Jersey State Archives; John Beekman, Jersey City Free Public Library; Ruth Janson, Brooklyn Museum; Liz Kurtulik, Art Resource; Mark Renovitch, Franklin D. Roosevelt Presidential Library and Museum; Joseph Myers, Coopers Ferry Partnership; Michael Siegel, Rutgers University Cartography Lab; Joseph Seneca and Richard Hughes, Edward J. Bloustein School of Planning and Public Policy, Rutgers University; and Dr. Joseph Salvatore, Naval Air Station Wildwood Aviation Museum.

The Rutgers University Special Collections and University Archives for help with research, images, and much more: David Kuzma, Fernanda Perrone, Ronald Becker, Bonita Craft Grant, Thomas Frusciano, Michael Joseph, Al King, Erica Gorder, and others on the staff.

For assistance with grant applications: Robert Apgar, Sara Cureton, and Niquole Primiani.

And of course all those at Rutgers University Press who have helped, including Marlie Wasserman, Allyson Fields, Anne Hegeman, and Marilyn Campbell, as well as Gretchen Oberfranc for her work in copyediting this volume.

Funding for this book has been provided by the New Jersey Council for the Humanities, the New Jersey Historical Commission, Seton Hall University, the Society for the Colonial Wars of New Jersey, the General Society of Colonial Wars, Thomas Higgins, Barry Kramer, Robert E. Mortensen, and Anne Moreau Thomas.

ABBREVIATIONS

ASNJ	*Bulletin of the Archaeological Society of New Jersey*
JAH	*Journal of American History*
NJH	*New Jersey History*
PMH&B	*Pennsylvania Magazine of History and Biography*
Proc. NJHS	*Proceedings of the New Jersey Historical Society*
W&MQ	*William and Mary Quarterly*

NEW JERSEY

INTRODUCTION

New Perspectives on New Jersey History

MARC MAPPEN

The written historical study of New Jersey began in 1765 when Samuel Smith, a merchant and political figure in south Jersey, published a book with the lengthy title *The History of the Colony of Nova-Caesaria, or New-Jersey, Containing an Account of Its First Settlement, Progressive Improvements, the Original and Present Constitution, and Other Events, to the Year 1721, with Some Particulars Since; and a Short View of Its Present State*. In his preface, Smith explained that his book was "designed for the publick" and undertaken "with hopes of service to the province." It was said of Smith's book in the next century that it was "the fruit of careful research, and a clear and agreeable style."[1]

The book you hold in your hands now (or perhaps have downloaded from the Internet to a digital reader) is a direct descendant of Smith's *History* and benefits from the same attention to sound research and accessible writing. Like its predecessor two and a half centuries ago, it is a one-volume work aimed at a general audience. And thanks to advances in such history-related fields as archaeology, archival research, ethnography, sociology, and economics, it ranges far beyond the realms of knowledge that Smith could draw upon. Indeed, Smith focused almost exclusively on white, male members of the upper class, with some passing references to Native Americans. In contrast, this book shares historians' perspectives on the men and women, immigrants and natives, workers, soldiers, politicians, and farmers who shaped New Jersey's past. The cast of characters is broad. They include Puritan divines, Native American leaders, political and social reformers, military heroes such as the seemingly omnipresent George Washington, inventors and scientists from Edison to Einstein, and unsung heroes such as James Still, the "Black Doctor of the Pines," and his abolitionist brother William Still. This volume incorporates a significant amount of scholarly research on New Jersey that has appeared recently and is truly a new history of New Jersey.

Smith observed that there was a need for his book; a century had passed since New Jersey was established, and very little had appeared in print about the colony's progress. In the same way, *New Jersey: A History of the Garden State* responds to a considerable need. With the exception of pre–high school textbooks, no general history of the state has appeared since 1977. In general, historical publications about New Jersey have been lacking. In 1964, the 300th anniversary of the establishment of the colony of New Jersey, the distinguished Rutgers University historian Richard P. McCormick observed that the citizens of the state "have lacked the strong sense of pride in their commonwealth that characterized the inhabitants of many other states."[2] In 1997, the report of the Task Force on New Jersey History, a body established by the state legislature, calculated that of the original thirteen states, New Jersey ranked last in the number of history publications relative to state population. This book represents a determined effort to correct that lamentable situation.

Samuel Smith saw the history of New Jersey as connected to the saga of the thirteen English colonies. In the same way, *New Jersey: A History of the Garden State* illuminates how events in New Jersey relate to the larger history of the American nation. In fact, historians have long appreciated the ways in which local history can inform broader historical knowledge. Thus, the topics covered in this book correspond to the major eras and issues in American history.

The volume begins with a brief examination of New Jersey's earliest inhabitants, the Lenape or Delaware Indians and their precursors. New Jersey's Native American heritage stretches back some 13,000 years and is represented by thousands of archaeological sites from High Point to Cape May. In the nineteenth century New Jersey was at the center of a great archaeological controversy regarding when the first human inhabitants arrived in the New World. The debate continues today, although the sites examined are much farther afield. Archaeology and the changing patterns of Native American lives during the period before written history are only part of the story of our state's rich Native American heritage. Indeed, New Jersey still has vibrant Native American communities that maintain an abiding interest in their past and aspirations for their future.

In the second chapter Maxine N. Lurie examines colonial New Jersey in all its complexity. Dutch, Swedes, Scots, and Englishmen all cast a covetous eye on New Jersey. One result was a colony that, much like the modern state of New Jersey, was noteworthy for its diversity. African Americans were also present from the earliest days, and their story is treated here. Lurie carefully guides readers through the contentious proprietary period, when New Jersey was divided into two colonies, and highlights its relevance to the state's later history. Land riots, colonial wars, and massive religious revivals played major roles in shaping colonial New Jersey.

Of course, no period of New Jersey history is better known than the Revolutionary era. John Fea takes readers through the Revolution and on to the post-Revolutionary period under the Articles of Confederation. He describes an agricultural colony transformed into the crossroads of the Revolution, the scene of major battles, the site of army encampments, and the home of a populace deeply divided in its loyalties. Fea provides a comprehensive view of the war's causes, course, and effects.

Graham Hodges, who takes up where Fea leaves off, examines the characteristics of New Jersey's population in the early Republic before turning his attention to the politics of the period and the role of New Jerseyans, such as William Paterson, in the national issues of the era. Slavery and race and their local manifestations are discussed, with an emphasis on New Jersey's fitful steps toward emancipation and on the role of the American Colonization Society. Although New Jersey's economy remained largely agricultural during this period, the relatively modest industrial centers of Paterson and Newark foreshadowed growth to come.

During the first half of the nineteenth century, New Jersey inventors and entrepreneurs sought to improve the state's transportation infrastructure. As Michael Birkner notes, this was also a time when agricultural production increased, industries expanded, and cities grew. The power of the Great Falls of the Passaic was harnessed for industrial purposes, and craft traditions began to be supplanted by industrial processes. Jacksonian Democrats and Whigs espoused very different views regarding the role and nature of government, and New Jerseyans were active participants in these debates. Although slavery persisted, it was clearly declining, and a free African American middle class was slowly developing. The economic transformations of the nineteenth century led to a variety of responses, from utopian communities to the development of mental hospitals, improved prison conditions, and wider access to education.

Larry Greene looks at New Jersey during the Civil War era. Although some scholars have characterized New Jersey as a border state with southern leanings, Greene sees a conservative state that robustly supported the war effort while questioning some of the policies of the federal government. He carefully situates these issues within the larger debate about slavery that was central to the Civil War. Finally, he looks at how political debates about emancipation and the status of African Americans continued into the Reconstruction period.

During the late nineteenth century, inventors such as Thomas Edison, new immigrants, and the second industrial revolution transformed cities like Newark, Elizabeth, Trenton, Paterson, and Jersey City. Paul Israel points out that, even as the growth of industry was facilitated by liberal incorporation laws, agriculture remained important. At the same time, resorts at the Jersey Shore provided an escape for the masses and spurred the growth of communities such as Asbury Park. It was an exciting, heady time; however, the benefits and the costs of industrialization were unevenly distributed.

Brian Greenberg illuminates the responses to the issues that plagued late nineteenth-century America. Progressives developed settlement houses and other educational institutions to counterbalance the gritty factory work that consumed so many new immigrants. Some individuals opted for radical fixes, such as the idealists who founded the Helicon Hall Colony, Free Acres, and other communities. Other reformers worked within the political system for suffrage, temperance, and improved working conditions. City bosses such as Frank Hague organized new immigrants into potent political blocks. Generally speaking, New Jersey welcomed corporations, but some politicians, most notably Woodrow Wilson, attempted to rein in corporate oligarchs. It was also during this period that, at long last, New Jersey's women gained the right to vote.

Kurt Piehler examines the period of the Great Depression and World War II. State and federal responses to the Depression took a variety forms, including back-to-work projects and the establishment of new institutions of higher learning (what are now Union County College and Monmouth University). The local rise of the Ku Klux Klan and the German American Bund were sad episodes in the prewar period. Finally, New Jersey's industries and people played significant roles in World War II. African Americans in the armed forces fought a dual battle against fascism abroad and racism at home, a struggle that affected postwar life in the state.

The postwar period saw the rise of the suburbs. Howard Gillette shows how the interstate highway network, shopping malls, suburbanization, and the decline of cities shaped a new New Jersey. Deep-seated racial inequities led to unrest in the streets of many New Jersey cities, as well as political change, including the landmark Mount Laurel decision. The legacy of this period is very much alive in twenty-first-century New Jersey

Samuel Smith modestly admitted that New Jersey was "not in many respects to be compared to colonies of greater extent and growth," meaning that it did not match the influence and power of New York, Massachusetts, Pennsylvania, and Virginia.[3] And in fact, New Jerseyans have long been resigned to living in a state that is the butt of jokes. More recently, television programs such as *The Sopranos, Jersey Shore,* and *Real Jersey Housewives* have given viewers around the world an unflattering portrait of our state.

New Jersey deserves better. The state and its citizens have contributed significantly to the development of the American nation through pioneering roles in industry, science, and technology. The state's admirable 1947 Constitution provided an innovative model for governance by banning discrimination and establishing a strong governor, an exemplary judicial system, and an integrated law enforcement structure. Academic historians do not normally regard the enhancement of local pride as a primary goal of their research. But if that kind of pride is encouraged by this book, it is a worthy by-product.

NOTES

1. Samuel Smith, *The History of the Colony of Nova Caesaria . . .* , 2nd ed. (Trenton: Wm. S. Sharp, stereotyper and publisher, 1877), v, xiii.
2. Richard P. McCormick, *New Jersey from Colony to State, 1609–1789* (Princeton: Van Nostrand, 1964), ix.
3. Smith, *History*, xii.

1 · SETTING THE STAGE

Archaeology and the Delaware Indians, a 12,000-Year Odyssey

RICHARD VEIT

Individuals interested in understanding the history of New Jersey's native populations are dependent upon a handful of sources. These include archaeological evidence, historic and ethnographic sources, oral traditions, and comparative evidence derived from other societies that lived in similar environments or employed similar technology. The archaeological remains from New Jersey's early Native American inhabitants can provide material evidence about where they lived, the tools they made, the dwellings they inhabited, what they ate, their physical appearance, and, to some extent, their cultural practices and religious beliefs. However, it is an imperfect record. Much of the material culture that our state's ancient inhabitants once produced—wooden objects, textiles, foodstuffs, and dwellings—has been lost to natural processes of decay. Human remains from the earliest periods of native occupation 12,000 years ago are quite rare. Furthermore, many of the sites Native Americans once found attractive for habitation now lie buried beneath urban centers or have been erased by suburban sprawl. Others have been inundated by rising tides.[1] Nevertheless, extraordinary archaeological discoveries have been made and continue to be made, revealing tantalizing glimpses of the first New Jerseyans.[2]

Written records from the colonial period also provide a lens through which to view the lives of the state's first inhabitants. We catch glimpses of New Jersey's seventeenth- and eighteenth-century Native Americans in diaries, in promotional tracts encouraging settlers to come to New Jersey, in merchants' ledgers, and even in newspaper advertisements and court records. Hundreds of deeds documenting land transactions between Native Americans and early settlers survive in government archives, historical societies, and private collections. They provide a significant body of information not just about the processes through which Native Americans sold their land, but also about who participated in these sales, what payments were made to natives for the land, which parcels of land were sold and when, and even how the social organization of native groups changed. But such documents provide information only about the most recent periods of Native American history, and very rarely do they reflect the perspectives of Native Americans themselves.[3]

Oral histories are also important sources of information. Unlike the incomplete but extensive archaeological record and the documents written by early white settlers, oral histories and traditions reflect Native American perspectives about their origins, history, religion, and beliefs. Undoubtedly, information was lost as Native American populations were displaced from their lands, saw their cultural beliefs challenged, and suffered population decline because of disease and conflict. Nevertheless, oral traditions maintained by modern Native Americans provide us with an insider's view that is otherwise missing.

In an effort to fill in the gaps in our understanding of how ancient Native Americans lived, some archaeologists have also experimented with re-creating the technologies once employed by Native Americans, from pinching and coiling clay to make pots, to weaving textiles, knapping flint, and hollowing out logs for canoes.[4] Experimental archaeology can tell us how people may have lived in the past. By tacking back and forth between these various sources, archaeologists, historians, and other scholars are working to expand our understanding of the distant past.

THE LENAPE OR DELAWARE INDIANS

New Jersey's Native American inhabitants are generally referred to as Lenape or Delaware Indians. "Lenape," sometimes "Renappi" or "Lenni Lenape," means "ordinary, real, or original people."[5] "Delaware," derived from the name of a seventeenth-century English governor of Virginia, Lord De La Warr, is a term used to refer to the culturally similar bands that occupied the Delaware Valley and adjacent areas at the beginning of the seventeenth century. Most Native Americans were described by others, and thought of themselves, as members of particular bands, of which there were several dozen, for example, Raritans, Sanhickans, Navesink. The name "Delaware" was initially limited to natives living in the middle Delaware Valley, but over time came to be applied to all of the region's native people. The Delaware spoke related Eastern Algonquian languages known to scholars as Munsee and Unami. The Native Americans of northern New Jersey and adjacent portions of Pennsylvania and New York spoke Munsee; those of southern New Jersey and adjacent parts of Pennsylvania and Delaware were Unami speakers. The Munsee were also a distinct group of people who inhabited both northern New Jersey and adjacent parts of New York State, including Staten Island, Manhattan, the lower Hudson Valley, and western Long Island.[6] An added complication is the use of such terms as "Jersies" and "River Indians" for New Jersey's Native Americans during the colonial period.[7] In this chapter, for simplicity's sake, the terms "Delaware" and "Lenape" will be used to refer to New Jersey's Native American inhabitants during the colonial period and afterward. Earlier groups, whose names have been lost to time, will be referred to as Native Americans.[8]

A BRIEF HISTORY OF ARCHAEOLOGICAL EXPLORATION IN NEW JERSEY

During the nineteenth century, American archaeologists began to explore the material traces of the continent's first inhabitants. They focused on determining who the people were, when they had arrived in the Americas, and where they came from. Early researchers sought parallels with Old World societies. Some of the first archaeological investigations into the prehistory of New Jersey centered on the most visible of Native American sites, the great shell mounds at Keyport and Tuckerton.[9] However, the most intriguing question addressed by these early scholars was the issue of when the first human inhabitants arrived in the Americas. The development of New Jersey archaeology was intimately linked to this controversy. In the 1870s, pioneering archaeologist Charles Conrad Abbott, a physician and naturalist

William Sauts Netawuxme Bock, *The Lenape Creation Myth*, 1989. (Reproduced with permission of the artist.)

from Hamilton Township, began collecting artifacts on his farm.[10] The crude artifacts that Abbott found in local gravel deposits strongly resembled Paleolithic hand axes being found in France and England.[11] Abbott concluded that truly ancient human beings had once lived in the Delaware Valley, followed by a culture he termed the Argillite Culture and, more recently, by the historic Lenape.[12] Ultimately, Abbott's ideas were shown to be incorrect, but his belief in a long human prehistory for North America has been vindicated.

The Lenape had their own understanding of their distant history. They believed that Kishelemukong, their creator, brought a giant turtle up from beneath the ocean at a time when the entire world was covered with water. As it grew, soil accumulated around it until it became North America. A tree sprouted from the turtle's back, and a shoot from the tree created the first man. The tree then bent over and touched the earth, and from a second sprout woman was created. From these two individuals all later people sprang.

A second tale, known as the *Walum Olum* or "painted record" and based on a collection of now lost wooden tablets, purports to recount the ancient history of the Delaware people from their origin across the Bering Strait to their recent arrival in the Delaware Valley. Careful scholarship by David Oestreicher has shown that this tale is probably the work of a nineteenth-century antiquarian, Constantine Rafinesque, to fit then current beliefs about Native Americans.[13]

The first systematic efforts to record New Jersey's archaeological heritage occurred in the early twentieth century when the State Geological Survey organized a series of archaeological surveys.[14] Many of the sites recorded then have since been lost to development. During the Great Depression an intensive program of archaeological fieldwork began to take shape as part of the effort to hire the unemployed. Under Dorothy Cross, New Jersey's first state archaeologist, local prehistoric archaeology became a major focus of the New Jersey State Museum. Between 1936 and 1942, the Indian Site Survey of the Works Project Administration carried out twenty-two major excavations, surveyed 1,700 sites, developed several exhibitions, inventoried hundreds of private collections, and cataloged thousands of artifacts.[15]

A new era of archaeological research began after World War II. In 1966 a landmark piece of legislation, the National Historic Preservation Act, required archaeological studies of properties threatened by federal activities. In a short period of time, archaeology, once a weekend avocation and the domain of a handful of college professors and museum professionals, was transformed into an industry known as "cultural resource management." One result has been a greatly enriched understanding of New Jersey's prehistoric past as hundreds of projects are carried out in areas never before examined. Nevertheless, questions remain, such as when the first humans arrived in New Jersey, how they supported themselves, when domestic crops were introduced by Native Americans, the extent of ancient trade networks, the influence of environment on culture, pre-contact settlement patterns, the impact of European settlement on Native American societies, and issues of social and religious organization. Increasingly, new scientific techniques are allowing archaeologists to answer old questions and ask ones previously deemed irresolvable.[16]

NEW JERSEY'S PREHISTORIC PAST

Based on a century and a half of research, New Jersey's archaeologists have constructed a chronology of cultures for the prehistoric people who once inhabited the state. The ancient cultures of the region are generally divided into three broad temporal divisions: Paleo-Indian, Archaic, and Woodland. Other scholars prefer more descriptive terms and call these periods the Hunter Gatherer I, Hunter Gatherer II, Intensive Gathering–Formative Cultural Period, and the Village Life Cultural Period.[17] Today, it appears that the divisions between these periods may be somewhat more arbitrary than long believed; moreover, recent discoveries are pointing to the presence of a pre–Paleo-Indian occupation in parts of the Americas.

The Paleo-Indian period lasted from approximately 12,000 to 8,000 years before the present. This period began at the end of the Pleistocene epoch, the last major Ice Age. Much of the continental shelf was dry land that was inhabited. Glaciers extended as far south as Metuchen and Perth Amboy before they began to retreat. The enormous amounts of water incorporated in these glaciers exposed land in what today is the region of the Bering Strait, which would have allowed humans and animals to cross from northeastern Asia to what is now Alaska. Archaeologists are also exploring the possibility that migrating populations may have worked their way down the Pacific coast using watercraft, and some scholars see similarities between the stone tools of the Paleo-Indians and those produced in France during a period archaeologists call the Solutrean, between 22,000 and 17,000 years ago. Still, linguistic evidence points to an Asian origin for the first Americans and seems to indicate several successive waves of immigrants rather than a single group.

The first settlers to reach what is now New Jersey probably did so during or before the Paleo-Indian period. Archaeological sites from this period are quite rare. The environment would have been cool and moist, tundra-like in some areas.[18] As the glaciers melted and sea levels rose, the continental shelf was submerged. River systems realigned, land freed from the weight of the glaciers rose, and large lakes and marshes were left behind. Today, landscape features created by the glaciers, from car-sized boulders called erratics, to marshes such as the Meadowlands and the Great Swamp, and even small ponds and waterholes, periglacial features, survive to remind us of the glaciers' massive power. Large animals, collectively called megafauna, such as the American mammoth and mastodon, as well as elk-moose, ground sloth, and caribou, were present in the state during this period. Although there is considerable evidence for Native Americans hunting these large mammals in the western United States, the evidence is more equivocal in the east. During the Paleo-Indian period, human populations seem to have been small and very mobile. Groups of thirty to fifty people may have exploited hunting ranges of roughly two thousand square miles.[19]

Paleo-Indians often crafted fluted projectile points from high-quality chert or flint, which came from the Hudson Valley and eastern Pennsylvania and perhaps elsewhere. Paleo-Indian artifacts have been found across nearly the entire state, but only a handful of Paleo-Indian sites have been carefully excavated. These include the Zierdt site in Sussex County, the Plenge site in Warren County, Turkey Swamp in Monmouth County, and the Sam's Club site in Ocean County. There are also Paleo-Indian sites nearby on Staten Island and in other parts of New York State and Pennsylvania. Excavations at the Plenge site in the early 1970s recovered a large collection of artifacts, including numerous fluted projectile points, scrapers, gravers, and other tools.[20] It appears that Paleo-Indian hunters revisited this site periodically as they traveled between the Delaware River and the lake regions of northern New Jersey and New York. The Turkey Swamp site near Freehold is a late Paleo-Indian site; the distinctive fluted points of earlier sites are not present, but knives, scrapers, and basally thinned triangular projectile points have been found there.[21] The Sam's Club site, located near the headwaters of Kettle Creek in Ocean County, seems to have been a place where Paleo-Indians briefly stopped and fixed tools. By 10,000 years ago, the megafauna had become extinct, the environment was changing, and new cultural adaptations were occurring.

The next cultural period in the history of eastern North America is termed the Archaic (8000 B.C.–1000 B.C.). William Ritchie, who coined the term, defined the period as "an early level of culture based on hunting, fishing, and gathering of wild vegetable foods, and lacking pottery, the smoking pipe, and agriculture."[22] Archaeologists typically divide the Archaic into three sub-periods (Early, Middle, and Late) based on the types of artifact and what is inferred from them about social organization. The transition from the Paleo-Indian to the Archaic period is not well understood. Some archaeologists see the Early Archaic as a continuation of the Paleo-Indian period rather than a clear break. Small bands of hunters, fishers, and gatherers were the norm. They appear to have settled on high ground overlooking coastal estuaries.[23] They also ate shellfish and took advantage of seasonal fish runs. Some of the earliest human remains ever found in New Jersey are cremation burials dating from the Early Archaic period, unearthed at West Creek in Ocean County.[24]

New forms of projectile points, with notched and bifurcate stems, also appeared at the beginning of the Archaic period. They were likely used in association with atlatls (spear throwers), enabling a new and more efficient form of hunting at longer range from prey. Fishing may also have increased, as evidenced by the archaeological discovery of net sinkers, both notched and perforated, and spears.

By roughly 8000 B.C., the pattern of vegetation had acquired a modern appearance.[25] New technologies, particularly polished and ground stone tools, appeared during this period, which is called the Middle Archaic. These tools would have been used to fell trees, to shape canoes, and to dispatch wounded prey. Tools for grinding nuts and other plant foods became more common, perhaps reflecting a greater reliance on new food sources present in an increasingly forested environment. New forms of projectile points also characterize the Middle Archaic.

Approximately 6,000 years ago a new archaeological period, the Late Archaic, began. Some scholars link this period with the following Early and Middle Woodland Chronological periods (3000 B.C.–A.D. 1000), describing it as the Intensive Gathering–Formative Cultural period.[26] Settlements were near major rivers, and food sources included small game, shellfish, nuts, and other plants. Mortars and pestles were used to process seeds and nuts into flour. Settlement sites were much larger than in earlier periods, possibly reflecting recurrent use of certain favored locations or more efficient exploitation of natural resources. Mobility seems to have lessened, perhaps as populations grew. Local shale, argillite, quartzite, flint, and jasper were used for tools. Ground stone semi-lunar knives, or ulus, also appeared and may have been used for hide processing. Stemmed projectile points and broadspears became common, and well-formed bannerstones or atlatl weights were also common. Some materials were traded long distances.

Finally, bowls carved out of soapstone, probably patterned after baskets or wooden containers, appeared at the end of the Late Archaic. There is also considerable evidence for hunting, gathering, and fishing, as well as hot-rock cooking or stone-boiling. Shellfish became a major food source, and oysters were harvested in great numbers. Some shellfish beds may have been exploited for the first time, given the large size of some oyster and clam shells. Large shell mounds, like the ones at Tuckerton and Keyport, probably began to rise above the marshes during this period. Circular houses and pit houses created during the Late Archaic are some of the state's oldest known structures. Burials, particularly cremation burials and bundle burials, have been recovered from the Abbott Farm near Trenton and from the Savich Farm and Koens-Crispin sites in Burlington County. At the Koens-Crispin site, artifact caches or purposefully buried collections containing bannerstones, unusual "ceremonial" objects, and large projectile points were found in pairs with large projectile points and associated bones. Today the site is recognized as a cemetery where cremated human remains, accompanied by the finest artifacts of the Late Archaic period, were interred. It is possible that the differential distribution of artifacts indicates that a new elite class was developing, which was able to acquire and distribute scarce commodities.[27]

On a broader scale, the Late Archaic saw a transition from a foraging to a collecting pattern, which correlated with a warm, dry climatic episode. At the end of the Late Archaic period the first pottery appears in the state. When the climate became cooler and wetter at the beginning of the Early Woodland period, populations may have returned to a foraging pattern.

The final culture phase in New Jersey prehistory is known as the Woodland period. It began roughly 3,000 years ago and ended with the beginning of the Contact period 500 years ago. Environmental conditions were generally similar to those today. The simple circular structures known from remains at sites in nearby New York were probably used in New Jersey as well. Perhaps the most significant change at the beginning of the Woodland period was the expanded use of pottery. At first, both flat-bottomed and cone-shaped vessels were produced. The latter continued to be made until approximately 400 years ago, with later examples often extensively decorated. Ceramic vessels were an important technological innovation and made cooking and food storage much more efficient. The use of pottery vessels was likely linked to an increasingly sedentary lifestyle.

New forms of stone tools, such as fishtail bifaces that resemble the famous goldfish crackers and roughly triangular Meadowood points, crafted from Onondaga chert from New York State, became common. Soapstone

Dorothy Cross excavating a large Middle Woodland pottery vessel at the Abbott Farm, 1937. (Courtesy of the New Jersey State Museum.)

bowls, pendants, and ornaments were sometimes included in graves. Some of these tough stone bowls had holes punched through them or had been purposefully broken before burial.

New forms of religious expression also occurred, which are known as the Middlesex and Meadowood Complexes. In Ohio and adjacent states, Native Americans were building elaborate earthen mounds during this period; some functioned as temples, and others served as sepulchers. Archaeologists term these mound-building cultures the Adena and the Hopewell. In New Jersey, elaborate grave goods such as stone pipes, copper artifacts, and amazingly large, thin, leaf-shaped bifaces appear to be an eastern manifestation of these new cultural traditions. What are locally termed Middlesex-phase burial sites may be associated with the mound-building Adena culture of Ohio. The Rosenkrans Ferry site in Sussex County is one of the richest of the Adena-related Middlesex sites.[28] Eight individuals have been identified there. Infants and children were buried with copper bead necklaces and bracelets; adults were buried with spearpoints, pendants, gorgets, and tobacco pipes. The copper artifacts are particularly intriguing. Similar artifacts have been found at other sites in southern New Jersey, such as the

Scott site on Beesley's Point, the Vanaman site in Port Elizabeth, and the Canton site in Salem County.

Copper artifacts became common during the Late Archaic period in Michigan and the upper Midwest, reflecting the presence of copper deposits in that area. There, copper tools seem to have functioned as emblems of achieved status, though they resembled everyday tools manufactured from stone.[29] New Jersey archaeologists have long wondered whether the copper artifacts found in this state originated in the Midwest or were produced from local copper sources. Recent research seems to show that copper from both distant and local sources was employed, though with different sources dominating at different times.[30] On rare occasions, obsidian (volcanic glass) projectile points have been recovered in New Jersey. Some of these finds date from the Late Archaic and Early Woodland periods.[31] Because the nearest source of obsidian to New Jersey is the Yosemite Valley, the few obsidian artifacts from the state point to incredibly long-distance trade during some periods of prehistory.

Somewhat later, during the Middle Woodland period, Fox Creek points, which probably functioned as knives, became common, particularly around the Falls of the Delaware. Large and roughly oval in form, these projectile points were typically made from argillite, a material quarried in the area around Flemington, and are often associated with net-impressed pottery vessels.[32] It seems likely that these bifaces were associated with the processing of large numbers of fish, such as shad and sturgeon, which made seasonal runs up the Delaware River and its tributaries.[33] The fish may have been dried or processed into fish oil. In contrast to Fox Creek ceramics, which are almost always prosaic, other Middle Woodland ceramics are elaborately ornamented.[34]

During the Late Woodland period, which began roughly 1,000 years ago and continued until contact, there seems to have been an increase in population and a greater use of storage pits for food. Ceramics tend to vary from region to region. Small triangular projectile points supplanted the larger, finely made stone tools. Clay tobacco pipes and pendants became more common. Conoidal pottery continued to be used in southern New Jersey, though often with more elaborate decoration. In the northern part of the state, more globular vessels, with raised, highly decorated collars, became popular. Sometimes, small human faces were molded on these collars. These vessels resemble pre-Iroquoian ceramics from New York State, which after A.D. 1350 take on their own local characteristics associated with the Munsee people.[35] Although there are marked similarities between the pottery of northwestern New Jersey and that of the Iroquoian cultures of New York State, the resemblances end there. There is also convincing evidence for horticulture in the upper Delaware Valley, while in southern New Jersey foraging seems to have remained the main form of sustenance.

To some extent, our understanding of the Late Woodland period is hampered by the limited number of excavations. Noteworthy studies have been done to the north of the Delaware Water Gap, in small areas of the Inner Coastal Plain, and near the Maurice River.[36] However, archaeologists have begun to synthesize the available data on the coastal portions of the state, much of which is derived from cultural resource management projects. Patterns of postholes relating to prehistoric structures have been found at sites in Monmouth County.[37] Indeed, Native American occupation of the coastal zone appears to have been much more extensive than previously assumed. One particularly significant site is at Kimble's Beach on the Delaware Bay in Cape May County. Excavations there have provided new insights into how Native Americans in southern New Jersey made stone tools from locally available gravel sources.[38]

Renowned archaeologist Herbert C. Kraft argued for the presence of a Pahaquarra, or proto-Munsee, culture in northern New Jersey between A.D. 1000 and 1350, with individuals speaking a Munsee dialect of the Eastern Algonquian language, living in small, unfortified oval houses and longhouses, and using celts or ungrooved axes for woodworking. There is evidence for the cultivation of maize, beans, squash, pumpkins, and tobacco. Triangular Levanna and Madison points were used to hunt with bows. Fishing continued to be important, as evidenced by notched pebble netsinkers, bone fishhooks, and harpoons. Freshwater mussels were gathered and eaten. Canoes provided transportation. Human remains were tightly flexed or folded in graves, and grave goods were rare. Cremation burial, which had been practiced earlier, seems to have ceased. Pottery vessels, both collarless and low collared, were produced. The proto-Munsee lived in small communities consisting of a handful of round-ended longhouses, generally with an entrance at the side. Smaller structures and deep, silo-like food storage pits were created. Pipes, sometimes ornamented with effigy faces, were produced. These faces and effigies may represent the Living Solid Face, a god who watched over the game animals.[39]

A visitor to New Jersey in A.D. 1600 would have found a land populated by roughly 12,000 Native Americans.[40] They lived in relatively small groups, called bands by anthropologists. Their society was organized in an egalitarian manner, which emphasized flexibility and consensus over hierarchy. Indeed, this flexibility in the face of adversity was to characterize their behavior through much of the colonial period.[41]

Their technology, though simple by today's standards, was effective and included flaked and ground stone tools, pottery, and small quantities of copper, not to mention a broad array of items fashioned from wood, bark, bone, antler, and animal hides. Evidence for longhouses as well as smaller wigwams has been found in northern New Jersey, though only wigwams have been noted in southern New Jersey.[42] Subsistence focused on hunting and gathering among most Native American groups until very late in the prehistoric period. The bow and arrow was introduced about A.D. 1000. Animals were also driven into pounds and natural impasses to facilitate hunting. Fish, such as shad, sturgeon, and eels, were caught and processed. Corn was a staple crop, as were beans. Garments were made of deerskin, moccasins of hide, and in the historic period large blankets called matchcoats or duffels were worn. Ornaments of stone, shell, bone, and copper were used, as well as earrings and bracelets. Face painting and tattooing were common.

In terms of political and social organization, certain lineages seem to have been dominant. Chiefs acted as mediators and performed ceremonies, but they lacked the ability to coerce followers and instead led by example. Delaware society had a strong matrilineal focus, with a husband often moving into a new wife's household.[43] Information from the historic period indicates that natives traveled and traded quite widely.

A WORLD TRANSFORMED: NATIVE AMERICANS IN COLONIAL NEW JERSEY

Although European explorers almost certainly sailed up and down the coast of New Jersey in the sixteenth century,[44] the earliest surviving reports date from 1524, when Giovanni da Verrazzano, an Italian navigator sailing for the French, explored the Atlantic coast of North America. He described the natives as most loving. Almost a hundred years later, in 1609, Henry Hudson, a Dutchman sailing for the English, explored the New England coast. He traded with natives in Sandy Hook Bay, but also was attacked by natives in canoes who appear to have had some knowledge of firearms, because they waited for rain to render his men's guns useless before launching their attack. What may be a Lenape record of this early encounter between natives and Europeans was recorded in 1819 by the Moravian missionary John Heckewelder while living with Delaware refugees in Ohio. In this account, when the natives first saw a ship, they interpreted it as a very large fish or a very big house floating on the sea, and they gathered to observe the marvelous vessel. At length the vessel stopped moving, canoes left it for the shore, and curiously dressed people who spoke an unintelligible language disembarked from them. They proffered a vessel containing a strange liquid, which the natives at first were wary about drinking. Eventually, one native did drink from the cup, and after briefly appearing ill or asleep, he revived. Then the visitors gave them presents and asked for land for a garden. The strange men from beyond the sea asked for more and more land over time, and ultimately, "The Indians began to believe that they would soon want all their country, which in the end proved true."[45] Although this story may be an amalgam of several encounters, it is a striking representation of the first encounters between New Jersey's Native Americans and European mariners.

The Dutch also explored Delaware Bay and what they called the South River, today's Delaware. Hudson entered its mouth in 1609; the following year, the English navigator Samuel Argall sailed into the bay, which he named after Lord de la Warr. Both nations claimed the area, and Dutch explorers Cornelis Hendricksen and Cornelis Jacobsen May visited the region in 1616 and 1620. In 1624 May returned to North America with a party of thirty families who were religious refugees from Holland known as Walloons. They settled at Manhattan, at Fort Orange (Albany), along the Connecticut River, and on Burlington Island in the Delaware. Apparently, Burlington Island was intended to serve as the seat of Dutch government in New Netherland,[46] but the settlement there appears to have been short-lived. Soon, other Dutch settlements were established along the Delaware, including Fort Nassau at today's Gloucester City, in an attempt to control trade on the river.

The Dutch and their English contemporaries were particularly interested in furs, which were in great demand in Europe because overhunting had greatly reduced the number of available fur-bearing animals there. Beaver fur for hats became particularly valued. The Delaware found this fascination with furs quite curious, particularly as those furs that were most valuable for trade had already been worn, which apparently improved the condition of the pelt. In return for the furs, the Delaware received beads, brass kettles, tools, European clothes, tobacco pipes, guns, knives, fishhooks, and swords. It would be a mistake to underestimate the value of these seemingly trivial items to the Lenape. Thrust from a Stone Age society into a puzzling market economy, the Lenape lacked the technology to produce these items, which had great value in trade with more isolated Native American groups and in many cases readily fit into existing belief systems.[47] Copper, which had long been valued by Native Americans, and other metals were now readily available through trade. In fact, the appearance of large quantities of copper in Virginia served to depress the market for the material among natives after an initial period of euphoric consumption.[48] In some cases, they reworked these items, turning brass kettles into fishhooks, ornaments for clothes, bracelets, and projectile points. Metal axes were broken up to make other objects and even worn as ornaments. Rather than adopting European lifestyles, Native Americans took items that to them were precious and turned them into useful objects that suited their purposes. Native artisans showed incredible resourcefulness. Shattered bottles were reused as scrapers in place of stone tools. Metal tools helped facilitate the production of shell beads or wampum, which functioned as a form of currency as well as for ornamentation, diplomacy, and symbolic communication. Curious tobacco pipes and animal effigies made from lead and pewter may have been made by Native Americans or perhaps by European craftsmen hoping to appeal to Native tastes. Elaborate shell disks, called runtees, were cut from conch shells and used as ornaments. Other perishable commodities, such as alcoholic beverages, lubricated these transactions and ultimately proved troublesome to the Native Americans, who had no cultural norms regarding alcohol use.

The impact of disease on Native American populations was disastrous. Population estimates for the Lenape vary significantly, with some scholars arguing for 12,000 natives at the time of European contact and others for much smaller numbers.[49] In the seventeenth century smallpox epidemics, malaria, measles, and influenza significantly reduced the Native American population.[50] Although the exact losses suffered by the natives are unknown, a missionary named Jasper Danckaerts reported, "I have heard tell by the oldest New Netherlanders that there is now not 1/10th part of the Indians there once were, indeed not 1/20th or 1/30th."[51] The cultural dislocations caused by these diseases would also have been devastating, as young individuals, the future of the society, died and older individuals (with their years of knowledge and wisdom) passed away.

Under the Dutch regime, there was very little European settlement in New Jersey. Small Dutch settlements or patroonships had been established in Hudson and Bergen Counties and adjacent parts of Staten Island. Dutch businessmen, dissatisfied with their countrymen's lackadaisical colonial efforts in the New World, encouraged Sweden to establish a colony within the Delaware Valley. In 1638 New Sweden established its first settlement at Fort Christina near Wilmington, Delaware. Colonists from New Haven, Connecticut, also moved into southwestern New Jersey during this period, but these efforts were short-lived. Archaeological traces of Sweden's New World empire survive in southeastern Pennsylvania at the site of the Printzhof, a fortified house occupied by Governor Johan Printz and excavated by Marshall Becker.[52] Governor Printz had little sympathy for native peoples, even though he was dependent upon them for his colony's survival. The handful of archaeological sites that relate to this period show small quantities of artifacts, primarily fragments of copper kettles, tobacco pipes, and occasionally beads, in otherwise Native American contexts.[53]

The Dutch and the Swedes built forts on the Delaware, which helped control trade. Conflict, both between Native American groups and between Native Americans and traders/settlers, grew during this period. Misunderstandings led to the destruction of some European settlements, such as Swanendael in Lewes, Delaware. In 1637 Willem Kieft became director general of New Netherland. Relations with the Native Americans deteriorated under Kieft, as he attempted to tax them, ostensibly for protecting them. Upon hearing of the theft of a pig from a settler, Kieft sent troops to restore order. Sadly, the troops attacked a group of Raritans, who in turn began driving settlers off Staten Island. Ironically, after much loss of life, it became clear that the missing hog had been stolen by a Dutch servant.[54] Later, in 1642–1643, a group of Wiechquaeskeck Indians, harried by more northerly groups, fled to the Dutch settlement at Pavonia, today's Jersey City, hoping for protection. The duplicitous Kieft, rather than offering refuge, sent a group of soldiers to murder them. Once again, the Lenape retaliated, decimating the Dutch settlements in northeastern New Jersey and

Staten Island. This period also saw disease strike down survivors of the conflicts, further damaging native populations. A new governor, Peter Stuyvesant, arrived in 1649. Considerably more competent than his predecessors, he emphasized diplomacy rather than confrontation. Nevertheless, fighting continued sporadically through the early 1660s, with particularly troubled periods known as the Peach Tree War and the Esopus Wars.

Lenape social organization seems to have been largely matriarchal in Late Woodland times but began to change in response to the largely male traders entering New Jersey during the seventeenth century. Increasingly during this period, Native American leaders, generally men, are described as captains, chiefs, and kings. Some of the more noteworthy leaders were Oratam, Teedyuskung, and Weequehela.[55] These new leaders excelled at trade and diplomacy, and led their communities as best they could in a time of extraordinary change.

The Dutch conquered New Sweden in 1655, and in 1664 the English conquered New Netherland. The impact on the Lenape was substantial. English settlers in New England and on Long Island had long coveted the fine farmlands of New Jersey. Whereas the Dutch and Swedes had primarily supported themselves through trade, the English almost immediately set about establishing settlements. Hundreds of deeds for land sales survive from this period.[56] Those from northern New Jersey and Monmouth County have been the subject of considerable study and provide significant insights into how Native Americans used the land, where they lived, and how they dealt with settlers desiring their property.[57] The history of land transactions in early colonial New Jersey is complicated by the fact that Colonel Richard Nicolls, the leader of the English expedition that captured New Netherland, allowed settlers to enter the newly conquered territories under liberal terms before learning that the English proprietors intended to control the sale of land to settlers and establish a system of quitrents on property. As a result of this miscommunication, exact ownership of land was often in question. A good example of the resulting confusion is seen in the case of Richard Hartshorne, a Quaker who settled in Monmouth County in the 1670s. In May 1676 Hartshorne wrote, "The Indians came to my house and laid their hands on the post and frame of the house and said that the house was theirs; they never had anything for it, and told me if I would not buy the land, I must be gone. But I minded it not . . . they at last told me they would kill my cattle and burn my hay if I would not buy the land or begone; then I went to the Patentees . . . [and] bought William Goulder out."[58] Roughly a decade later, Hartshorne recorded other land troubles:

[T]he Indians pretend that formerly, when they sold all the land upon Sandy Hook, they did not sell, or did except liberty to plums, or to say the Indians should have liberty to go on Sandy Hook, to get plums when they please, and to hunt upon the land, and fish, and to take dry trees that suited them for cannows [sic] . . . for peace and quietness sake, and to the end there may be no cause of trouble with the Indians and that I may not for the future have any trouble with them as formerly I had, in their dogs killing my sheep, and their hunting on my lands, and their fishing . . . purchased their land.[59]

Hartshorne purchased land that did not have clear title. He then had to repurchase the land and subsequently made an additional payment to Native Americans who appear to have regarded the purchase agreement for Sandy Hook as allowing shared use of the tract, rather than dispossessing them entirely. Despite these multiple purchases, it appears that as late as the 1740s Indians were living on Sandy Hook.

During the eighteenth century New Jersey's Native American populations continued to shrink in size and to move increasingly toward refuge areas. Many of the Munsee of northern New Jersey migrated toward the Forks area, the Lehigh Valley of Pennsylvania, and the area of Minisink Island. Here, too, their lands were contested, and in 1737 the infamous Walking Purchase defrauded them of considerable land in eastern Pennsylvania. The Walking Purchase led to years of recriminations and bad feelings. Increasingly isolated, New Jersey's Native Americans attempted to preserve their traditional lands. A few became powerful and rich through land sales. Most did not. One extraordinary Delaware leader during this period was Weequehela, whose name means "weary or exhausted." He rose to prominence in East Jersey in the early eighteenth century. Contemporary accounts note that he wore European clothes and lived in a frame house after the fashion of his wealthy English neighbors.[60] In a confusing incident, he apparently killed his neighbor Samuel Leonard in 1727. Shortly thereafter, Weequehela was hanged, and his descendents began a long struggle to hold on to what remained of their land.

For the increasingly embattled Delaware, dispossessed of their land, religion provided some solace. Moravian and Presbyterian missionaries were particularly active among the Lenape. The Moravians were evangelical Protestants from what today is the Czech Republic. They established major communities in North Carolina, in eastern Pennsylvania (especially at Nazareth and Bethlehem), and in northwestern New Jersey at Hope. The Moravians were sympathetic to Native Americans, and it is from their writings that we get some of the best information about Lenape life during the eighteenth and early nineteenth centuries.[61]

Presbyterian missionaries also were active among the Delaware. In 1745 David Brainerd, a young Presbyterian minister who belonged to the New Light faction of the church, which emphasized personal salvation and evangelical zeal, began mission work among the Lenape.[62] After several failures, he began preaching to Lenape groups near Crosswicks and at the Forks of the Delaware. Brainerd succeeded in drawing converts, but found that the community at Crosswicks faced considerable challenges, including worn-out fields, debts, and widespread alcohol abuse.

In May 1746 Brainerd established a new community called Bethel in what is now Monroe Township, in Middlesex County, New Jersey. The settlement covered some eighty acres and included cabins for the converts, a home for David Brainerd, who was dangerously ill, a church, and a schoolhouse. Brainerd hoped to teach the Delaware to farm on the English model, with men, rather than women, working in the fields.[63] When David Brainerd died in 1747, his brother John succeeded him. The community's population had grown to 160 individuals. Despite initial successes, disease carried off many of the converts and led to disaffection among the survivors. The land where Bethel was established was also contested. Brainerd and the Bethel Indians eventually lost their land to Robert Hunter Morris, then chief justice of New Jersey. After the Bethel community disbanded in 1755,[64] William Tennent of Freehold began to minister to dispersed survivors. The French and Indian war posed another challenge. Indians had to register as loyal subjects or they might be charged with working for the enemy; even then some of them were killed.

In an attempt to redress the precarious situation of the Indians, the colonial government of New Jersey held two conferences at Crosswicks. The first, in 1756, resulted in the restriction of the sale of liquor to Indians, prevented their imprisonment for debt, and clarified the process of purchases and selling Indian lands. At a second meeting, held in 1758, the Crosswicks

Indians were well represented, as were other Indian groups. The goal was to settle any remaining land claims in the colony and establish a reservation for the Indians living south of the Raritan River.[65] Later, in 1758, at Easton, Pennsylvania, negotiations between the governments of Pennsylvania and New Jersey and the region's Indian inhabitants led to the sale of the remaining Indian lands in northern New Jersey to Governor Francis Bernard for a payment of 1,000 Spanish dollars.[66] In that same year, Benjamin Springer sold 3,044 acres of land in and around today's Indian Mills, New Jersey. John Brainerd was appointed superintendent and guardian of the Indians at Brotherton, as the place was then known.[67] Brotherton was arranged with the houses close together and farm lots near them. A store, gristmill, sawmill, church, and burying ground served the residents. Sources indicate that the Indians at Brotherton struggled to survive and descended into poverty. Jean Soderlund argues that their poor condition resulted not so much from physical poverty as from the attempt to maintain their traditional identity "in the midst of rising consumerism among whites."[68] Some apparently wished to move west to Ohio but were unable to sell the land. After John Brainerd moved to Deerfield in Cumberland County, contemporary sources, most notably the diary of John Hunter, a local Quaker who visited the Indians, describe them as "in a very poor suffering condition as to food and raiment."[69]

Apparently, the Brotherton Indians lived in a style quite similar to that of local whites and no longer employed stone tools.[70] In the 1990s archaeologists working on the border of the reservation identified a house site occupied between 1745 and 1765. Based on the artifacts they recovered, which included remnants of European clothes, weapons, and English clay tobacco pipes, interspersed with bone, stone, and antler tools, trade beads, and the remains of wild animals, it seems very likely that this was a home once occupied by Native Americans related to the Brotherton community. Moreover, the building, which was partially dug into the ground, resembles some Native American structures.[71] These findings contrast with Lenape sites in Pennsylvania from this time period, most notably the Playwicki site, which show a persistence of Native American technology and house forms well into the eighteenth century.[72] A sister community to Brotherton, called Wepink, was located to the west of present-day Vincentown. Though less well documented, it too appears to have been occupied during the second half of the eighteenth century.

In 1802 the Brotherton Indians sold their lands and moved to New York State, where they settled among the Stockbridge Indians. In 1832 the descendants and survivors of this group, now living in Wisconsin, successfully petitioned the State of New Jersey for further compensation based on claims to fishing and hunting rights in New Jersey, which they could no longer enjoy.

DIFFERENT PATHS TO THE FUTURE: THE DELAWARE IN THE NINETEENTH AND TWENTIETH CENTURIES

Although some of New Jersey's eighteenth-century Indian people moved to Brotherton, others followed different paths. A handful attended Princeton, sent there to learn more about Western culture.[73] Others moved west, attempting to escape the settlers and live more traditional lives. In 1762 a Delaware prophet named Neolin claimed that if native people rejected European goods and ideas and returned to the ways of their ancestors, the Great Spirit would drive the whites away. Pontiac, an Indian war leader, led the campaign against the English, and many western forts fell. Peaceful Indians, including the old chief Teedysukung, were killed by white vigilantes. As Pontiac's rebellion ended, Delaware survivors continued to move west.

In 1778, during the American Revolution, one group of Delaware signed a treaty with the United States,[74] the first Indian nation to do so. Moreover, this treaty alluded to the creation of an Indian state as part of the new American confederation.[75] However, in the Ohio country, American troops attacked and burned Indian villages, and some Delaware sided with the British. After the war, the Delaware moved farther west into Indiana. One group moved into Canada and settled at Muncy near Thamesville, Ontario. Others settled on the Moraviantown Reserve in Ontario. Some sided with the prophet Tenskwatawa, "the open door," who led military resistance to American expansion during the War of 1812.

The odyssey of the Delaware Indians continued during the nineteenth century as they moved farther west to Wisconsin, Missouri, Kansas, and Oklahoma. One large group of Delaware settled among the Cherokees in Oklahoma. Others intermarried with whites and renounced their Indian status. By the early twentieth century, the remaining Delaware were primarily living in Oklahoma, Kansas, Wisconsin, and Ontario, Canada. However, some Delaware remained on the East Coast. The Indian School movement broke bonds between the Delaware and their traditional society as many children were sent to schools in the East. The native language declined, and the Big House Ceremony, an important ritual, ceased.

Today, only a handful of individuals can speak the language fluently, but some elders have continued to pass on their traditions to their children. Native Americans in New Jersey and surrounding states, descendants of the Lenape and other Native American groups, such as the Ramapough Mountain Indians, Sand Hill Band, the Nanticoke Lenni Lenape, and others, have worked to determine the best paths for their groups in the twenty-first century and continue to celebrate their rich heritage.[76] They are playing an increasing role in shaping their own future by determining how their past is interpreted. For instance, at the Black Creek site in Vernon, New Jersey, a significant and endangered archaeological site was preserved in large part thanks to the concerns of the Nanticoke Lenni Lenape.[77]

The history of New Jersey's Native Americans is long, complicated, and not yet fully written. Along with the careful study of oral histories and preserved documents, archaeology provides insights into their lives. New technologies and archaeological techniques allow scientists to track ancient trade routes, recover subtle clues about the foods people ate, and learn how they created and used their tools. Although the story of New Jersey's native peoples stretches back thousands of years, our understanding of it is still evolving.

ACKNOWLEDGMENTS

I would like to acknowledge the following individuals and institution: Gregory D. Lattanzi, R. Alan Mounier, Ilene Grossman Bailey, R. Michael Stewart, Jesse Walker, and the Monmouth University Department of History and Anthropology.

NOTES

1. Daria Merwin, "The Potential for Submerged Prehistoric Archaeological Sites off Sandy Hook," *ASNJ* 57 (2002): 1–10.
2. William Schindler, "All Washed Up: A Prehistoric Dugout Canoe Discovered on the Jersey Shore" (paper presented at the 2008 Middle Atlantic Archaeological Conference, Ocean City, Md.); Steven Tull, M. Brown, and B. Sterling, *Archaeological Investigations at Sites 28PA39, 28PA40, 28PA145, the Early Dundee Canal Terminus Area, and the Eagle*

Foundry Site, Route 21 Extension Cultural Resources Mitigation, Passaic County, New Jersey (report prepared for the New Jersey Department of Transportation, Trenton, 1999).

3. Amy Hill Hearth, *Strong Medicine Speaks: A Native American Elder Has Her Say, An Oral History* (New York: Artria Books, 2008).

4. William Schindler, "Middle Woodland Exploitation of Migratory Fish in the Delaware Valley" (Ph.D. diss., Temple University, 2006).

5. Ives Goddard, "Delaware," in *Handbook of North American Indians*, vol. 15, *Northeast*, ed. Bruce G. Trigger (Washington, D.C.: Smithsonian Institution, 1978), 213–239.

6. Robert Grumet, *The Munsee Indians: A History* (Norman: University of Oklahoma Press, 2009), 12.

7. Marshall J. Becker has argued that these commonly employed names are incorrect, that other designations, such as "Jersies" and "River Indians," were more commonly used, and that the term "Delaware" seems to have been employed largely for individuals residing in Pennsylvania. This ongoing debate is beyond the scope of this chapter. See Marshall J. Becker, "Lenopi; or, What's in a Name? Interpreting the Evidence for Cultures and Cultural Boundaries in the Lower Delaware Valley," *ASNJ* 63 (2008): 11–32; Marshall J. Becker, "Cultural Diversity in the Lower Delaware River Valley 1550–1750: An Ethnohistorical Perspective," in *Late Woodland Cultures in the Middle Atlantic Region*, ed. Jay F. Custer (Newark: University of Delaware Press, 1986), 90–101; and Marshall Becker, "Mehoxy of the Cohansey Band of South Jersey Indians: His Life as a Reflection of Symbiotic Relations with Colonists in Southern New Jersey and the Lower Counties of Pennsylvania," *ASNJ* 53 (1998): 40–68.

8. Some scholars and indeed some Native Americans prefer the terms "American Indians" or simply "Indians."

9. Sean McHugh, "Charles Rau and the Keyport Shell Heap," *Journal of Middle Atlantic Archaeology* 25 (2009): 20.

10. Dorothy Cross, *Archaeology of New Jersey*, vol. 2 (Trenton: New Jersey State Museum, 1956), 1–11; Lucy Aiello, "Charles Conrad Abbott, M.D., Pick and Shovel Scientist," *NJH* 85 (1967): 208–216; Sharon Horan, "Charles Conrad Abbott: Associations with the Peabody and the Museum of Archaeology and Paleontology," *ASNJ* 47 (1992): 29–36.

11. Herbert C. Kraft, "Dr. Charles Conrad Abbott, New Jersey's Pioneer Archaeologist," *ASNJ* 48 (1993): 1–13.

12. Charles Conrad Abbott, *Primitive Industry* (Salem, N.J.: G. A. Bates, 1881), 471–551.

13. David Oestreicher, "Unmasking the *Walam Olum*, a 19th-Century Hoax" *ASNJ* 49 (1994): 1–44.

14. Alanson Skinner and Max Schrabisch, comp., *A Preliminary Report of the Archaeological Survey of the State of New Jersey*, Bulletin 9 (Trenton: New Jersey Geological Survey, 1913); Max Schrabisch, *Indian Habitations in Sussex County, New Jersey*, and Leslie Spier, *Indian Remains Near Plainfield, Union Co., and Along the Lower Delaware Valley*, Bulletin 13 (Union Hill: New Jersey Geological Survey, 1915); Max Schrabisch, *Archaeology of Warren and Hunterdon Counties*, Bulletin 18 (Trenton: New Jersey Geological Survey, 1917).

15. Gregory D. Lattanzi, "New Jersey's Golden Age: The Contributions of Dorothy Cross to the Archaeology of New Jersey" (paper presented at the annual meeting of the Eastern States Archaeological Federation, Mount Laurel, N.J., 2002), 4.

16. William Sandy, "Flotation Studies and Their Value for New Jersey Archaeology" (M.A. thesis, Rutgers University, 1985); Carolyn D. Dillian, Charles A. Bello, and Stephen M. Shackley, "Long Distance Exchange of Obsidian in the Mid-Atlantic United States," in *Trade and Exchange: Archaeological Studies from History and Prehistory*, ed. Carolyn D. Dillian and Carolyn White (New York: Springer, 2010), 17–36; Gregory D. Lattanzi, "Elucidating the Origin of Middle Atlantic Pre-Contact Copper Artifacts using Laser Ablation ICP-MS" (paper presented at annual meeting of the Eastern States Archaeological Federation, Burlington, Vt., 2007); Timothy Messner, "Woodland Period People and Plant Interactions: New Insights from Starch Grain Analysis" (Ph.D. diss., Temple University, 2009); George L. Pevarnik, Matthew T. Boulanger, and Michael D. Glascock, "Instrumental Neutron Activation Analysis of Middle Woodland Pottery from the Delaware Valley," *North American Archaeologist* 29, nos. 3–4 (2008): 239.

17. Jay F. Custer, *Classification Guide for Arrowheads and Spearpoints of Eastern Pennsylvania and the Central Middle Atlantic* (Harrisburg: Pennsylvania Historical and Museum Commission, 2001).

18. Herbert C. Kraft, *The Lenape-Delaware Indian Heritage 10,000 B.C. to A.D. 2000* (Elizabeth, N.J.: Lenape Books, 2001), 55.

19. Ibid., 61.

20. R. Alan Mounier, *Looking Beneath the Surface: The Story of Archaeology in New Jersey* (New Brunswick: Rutgers University Press, 2003), 19.

21. Ibid., 199.

22. William A. Ritchie, *The Lamoka Lake Site: The Type Station of the Archaic Algonkin Period in New York*, New York State Archaeological Association, Researches and Transactions, vol. 7, no. 4 (Rochester: Lewis Morgan Chapter, 1932), 79–134.

23. Herbert C. Kraft and R. Alan Mounier, "The Archaic Period in New Jersey: ca. 8000 B.C.–1000 B.C.," in *New Jersey's Archaeological Resources: A Review of Research Problems and Survey Priorities, The Paleo-Indian Period to the Present*, ed. Olga Chesler (Trenton: New Jersey Historic Preservation Office, 1982), 52–103.

24. Andrew J. Stanzeski, "Two Decades of Radiocarbon Dating from the New Jersey Shore," *ASNJ* 51 (1996): 42–45.

25. James B. Griffin, "The Midlands and Northeastern United States," in *Ancient Native Americans*, ed. Jesse D. Jennings (San Francisco: W. H. Freeman, 1978), 226–239.

26. Custer, *Classification Guide*, 70.

27. Mounier, *Looking Beneath the Surface*, 173.

28. Ibid., 177.

29. Lewis Binford, "Archaeology as Anthropology," *American Antiquity* 28 (1962): 217–225; Susan Martin, *Wonderful Power: The Story of Ancient Copper Working in the Lake Superior Basin* (Detroit: Wayne State University Press, 1999).

30. Lattanzi, "Elucidating the Origin."

31. Dillian, Bello, and Shackley, "Long Distance Exchange of Obsidian," 17–36.

32. Jesse O. Walker, "Alternative Mitigation Flemington Argillite Quarry Study, Raritan Township, Hunterdon County, New Jersey" (prepared by Richard Grubb and Associates for Hunterdon County Department of Roads, Bridges, and Engineering, 2009).

33. John Cavallo, "Fish, Fires, and Foresight: Middle Woodland Economic Adaptations in the Abbott Farm National Landmark," *North American Archaeologist* 5, no. 2 (1984): 111–139; Poul Erik Graversen, "An Analysis of Petalas Blade Caches in New Jersey and Eastern Pennsylvania" (M.A. thesis, Monmouth University, 2011).

34. Lorraine. E. Williams and Ronald A. Thomas, "The Early/Middle Woodland Period in New Jersey: ca. 1000 B.C.–A.D. 1000," in *New Jersey's Archeological Resources: A Review of Research Problems and Survey Priorities: The Palo-Indian Period to the Present*, ed. Olga Chesler (Trenton: New Jersey Historic Preservation Office, 1982), 103–138.

35. Kraft, *Lenape-Delaware Indian Heritage*, 208.

36. Herbert Kraft and R. Alan Mounier, "The Late Woodland Period in New Jersey: ca. A.D. 1000–1600," in Chesler, ed., *New Jersey's Archaeological Resources*, 139–184.

37. Paul Boyd, "Settlers Along the Shore: Lenape Spatial Patterns in Coastal Monmouth County 1600–1750" (Ph.D. diss., Rutgers University, 2005), 107.

38. James P. Kotcho, "The Lithic Technology of a Late Woodland Occupation on the Delaware Bay: Kimble's Beach Site (28CM36A), Cape May County, New Jersey" (M.A. thesis, Rutgers University, 2009).

39. Kraft, *Lenape-Delaware Indian Heritage*, 328–329.

40. This figure varies. Grumet notes a population range of 10,000–30,000 and settles on the median of 15,000. Grumet, *Munsee Indians*, 15.

41. Amy C. Schutt, *Peoples of the River Valleys: The Odyssey of the Delaware Indians* (Philadelphia: University of Pennsylvania Press, 2007).

42. Mounier, *Looking Beneath the Surface*, 130–134.

43. Grumet, *Munsee Indians*, 18.

44. Goddard, "Delaware," 213–239.

45. "'Between Hope and Fear': A Legend of the First Lenape Encounter with Europeans," in *Words That Make New Jersey History: A Primary Source Reader*, ed. Howard Green (New Brunswick: Rutgers University Press, 1995), 4–6.

46. Richard Veit and Charles A. Bello, "A Unique and Valuable Historical and Indian Collection: Charles Conrad Abbott Explores a 17th-Century Dutch Trading Post in the Delaware Valley," *Journal of Middle Atlantic Archaeology* 15 (1999): 95–124.

47. George R. Hamell, "The Iroquois and the World's Rim: Speculation on Color, Culture, and Contact," *American Indian Quarterly* 16 (1992): 451–469.

48. William M. Kelso, *Jamestown: The Buried Truth* (Charlottesville: University of Virginia Press, 2006).

49. Clinton A. Weslager, *The Delaware Indians: A History* (New Brunswick: Rutgers University Press, 1972); Marshall Joseph Becker, "Lenape Population at the Time of Contact: Estimating Native Numbers in the Lower Delaware Valley," *Proceedings of the American Philosophical Society* 133, no. 2 (1989): 112–122.

50. Grumet, *Munsee Indians*, 63–64, 151, 152, 182.

51. Charles T. Gehring, and Robert S. Grumet, "Observations of Indians from Jasper Danckaerts's Journal, 1679–1689," *W&MQ* 44 (1987): 105–120.

52. Marshall J. Becker, "Ethnohistory and Archaeology in Search of the Printzhof: The 17th Century Residence of Swedish Colonial Governor Johan Printz," *Ethnohistory* 26, no. 1 (1979): 15–44.

53. Peter Pagoulatos, "Native American Contact Period Settlement Patterns of New Jersey," *ASNJ* 62 (2007): 23–40; Edward J. Lenik, "New Evidence on the Contact Period in Northeastern New Jersey and Southeastern New York," *Journal of Middle Atlantic Archaeology* 5 (1989): 103–120.

54. Grumet, *Munsee Indians,* 57.

55. Robert S. Grumet, "The King of New Jersey," *ASNJ* 48 (1993): 45–52; Edward J. Lenik, "Chief Oratam's Burial Site: The Making of a Legend," *ASNJ* 45 (1990): 29–41; Anthony F. C. Wallace, *King of the Delawares: Teedyuscung, 1700–1763* (Philadelphia: University of Pennsylvania Press, 1949); Stephen R. Wilk, "Weequehela," *NJH* 111, nos. 3–4 (1993): 1–18.

56. Frank H. Stewart, *Indians of Southern New Jersey* (Woodbury, N.J.: Gloucester County Historical Society, 1932).

57. Robert S. Grumet, "'We Are Not So Great Fools': Changes in Upper Delawaran Socio-Political Life, 1630–1758" (Ph.D. diss., Rutgers University, 1979); Boyd, "Settlers Along the Shore."

58. Franklin Ellis, *History of Monmouth County, New Jersey* (Philadelphia: R. T. Peck and Co., 1885), 700.

59. Ibid.

60. Wilk, "Weequehela," 1–18.

61. Archer Herbert Butler and William Nathaniel Schwarze, eds., *David Zeisberger's History of the Northern American Indians in 18th Century Ohio, New York, and Pennsylvania* (1910; reprint, Lewisburg, Pa.: Wennawoods Publishing, 1999); John Gottleib Ernestus Heckewelder, *History, Manners, and Customs of the Indian Nations Who Once Inhabited Pennsylvania and the Neighboring States* (1819; reprint, New York: Arno Press and New York Times, 1971).

62. George D. Flemming, *Brotherton: New Jersey's First and Only Indian Reservation and the Communities of Shamong and Tabernacle That Followed* (Medford, N.J.: Plexus Publishers, 2005), 31.

63. Jean R. Soderlund, "The Delaware Indians and Poverty in New Jersey," in *Down and Out in Early America*, ed. Billy Gordon Smith (University Park: Pennsylvania State University Press, 2004), 302.

64. Flemming, *Brotherton,* 37.

65. Frank J. Esposito, "Indian-White Relations in New Jersey" (Ph.D. diss., Rutgers University, 1976), 298–300.

66. Kraft, *Lenape-Delaware Indian Heritage,* 466.

67. Flemming, *Brotherton,* 53.

68. Soderlund, "Delaware Indians and Poverty in New Jersey," 305.

69. Flemming, *Brotherton,* 56.

70. Henry Kammler, "J. F. H. Autentieth's 'Description of a Short Walking Tour in the Province of New Jersey . . .' [A Report from 1795 about the Brotherton Reservation]," *ASNJ* 51 (1996): 34–41.

71. Betty Cosans-Zeebooker and Ronald A. Thomas, "Excavations at the Burr/Haines Site, Burlington County, New Jersey," *ASNJ* 48 (1993): 13–20.

72. R. Michael Stewart, "The Indian Town of Playwicki," *Journal of Middle Atlantic Archaeology* 15 (1999): 35–54.

73. Anne Gossen, *Princeton 1783: The Nation's Capital* (Princeton: Morven Museum and Garden, 2009), 63.

74. Lorraine E. Williams, "Caught in the Middle: New Jersey's Indians and the American Revolution," in *New Jersey in the American Revolution*, ed. Barbara Mitnick (New Brunswick: Rutgers University Press, 2005), 109.

75. Ibid., 112.

76. Blair Fink, "Understanding the Struggle for Federal Recognition: Two New Jersey Native American Tribes' Perspectives on the Process and Expected Outcomes" (Honors thesis, Monmouth University, 2009).

77. Cara Lee Blume, "Healing the Scar: Recent Archaeological Research at the Black Creek Site" (prepared for the Vernon Historical Society, 2009).

2 · COLONIAL PERIOD

The Complex and Contradictory
Beginnings of a Mid-Atlantic Province

MAXINE N. LURIE

When Europeans (possibly fishermen, perhaps John Cabot, surely Giovanni da Verrazzano) first traveled along the coast of what would become New Jersey, Native Americans had been present for more than 12,000 years. But after 1609, when Henry Hudson and his crew explored the river that now bears his name, the area was more directly drawn into the Atlantic world. Part of three different empires in the seventeenth century —Dutch, Swedish, and then British—it was held after 1664 by a succession of proprietors (lords of the land, and landlords to its settlers). In the eighteenth century New Jersey became a royal colony, governed by the king's appointee. It was unlike Puritan New England or the plantation south, although it had both Congregationalists and slaves; no one religion dominated, and it was a "slave-owning society" rather than a "slave society" (that is, dependent on one crop and extensive use of unfree labor). In its economy and diversity, it resembled and was part of the Mid-Atlantic region, with New York and Pennsylvania, and even shared some of those colonies' very early history.[1] Because New Jersey is less often studied than its neighbors, its differences from them have been neglected. In fact, an examination of New Jersey in its colonial era, from 1609 to 1776, shows that it was the most complex and diverse of these three colonies. The patterns of this early period had significant consequences for the state's subsequent history and foreshadowed characteristics of the present-day United States.[2]

THE SEVENTEENTH CENTURY

At the beginning of the seventeenth century, when the Spanish and Portuguese had been developing their empires for more than a hundred years, more northern European nations began to stake their own conflicting claims in what they saw as a "new world." The French headed up the St. Lawrence River and down the Mississippi, the English looked to the eastern coast of North America and the Caribbean islands, and the Dutch spread from the east to the west "Indies." But the lands along and between the south (Delaware) and north (Hudson) rivers interested the Dutch, Swedes, and English. Settlers from all three nations moved into what later became New York, New Jersey, Delaware, and Pennsylvania, fighting each other as well as local natives for control. Once the English gained power over what became New Jersey, a series of proprietors attracted a diverse group of settlers in the late seventeenth century, established representative government and religious toleration, but also sowed the seeds of problems that would later haunt the colony.

Dutch and Swedes

First on the scene were the Dutch, who followed Hudson's exploration with the creation of the West Indies Company in 1621, which spread its colonists from Orange (Albany) to New Amsterdam (Manhattan) to the lower Delaware. The interest of Holland, increasingly a commercial nation, initially was in trade, particularly for furs, and later in establishing farms. By the early 1630s there were Dutch settlers on the west bank of the Hudson.

Sweden, then at the height of its military power, looked to create its own overseas empire and established the New Sweden Company. From 1638 to 1655 it fitfully sent settlers and a series of governors to the lower Delaware. When the Dutch successfully eliminated this rival, there were probably about three hundred Swedish-sponsored settlers, most but not all along the west bank of the river. Their legacy remains in place-names and in the log cabins and rail fences (introduced by the Finns) usually associated with the American frontier.[3]

Dutch dominance was short-lived though, as predicted by the Swedes when they surrendered: "Hode mihi, cras tibi" (my turn today, yours tomorrow).[4] Increased commercial competition with England for trade in Europe and America, as well as the fact that New Netherland physically cut the English colonies in two, led to a series of wars. In 1664 an English expedition took control of New Netherland. Although the Dutch briefly returned in 1673, from 1674 the region was part of the British Empire.

This brief summary indicates the ways in which the region was tied to the Atlantic world and to the competition of its nations for territory. The people involved in these shifting claims further complicate the story and help us to understand why New Jersey became so very diverse early on. Hudson, who sailed for the Dutch, was English; nearly half of the initial investors in the New Sweden Company were Dutch; the company's settlers were often Finns; and the "Dutch" themselves were of many nationalities, including French, Walloon, Scandinavian, Pole, Hungarian, Italian, German, and Flemish.[5]

English New Jersey

The expedition sent by England in 1664 in the name of the duke of York, the brother of King Charles II, created a proprietorship that extended from Martha's Vineyard to what became Delaware. The duke sent Richard Nicolls to govern his colony, but even before Nicolls arrived, the duke had given some of the lands to two loyal followers, Sir George Carteret and John Lord Berkeley. From 1664 to 1702 New Jersey's proprietary government underwent a dizzying series of changes—held briefly by the duke, then jointly by Carteret and Berkeley. Their tenure was interrupted by the Dutch reconquest in 1673–1674, after which Berkeley sold his share of the province to two Quakers, John Fenwick and Edward Byllynge. The result was the division in 1674 into two colonies: West New Jersey and East New Jersey. Here the story gets even more complicated, with important consequences for New Jersey's political history and land titles.[6]

In England, West Jersey proprietors Fenwick and Byllynge had a falling out. A group of Quaker trustees that included William Penn tried to mediate, but an impatient Fenwick headed for the Delaware in 1675, where he established his own settlement at Salem and attempted to exercise authority as governor over other settlers who followed. After 1680 Byllynge claimed that he alone had political authority, and he later sold his portion of West

Jersey, along with its government, to Daniel Coxe, an English investor who then sold it to the West Jersey Society, a group of investors.

In East Jersey, authority was first exercised by Governor Philip Carteret, a relative of Sir George, with a break in 1672, when he was overthrown and sought aid in England, returning after the Dutch interlude of 1673–1674. In 1682 Sir George's widow sold East Jersey to a consortium of twelve, then twenty-four mostly Quakers. The new East Jersey proprietors appointed Robert Barclay, a prominent Scotch Quaker, as governor; in practice, first he, and after his death the group, sent a series of deputy governors to the colony. These frequent changes in who claimed the right to govern only exacerbated the proprietors' problems in maintaining authority over settlers.

New Jersey's proprietors, starting with Berkeley and Carteret, allowed a measure of local self-government in the colony. Their Concessions of 1664/1665 provided representative government: an assembly of twelve deputies elected yearly had to consent to all taxes. The assembly and an appointed governor and council were to make the laws and constitute the courts. The first assembly met in 1668, although several of the towns settled by New Englanders refused to participate, claiming an even more local right to government. After the division in 1674, proprietors of the two Jerseys wrote their own concessions/constitutions: the West Jersey Concessions of 1676/1677, a radical Quaker document; the Fundamental Agreements of West Jersey of 1681; and the Fundamental Constitutions of East New Jersey of 1683. The 1676/1677 document clearly stated there were to be no taxes "without their owne consent" through an assembly; it also provided for a secret ballot, allowed Indians to serve on juries, and gave individuals the right to "plead" their own cause in court cases (avoiding lawyers). The colonists rejected both "fundamental" constitutions, apparently relying instead on the original Concessions of 1664/1665.[7] In both provinces elected representatives proved to be a feisty lot, insisting on their rights, questioning the authority of the deputy governors, and, in East Jersey especially, disputing land titles and quit rents.

The proprietors were also challenged from another direction. After the restoration of the monarchy in 1660, the English government created a series of proprietary colonies and then moved to consolidate the empire. It questioned whether anyone but the king could grant the right to govern. This challenge was of concern because New Jersey's grant was from the duke of York, not the king. In 1678 Edmund Andros, as governor of New

York, arrested Fenwick and then in 1680 Philip Carteret for what he stated was their illegal exercise of authority as governors of West and East Jersey, respectively. Consolidation led to the creation of the Dominion of New England in 1686, which included the New England colonies, New York, and in 1688 the two Jerseys, only to be dissolved in 1689 following the Glorious Revolution of 1688.[8] The proprietors again appointed deputy governors after 1692, but their ability to keep order in both colonies seriously deteriorated as their authority was increasingly challenged by settlers. With the turn of the century and a second effort to consolidate the empire, both sets of proprietors agreed to surrender their claims to govern to the crown. Once again there was only one New Jersey, now a royal colony.

Although the proprietors surrendered the governments of East and West Jersey, they did not cede their claims to the land.[9] Land titles had been the source of much disagreement since the beginning of English rule, and the issues continued into the eighteenth century and beyond. The first and most persistent problem stemmed from the two grants made by the duke of York's governor, Richard Nicolls, when he first arrived, known as the Elizabethtown and Monmouth patents. Every subsequent group of proprietors refused to recognize these as legitimate, demanding that settlers take out new titles and pay quit rents. Some settlers complied, but others, emboldened by court cases that sometimes went in their favor, refused. The second source of difficulty was the insistence by those who settled in and then west of Newark that Indian titles alone were sufficient. Third, the proprietors' methods of handling their lands sometimes produced conflicting titles to the same parcels. The East Jersey Board of Proprietors, created in 1685, divided into twenty-four shareholders. The West Jersey Council of Proprietors, formed in 1688, marked out one hundred shares. All of these shares were subdivided, so that an investor could hold a fraction of a share, and dividends were given in the form of land. Some shareholders moved to New Jersey, but others remained in Britain. To obtain a land grant in New Jersey, a prospective owner was supposed to go through a proprietary shareholder, essentially using the proprietor's land dividend. Surveyors appointed by the proprietary groups then laid out the lands. This convoluted system at times produced overlapping titles, with mistakes compounded by inaccurate early instruments, unscrupulous proprietors, devious settlers, and Native Americans who sometimes sold lands claimed by others.

Finally adding to the confusion were boundary disputes between New

York and New Jersey and between the eastern and western sections of the colony.[10] The grant of New Jersey from the duke of York, based on an early inaccurate map, specified the northern boundary to run from 41° 40' on the Hudson west to a nonexistent branch of the Delaware. The resulting dispute was settled by a Royal Boundary Commission just before the American Revolution; meanwhile, both New York and New Jersey granted lands in the disputed area. Several attempts were made after 1676 to demarcate East and West Jersey by running a line at an angle northwest from Little Egg Harbor on the Atlantic to the illusive point on the Delaware where New York started. There was no resolution of this province line in the colonial period, resulting in more overlapping grants. The land problems, especially the arguments over the Nicolls patents, boiled over into politics in the late seventeenth and mid-eighteenth centuries. Some historians have seen the major fault lines in both periods as between proprietary and antiproprietary groups, but in fact the colony was also divided by sectional, ethnic, and religious differences.

Settlers and Settlement Patterns

Despite the shifts in government and problems with land titles, numerous settlers came to New Jersey in the late seventeenth century.[11] They were attracted by the fertile lands (Nicolls thought them the "most improveable") along the Delaware, Raritan, Passaic, Hackensack, and other rivers. But they also came because of the terms the proprietors offered under the Concessions of 1664/1665 and later constitutions. As well as grants of land for each settler and for those they brought with them, these included participation in the government and religious toleration. The Concessions of 1664/1665 stated that "noe person . . . shalbe any waies molested punished disquieted or called in Question for any difference in opinion or practice in matters of Religious concernments." The West Jersey Concessions of 1676/1677 were more direct: "That no Men nor number of Men upon Eearth hath power or Authority to rule over mens consciences in religious matters." Although the 1676/1677 document was never put into effect, its provisions were not forgotten. The policies of toleration not only drew a religiously diverse population but also, in the long run, ensured that the colony never had an established church, even though the 1702 instructions to the first royal governor opened the possibility of an Anglican establishment.[12]

The settlers who came to New Jersey were a mixed group. In 1664 Dutch settlers in northeastern New Jersey occupied the fortified town of Bergen, and colonists of New Sweden remained along the southern reaches of the Delaware. In the 1690s more Dutch moved from New York as part of the fallout from the failed Leisler's Rebellion, settling along the Raritan and Hackensack. New Englanders came by way of Connecticut and Long Island into the Elizabethtown and Monmouth patents, establishing towns at Woodbridge, Piscataway, Shrewsbury, and Middletown, and then settled in Newark. With the takeover by the twenty-four proprietors, they were joined by an influx of Scotch settlers into Perth Amboy. The West Jersey proprietorship brought settlers from England, Ireland, and Wales to the banks of the Delaware, founding the towns of Salem and Burlington as well as scattered farms. English planters from Barbados arrived with their slaves. Lewis Morris Sr. used the largest number of them (sixty) on his estate in Tinton Falls to produce iron. Although Native Americans came into conflict with arriving Europeans and pushed the Dutch east across the Hudson in both the 1640s and 1650s and occasionally fought with Swedes, they were a declining, though mostly peaceful, presence once the English arrived.

By 1700 this ethnic and racial mix was matched by a religious plurality that included Dutch Reformed, Swedish Lutherans, French Huguenots, Quakers, Puritans (Congregationalists), Presbyterians, Baptists, and Anglicans. Although some towns and areas were dominated by one religious or ethnic group, increasingly there was a mix and the presence of more than one church in a town. George Keith, for example, who ran the first survey of the boundary between East and West Jersey, arrived as a Quaker, then became an Anglican missionary and inspired followers who helped diversify West Jersey.[13] The pattern of settlement is interesting not only because of the ethnic and religious diversity it so early brought to the colony, but also because movement spread from both the east and west at the same time. New Jersey never had one frontier line moving west.

Legacy of the Seventeenth Century

If New York, Pennsylvania, and New Jersey shared an early seventeenth-century history that included settlement by the Dutch and/or Swedes, by 1700 there were significant differences. Under English rule, all three were originally proprietary colonies. New York became a royal colony in 1685 at the death of Charles II, and Pennsylvania remained in the Penn family until the American Revolution. Neither experienced division into two colonies, a multiplication of proprietors, or questionable rights to the government. At the end of the seventeenth century New York, though including New England Congregationalists and Anglicans, was still heavily Dutch, while Quakers dominated Pennsylvania. No one religious or ethnic group prevailed in New Jersey in 1700 or afterward. Even towns founded by strict Congregationalists (for example, Newark) no longer collected tithes. Support for ministers was voluntary.

At the end of the seventeenth century both East and West Jersey were in turmoil. In East Jersey from 1664 to 1700, there were eight different governments; in West Jersey from 1674 to 1700, six.[14] Both sections were roiled by conflicting land titles and the uncertain political authority of the proprietors. Yet early settlement patterns left important and lasting legacies: a broad range of ethnic, religious, and racial groups; a heritage of self-government through local assemblies; and religious toleration.

EIGHTEENTH CENTURY

The division into two colonies left its imprint even after the proprietors surrendered their claims to govern in 1702. During the eighteenth century the legislature alternated its meetings between the two former capitals, Burlington and Perth Amboy; there were two colonial treasurers, two landed proprietary groups, and at times political divisions based on section. The merger of the two Jerseys and the appointment of a royal governor meant both greater oversight and more direct participation in the British Empire. Colonists traveled to London to advocate for positions and policies, and proprietors and legislators hired lobbyists to further their causes. The spread of religious revivalism also increased ties and connections, as ministers and congregants crossed the ocean or exchanged letters seeking ideas and support. As the colony continued to grow, it was if anything more connected to the larger Atlantic world through immigration, trade (both the export of its produce and the increased importation of goods, including slaves), and war. European conflicts spread in what the colonists knew as Queen Anne's War, King George's War, and then the French and Indian War. The latter, which concerned much of the interior of North America, has also been called the Great War for Empire because the conflict extended around the globe. When it ended in 1763, New Jersey's colonists were proud of Britain's victories and welcomed young William Franklin as their governor. But efforts to settle war debts and consolidate a now larger empire led to conflict that ended his tenure and forever defined him as the last royal governor. In 1776 the colony became a state.[15]

Politics

When the proprietors negotiated the terms of the surrender of their governments, they tried to protect their lands and ensure continued political power. Though not entirely successful on either score, they remained an important political presence for the remainder of the colonial period. What changed was that the governor and the members of his council (upper house of the legislature) were now royal appointees. Selection and tenure were connected to British politics, and patronage was crucial. For example, the first royal governor, Edward Hyde, Lord Cornbury (served 1701–1708), was a cousin of Queen Anne; another, Robert Hunter (1710–1720), had ties to prominent Whig politicians during a period of their dominance; and a third, William Burnet (1720–1728), was the son of Gilbert Burnet, an Anglican bishop and early supporter of William and Mary in the Glorious Revolution of 1688. From 1702 to 1738, these royal governors were shared with New York. Although the importance of political connections did not change after separation in 1738, the time and attention given to the smaller colony increased once it had its own governor.[16]

The quality of New Jersey's governors varied in this period. Traditionally, Cornbury has had the worst reputation, denigrated by his opponents as a "despicable maggot" who walked the ramparts of New York City in female dress. Criticized by chroniclers then and by historians since for corruption, he has been defended more recently by Patricia Bonomi, who argues that he represented the strong centralizing bureaucrat of a modernizing empire and was unfairly caught in the slander machine of the new Fleet Street press. Hunter, an able administrator and literary figure, has been given credit for moderating the political divisions in the colony. On the other hand, the first governor of the separate colony of New Jersey, Lewis Morris (1738–1746), was a popular "native son" who had been long involved in the colony's politics but was widely disliked by the time of his death. Ironically, William Franklin (1763–1776), also colonial born, was initially quite successful until overwhelmed by events leading to the Revolution, which he was unable to prevent and unwilling to join.

Lewis Morris (1671–1746) played a prominent role in New York and New Jersey politics. He served on the governor's council for New Jersey, as acting governor, and, from 1738, as the first royal governor of the separate colony. (John Watson [American, 1685–1768], *Governor Lewis Morris*, ca. 1726. Oil on canvas, 30 1/16 x 25 in. [76.3 x 63.5 cm]. Brooklyn Museum, purchased with funds given by John Hill Morgan, Dick S. Ramsay Fund, and Museum Collection Fund, 43.196.)

All of New Jersey's royal governors were called upon to enforce imperial policies in a colony divided by section, religion, ethnicity, and proprietary groups (as well as among proprietors). Governors had few patronage positions they could bestow to strengthen their influence, and they faced a legislative assembly whose power steadily grew because it controlled the purse strings (including salaries). This situation was found in all of the eighteenth-century colonies, but New Jersey's assemblymen appear to have been particularly adept and determined at getting their way. They repeatedly held governors' salaries and general appropriations for administrative costs hostage for legislation they wanted, especially authorization to issue paper money. In Lewis Morris's case, they refused to pay his salary, even to his widow after his death, because he vetoed popular bills. Several governors violated their royal instructions in order to obtain appropriations and their salaries, including Francis Bernard (1758–1760), Thomas Boone (1760–1761), and Josiah Hardy (1761–1763). The assembly also pushed for control of money once appropriated and even, in an increasingly nasty dispute with Franklin, who was usually skilled in dealing with the body, gained control in 1774 over the appointment of the two colonial treasurers.

Only one of the early proprietary concessions/constitutions specified who could vote or hold office, but the document was never accepted, and so the seventeenth-century standards are not clear.[17] With the surrender, the proprietors pushed for a high requirement to maintain control over politics and hence their lands. The royal instructions of 1702 directed that individuals must own 1,000 acres to hold office and 100 acres to vote. These requirements were removed for freeholders in 1704, but restored after 1709 to 1,000 acres or £500 of property to hold office and 100 acres or £50 of property to vote. These laws restricted officeholding but had less effect on voting.[18] Even without the property qualifications, it is likely that the legislature would be composed of substantial landowners, because only a relatively wealthy man could afford the time and expense of attending sessions on small compensation. The costs were sufficient that many did not run again, producing a political establishment characterized by both a large number of family connections (fathers and then sons serving) and high turnover. Furthermore, while members of the proprietary groups dominated the governor's council (because they owned more property and had more political connections), they had to be elected to serve in the assembly —and they were not always successful.[19]

Some historians of the politics of this period have viewed the conflicts between the legislature and the royal governors simply as a proprietary versus anti-proprietary split, stemming from the East Jersey pattern in the late seventeenth century.[20] In contrast, Michael Batinsky, who did a roll-call analysis of assembly votes, described politics as "fractional" or "inchoate," characterized by shifting alliances among New Jersey's ethnically and religiously diverse population, two sections, and proprietary groups. Larry Gerlach has described "ad hoc" factions. Thomas Purvis also looked at votes and found substantial agreement on issues such as paper money. This being New Jersey, probably all versions are accurate to some degree, depending on the period and the issue examined.

The complexities are illustrated by the situation facing Lord Cornbury when he arrived. One faction included West Jersey Quakers, East Jersey Scotch proprietors, and the West Jersey Society. It was opposed by a group of West Jersey Anglicans, East Jersey English proprietors, and Nicolls patentees. Cornbury and his allies, called the "Cornbury Ring," became the focus of increasingly bitter accusations of attempted bribery from both factions. Cornbury clearly tried to reduce the power of the Quakers (by disqualifying them from serving in the assembly), as well as that of both proprietary boards, while supporting Anglicans. When Robert Hunter arrived in 1710, he worked to reduce the power of the ring and the level of conflict, but continued to favor the first faction. By the time he left, disagreements had moderated, but heated political divisions returned with Lewis Morris's appointment and a revival of land disputes.

Certainly during the administration of Jonathan Belcher (1747–1757), Lewis's successor, the proprietors who sat on and controlled the council viewed the governor and the assembly as hostile and supporting the land rioters. Thomas Purvis has argued that the assembly actually tried to stay neutral in these disputes. Finally, although conflict over land was important, other issues also divided New Jersey residents in the middle of the eighteenth century, such as support for imperial wars, religion, and college charters. Probably all that can be said in the end is that New Jersey's colonial politics defies easy classification, not surprising in a colony characterized by sectional, ethnic, religious, and economic differences. Politics seem clearer in neighboring New York and Pennsylvania, where divisions into Delancys-Livingstons and Quakers-Proprietors have been seen by some historians as the origins of modern political parties. Such patterns do not appear as obvious in New Jersey until the 1790s.

Land Disputes and Other Issues

The land disputes that ended in violence in the 1740s and 1750s and impinged on politics originated in the seventeenth century and became progressively more complicated. Cornbury and his friends, after obtaining control of the records of the East and West proprietors, made a number of large and later questioned land grants (for example, the Ramapo grant in northeastern New Jersey).[21] In West Jersey, Daniel Coxe's son continued to grant land after his father sold out to the West Jersey Society. But the primary source of problems was the East Jersey proprietors' continued refusal to recognize the Elizabethtown and Monmouth heirs of the Nicolls grants and the Indian titles used by Newark, even as these groups expanded on what they claimed (from 40,000 to 450,000 acres or more).

By 1745, ownership of 500,000 to 700,000 acres was contested. Facing both squatters and individuals who stole lumber from unpatented lands, the proprietors moved aggressively to counter what they viewed as theft. Settlers, on the other hand, were angered at being hauled into court and asked to pay for the same land twice. The East Jersey proprietors, led by lawyer and surveyor James Alexander and assisted by all the lawyers who could be put under retainers, spent four years writing the Elizabethtown Bill in Chancery, which, when filed in 1745, was the largest lawsuit in colonial America. The Elizabethtown Associates submitted a rejoinder in 1751, written in part by then New York lawyer William Livingston. In the meantime, twenty-three incidents in six counties involved the use of force or intimidation. Men arrested for "trespass" were freed from jail by friends wielding clubs. Proprietors complained of unfair juries that let their peers off; landholders decried unfair judges, either the proprietors themselves or men beholden to them; and both sides grumbled about lawyers' fees.

This dispute pitted proprietors in the governor's council and legislative assembly (or their allies) against colleagues who held Newark or Elizabethtown titles. The council pushed for stringent laws against rioting, the assembly for bills offering amnesty. In the end, new laws imposed penalties and also offered amnesty. Governor Belcher tried to mediate, but as violence continued, he sought assistance from England, where his request received serious consideration by the Lords of Trade.[22] The possibility that troops might be sent to quell the violence, along with the outbreak of war in the west, put a damper on protests. Calm was restored by 1754, although protests erupted briefly again in 1769–1771. The disputes did not prevent proprietors from being elected to the assembly and even to the post of speaker (Samuel Neville and Cortland Skinner). In the end, the Newark claimants lost when their case went to arbitration in 1769. The Elizabeth-town Bill in Chancery was never resolved in the courts, as first one side and then the other delayed, depending on the sitting governor (as chancellor, he would decide the case). In the long run, title appears to have been settled by possession. Some historians have connected the land disputes to economic differences between wealthy proprietors and poor landholders, though some of the rioters claimed sizeable holdings. Still others have seen a relationship to the Great Awakening and political divisions over chartering colleges, with New Side ministers concentrated in areas of the Nicolls grants.[23]

If land issues sometimes divided New Jersey politicians, paper money brought them together in opposition to most royal governors and their instructions from England.[24] New Jersey, like other mainland colonies, experienced a shortage of money resulting from an imbalance of payments. Hard money flowed out of the colonies to pay for imports and customs duties, leaving locals to settle bills by barter and even pay taxes with produce. The solution was the use of paper money, which the colonists wanted to have recognized as legal tender so that it had to be accepted in payment and thus retain its value. New Jersey first issued paper money in 1709, distributing it as loans secured by land. Farmers used it to purchase more land, everyone (including colonists in New York and Pennsylvania) used it to conduct business, and the interest paid on it covered the cost of the colonial government. When used to pay taxes, it was usually "retired" (burned), which meant the supply dwindled, the economy contracted, and colonists called for another issue. British merchants did not trust paper money and pressured the king and Parliament to outlaw it. But it solved the colonists' economic problems and eliminated the requirement for taxes in New Jersey. This need was highest in wartime, when the British government demanded men and equipment supplied by the colonial legislature. The result was frequent conflict between governors and legislatures.

The first serious conflict over paper money came when Lewis Morris was governor (1738–1746). The legislature approved paying his salary on the assumption that he would sign its paper money bill and was furious when he accepted the salary and vetoed the bill. The rest of his term was a stalemate—no paper money and no salary.[25] This situation became most serious when funds were needed for war. New Jersey's stock answer was that the colony was too "poor" to provide much assistance, but the real

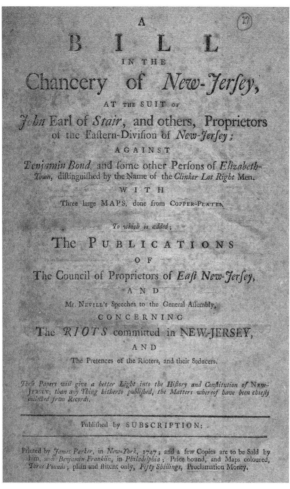

A *Bill in the Chancery of New-Jersey, at the Suit of John Earl of Stair,
and Others, Proprietors of the Eastern-Division of New-Jersey;
Against Benjamin Bond, and Some Other Persons of Elizabeth-
Town, Distinguished by the Name of the Clinker Lot Right Men . . .*
(New York: Printed by James Parker, 1747), title page. The East
Jersey proprietors prepared this statement of their case against
the Elizabethtown settlers. The largest legal conflict in colonial
New Jersey, it never came to trial. (Sinclair New Jersey Rare
Book Collection, Special Collections and University Archives,
Rutgers University Libraries.)

reasons included the desire to keep paper money in circulation, prevent high taxes, and avoid a crisis of conscience for the colony's Quakers.

Colonial Wars

In the first three-quarters of the eighteenth century, with one brief exception, no wars were fought on New Jersey soil.[26] The same cannot be said for Pennsylvania, New York, Massachusetts, Virginia, Georgia, and the Carolinas. New Jersey's good fortune was a consequence of geography, settlement patterns, and the fact that the relatively few remaining Indians were peaceful. In a colony bound on three sides by water, settlement spread from east and west into the center, leaving the southeastern section, known as the "pine barrens," the most sparsely settled area. The only areas exposed to attack were in the northwest corner (where raiding parties during the French and Indian War came across the Delaware River from Pennsylvania). The governor and legislature responded by sending militia and fortifying several places with blockhouses. Otherwise, New Jersey was not subject to *direct* attack by the French, Spanish, or Indians; its citizens were not dragged off to Canada, held for ransom, or adopted into tribes.

This relative security did not mean that New Jersey escaped fear of attack by French or Spanish ships along its coast or that it missed participating in colonial wars.[27] English officials asked for and received men and materials, even though the colony was often slow to act and then provided only a portion of its allotment. Several reasons explain this tendency: the colony was less directly threatened, remained largely agricultural, and had a substantial Quaker population (primarily in West Jersey). As pacifists, the Quakers were opposed to military service and appropriations. Although they remained politically important up to the American Revolution, after 1700 they never held a majority in the legislature (as they did in West Jersey before the merger) and could rarely block appropriations. They did not, as Pennsylvania Quakers did after 1754, withdraw from politics during wartime; rather, they voted no or absented themselves when votes were taken on military matters. (Only in 1776 did Quaker political leaders, including James Kinsey, who had been the speaker of the New Jersey assembly and a delegate to the Continental Congress, leave the political scene.)[28] Even if the opinions of this substantial minority had to be taken into consideration, the presence of Quakers is only a partial explanation for the legislature's lack of full compliance. New Jersey was neither wealthy nor poor, but as it had little direct trade, taxes would be based on land. Legislators were loath to impose such taxes, especially if they could raise funds by loaning out paper money and using the interest payments instead.

Despite New Jersey's hesitancy to raise troops and funds, its soldiers fought, suffered imprisonment, and died in one colonial war after another. Only during King William's War (1689–1697), a time of turmoil in the colony, did it offer little help. In Queen Anne's War (1702–1713) troops were sent to New York, although not used. Thereafter the Jersey Blues, as they were later called, fought the Spanish during the War of Jenkins' Ear (1739–1741) in the Caribbean, the French during King George's War (1744–1748) at Louisburg and Crown Point, and again during the French and Indian War (1754–1763) at Oswego and Fort William Henry. In the last two engagements New Jersey forces were caught in the worst of the action, including the so-called massacre when Fort William Henry surrendered to the French. As many as five hundred Jersey men were captured. One poor sergeant went from New York to Quebec to France, then to England, and finally returned home six and a half years later.[29] When forces from England massed to fight the French after 1754, New Jersey towns were overwhelmed with soldiers stationed in their midst (sometimes twelve to fifteen put up in private homes). In response, the colony built a series of barracks in Trenton (which still remain), Perth Amboy, Elizabethtown, Burlington, and New Brunswick. In this, the largest imperial war, New Jersey supplied well over three thousand men, including some involved in the 1760 victory at Montreal. The prospect of conclusively removing the French from Canada encouraged participation, as did British promises to reimburse expenses.

During this costly imperial war, royal governors agreed to issue paper money. By the time the war was over, the colony had become so dependent upon the expediency that it had borrowed £347,000 and had £275,000 outstanding, the highest debt of any colony. More was added when New Jersey contributed to fighting Pontiac's Rebellion in the west. Retiring this debt became problematic after 1764, when Parliament passed a law prohibiting paper money. In the end, even though fighting in the colony was minimal, the French and Indian War left New Jersey with a large debt, a collection of barracks, and numerous veterans with military experience.

Religion and the Great Awakening

Historians have debated whether the term "Great Awakening" was used in the eighteenth century, and even whether it should be used today, but it seems appropriate for colonial New Jersey, which was roiled by religious revivalism.[30] Brought by pietists from Holland and influenced by Scotch and Irish ministers, this movement spanned the Atlantic world and spread in the colony across multiple denominations through much of the century. It was especially potent in the Dutch Reformed and Presbyterian churches, producing not only discord, but also greater toleration, religious diversity, and three colleges. George Whitefield, the Anglican minister who traveled through all of the colonies many times between 1740 and his death in 1770, found New Jersey undergoing revival on his several visits there, and Jonathan Edwards, whose preaching helped ignite New England revivalism, spent the last weeks of his life as president of the College of New Jersey in 1758. The colony was as much the crossroads of revivalism as of the Revolution.[31]

Disruptive revival religion appeared in New Jersey from 1720, if not earlier, introduced by Dutch ministers such as Guiliam Berthoff, who preached in the Hackensack Valley, and then Theodorus Jacobus Frelinghuysen in the Raritan Valley. William Tennent Sr., an Anglican immigrant from Ireland who became a Presbyterian, established the "log college" in Pennsylvania to train young men, and he fathered future ministers, several of whom served in New Jersey. The best known, Gilbert Tennent, exemplifies the issues. He insisted that only converted ministers should lead churches: "That such who are contented under a *dead Ministry*, have not in them the Temper of that Savior they profess. It's an awful Sign, that they are as blind as Moles, and as dead as Stones, without any spiritual Taste and Relish."[32] He thought emotional sermons freshly given were more important than learned prepared texts and that traveling evangelical ministers (such as Whitefield) ought to be welcomed, even if they were from different sects. Frelinghuysen, who along with his friend Tennent headed a church in New Brunswick, also argued that ministers should be trained and ordained in the colonies, rather than be required to make long and expensive trips abroad. Early in his career, Frelinghuysen warned those members of his congregation "at ease in sin" that they would go to hell: "you carnal and earthly-minded ones; you unchaste whoremongers and adulterers; you

proud, haughty men and women; you seekers after pleasure; you drunk-
ards, gamblers, disobedient and wicked rejectors of the Gospel; you hypo-
crites and dissemblers."[33] Not surprising, some parishioners were offended.
Debates over these and other issues divided church members into New
Sides or New Light/Coetus (supported) and Old Sides or Old Light/Con-
ferentie (opposed).

Another issue was who would control colonial churches and their doctrine. For the Dutch, the questions centered on the power of the Classis of
Amsterdam and the use of Dutch or English in their churches. This situation was complicated for the Presbyterians by their European and local
history. In New Jersey, early eighteenth-century English Congregationalists (Puritans), Scotch Presbyterians, and Irish Dissenters joined forces to
form a Presbyterian synod of Philadelphia, but they came from different
traditions of church hierarchy and disagreed about the need to sign a strict
confession of faith.[34] Arguments over revivalism overlapped other controversies, and in 1745 a group led by John Dickinson of Elizabethtown and
Gilbert Tennent formed a new synod. This group also pushed for the establishment of a college to educate New Side ministers.

The College of New Jersey (now Princeton University) started in Newark and moved to Princeton. It obtained a charter with the assistance of
Governor Belcher in 1746, over the opposition of the colony's Anglicans,
Quakers, and Old Side Presbyterians. To obtain support, the college's
founders broadened its mission to train men to be "ornaments of the State
as well as the Church" and pledged to include members of other denominations as trustees.[35] By the time of the Revolution, the college was attracting
students from other colonies, including James Madison, an Anglican from
Virginia. By then, the Presbyterians had patched up their differences, at least
for the time, and in 1768 the college hired John Witherspoon from Scotland, who taught young men the moral philosophy of the Enlightenment.

In 1766 the New Side (Coetus) Dutch Reformed followed this model
when creating Queen's College (now Rutgers University). The college
barely survived into the next century because the Dutch remained deeply
divided by the Awakening (with consequences in the American Revolution, when revivalists tended to be patriots and their opponents loyalists).
Meanwhile, Baptists in New Jersey also started an academy at Hopewell,
which later moved to Providence and became the College of Rhode Island
(now Brown University).[36]

Although some Old Side ministers closed their churches to revival preachers (including Whitefield), others shared their pulpits (as did Frelinghuysen and Tennent when both were in New Brunswick). At times, congregations also shared their church buildings with other faiths and invited ministers from other sects to preach. There were limits to this toleration—even Tennent was horrified by Count Nikolaus von Zinzendorf and the beliefs of the Moravians. And Anglicans in New Jersey, who watched religious diversity spread (including what was the beginnings in their midst of Methodism), pushed especially in the 1760s for an Anglican religious establishment and a bishop for the colonies, with Jonathan Odell and William Bradbury Chandler of New Jersey seeing themselves as candidates for the position.

Looking at the increasingly diverse religious mosaic that was New Jersey in the eighteenth century and at the cooperation which at times existed, historian Douglas G. Jacobsen has argued that this was the one place in colonial America where competing groups—New Side/Old Side clusters among the Presbyterians, Dutch Reformed, and Anglicans, plus Seventh Day Baptists and Methodists, German Lutherans, German Reform, Moravians, and others—learned to live and practice religious toleration.[37] They also came to value it. The state constitution of 1776 explicitly provided for toleration, stating that no person should ever be "deprived of the inestimable Privilege of worshipping Almighty God in a Manner agreeable to the Dictates of his own Conscience" and that there never would be an "Establishment of any one religious Sect . . . in Preference to another."

Settlement

As already noted, during the eighteenth century settlement spread into the colony's interior even as its small towns and rural areas continued to grow. The population increased from an estimated 10,000 in 1700 to 130,000 in 1776.[38] This growth was significant, although less than that of its neighbors New York (190,000) and Pennsylvania (260,000). Increased numbers also brought greater ethnic and religious diversity. Included in the mix were some Palatine refugees early in the century and German Moravians who established a settlement at Hope, in northern New Jersey near the Delaware. The number of Scotch-Irish also grew and spread beyond the Perth Amboy area.

At the same time the number of blacks, almost all slaves, increased from

200 in 1680 to approximately 8,220 in 1776, or 7.5 to 8 percent of the population.[39] Slavery was an accepted institution in colonial America, with bound
labor used everywhere. The Concessions of 1664/1665 recognized its existence, and both English and Dutch settlers brought slaves with them. Although the numbers were higher in the southern colonies, where there was
a longer growing season and greater dependence on staple crops (in this
period, tobacco and rice), slave labor was used on New Jersey farms, in the
iron industry, and as household help. If the number of slaves owned by each
family was significantly smaller than in the south, the legal system and their
treatment were often similar. A Slave Code written in 1704, and revised in
1713 because of increased fears of revolt, provided separate trials and more
stringent penalties for blacks. It originally included forty lashes, branding,
burning, and even castration, depending on the crime, and later execution
for "arson, rape, or murder." Smaller holdings than in the southern colonies
made it more difficult for the enslaved to have families and to continue African traditions, but evidence indicates both.

From the late seventeenth century, the majority of black slaves were
held in East Jersey, where several large slaveholders from Barbados settled,
where the Dutch (accustomed to slavery) were concentrated, and where
proprietors owned a number of large estates. This concentration increased
after 1750 as Quakers, led by John Woolman, began to question slavery and
advocate abolition. Woolman, first a small farmer, then a shopkeeper, was
influenced by the Quaker idea of the equality of all humankind and ap-
palled by the treatment he observed of slaves. He urged a boycott of dyed
clothing, sugar, and other products of slave labor. Increasingly, Quakers
freed (or sold) their slaves, and in 1776 the Society of Friends forbade its
members to hold slaves.[40] As a result, the number of slaves in West Jersey,
where Quakers were concentrated, declined toward the end of the colonial period. At the same time, the number of free blacks began to increase
(about 5 percent of the total population in 1776), as did the number (slave
and free) who were skilled craftsmen (from builders to bakers, shoemakers
to barbers). Changes came despite the requirement that owners put down a
substantial bond when manumitting their slaves.

While other groups grew, the one segment of the population that declined in the eighteenth century was the Native American, not only because
of disease but also because of the movement of tribes both west and north.
Those left in New Jersey intermarried or blended into the white population

(some intermarried with African Americans). During the French and Indian War, when the remaining Indians were viewed with fear, Governor Belcher helped negotiate the Treaty of Easton in 1758, by which residual land claims were exchanged for a reservation. Responding to the efforts of Presbyterian ministers David and John Brainerd to convert them, some three hundred natives moved to Brotherton, in the center of the colony. Still, the number of Indians in New Jersey continued to decline, and by 1800 the reservation was gone.

Despite recent scholarship on women in New Jersey, little has been written about them in the colonial period.[41] What is clear is that their legal status, like that of women in other colonies, was restricted, their education limited, and their work usually domestic. Differences depended in part on religion and ethnicity, as well as race and class. The Quaker emphasis on equality meant the early creation of women's and men's meetings, examples of female ministers, and provisions for partible inheritance. Early Dutch settlers also were more likely to divide estates equally among all children or to have wives inherit all, rather than following the English pattern of favoring sons, especially the eldest. Even among the English, however, there are examples in the seventeenth century of women owning property, including Elizabeth Carteret after her husband's death and Sara Reape, a Quaker widow who managed the family property in Monmouth County. As the eighteenth century progressed, elite women received more education. Esther Edwards Burr and Annis Boudinot Stockton kept diaries and corresponded with literary and political figures of their day; Stockton also composed poems that show her familiarity with intellectual works of the period. By the 1760s and 1770s, even young women in Cohansey, down along the Delaware, were participating in what John Fea has called a "rural enlightenment," joining young men to discuss literature.[42]

Economy

Throughout the colonial period, New Jersey was primarily rural and agricultural, tied to the Atlantic world by the goods that it exported and imported.[43] The largest of its trade centers were Burlington and Perth Amboy. Other small ports collected goods (for example, wheat at Raritan Landing) or ferried people from one side of a river to the other (New Brunswick and Lambertville), sending them on their way to larger cities. Cape May served as an early whaling port, and Trenton was a milling center. But despite efforts to promote its ports throughout the eighteenth century, most trade went through New York and Philadelphia, then abroad. The largest New Jersey city in 1776 was Elizabethtown with all of 350 households.[44]

New Jersey was one of the "bread colonies," along with New York and Pennsylvania, producing a surplus of grains. A portion went to Europe, but most was shipped to the West Indies to feed slaves and plantation owners who concentrated on sugar. In addition to wheat, farmers grew oats, rye, barley, buckwheat, and Indian corn. To these staples were added beef, cheese, pork products, and some lamb. As urban areas developed, a wide variety of vegetable crops went to market, including potatoes, peas, turnips, cabbages, asparagus, and pumpkins.[45] Orchards were common, planted with apples, plums, pears, cherries, peaches, grapes, and other fruits that were used to produce cider and brandy. Flax, used for linen, was raised, along with hemp, used for rope. Fish and oysters were harvested. White cedar trees, especially abundant in the southern part of the colony, were cut down to make shingles and barrel staves, both exported. At times, ethnicity helped determine what was produced (and grown for home consumption); English farmers preferred sheep, for example, the Swedes, horses and cattle. For labor, farmers depended upon family members and sometimes a few slaves; frequently during planting and harvest times, they hired neighbors and their grown children.[46]

Nascent industries included the milling of flour and lumber.[47] There were early copper mines near Belleville, Bound Brook, New Brunswick, and Rocky Hill. Although the earliest effort to produce iron in the colony, at Tinton Falls, had ended by 1715, new interest grew by midcentury. In south Jersey, Charles Read and others scooped muck out of bogs to extract limonite; in north Jersey, William Alexander and Peter Hasenclever, the latter hired from Germany by English investors in the American Iron Company, dug magnetite rocks from mines. Trees in the then abundant forests in both areas were used to produce charcoal to stoke the furnaces that melted and extracted the ore. By the 1760s, New Jersey ironworks were producing bar and pig iron, though the process proved expensive and not all the enterprises survived. Those that did served the patriots in the Revolution. At the same time, Casper Wistar hired European experts to produce glass, using the prevalent sand of south Jersey, and established the factory town of Wistarburg to furnish bottle and window glass.

In 1748 Governor Belcher described the colony as "the best country I have seen for people who have to live by the sweat of their brows."[48] Colonial America as a whole has been seen as a place where inhabitants enjoyed an abundance of food and a high standard of living, compared with other parts of the world. Nevertheless, even as goods were more widely available in eighteenth-century America, the differences between those at the top and at the bottom of the economic scale increased.[49] An estimated two-thirds of New Jersey farmers and artisans were of middling income, but the range widened. Tenancy, renting land and city houses, was common and not necessarily an indicator of low status. Better gauges were the size of a farm or estate, the clothing worn and the goods accumulated, and especially the kind and size of houses.[50]

Historians have recently noted that a consumer revolution took place in colonial American from about 1750. The amount of household goods grew, clothing and furniture reflected more recent styles, and the consumption of tea (and with it sugar) increased, as did the use of the cups, pots, and linens associated with it.[51] The changes can be traced through newspaper advertisements and through items listed in wills. Whereas a local farmer's wife might use some mismatched pieces of pottery, wealthy families acquired sets of fine china and silver. Landowners and merchants in New Jersey enjoyed the same amenities as the urban elite of Boston and Charleston. William Franklin, for example, had a wine cellar in his house in Perth Amboy and served tea to guests in his formal sitting room.

New Jersey's architecture in the eighteenth century, like its food crops, reflected the ethnic origins of the settlers. The Dutch and English built distinctively different barns, for example, and those who could afford to impress their neighbors constructed homes in the Georgian style favored in contemporary England. Remnants of these grand buildings remain today: the William Trent House on the Delaware (1720s), the Cornelius Low House (1741) in Piscataway, which once overlooked Raritan Landing, the Ford Mansion (1772) at Morristown National Historic Park, and the large proprietary house in Perth Amboy (completed 1764) designed for the colony's governor (where Franklin served his tea).[52] These residences and their contents were meant to indicate high status; they were deliberately more elegant than the homes of small farmers, such as the modest Wick house (1746), also at Morristown, with its dirt floor and multipurpose front room. Even this dwelling differs significantly from the small log cabins built by the Swedes on the lower Delaware early in the previous century.

Legacies of the Eighteenth Century

In the third quarter of the eighteenth century New Jersey was a generally prosperous though largely rural colony. It had gained in population, and also in ethnic, religious, racial, and economic diversity. Its residents were primarily concerned with local affairs, and their differences meant that they could split many ways over political issues. But by the 1770s they had long become accustomed to representative self-government and religious toleration, building on the cherished inheritance of the seventeenth century. In 1758 Aaron Leaming and Jacob Spicer, two long-time members of the legislature, compiled the records of the colony and published them as *The Grants, Concessions, and Original Constitutions of the Province of New-Jersey*; in 1765 Samuel Smith published his *History of the Colony of Nova-Caesaria*, in which he liberally quoted from these early documents and explicitly stated that they were the sources of "religious and civic freedom."[53] Of course, these early historians could not know that the way of life that had been established in colonial New Jersey was about to be challenged.

CONCLUSION

New Jersey as a colony was part of the Atlantic world, as seen in its population, trade, participation in wars, and religious and intellectual controversies. In some ways it was overshadowed by its neighbors New York and Pennsylvania, both larger territories with important ports, so that it has been described as an "agricultural warehouse with a door at both ends."[54] Never in the colonial period did it have its own newspaper. At the same time, New Jersey was distinctive—certainly in the history of its proprietorships, lack of an eighteenth-century frontier, extent of its ethnic and religious diversity, and its politics. Lumping it together with the other middle colonies does not tell the whole story.[55]

ACKNOWLEDGMENTS

The author would like to thank Peter O. Wacker, Jonathan Lurie, and Richard Veit for their close reading and helpful comments on this chapter. The conclusions are of course my own.

NOTES

1. For the debate on the middle colonies, whether and how they are distinctive, see: Wayne Bodle, "The Myth of the Middle Colonies Reconsidered: The Process of Regionalization in Early America," *PMH&B* 62 (1989): 527–548; Patricia U. Bonomi, "The Middle Colonies: Embryo of the New Political Order," in *Perspectives on Early American History: Essays in Honor of Richard B. Morris*, ed. Alden T. Vaughan and George Athan Billias (New York: Harper & Row, 1973), 63–92; Robert J. Gough, "The Myth of the 'Middle Colonies': An Analysis of Regionalization in Early America," *PMH&B* 107 (1983): 393–419; Douglas Greenberg, "The Middle Colonies in Recent American Historiography," *W&MQ*, 3d ser., 36 (1979): 396–427; Michael Zuckerman, "Puritans, Cavaliers, and the Motley Middle," in *Friends and Neighbors: Group Life in America's First Plural Society*, ed. Michael Zuckerman (Philadelphia: Temple University Press, 1982), 3–25; Ned C. Landsman, *Crossroads of Empire: The Middle Colonies in British North America* (Baltimore: Johns Hopkins University Press, 2010).

2. For overviews see: John Pomfret, *Colonial New Jersey: A History* (New York: Scribner, 1973); Richard P. McCormick, *New Jersey from Colony to State*, rev. ed. (Newark: New Jersey Historical Society, 1981).

3. Carol E. Hoffecker et al., eds., *New Sweden in America* (Newark: University of Delaware Press, 1995); Adrian Leiby, *Early Dutch and Swedish Settlers of New Jersey* (Princeton: D. Van Nostrand, 1964); Randall Balmer, *A Perfect Babel of Confusion: Dutch Religion and English Culture in the Middle Colonies* (New York: Oxford University Press, 1989).

4. Charles T. Gehring, "'Hodie Mihi, Cras Tibi': Swedish/Dutch Relations in the Delaware Valley," in Hoffecker et al., eds., *New Sweden in America*, 69.

5. David S. Cohen, "How Dutch Were the Dutch of New Netherland?" *New York History* 62 (1981): 43–60.

6. Wesley Frank Craven, *New Jersey and the English Colonization of North America* (Princeton: D. Van Nostrand, 1964); John Pomfret, *The Province of East New Jersey 1609–1702: The Rebellious Province* (Princeton: Princeton University Press, 1962); John Pomfret, *The Province of West New Jersey 1609–1702: A History of the Origins of an American Colony* (Princeton: Princeton University Press, 1956); Edwin P. Tanner, *The Province of New Jersey, 1664–1738* (New York: Columbia University Press, 1908); Eugene R. Sheridan, *Lewis Morris, 1671–1746: A Study in Early American Politics* (Syracuse: Syracuse University Press, 1981); Daniel Weeks, *Not for Filthy Lucre's Sake: Richard Salter and the Antiproprietary Movement in East New Jersey, 1665–1707* (Bethlehem, Pa.: Lehigh University Press, 2001); Maxine N. Lurie, "The Case of the Founding of Monmouth County," *NJH* 126, no. 1 (2011): 84–95.

7. All quotations from documents are from Julian P. Boyd, ed., *Fundamental Laws and Constitutions of New Jersey, 1664–1964* (Princeton: D. Van Nostrand, 1964). On the 1676/1677 document, which was never officially accepted, see: John Pomfret, "The Problems of the West Jersey Concessions of 1676/7," *W&MQ*, 3d ser., 5 (1948): 95–105; *West Jersey Concessions and Agreements of 1676/77: A Round Table of Historians* (Trenton: New Jersey Historical Commission, 1979).

8. Carlos E. Godfrey, "When Boston Was New Jersey's Capital," *Proc. NJHS* 51 (1933): 1–23; Eugene R. Sheridan, "Daniel Coxe and the Restoration of Proprietary Government in East Jersey, 1690—A Letter," *NJH* 92 (1974): 103–109.

9. John Pomfret, *New Jersey Proprietors and Their Lands, 1634–1776* (Princeton: D. Van Nostrand, 1964); John Cunningham, *East of Jersey: A History of the General Board of Proprietors of the Eastern Division of New Jersey* (Newark: New Jersey Historical Society, 1995); Maxine N. Lurie, "New Jersey: The Unique Proprietary," *PMH&B* 111 (1987): 76–97; Maxine N. Lurie, "New Jersey: The Long Lived Proprietary," in *Constructing Early Modern Empires: Proprietary Ventures in the Atlantic World, 1500–1750*, ed. L. H. Roper and B. Van Ruymbeke (Leiden: Brill, 2007), 327–355. The East Jersey Board of Proprietors survived until 1998; the West Jersey Council of Proprietors still exists and owns never patented lands.

10. Philip Schwartz, *Jarring Interests: New York's Boundary Makers, 1664–1776* (Albany: State University of New York Press, 1979); Maxine N. Lurie, "Colonial and State Boundaries," in *Mapping New Jersey*, ed. Maxine N. Lurie and Peter O. Wacker (New Brunswick: Rutgers University Press, 2009), 202–204.

11. Peter O. Wacker, *Land and People: A Cultural Geography of Preindustrial New Jersey Origins and Settlement Patterns* (New Brunswick: Rutgers University Press, 1975); Ned C. Landsman, *Scotland and Its First American Colony* (Princeton: Princeton University Press, 1985).

12. Although the 1702 royal instructions urged the governor to take special care that the Book of Common Prayer should be read on Sundays and that holy days be celebrated, it also provided "Liberty of Conscience to all Persons"—except Catholics.

13. J. William Frost, "George Keith," in *Encyclopedia of New Jersey*, ed. Maxine N. Lurie and Marc Mappen (New Brunswick: Rutgers University Press, 2004), 437.

14. Counted for East Jersey: Dutch, Carteret and Berkeley, Revolution of 1672, Dutch, Carteret, Twenty-four Proprietors, Dominion of New England, Twenty-four Proprietors. For West Jersey: Fenwick/Trustees, Byllynge, Coxe, Dominion of New England, Coxe, West Jersey Society.

15. General works on the eighteenth century are: Edgar Jacob Fisher, *New Jersey as a Royal Province, 1738–1776* (New York: Columbia University, 1911); Donald L. Kemmerer, *Path to Freedom: The Struggle for Self-Government in Colonial New Jersey, 1703–1776* (New Brunswick: Rutgers University Press, 1940); and Tanner, *Province of New Jersey.*

16. On politics, see above and: Michael Batinski, *The New Jersey Assembly, 1738–1775: The Making of a Legislative Community* (Lanham, Md.: University Press of America, 1987); Larry R. Gerlach, "'Quaker' Politics in Eighteenth Century New Jersey: A Documentary Account," *Journal of the Rutgers University Library* 34 (1970): 1–12; Thomas L. Purvis, *Proprietors, Patronage, and Paper Money: Legislative Politics in New Jersey, 1703–1776* (New Brunswick: Rutgers University Press, 1986); Benjamin H. Newcomb, *Political Partisanship in the American Middle Colonies 1700–1776* (Baton Rouge: Louisiana State University Press, 1995). On politics and specific governors, see: Paul Stellhorn and Michael Birkner, eds., *Governors of New Jersey, 1664–1974* (Trenton: New Jersey Historical Commission, 1982); Michael Batinski, *Jonathan Belcher, Colonial Governor*

(Lexington: University Press of Kentucky, 1996); Patricia Bonomi, *The Lord Cornbury Scandal: The Politics of Reputation in British America* (Chapel Hill: University of North Carolina Press, 1998); Mary Lou Lustig, *Robert Hunter, 1666–1734: New York's Augustan Statesman* (Syracuse: Syracuse University Press, 1983); Colin Nicolson, *The "Infamous Governor": Francis Bernard and the Origins of the American Revolution* (Boston: Northeastern University Press, 2001); and Sheridan, *Lewis Morris*.

17. The provision in the Declaration of Intent of 1672 that required an individual to hold a proprietary land title in order to vote and hold office was contested by the settlers. The Fundamental Constitutions of East Jersey (1683) would have required fifty acres, or a house and three acres, or £50 property. See Richard P. McCormick, *The History of Voting in New Jersey: A Study in the History of Election Machinery, 1664–1911* (New Brunswick: Rutgers University Press, 1953).

18. The requirement for voting was changed again in 1776, first by law and then in the state constitution, to £50 property. All property was valued in New Jersey paper currency, which made it easier to qualify.

19. Purvis, *Proprietors, Patronage, and Paper Money*; Thomas L. Purvis, "'High-Born, Long-Recorded Families': Social Origins of the New Jersey Assemblymen, 1703 to 1776," *W&MQ*, 3d ser., 37 (1980): 592–615.

20. See: Weeks, *Not for Filthy Lucre's Sake*; Brendan McConville, *These Daring Disturbers of the Public Peace: The Struggle for Property and Power in Early New Jersey* (Ithaca: Cornell University Press, 1999); Newcomb, *Political Partisanship*. Newcomb calls the division, which he sees as consistent from the 1740s, administration/opposition; he sees the same pattern in all of the middle colonies. He argues that this was the beginning of modern political parties.

21. Fisher, *New Jersey as a Royal Province*, 181.

22. James A. Henretta, *"Salutary Neglect": Colonial Administration under the Duke of Newcastle* (Princeton: Princeton University Press, 1972), 298–304.

23. Gary S. Horowitz, "New Jersey Land Riots, 1745–1755," in *Economic and Social History of Colonial New Jersey*, ed. William Wright (Trenton: New Jersey Historical Commission, 1974), 24–33; McConville, *Daring Disturbers*, 79–87, 107–201; Purvis, *Proprietors, Patronage, and Paper Money*, 200–231; Thomas L. Purvis, "The Origins and Patterns of Agrarian Unrest in New Jersey, 1735–1754," *W&MQ*, 3d ser., 39 (1982): 600–627; Kemmerer, *Path to Freedom*, 190–236; Alison B. Olson, "The Founding of Princeton University: Religion and Politics in Eighteenth Century New Jersey," *NJH* 87 (1969): 133–150.

24. Purvis, *Proprietors, Patronage, and Paper Money*; Donald L. Kemmerer, "A History of Paper Money in Colonial New Jersey, 1668–1775," *Proc. NJHS* 124 (1956): 107–144.

25. Sheridan, *Lewis Morris*, 181–201; Maureen McGuire, "Struggle Over the Purse: Governor Morris vs New Jersey Assembly," *Proc. NJHS* 82 (1964): 200–207.

26. Fred Anderson, *The Crucible of War: The Seven Years' War and the Fate of Empire in America, 1754–1766* (New York: Knopf, 2000); Anthony Nicolosi, "Colonial Particularism and Political Rights: Jacob Spicer II on Aid to Virginia, 1754," *NJH* 88 (1970): 69–88; Carl Raymond Woodward, *Ploughs and Politics: Charles Read of New Jersey and His Notes*

on Agriculture, 1715–1774 (New Brunswick: Rutgers University Press, 1941), 164–176; Richard Wayne Parker, "New Jersey in the Colonial Wars" *Proc. NJHS* 6 (1921): 193–217.

27. French privateers did appear on the Delaware River in 1748, and there were alarms at other times.

28. Michael Batinski, "Quakers in the New Jersey Assembly, 1738–1775: A Roll-Call Analysis," *Historian* 54 (1991–1992): 65–78.

29. Ian K. Steele, *Betrayals: Fort William Henry and the "Massacre"* (New York: Oxford University Press, 1990), 17, 96, 135, 142–143.

30. Jon Butler, "Enthusiasm Described and Decried: The Great Awakening as Interpretative Fiction," *JAH* 68 (1982): 305–325; Frank Lambert, *Inventing the "Great Awakening"* (Princeton: Princeton University Press, 1999).

31. On religion in general, see: Wallace N. Jamison, *Religion in New Jersey: A Brief History* (Princeton: Van Nostrand, 1964); Nelson R. Burr, *The Anglican Church in New Jersey* (Philadelphia: Church History, 1954); Norman H. Maring, *Baptists in New Jersey: A Study in Transition* (Valley Forge, Pa.: Judson Press, 1964). On the Great Awakening, see: Milton J. Coalter Jr., *Gilbert Tennent, Son of Thunder: A Case Study of Continental Pietism's Impact on the First Great Awakening in the Middle Colonies* (New York: Greenwood Press, 1986); Ned Landsmen, "Revivalism and Nativism in the Middle Colonies: The Great Awakening and the Scots Community in East New Jersey," *American Quarterly* 34 (1982): 149–64; Landsman, *Crossroads of Empire*, 162–181; John B. Frantz, "The Awakening of Religion among the German Settlers in the Middle Colonies," *W&MQ*, 3d ser., 33 (1976): 266–288; Bryan F. Le Beau, *Jonathan Dickinson and the Formative Years of American Presbyterianism* (Lexington: University Press of Kentucky, 1997); James Tanis, *Dutch Calvinistic Pietism in the Middle Colonies: A Study in the Life and Theology of Theodorus Jacobus Frelinghuysen* (The Hague: Martinus Nijhoff, 1967); Edward J. Cody, "The Growth of Toleration and Church-State Relations in New Jersey, 1689–1763: From Holy Men to Holy War," in Wright, ed., *Economic and Social History of Colonial New Jersey*, 42–63; Martin Lodge, "The Crisis of the Churches in the Middle Colonies, 1720–1750," *PMH&B* 95 (1971): 195–220; Firth Haring Fabend, *Zion on the Hudson: Dutch New York and New Jersey in the Age of Revivals* (New Brunswick: Rutgers University Press, 2000).

32. Gilbert Tennent, *Danger of an Unconverted Ministry* (1740; reprint, Boston: Rogers and Fowle, 1742), 12.

33. *Forerunner of the Great Awakening: Sermons by Theodorus Jacobus Frelinghuysen (1691–1747)*, ed. Joel R. Beeke (Grand Rapids, Mich.: Eerdmans, 2000), xv.

34. Elizabeth Nybakken, "New Light on the Old Side: Irish Influences on Colonial Presbyterianism," *JAH* 68 (1982): 813–832; Marilyn J. Westerkamp, *Triumph of the Laity: Scots-Irish Piety and the Great Awakening, 1625–1760* (New York: Oxford University Press, 1988).

35. Francis L. Broderick, "Pulpit, Physics, and Politics: The Curriculum of the College of New Jersey, 1746–1794," *W&MQ*, 3d ser, 6 (January 1949): 56–57.

36. George P. Schmidt, *Princeton and Rutgers: The Two Colonial Colleges of New Jersey* (Princeton: D. Van Nostrand, 1964); David C. Humphry "The Struggle for Sectarian

Control of Princeton 1745–1760," *NJH* 91 (1973): 77–90; Richard P. McCormick, *Rutgers: A Bicentennial History* (New Brunswick: Rutgers University Press, 1966), 1–12; Broderick, "Pulpit, Physics, and Politics"; Olson, "Founding of Princeton University."

37. Douglas G. Jacobsen, *An Unprov'd Experiment: Religious Pluralism in Colonial New Jersey* (Brooklyn, N.Y.: Carlson Pub., 1991).

38. Pomfret, *Colonial New Jersey*, 92, 192.

39. Giles R. Wright, "Moving Toward Breaking the Chains," in *New Jersey in the American Revolution*, ed. Barbara Mitnick (New Brunswick: Rutgers University Press, 2005), 113–137; Graham Russell Hodges, *Slavery and Freedom in the Rural North: African Americans in Monmouth County, New Jersey, 1665–1865* (Madison, Wis.: Madison House, 1997), 1–90; Graham Russell Hodges, *Root & Branch: African Americans in New York and East Jersey, 1613–1863* (Chapel Hill: University of North Carolina Press, 1999), 6–138; Frances D. Pingeon, "Slavery in New Jersey on the Eve of the Revolution," in *New Jersey in the American Revolution: Political and Social Conflict*, ed. William C. Wright (Trenton: New Jersey Historical Commission, 1970), 48–65; Clement Alexander Price, *Freedom Not Far Distant: A Documentary History of Afro-Americans in New Jersey* (New Brunswick: Rutgers University Press, 1980), 1–50.

40. Thomas P. Slaughter, *The Beautiful Soul of John Woolman, Apostle of Abolition* (New York: Hill & Wang, 2008); Jean R. Soderlund, *Quakers and Slavery: A Divided Spirit* (Princeton: Princeton University Press, 1985).

41. Joan Burstyn, ed., *Past and Promise: Lives of New Jersey Women* (Syracuse: Syracuse University Press, 1997), 1–44; Carmela Ascolese Karnoutsos, *New Jersey Women: A History of Their Status, Roles, and Images* (Trenton: New Jersey Historical Commission, 1997), 9–24; Carol F. Karlsen and Laurie Crumpacker, eds., *The Journal of Esther Edwards Burr* (New Haven: Yale University Press, 1984); Claribel Young, "Women and Landownership in Proprietary East Jersey: The Case of Sarah Reape, Quaker," *NJH* 117 (1999): 47–63; Firth Haring Fabend, *A Dutch Family in the Middle Colonies, 1660–1800* (New Brunswick: Rutgers University Press, 1991).

42. John Fea, *The Way of Improvement Leads Home: Philip Vickers Fithian and the Rural Enlightenment* (Philadelphia: University of Pennsylvania Press, 2008).

43. Paul G. E. Clemens, *The Uses of Abundance: A History of New Jersey's Economy* (Trenton: New Jersey Historical Commission, 1992), 10–30; Peter O. Wacker and Paul G. E. Clemens, *Land Use in Early New Jersey* (Newark: New Jersey Historical Society, 1995); David J. Fowler, " 'These Were Troublesome Times Indeed': Social and Economic Conditions in Revolutionary New Jersey," in Mitnick, ed., *New Jersey in the American Revolution*, 15–30; Carl Raymond Woodward, "Agriculture in Colonial New Jersey," in *New Jersey: A History*, ed. Irving Kull, vol. 1 (New York: American Historical Society, 1930), 263–300; Hubert G. Schmidt, *Agriculture in New Jersey: A Three-Hundred-Year History* (New Brunswick: Rutgers University Press, 1973).

44. James H. Levitt, *For the Want of Trade: Shipping and the New Jersey Ports, 1680–1783* (Newark: New Jersey Historical Society, 1981).

45. Woodward, "Agriculture in Colonial New Jersey," 272, said the list of crops "reads almost like the table of contents of a modern seed catalogue."

46. Paul G. E. Clemens and Lucy Simler, "Rural Labor and the Farm Household in Chester County, Pennsylvania, 1750–1820," in *Work and Labor in Early America*, ed. Stephen Innes (Chapel Hill: University of North Carolina Press, 1988), 106–143.

47. Jeannette P. Nichols, "The Colonial Industries of New Jersey, 1618–1815," in Kull, ed., *New Jersey*, 228–262; Richard W. Hunter, "Early Milling and Water Power," in Lurie and Wacker, eds., *Mapping New Jersey*, 170–171; Collamer W. Abbott, "Colonial Copper Mines," *W&MQ*, 3d ser., 27 (1970): 293–309; Charles S. Boyer, *Early Forges of New Jersey* (Philadelphia: University Pennsylvania Press, 1931); Arthur P. D. Pierce, *Iron in the Pines* (New Brunswick: Rutgers University Press, 1957); James M. Ransom, *Vanishing Ironworks of the Ramapos* (New Brunswick: Rutgers University Press, 1960); Woodward, *Ploughs and Politics*; Rosalind Beiler, *Immigrant and Entrepreneur: The Atlantic World of Caspar Wistar, 1650–1750* (University Park: Pennsylvania State University Press, 2008).

48. Quoted in Pomfret, *Colonial New Jersey*, 205.

49. Marc Mappen, "The Paupers of Somerset County," *Journal of the Rutgers University Library* 33 (1970): 33–45; John A. Grigg, "'Ye relief of ye poor of sd towne': Poverty and Localism in Eighteenth-Century New Jersey," *NJH* 125 (2010): 23–35.

50. Coming up with a precise description of the size of landholdings is complicated by insecure titles and boundary disputes. See Wacker, *Land and People*, 399–408.

51. T. H. Breen, *The Marketplace of Revolution: How Consumer Politics Shaped American Independence* (New York: Oxford University Press, 2004); Carole Shammas, *The Preindustrial Consumer in England and America* (New York: Oxford University Press, 1990).

52. Harriette C. Hawkins, "New Jersey Architecture in the Revolutionary Era," 77–100, and Barbara Mitnick, "Picturing Revolutionary New Jersey: The Arts," 61–76, both in Mitnick, ed., *New Jersey in the American Revolution*; Suzanne Hand, *New Jersey Architecture* (Trenton: New Jersey Historical Commission, 1995), 20–48; McConville, *Daring Disturbers*, 223–228; Thomas Jefferson Wertenbaker, *The Founding of American Civilization: The Middle Colonies* (New York: Charles Scribner's Sons, 1938).

53. Newcomb, *Political Partisanship*, 85–87; Carl E. Prince, "Samuel Smith's History of Nova-Caesaria," in *The Colonial Legacy*, ed. Lawrence H. Leder, vol. 2 (New York: Harper, 1971), 163–180; Samuel Smith, *The History of the Colony of Nova-Caesaria, or New-Jersey* (Burlington, N.J.: Printed by James Parker, 1765), 11, 265–274.

54. Levitt, *For Want of Trade*, 44.

55. Landsman, *Crossroads of Empire*, does note some of the ways New Jersey is different from its mid-Atlantic neighbors.

3 · REVOLUTION AND CONFEDERATION PERIOD

New Jersey at the Crossroads

JOHN FEA

The American Revolution came slowly to the colony of New Jersey. There were no dramatic revolutionary moments such as the Boston Massacre or the Boston Tea Party (although New Jersey did have a couple of "tea parties" of its own). There was no equivalent of Patrick Henry's famous "Give Me Liberty or Give Me Death" speech.[1] New Jersey was a relatively quiet place during the late colonial period. Most of the 122,000 inhabitants at the time of the American Revolution were planters who owned modest tracts of farmland. The colony had no major cities, few large merchants, and a heterogeneous population that made unified political action difficult.

When the American Revolution eventually did overtake New Jersey, it came with a bang. The state was the site of some of the most important battles in the war. This "Crossroads of the Revolution" was trampled upon and severely damaged by British and American forces. In the wake of the war, thousands of damage claims were filed. New Jersey also served as winter headquarters for both armies. And it was the site of fierce civilian conflict between patriots and loyalists. According to one estimate, more than six hundred battles and skirmishes took place on New Jersey soil.[2] As a small state, New Jersey had its doubts about the Articles of Confederation, but its leadership ratified the document nevertheless. In 1787 it was the third state to ratify the U.S. Constitution. New Jersey's postwar economic ills and its commitment to remedying those ills, particularly as they related to trade and monetary policy, made its political leaders strong supporters of a federal union.

PROLOGUE

Following the French and Indian War, the British government, under the leadership of Prime Minister George Grenville, turned its attention to the American colonies in a way that it had never done before. Given the need to govern and bring order to newly acquired territory in Canada and the trans-Appalachian west, the presence of nearly 20,000 French troops in the West Indies, and a renewed interest in stopping illegal trade, Grenville saw fit to increase the number of British troops in America. To help pay the expenses of close to 10,000 new troops, the prime minister initiated a series of new colonial taxes. The first, a levy on imported molasses (often referred to as the Sugar Act), was followed by a controversial tax known as the Stamp Act, which required newspapers and legal documents to be printed on paper bearing a revenue stamp. The money raised from both taxes would be used to support the British troops in the colonies.

Colonial leaders were not bothered so much by the way the tax would affect their wallets as they were by the fact that Parliament claimed the right to impose the tax in the first place. Because the colonists were not represented in Parliament, they believed that only their colonial assemblies had the power to levy direct taxes. In Virginia, the House of Burgesses responded to the Stamp Act with the "Virginia Resolves," a document affirming the belief that the colonies could not be taxed without their consent. In Boston, opponents of the Stamp Act took to the streets. The local tax collector was hung in effigy, and the home of Lieutenant Governor Thomas Hutchinson was ransacked. In October 1765, nine of the thirteen colonies, including New Jersey, sent delegates to New York to defend the idea of "no taxation without representation." The gathering was known as the Stamp Act Congress.[3]

In New Jersey itself, there was no immediate response to the Stamp Act. The colony had few merchants and even fewer printers. In fact, the colonial assembly initially chose not to send delegates to the Stamp Act Congress. Princeton lawyer Richard Stockton had to convince the members that it was important for New Jersey to unite with the other colonies. If New Jersey did not participate in the congress, he claimed, the colony would "not only look like a speckled bird among our sister Colonies, but we shall say implicitly that we think it no oppression."[4] Royal Governor William Franklin was "not a little Supriz'd" when stamp collector William Coxe resigned his position in early September 1765. Franklin surmised that Coxe had been intimidated by the protests taking place in other colonies.

Following the Stamp Act Congress, resistance to the new tax intensified. The New Jersey assembly drafted a declaration of rights and grievances and met in Perth Amboy to declare the Stamp Act "unconstitutional" and in direct violation of freedom of the press. In October and November an increasing number of local protests took place in New Jersey towns. Woodbridge condemned the Stamp Act, claiming that its residents would "pay no Sort of Regard to it."[5] On October 29, 1765, the inhabitants of New Brunswick hung an effigy of Speaker of the House Robert Ogden, a representative to the Stamp Act Congress who refused to endorse its "Declaration of Rights."[6] The residents of Elizabethtown threatened to ostracize "all and every Stamp Pimp, Informer, Favourer, and Encourager of the said Act."[7] And when the opponents of the Stamp Act in Salem heard a rumor that John Hatton, a local customs collector, was lobbying to replace Coxe as colonial stamp agent, they sent a delegation to his house "in order to know the Truth of the Report."[8]

The resistance to the Stamp Act placed Governor William Franklin at odds with his assembly, a position in which he would find himself often over the course of the next decade. Franklin's job was to enforce the Stamp Act, but he was also sensitive to the social disorder that might ensue if he carried it out with too much force. He worried that he might suffer the fate of Thomas Hutchinson or perhaps trigger mob violence like that in Boston. In the end, Franklin did not have to make a decision about whether to enforce the act because Parliament repealed it in March 1766. The stamps, which were being held on a ship docked at New Castle, Delaware, never made it to New Jersey shores. The Stamp Act controversy passed without any mob activity, violence, or destruction of property in the colony.[9]

In the meantime, the additional troops sent to the colonies needed places to sleep. In March 1765 Parliament passed the Quartering Act, which directed that British troops stay in public buildings when barracks or other forms of lodging were unavailable. The people of New Jersey had seen their fair share of British soldiers before. During the French and Indian War they had built barracks in five towns, including Trenton, to meet the needs of the troops. Although the colony had ample space to house soldiers, most New Jersey residents—especially peaceful Quakers—did not feel comfortable with British regulars in their communities. And they certainly did not want to pay for their support through troop supply bills. When William Franklin asked the assembly to pass a bill that "would make suitable Provision for the Supply of His Majesty's Troops stationed in this Province," it was overwhelmingly defeated, prompting General Thomas Gage to inform the governor that if the assembly would not fund the troops, he would have to supply them "by some other Means, with the necessarys they cannot dispense with."[10] A potential conflict was avoided in September 1771, when the army decided to move the 29th Regiment, which was stationed in Elizabethtown, to an outpost in St. Augustine, Florida.

In 1767 a new set of taxes, known as the Townshend Acts (proposed by Charles Townshend, chancellor of the Exchequer), were levied on the colonies. Unlike the Stamp Act, which taxed documents that were essential to colonial life, the Townshend duties were aimed at luxury items, such as wine, fruit, glass, lead, paint, and tea. The colonists once again protested that Parliament had no legal right to tax them for the sole purpose of raising revenue.

The Townshend duties went into effect in September 1767, but New Jersey showed little sign of resistance until the assembly received the Massachusetts "Circular Letter" sometime after February 1768. The circular letter, which was distributed to the legislatures of all British American colonies, argued that the Townshend duties were a violation of natural and constitutional rights because the colonists did not have direct representation in Parliament. The New Jersey assembly fully endorsed the letter in May 1768 and encouraged its inhabitants to join other colonies in boycotting British manufactured goods. When Lord Hillsborough, the secretary of state for the American Department, learned about the circular letter, he urged all colonial governors to do everything in their power to prevent their legislatures from responding to it. The New Jersey assembly's positive response to the letter led Hillsborough to reprimand Governor William Franklin and admonish the assembly.[11]

Meanwhile, New Jerseyans did what they could to support the non-importation movements. Some began wearing homespun. Upon intercepting a letter from New York merchants announcing that they would no longer participate in the boycotts, students at the College of New Jersey at Princeton publicly burned the missive in front of Nassau Hall.[12] Several New Jersey towns and counties formed committees of correspondence to share information and enforce non-importation agreements. Though these acts of protest were few in number, they are evidence of a growing movement of colonists seeking political unity around what they perceived to be the tyranny of British taxation schemes.

Despite the ever-increasing resistance to British policies, the biggest news of the 1760s was the robbery of the colonial treasury in Perth Amboy. On July 21, 1768, someone broke into the house of East Jersey treasurer Steven Skinner and stole more than £6,000 from a steel chest in his first floor office. Governor Franklin ordered an investigation, and Skinner offered a handsome reward, but the money was never found. Up until this point in his administration, Franklin had managed to withstand public controversies largely unscathed. But in the fall of 1770, the assembly conducted its own investigation of the robbery and concluded that Skinner, now a member of Franklin's governing council, had not shown the proper "Security and Care" necessary to keep the money safe. The assembly leadership demanded that he reimburse the colony for its loss. When Skinner refused, the assembly asked Franklin to require him to do so. The governor found himself in a stand-off with the assembly as he refused this request and another to remove Skinner from his treasurer's post. Skinner eventually resigned amid the controversy (and would later become a prominent Tory). In Franklin's opinion, the assembly had used the incident to exert its power and disrupt the delicate balance between royal governor and colonial legislature.[13]

Although the Townshend duties were repealed in 1770, the tax on tea continued, and the colonial boycotts persisted. In 1773 Parliament added to the controversy by passing the hated Tea Act, which, ironically, *lowered* the price of tea in the colonies. The British East India Company's warehouses were full of tea, but the strength of the boycotts was making it difficult to sell the beverage in America. In order to aid the company, Parliament allowed it to choose a select group of colonial merchants who would be permitted to sell tea at a special discount.

Opposition to the Tea Act came from three different segments of the colonial population. First, some believed that the lower price was a clever attempt by England to trick the colonies into forgetting about the already existing tax on tea. Parliament may have been benefiting American consumers, but it was still taxing the colonies without representation. Second, merchants who were not chosen to sell the cheap East India Company tea were unhappy about being left out of what they saw as an excellent business opportunity. Third, the reduced tea prices hurt smugglers, who now found it difficult to compete with legitimate merchants selling East India Company tea.

The first attempts to ship East India Company tea to America occurred in the summer of 1773. Patriots in New York and Philadelphia did not allow the tea to be unloaded, but there was very little confrontation. The resistance reached violent proportions in Boston, however. When a shipment of East India Company tea arrived in Boston Harbor, Thomas Hutchinson, now the colonial governor, demanded that the cargo be unloaded and refused to allow the ships to leave port until it was safely stored. On December 16, 1773, a group of men dressed as Indians climbed aboard the ships and threw some 340 casks of tea into the water. Similar "tea parties" occurred throughout the colonies. In New Jersey, less than a week after the Boston event, a group of young patriots in the Cumberland County town of Greenwich seized a supply of tea from a local storehouse and burned it in the center of town. The following month, students at the College of New Jersey burned the school's supply of tea and an effigy of Hutchinson with a tea canister tied around his neck.[14]

The British response to the so-called Boston Tea Party was harsh. In a series of Coercive Acts, the English closed Boston Harbor, limited the number and scope of town meetings in Massachusetts, raised the number of British troops in the colony, and required that the trials of royal officials indicted of a crime be held in England, where those loyalists might find a sympathetic jury. As news of the Coercive Acts spread down the eastern seaboard, patriots in other colonies rallied. Because New Jersey conducted very little trade with New England, news of the closing of Boston Harbor did not provoke a strong response. Yet there were local manifestations of support for the Boston patriots. In June, the Monmouth County government issued a statement demanding the repeal of the Boston Port Act. Patriotic leaders in Essex County also went on record in opposition to the Coercive Acts. New Jersey committees of correspondence burst into action to provide the protest movement with a sense of community and common purpose.[15]

On July 21, 1774, seventy-two men from the various committees of correspondence gathered in New Brunswick to make a more formal declaration of their allegiance to the Boston patriots and to work toward grounding "the constitutional rights of America on a solid and permanent foundation." The meeting also selected James Kinsey, William Livingston, John de Hart, Stephen Crane, and Richard Smith—all prominent New Jersey lawyers— to represent the interests of the colony in the First Continental Congress, to be held later that summer in Philadelphia. The illegal meeting in New Brunswick was a turning point in New Jersey Whig politics. The colony had come to the aid of a neighboring colony suffering under British tyranny and, in the process, had been drawn into the revolutionary movement.[16]

As the First Continental Congress got under way, a noticeable change took place in the makeup of the colony's political leadership. Prior to the Coercive Acts, most of the major political offices in the state were held by wealthy and prominent landholders of the Anglican or Quaker religious persuasion. After the New Brunswick meeting, a new group of politicians emerged. Equal in wealth and prestige to the men whom they replaced, they worshiped in Presbyterian churches. Members of the largest denomination in the colony, Presbyterians were some of the most radical supporters of American independence, dominating the revolutionary movement in Cumberland, Middlesex, Essex, and Morris Counties. Presbyterian clergymen like John Witherspoon, president of the College of New Jersey, Jacob Green, pastor of the Hanover Presbyterian Church, and James Caldwell, minister at Elizabethtown, used their pulpits to promote political radicalism. Witherspoon would serve as a delegate to the Second Continental Congress and become the only clergyman to sign the Declaration of Independence. Green would head the committee that wrote the state's first constitution. These Presbyterians blended traditional Whig political ideas with a firm belief in God's providence. This powerful combination motivated many New Jerseyans to follow them into revolution.[17]

Presbyterians and other New Jersey patriots became active participants in promoting the "Association," the First Continental Congress's most important resolve. The Association was the means by which Congress

John Witherspoon (1723–1794), Presbyterian minister, president of the College of New Jersey, and signer of the Declaration of Independence, was a strong supporter of the Revolution. (Engraved by J. B. Longacre, from a painting by Charles Willson Peale. New Jersey Portraits Collection, Special Collections and University Archives, Rutgers University Libraries.)

enforced its non-importation, non-consumption, and non-exportation requirements. The orders of the Association were enacted by local governments. Congress asked the colonies to "encourage Frugality, Economy, and Industry" and to promote "Agriculture, Arts, and Manufacturing of this Country, especially that of Wool." The Association called on the colonists to behave in a moral fashion by ceasing the kind of "extravagance and dissipation" often linked to horse racing, gaming, cockfighting, and attendance at plays. Those who failed to abide by these rules were to have their names "published in the Gazette, to the end that all such foes to the rights of *British America* may be publicly known, and universally condemned as enemies

of *American Liberty*, and thenceforth we respectively will break off all dealing with him or her."[18]

In November the Essex County Committee of Correspondence formed
committees "for the more extensive observation of the conduct of individuals" in their districts. Seven other counties soon followed its lead. Known
as "committees of observation" or "committees of inspection," these local
patriot groups burned pro-British literature, arrested neighbors who expressed loyalist sentiments, and committed a host of other vigilante-style
acts.[19] Not everyone responded positively to the Association. Towns with
large loyalist or Quaker populations refused to participate. Others worried
about the potential for anarchy and social chaos stemming from the revolutionary behavior of committee members. Governor Franklin did everything he could to discredit the Continental Congress.[20]

The revolutionary movement in New Jersey became formal on May 23,
1775, a few weeks after the Battles of Lexington and Concord, when eighty-
five delegates gathered in Trenton for the first meeting of the Provincial
Congress. Its members claimed to be the colony's legitimate government.
(For the next year it would exist alongside the colonial assembly.) The congress declared its ardent wish "for a reconciliation with our parent state on
constitutional principles," and its members committed themselves to "carry
into execution whatever measures may be recommended by the Continental and our Provincial Congress, for defending our Constitution, and
preserving the same inviolate."[21] In June the Congress discussed a plan for
organizing and preparing a colonial militia and imposed a tax on the counties for the purpose of funding its continued work. In addition, its members
asked each county to provide the congress with a list of individuals who
were unwilling to comply with the Association.[22]

Perhaps the most pivotal moment in New Jersey's revolutionary history
occurred in November 1775, when William Franklin, desperate to counter
the activity of the Provincial Congress and anxious to preserve his position
as royal governor, called the colonial assembly into session. The meeting
in Burlington must have been awkward for the many in attendance who
had actively participated in a meeting of the Provincial Congress only a
few weeks earlier. Franklin opened the session with a speech reminding
the assembly members that any movement toward independence or the
overthrow of New Jersey's colonial government would be met with British military force. Franklin felt that he came to the assembly in a position

of power. Not only did he have in his possession petitions from residents (mostly Quakers) of Burlington County asking the assembly to "discourage Independency," but he also had word that two New Jersey members of the Continental Congress, John de Hart and James Kinsey, had resigned. Although de Hart and Kinsey (a Quaker) claimed that they acted for personal reasons, Franklin suspected that they feared for their safety. Finally, the assembly formed a committee to send a petition to the king (separate from the petition of the Continental Congress) calling for the restoration of peace between the colonies and the crown.[23]

Not all went well for Franklin at the meeting. Near the end of the session the assembly finally responded to the governor's opening speech. The members chided him for assuming that they wanted to remove him from office and suggested that if he continued to submit to the will of the assembly, his job would remain secure. Franklin was angered that the assembly was setting the terms of the debate but did nothing that might give the assembly reason to remove him. Matters worsened on December 5, when delegates from the Continental Congress—John Dickinson, John Jay, and George Wythe—arrived in Burlington and convinced the assembly not to send its separate petition to the king. For all intents and purposes, Franklin no longer held any influence in the New Jersey government.[24]

Franklin's world came crashing down when a letter he had written to Lord Dartmouth, his superior in England, was intercepted by his former friend and now political enemy William Alexander, the self-appointed "Lord Stirling." The letter claimed that most Americans did not support the Continental Congress and that those who did were being selfish in their decision to separate from the country that had nurtured them for so long. Intent upon embarrassing his rival, Stirling sent troops to the governor's residence in Perth Amboy to place him under house arrest in Elizabethtown while awaiting news from the Continental Congress on how to punish him. Eventually, Royal Chief Justice Frederick Smyth came to Franklin's defense and convinced Stirling to allow the governor to remain in his residence in Perth Amboy. The Continental Congress did not act on the letters.

As 1776 approached, many New Jersey patriots were still skeptical about declaring independence, but the number of these moderates was growing smaller by the day. The colonists, including soldiers from New Jersey, were at war with British forces in Canada and New England. John Witherspoon defended Thomas Paine's *Common Sense* in the pages of the *Pennsylvania*

Packet, and Jacob Green's *Observations on the Reconciliation of Great-Britain and the Colonies* was the only pamphlet written in support of independence by a resident of New Jersey.[25] In Greenwich, a young Presbyterian minister named Philip Vickers Fithian described "Battalions of Militia & Minutemen embodying—Drums & Fife rattling—Military Language in every Mouth" and young men resolved "in steady manly Firmness, to support & establish American Liberty or die in battle."[26] Throughout the colony, committees of safety were rounding up Tories and punishing them for their counterinsurgency. The Provincial Congress formed a committee dedicated to removing royally appointed officials from office. One of them would be William Franklin.

Sometime in the spring of 1776, William Franklin received news that a British peace commission was on its way. He saw its arrival as his last opportunity to prevent his colony from joining with the Continental Congress in what was now a surge toward independence. Even though the Provincial Congress was serving as the de facto government in New Jersey, Franklin exercised his prerogative as royal governor and called for a meeting of the general assembly on June 20. Franklin still believed, perhaps naively at this point, that the majority of the inhabitants of New Jersey were opposed to independence.

The meeting of the assembly never took place. The Provincial Congress viewed Franklin's actions as a "direct contempt and violation of the resolve of the Continental Congress" and declared the governor "an enemy to the liberties of this country."[27] The Provincial Congress called for his immediate arrest and assigned Colonel Nathaniel Heard to carry out the order. On June 17 Heard arrived in Perth Amboy to find a recalcitrant William Franklin. As the royal governor awaited his arrest, he wrote feverishly to the Provincial Congress in an attempt to defend himself for calling the assembly and made a last-ditch effort to convince its members that they had been duped by the Continental Congress in Philadelphia into believing that a declaration of independence was in their best interest. Two days later Heard took Franklin to Burlington, where he was interrogated by the members of the Provincial Congress, who decided that he would be placed under house arrest in Connecticut.[28]

With the royal governor removed from office, the Provincial Congress focused its attention on the question of independence. At the time of Franklin's arrest, only Maryland, New York, and New Jersey had not given full support to the independence movement that was being seriously discussed and debated in the Continental Congress. That changed on June 21, when the Provincial Congress voted 54–3 to send delegates to Philadelphia with instructions to vote for independence. A new pro-independence delegation made up of Richard Stockton, Abraham Clark, John Hart, Francis Hopkinson, and John Witherspoon headed off to Philadelphia, and a committee was named to draw up a state constitution. New Jersey's revolution had begun.[29]

The 1776 constitution, which was written before the Continental Congress officially declared independence from England, invested power in the people as represented through the legislative branch. Council members, sheriffs, and coroners would no longer be appointed positions, but elected offices. The governor and justices of the supreme court, previously appointed by the crown, would now be chosen by a joint meeting of the upper council and the lower house. Members of the lower house were required to own £500 in landed or real property; those who sat on the council were required to own £1,000. The right to vote was given to any inhabitant who was a Protestant, who owned £50 in landed or real property, and who was willing to take an oath of "abjuration and allegiance." A lack of specificity in the text meant that women and blacks who met all of the qualifications were permitted to vote.

Perhaps the most curious part of the new constitution was its reference to New Jersey as a "colony" and its concluding statement: "Provided always, and it is the true Intent and Meaning of this Congress, that if a Reconcilation [sic] between Great Britain and these Colonies should take place, and the latter be again taken under the Protection and Government of the Crown of Great Britain, this Charter Shall be null and void, otherwise to remain firm and inviolable." Several members of the Provincial Congress felt that this phrase was too conservative and moved to have it changed, but on July 3 it was decided, by a 17–8 margin, that the original draft, with the "reconciliation" clause included, would be official.[30]

WAR

On July 8, 1776, a celebration of American independence was held in Trenton with "loud acclamations" from local patriots. The following night, in

Princeton, a "spectacular celebration" took place at the College of New Jersey. Nassau Hall, the main building on campus, was "grandly illuminated," and a "triple volley" of muskets was fired in "universal acclamation for the prosperity of the United States."[31] New Jersey had moved from colony to state, but in a few months it would become one of the fiercest battlegrounds in the Revolutionary War.[32]

As the Continental Congress was making its final revisions to the Declaration of Independence, a massive fleet of seventy British warships (roughly half of the Royal Navy) was approaching the coast of Staten Island. On July 1, Nathaniel Scudder, a militia colonel from Monmouth County and a future delegate to the Continental Congress, rode his horse through the night to warn the Provincial Congress in Burlington that the British forces had arrived. Throughout the summer of 1776 the British army under the leadership of General William Howe and the British navy under the leadership of his brother, Admiral Richard Howe, drove George Washington's army from its post on Long Island and eventually captured Manhattan, a conquest they held for the rest of the war. Howe appointed General Charles Cornwallis to follow the fleeing Continental Army through New Jersey. The goal was to remove it from the state before the winter set in and bring a quick end to the war.

Washington's army crossed the Hudson after the fall of Fort Washington, New York, on November 16, 1776, and Cornwallis soon followed, attacking Fort Lee on November 20 and driving the Continental Army out of Hackensack the following day. The abundant farms scattered across the valley landscape were rich in cattle, and the Dutch settlers in the region quickly became the object of foraging parties from both armies. As the war progressed, American and British soldiers passed in and out of the Hackensack Valley.[33] The Continental Army was now on the run. In what has been described as "the long retreat," Washington marched his army through Newark, New Brunswick, and Princeton.[34] Cornwallis remained in hot pursuit until he established headquarters with his army and accompanying Hessian troops at New Brunswick.

Washington's troops eventually made it all the way to Trenton and crossed the Delaware River into Pennsylvania. Howe decided that the British would not follow, and during the second week of December he sent troops, mostly Hessians from New Brunswick, to Trenton. While the Continental Army licked its wounds in Pennsylvania, Howe and Cornwallis set out to restore British order to the New Jersey countryside. Howe offered amnesty to patriots who were willing to swear an oath of allegiance to the crown. The plan appears to have been a success. The British commander claimed that more than three thousand colonists in the region took him up on the offer, including Richard Stockton, a signer of the Declaration of Independence. Stockton had been captured by loyalists and turned over to the British army; after receiving cruel treatment, he took Howe's oath of loyalty and was permitted to return to Morven, his stately Princeton manor house. Meanwhile, John Witherspoon, fearing British retaliation against the College of New Jersey, closed the school on November 29 and fled to Pennsylvania, where he briefly resided with his daughter and son-in-law Samuel Stanhope Smith. Howe thought that the colonial rebellion was over.

On Christmas night 1776, a major snowstorm blanketed the region, and even though Hessian officers in Trenton sent out patrols in the early morning, they were surprised by the day's events.[35] What the Hessians did not know was that in the midst of this storm Washington's troops had crossed the Delaware River to the north of Trenton and prepared for a march into the town. It was a terrible night for such a crossing. There were many in Washington's army who marched barefoot or with old rags on their feet for lack of shoes. One member of Washington's staff reported that despite the difficulties, he had "not heard a man complain. They are ready to suffer any hardship and die rather than give up their liberty."[36] Shortly after eight o'clock on the morning of December 26, two wings of American forces marched into Trenton and captured the town, taking 896 of the German mercenaries before heading back across the Delaware. No American soldier died in the battle, and only four were wounded. Upon hearing the news, Cornwallis canceled his plans to return to England and led 8,000 British soldiers toward Trenton.[37]

The Continental Army was not yet done in Trenton. On December 29, 1776, Washington's forces crossed the Delaware again to engage Cornwallis, who was planning a direct assault on the American army. Washington chose to occupy a hill just south of Assunpink Creek and fight from the high ground. On January 2, 1777, the Continental Army defended the bridge over the creek before eventually escaping to the east in the middle of night. The so-called Second Battle of Trenton was brief, but it proved to be another American victory.

Washington called a council of war and decided to march the Continental

Army toward Princeton, where it engaged the British in a major battle on January 3. With Washington rallying his troops, the Americans won another victory. Alexander Hamilton, the future secretary of the Treasury, served as the battery commander who drove the last British regulars from their position inside Nassau Hall. Following the battle, Washington chose not to continue on to New Brunswick, where the bulk of the British troops were still located. Instead, he marched his soldiers to Morristown, where they spent the rest of the winter.

With the arrival of spring, Washington moved his troops to the safety of Middlebrook in the Watchung Mountains. Perhaps remembering his costly removal of patriot forces from the high ground at Bunker Hill, Howe made every effort to lure the army down from the mountains. After a few minor skirmishes in June 1777, Howe decided to sail his army to Philadelphia via the Chesapeake Bay and Delaware River. The American forts guarding the Delaware—Fort Mifflin on the Philadelphia side and Fort Mercer on the New Jersey side of the river at Red Bank—delayed this effort but in the end were no match for the British navy. In October and November Howe's forces captured the forts, and the British occupied Philadelphia, where they spent the winter. Meanwhile, Washington's troops crossed the Delaware yet again and spent the winter at Valley Forge.

On June 18, 1778, the new British commander, Henry Clinton, abandoned Philadelphia, intent upon taking the war to the south. His plan was to march 12,000 troops across New Jersey to New York, where some would take ships to the Carolinas. After the long winter at Valley Forge, Washington followed Clinton to New York with a much improved army, thanks to the military training the soldiers received from Prussian officer Friedrich von Steuben. Washington's troops caught Clinton's forces on June 28 at Monmouth Court House, where the two armies engaged in one of the longest and bloodiest campaigns of the entire war. The battle was fought in excruciating summer heat, and it ended in a draw. But the Continental Army was able to hold the battlefield without retreating. In the end, Clinton and his forces escaped to Sandy Hook, where transport ships were waiting for them. Today, the Battle of Monmouth is remembered for George Washington's staunch rebuke to Major General Charles Lee after Lee ordered the Continental troops to retreat in the face of an assault by Cornwallis, and for the exploits of Mary Hays McCauly of Carlisle, Pennsylvania, immortalized in New Jersey folklore as "Molly Pitcher."[38]

Victory at Trenton, December 26, 1776. This engraving celebrates General George Washington's victory over the Hessian troops. (John W. Barber and Henry Howe, *Historical Collections of the State of New Jersey* [New York: S. Tuttle, 1845], frontispiece. Special Collections and University Archives, Rutgers University Libraries.)

Monmouth Court House was the last major battle in New Jersey. From this point forward, most of the fighting in the state occurred in smaller engagements and skirmishes. For example, in June 1780, Hessian commander Baron Wilhelm von Knyphausen led 5,000 British regulars, loyalist militia, and Hessian troops on a march through Elizabethtown toward the winter encampment at Morristown. The Continental Army had just suffered through its worst winter of the war in this small Morris County village. In addition to the cold and the snow, the army endured a smallpox epidemic, shortages of food, and a mutiny of Pennsylvania soldiers (as well as some at Pompton from New Jersey).[39] On June 8, as Knyphausen led his troops toward Morristown, he met resistance at Connecticut Farms (now Union). During the short fight, one of Knyphausen's men, a British soldier, shot and killed Hannah Ogden Caldwell, the wife of the Reverend James Caldwell, a patriot Presbyterian minister from Elizabethtown who had recently moved his family to Connecticut Farms to keep them safe while he served as a military chaplain. Hannah Caldwell's death received much publicity in colonial newspapers, where it was pictured as an atrocity. Kynphausen's mercenaries torched both Connecticut Farms and, two weeks later, Springfield after a brief skirmish with American troops.

Throughout the war the New Jersey countryside was riddled with violence and destruction. Some of it came from the intrusion of large armies into small communities. Elsewhere, fighting erupted between local patriots and their loyalist neighbors. Alexander MacWhorter, the Presbyterian clergyman in Newark, gathered stories of residents who were murdered, robbed, raped, and insulted by British troops. Ebenezer Hazard, the postmaster of New York who toured New Jersey in the fall of 1777, described a desolate landscape filled with damaged meetinghouses, courthouses, parsonages, and fences. In Somerset, he wrote, "Great Devastation was made by the Enemy. . . . The Dutch & Presbyterian Churches were stripped of their Pulpits & Pews, their Doors & Windows were broken, & the Boards torn off the Outside, so as to leave the Frames bare."[40]

In Gloucester County, Swedish Lutheran minister Nicholas Collin reported on April 4, 1778, that Hessian troops, in the wake of the British attack on Fort Mercer at Red Bank, burned down a schoolhouse because they had friends who had been kept as prisoners there. Collin urged them to stop such unchristian behavior, but the officer claimed to have lost all military discipline.[41] Two weeks earlier British troops under the command of

Colonel Charles Mawhood had attacked patriot militia at Quinton Bridge in Salem County and then used bayonets to massacre another group of soldiers who were sleeping at nearby Hancock's Bridge. In February of the following year, Governor William Livingston and his family were forced to flee from their Elizabethtown estate when a British raiding party attacked it by surprise. One historian has estimated that nearly 900 men were killed, wounded, or captured in the guerilla-style forage war that occurred just in the three months following the Battle of Princeton.[42] Revolutionary New Jersey was a dangerous place.

Monmouth County, perhaps more than any other New Jersey county, experienced some of the most intense fighting between patriots and loyalists. The news that the Continental Congress planned to declare independence provoked a small-scale civil war in the county. Slaves began to flee from their masters upon hearing about Virginia Governor Lord Dunmore's proclamation offering freedom to any slave who joined the British army. Loyalist insurgents briefly gained control of the county government, and Whigs mounted a counterattack in the wake of the Battle of Trenton. The loyalists staged their assaults from their base at "Refugeetown," a community of displaced loyalists on Sandy Hook. In 1778, Tories emerged from hiding in the Pine Barrens to wreak havoc on the houses and farms of their adversaries.[43] On multiple occasions, Governor William Livingston was forced to send militia from other counties to restore order in Monmouth.

African Americans played a prominent role during the civil war raging in Monmouth County and some of its neighbors. In 1770 New Jersey had 8,220 slaves, second only to New York among colonies in the north. Most of the slaves were concentrated in the eastern counties. As slaves started to escape from their masters and join the British army or loyalist factions, fear of social chaos arose in the state. The most notorious slave-turned-loyalist was Titus, who earned the unofficial title of "Colonel Tye." Tye gained local fame through his heroics at the Battle of Monmouth, where he captured a Monmouth militia captain. He spent most of the war stealing cattle and horses from patriot farms, kidnapping some of the county's leading patriot leaders, and, on at least two occasions, killing militia officers. Tye eventually met his fate when he attempted to capture Josiah Huddy, a militia captain who was known for his successful raids on British troops at Staten Island and Sandy Hook.[44] The war allowed many New Jersey slaves like Tye to find freedom behind the lines of the British army. It also provided an additional forum for Quaker and non-Quaker abolitionists to continue their argument against the peculiar institution. But in the end, the American Revolution did little to bring about emancipation in New Jersey in the way that the language of liberty brought slavery to an end in Pennsylvania and the New England states. New Jersey would not pass a gradual emancipation law until 1804.[45]

CONFEDERATION

As the war raged and state constitutions were written, the Continental Congress was faced with the task of creating a new federal government. Not the least of its challenges was to bring thirteen colonies with very different cultures, ethnic populations, religious convictions, and economies into a unified nation. Some wondered whether such a union was possible. In 1776 these colonies were able to unite around shared political beliefs about liberty and tyranny, but when the common enemy had been defeated, they were more than willing to return to their own independent enclaves as separate and sovereign entities.

After much deliberation, the Continental Congress approved the Articles of Confederation as the first official government of the United States of America. In 1781 the Articles were ratified by the states, and a new "national" government began to function. It is worth noting that the congress decided upon a "confederation" as the American form of government. A "confederation" is a group of states or sovereign units that come together for specific and limited purposes, usually related to the regulation of trade or protection from foreign invaders. The framers of the Articles intentionally created a very weak central government. The Congress under the Articles of Confederation could borrow money, conduct foreign affairs, issue coinage, establish a postal system, govern westward expansion, and supervise Indian affairs. But it was forbidden to levy taxes, control commerce, or pass any legislation without the approval of nine of the thirteen states.

Princeton's John Witherspoon was one of New Jersey's strongest supporters of a confederacy. In a speech delivered before the Continental Congress on July 30, 1776, he insisted that each state put aside its particular interests in favor of a national union. He realized that smaller states, such as his own New Jersey, ran the risk of being subjected to the power of the larger states, but he was willing to accept that risk if it resulted in unity.[46] When the drafting of the Articles of Confederation was complete, the New Jersey legislature did not immediately endorse the document. The fear of domination by the larger states was all too real. Yet, despite the imperfections, on November 20, 1778, the legislature voted 21–8 to ratify the Articles.

Some of the more thoughtful of New Jersey's citizens wondered how the new Confederation would foster a sense of national unity and common purpose. An unstable economy and an increase in popular participation in government was a recipe for individuals to place self-interest over the public good. Many of these observers knew that in order for a republic to survive, the people needed to be willing to sacrifice their own interests for the success of the republic whenever the two came into conflict. Calls for virtue were quite common in the 1770s and 1780s. In an August 7, 1776, address to the citizens of Cumberland County, Jonathan Elmer told his audience that a "new era in politics had commenced." The American Revolution would be successful in the long run only if the people were "actuated by principles of virtue and genuine patriotism" and would agree to "make the welfare of our country the sole aim of all our actions."[47] Later that summer Governor William Livingston urged the state legislature to "encourage a Spirit of Oeconomy, Industry, and Patriotism" and to work toward constructing a foundation for New Jersey that was "laid in Virtue and the Fear of God."[48] Writing in the *New York Gazette*, "Cato" (possibly John Witherspoon) defined a good "Assembly-Man" as someone who was able to "detach himself from local partialities, and county-interests" that were "inconsistent with the common weal."[49] Without virtue, the state would crumble under the weight of selfishness.

Although the 1776 state constitution allowed for increased political participation for many New Jersey residents, the Revolution brought very little social change to the state. A close study of the towns of Piscataway, Shrewsbury, Newark, Morristown, Woodbridge, and Middletown suggests that there was very little redistribution of wealth following independence. Property occasionally changed hands when loyalists fled the state, but those on the bottom rungs of New Jersey society did not benefit economically from the change in government.[50] There was, however, a significant change in inheritance laws. Primogeniture, the practice of passing an estate to the first-born male heir, was abolished. In 1780 the legislature passed a law providing for the division of property among all children, both male and female.

If the social structure of post-Revolutionary New Jersey stayed relatively stable, the same cannot be said for the state's economic climate. New Jersey's postwar economic woes were directly related to the reappearance of inexpensive British goods. With the reopening of British trade routes and a relaxation in political pressure to live self-sufficiently, New Jersey residents went on a spending spree, indulging in a host of British luxuries, from sugar and tea to glassware and silk handkerchiefs. Those who worried that the high level of consumer spending would drain the state of its cash were right. American merchants were racking up large debts to their British counterparts. Hard money became scarce, and the economy spiraled. This turn of events was not unique to New Jersey. A general economic depression gripped the entire nation in the mid-1780s. Many observers believed that the crisis stemmed from a lack of virtue, and some even called for a return to associations, not unlike the ones that enforced the non-importation agreements of the 1760s and 1770s, to curb exorbitant consumer spending.

New Jersey's merchants had hoped that political independence might provide them with greater commercial independence. In the colonial era, New Jersey trade always took a backseat to trade from the larger ports of New York and Philadelphia. After the revolution, state leaders tried their best to lure wealthy merchants to its ports and created a tariff on goods coming to New Jersey from other states. Most of these efforts failed. The state's only recourse was to push for central government regulation of trade. If customs revenues went directly to the federal government rather than the individual states, those states with a strong mercantile community would benefit from the more even economic playing field.

Monetary issues also plagued New Jersey in the 1780s. During much of the decade the state lacked an ample supply of paper currency. The Congress of the Confederation was in even worse financial shape. Farmers who had supplied the army with food during the war were paid with promissory notes that were hardly worth the paper they were printed on. Moreover, New Jersey was saddled with one-eleventh of the United States's total domestic debt—a large burden for such a small state.

As the state government sought to collect its debts through taxes, and the Congress under the Articles of Confederation failed to meet its obligations, New Jersey farmers cried out for the printing of more paper money. The educated leadership of the state, such as Princeton lawyer William

Paterson and Governor William Livingston, believed that the economic crisis required New Jersey citizens to tighten their belts, exercise frugality, and continue in their honest labors. Ignoring these calls to virtue, the hard-pressed people of New Jersey exercised their democratic rights under the New Jersey Constitution, and eventually, in May 1784, the legislature acceded to their demand and passed a loan-office bill that injected more than $266,000 of new paper into the economy.

But there were still problems. Near bankruptcy, the Congress of the Confederation was forced to call upon the states for help in paying off the nation's wartime debt. In September 1785 the members of Congress asked each state to pay $3 million to keep the federal government afloat. When the New Jersey legislature suggested raising this money through the sale of new certificates and the passage of new taxes, the proposal was roundly defeated. New Jersey refused to pay the requisitions, and its independent course sent a clear message to the rest of the states: the Articles of Confederation were broken. Some historians have suggested that New Jersey's refusal to pay the requisition played a more prominent role than Shays' Rebellion in the call for a new federal constitution. Thus, when it came time to revise the Articles, New Jersey was one of the first states to participate. The leadership of the state wanted a stronger national government that would have the power to collect tariffs and regulate commerce. These powers would bring funds to the national treasury and take the pressure off small states like New Jersey to raise taxes to meet congressional requisitions.[51]

New Jersey was the first state to appoint delegates to the Constitutional Convention in the summer of 1787. It was represented by David Brearley, William Paterson, William Livingston, William Churchill Houston, and Jonathan Dayton. From the outset, the New Jersey delegation, led by Paterson, opposed Virginia's attempt to create a two-house legislature in which representation would be based on population. Such a proposal favored the larger, more populated states over the smaller ones. Paterson's "New Jersey Plan" was quite similar to the Articles of Confederation. It called for each state to have an equal vote in a unicameral legislature. Eventually, a compromise adopted the best of both the Virginia Plan and the New Jersey Plan. Seats in the lower house, the House of Representatives, would be apportioned based on population, and seats in the upper house, the Senate, would be apportioned equally. New Jersey ratified the U.S. Constitution on December 18, 1787. It was the third state to do so.

CONCLUSION

New Jersey's revolutionary history is filled with interesting episodes. In addition to studies of some of the most important military engagements of the Revolutionary War, students of New Jersey's revolutionary past will find colorful stories about radical Presbyterians at Nassau Hall, black loyalists ravaging Monmouth County, bold confrontations between provincial troops and a royal governor, brutally cold winters at Morristown, and a surprise river crossing. By 1776, New England, the site of the Stamp Act riots, the Boston Massacre, the Boston Tea Party, and the Battles of Lexington and Concord, was no longer a major focus in the struggle for independence. Virginia, the home of George Washington, Thomas Jefferson, and Patrick Henry, would play a minor role in the events immediately following the Declaration of Independence. But New Jersey, with its strategic location between New York and Philadelphia, remained at the center of the American revolutionary experience. The colony took a gradual path toward independence, the state was the site of major military campaigns, and, in the post-Revolutionary period, its citizens confronted the economic struggles that led to the collapse of the Articles of Confederation. It is time to bring New Jersey more fully into our narrative of the American Revolution.

NOTES

1. For an overview of the Revolution as a whole, see Robert Middlekauff, *The Glorious Cause: The American Revolution 1763–1789*, rev. ed. (New York: Oxford University Press, 2005).
2. Mark Edward Lender, "The 'Cockpit' Reconsidered: Revolutionary New Jersey as a Military Theater," in *New Jersey in the American Revolution*, ed. Barbara Mitnick (New Brunswick: Rutgers University Press, 2005), 45.
3. The best treatment of the Stamp Act crisis remains Edmund Morgan and Helen Morgan, *The Stamp Act Crisis: Prologue to Revolution* (Chapel Hill: University of North Carolina Press, 1953).
4. Richard Stockton to Robert Ogden, September 14, 1765, cited in Larry Gerlach, *Prologue to Independence: New Jersey in the Coming of the American Revolution* (New Brunswick: Rutgers University Press, 1976), 107.
5. Resolutions of the Woodbridge Sons of Liberty, *New York Gazette; or, the Weekly Post-Boy*, March 6, 1766, in Larry Gerlach, *New Jersey in the American Revolution, 1763–1783: A Documentary History* (Trenton: New Jersey Historical Commission, 1975), 27–28.

6. "The Effigy of a Wretch," *New York Gazette; or, the Weekly Post-Boy,* October 31, 1765, in Gerlach, *New Jersey in the American Revolution,* 19–20.

7. Essex County Stamp Act Resolves, *Supplement to the New-York Gazette; or the Weekly Post-Boy,* October 31, 1765, in Gerlach, *New Jersey in the American Revolution,* 19.

8. Gerlach, *Prologue to Independence,* 120.

9. Ibid., 122.

10. Ibid., 74–76.

11. Ibid., 150–154.

12. "Protest Activities at the College of New Jersey," extracts of letters from Princeton and New Brunswick published in the *New York Gazette; or the Weekly Post-Boy,* July 16 and 30, 1770, in Gerlach, *New Jersey in the American Revolution,* 52–53.

13. Sheila Skemp, *William Franklin: Son of a Patriot, Servant of a King* (New York: Oxford University Press, 1990), 122–131; Gerlach, "Politics and Prerogatives: The Aftermath of the Robbery of the East Jersey Treasury in 1768," *NJH* 90 (1972): 133–168.

14. John Fea, *The Way of Improvement Leads Home: Philip Vickers Fithian and the Rural Enlightenment in Early America* (Philadelphia: University of Pennsylvania Press, 2008).

15. Gerlach, *Prologue to Independence,* 205–213; Essex County Resolves on the Boston Port Act, June 11, 1774, in Gerlach, *New Jersey in the American Revolution,* 69–72.

16. Resolves of the New Brunswick Convention, July 23, 1774, *Minutes of the Provincial Congress and the Council of Safety in the State of New Jersey,* in Gerlach, *New Jersey in the American Revolution,* 76–78.

17. Dennis P. Ryan, "Six Towns: Continuity and Change in Revolutionary New Jersey, 1770–1792" (Ph.D. diss., New York University, 1974); Mark Noll, *Princeton and the Republic, 1768–1822: The Search for a Christian Enlightenment in the Age of Samuel Stanhope Smith* (Princeton: Princeton University Press, 1989).

18. *Extracts from the Votes and Proceedings of the American Continental Congress* (Philadelphia: William and Thomas Bradford, 1774), 5.

19. "The Call for the Election of Essex County Committees of Observation," *New-York Gazette; and the Weekly Mercury,* December 5, 1774, in Gerlach, *New Jersey in the American Revolution,* 95–97.

20. Gerlach, *Prologue to Independence,* 244.

21. *The New Jersey Provincial Association,* May 31, 1775, in Gerlach, *New Jersey in the American Revolution,* 143–144; Gerlach, *Prologue to Independence,* 266.

22. Gerlach, *Prologue to Independence,* 269.

23. *Votes and Proceedings of the New Jersey Assembly, November 15–December 6, 1775,* in Gerlach, *New Jersey in the American Revolution,* 164; "A Burlington County Petition to the Legislature on Reconciliation," in ibid., 160–161; Gerlach, *Prologue to Independence,* 294–299.

24. Gerlach, *Prologue to Independence,* 296–297.

25. Ibid., 323 (Witherspoon wrote under the pseudonym "Aristedes"). Jacob Green, *Observations on the Reconciliation of Great-Britain and the Colonies* (Philadelphia: Robert Bell, 1776).

26. Journal of Philip Vickers Fithian, November 13, 1775, in *Philip Vickers Fithian:*

Journal, 1775–1776, ed. Robert Greenhalgh Albion and Leonidas Dodson (Princeton: Princeton University Press, 1934), 131. For a full treatment of Fithian's role in the Revolution, see Fea, *The Way of Improvement Leads Home*.

27. Minutes of the Provincial Congress and the Council of Safety of the State of New Jersey, June 14–15, 1776, in Gerlach, *New Jersey in the American Revolution*, 209–210.

28. Gerlach, *Prologue to Independence*, 307–310.

29. Minutes of the Provincial Congress and the Council of Safety of the State of New Jersey, June 22, 1776, in Gerlach, *New Jersey in the American Revolution*, 210–212.

30. For a good discussion of the "reconciliation clause," see Maxine N. Lurie, "New Jersey: Radical or Conservative in the Crisis Summer of 1776?" in Mitnick, ed., *New Jersey in the American Revolution*, 31–43.

31. *Dunlap's Pennsylvania Packet; or, the General Advertiser*, July 15, 1776, in Gerlach, *New Jersey in the American Revolution*, 219–220.

32. For a general overview of the war in New Jersey, see Alfred Hoyt Bill, *New Jersey and the Revolutionary War* (Princeton: D. Van Nostrand, 1964).

33. Adrian C. Leiby, *The Revolutionary War in the Hackensack Valley: The Jersey Dutch and the Neutral Ground* (New Brunswick: Rutgers University Press, 1962).

34. William M. Dwyer, *The Day Is Ours! The Inside View of the Battles of Trenton and Princeton, November 1776–January 1777* (New Brunswick: Rutgers University Press, 1983); Arthur S. Lefkowitz, *The Long Retreat: The Calamitous American Defense of New Jersey* (New Brunswick: Rutgers University Press, 1998).

35. David Hackett Fischer, *Washington's Crossing* (New York: Oxford University Press, 2004), 256.

36. William Stryker, *The Battles of Trenton and Princeton* (Boston, 1898), cited in Gerlach, *New Jersey in the American Revolution*, 289.

37. Fischer, *Washington's Crossing*.

38. Joseph G. Bilby and Katherine Bilby Jenkins, *Monmouth Court House: The Battle That Made the American Army* (Yardley, Pa.: Westhome Books, 2010); David G. Martin, *A Molly Pitcher Source Book* (Hightstown, N.J.: Longstreet Press, 2003).

39. John T. Cunningham, *The Uncertain Revolution: Washington & the Continental Army at Morristown* (West Creek, N.J.: Down the Shore Publishing, 2007); Thomas Fleming, *The Forgotten Victory: The Battle for New Jersey—1780* (New York: E. P. Dutton, 1973).

40. *Pennsylvania Evening Post*, April 12, 1776, in Gerlach, *New Jersey in the American Revolution*, 296–298; diary of Ebenezer Hazard, August 4–14, in ibid., 298–301.

41. *The Journal and Biography of Nicholas Collin, 1746–1831*, translated by Amandus Johnson (Philadelphia: New Jersey Society of Pennsylvania, 1936), 236–250.

42. Fischer, *Washington's Crossing*, 359.

43. David J. Fowler, "Egregious Villains, Wood Rangers, and London Traders: The Pine Robber Phenomenon in New Jersey during the Revolutionary War" (Ph.D. diss., Rutgers University, 1987); Michael Adelberg, *The American Revolution in Monmouth County: The Theatre of Spoil and Destruction* (Charleston, S.C.: History Press, 2010).

44. Graham Russell Hodges, *Slavery and Freedom in the Rural North: African-Americans in Monmouth County, New Jersey, 1665–1865* (Madison, Wis.: Madison House, 1997).

45. James John Gigantino II, "Freedom and Unfreedom in the 'Garden of America': Slavery and Abolition in New Jersey, 1770–1857" (Ph.D. diss., University of Georgia, 2010).

46. Witherspoon, speech in the Continental Congress, July 30, 1776, *Works of John Witherspoon*, vol. 9, cited in Gerlach, *New Jersey in the American Revolution*, 404–407.

47. Jonathan Elmer, speech to the residents of Cumberland County, *Pennsylvania Journal*, August 28, 1776, in Gerlach, *New Jersey in the American Revolution*, 135.

48. Livingston to the New Jersey State Legislature, September 13, 1776, in Gerlach, *New Jersey in the American Revolution*, 228–230.

49. *New Jersey Gazette*, January 7, 1778, in Gerlach, *New Jersey in the American Revolution*, 425–427.

50. Ryan, "Six Towns," 242, 259, 313.

51. Richard P. McCormick, *Experiment in Independence: New Jersey in the Critical Period, 1781–1789* (New Brunswick: Rutgers University Press, 1950); Mary Murrin, *To Save This State from Ruin: New Jersey and the Creation of the United States Constitution, 1776–1789* (Trenton: New Jersey Historical Commission, 1987).

4 · NEW JERSEY IN THE EARLY REPUBLIC

GRAHAM RUSSELL GAO HODGES

New Jersey rebounded dramatically after the ravages of the American Revolution. Most strikingly, the state's population doubled between 1790 and 1830. New Jersey politics gradually moved from colonial and revolutionary divisions into a vibrant, hotly contested two-party system, which greatly enlarged the white male electorate, created a strong party system, and initiated patronage. For a brief time, New Jersey allowed female suffrage, and women began to be educated in genuine schools in this period. State legislators also began the halting process of gradual emancipation, a reform not achieved until 1804. Free black New Jerseyans gathered in small communities, though many former slaves chose to leave the state. The economy remained largely agricultural, though enlivened by several widely heralded industrial efforts. Despite the conservatism of production, capitalist relations transformed how state residents regarded their land and movable property.[1]

DEMOGRAPHY

New Jersey's geographic boundaries did not change after the American Revolution, but the size of its white populace rose dramatically. The 1790

census enumerated 184,139 residents, of whom 169,954 were white. In succeeding decades the white population continued to grow: 195,125 by 1800;
226,861 by 1810; 257,409 by 1820; and 300,266 by 1830. It would more than
double again to 646,000 by 1860. New Jersey's population was overwhelmingly rural for decades. Urban development was not even measured until
1810, when census takers counted slightly fewer than 6,000 state residents
as city dwellers. Even by 1830, the 18,333 urbanites were just under 6 percent
of the state's population. The census did not record male and female ratios
until 1820, when men outnumbered women by 140,023 to 137,403.[2]

In 1786, New Jersey's population was the most diverse in the youth-
ful country. Fifty-eight percent of white inhabitants were English and
Welsh; Scots, Scotch-Irish, and Irish accounted for 14.8 percent; citizens
of Dutch descent amounted to 12.7 percent; French Huguenots (2.1 percent), Swedes and Finns (2.1 percent), and Germans (9.2 percent) rounded
out the remainder. New Jerseyans emphasized religious affiliation as self-
identification more than nationality. Presbyterians were nearly a quarter of
the population; Quakers made up 16 percent; Reformed Dutch and French
church members accounted for more than 20 percent; and Lutherans, Baptists, Episcopalians, and Mennonites composed smaller but significant portions. Moravians and Catholics were one percent or less. The state's ethnic
and religious population was geographically mixed, though Quakers clustered in the southern counties nearest Philadelphia and the Dutch dominated Bergen County.[3]

POLITICS

Revolutionary-era alignments strongly affected state politics for several decades. Conservative Whigs became Federalists; Popular Whigs joined the
anti-Federalist movement, which soon became Jeffersonian Republican-
ism. These fissures were plain among New Jersey's delegates to the Constitutional Convention of 1787: William Livingston, governor during the Revolution and after; David Brearley, chief justice of the state supreme court;
Jonathan Dayton, a Revolutionary War captain and land speculator who, at
twenty-six, was the youngest of all delegates; William Churchill Houston,
an assemblyman and clerk of the state supreme court; and William Paterson, a lawyer and former state attorney general. Houston withdrew from

the convention in ill health after only a week, the only member of the delegation not to sign the final document.

Paterson and Brearley had the greatest impact upon the convention when they devised, along with Roger Sherman of Connecticut, Luther Martin of Maryland, and John Lansing of New York, what became known as the New Jersey or Small States Plan. This proposal was a reaction to the Virginia Plan, which would scrap the Articles of Confederation, create a new government that would consist of supreme legislative, executive, and judicial branches, and give the new government the sole power to create treaties. The chief executive would be far more powerful than the existing president of the Confederation. The New Jersey Plan reasserted the original charge to the delegates that the "Articles of Confederation ought to be so revised, corrected, and enlarged, as to render the federal Constitution adequate to the exigencies of Government and the preservation of the Union." There was no call to replace the Confederation with a new national government. In other words, the New Jersey Plan proposed a government distinctly "federal," but increased its powers to levy taxes on imports and to regulate trade and commerce. The delegates were to amend the Articles of Confederation, not toss them out.

Paterson advocated a provincial, small state ideology. He wished to maintain the form of past representation, with each state delegation having only one vote in Congress. Whereas James Wilson of Pennsylvania and James Madison of Virginia had proposed a powerful chief executive, Paterson argued for multiple executives of limited powers who could be recalled by a majority of the executives of the states, which would make the executives subservient to Congress and Congress beholden to the individual state governments. Moreover, Paterson, cognizant of New Jersey's recent problems regarding paper currency and debt relief, saw the dangers to his state if a majority of federal legislators read the nation's needs differently or viewed such issues more from their states' self-interest. When Madison refused to consider Paterson's plan, the convention froze into a deadlock for a month, its success very much in jeopardy. If Madison took Paterson too lightly, the New Jersey delegate impressed others with his arguments. William Pierce, a delegate from Georgia, viewed Paterson as "a Classic, a Lawyer, and an Orator . . . everyone seemed ready to exult him with their praises."[4]

The deadlock broke after Alexander Hamilton and James Madison regrouped the nationalists in June. Madison directly confronted the Paterson plan by contending that it was a woefully inadequate solution to the convention's charge of uniting the country in remedying the weaknesses of the Confederation government. In particular, the Paterson plan would not prevent the states from encroaching on federal authority or on each other. With a reminder of the recent Shays' Rebellion, one of the reasons for calling the convention, Madison declared that the Paterson plan would not ensure the internal tranquility of the states themselves. After weeks of acrimonious debate, Roger Sherman of Connecticut devised a compromise that recommended a bicameral legislature: a lower house composed of representatives, elected by state citizens, in proportion to each state's population and an upper house with two representatives from each state, who would be chosen by the state legislature. This compromise reflected Madison's nationalist drive and sufficiently satisfied the smaller states that their rights were protected. William Paterson, who had abandoned the convention on July 23 and refused to return despite pleas from his colleagues, signed the new Constitution on September 17, though he remained anxious about diminution of small state powers within the new government. A few years later, his worries mollified, he took pride in his role in devising the Constitution.[5]

After the state delegation's key role in the Philadelphia convention, New Jersey's lawmakers quickly ratified the new federal constitution. The ratification convention met at the Blazing Star Tavern in Trenton on December 18, 1787, and the delegates approved of the new government by a vote of 38–0. A journal of the proceedings revealed that there was no published debate, no discussion in the newspapers, just unanimity. That came, speculates Pauline Maier, from a desire to stop paying duties on goods imported through New York and Pennsylvania, which would occur once Congress assumed powers to levy tariffs. In truth, the New Jersey delegates, like Connecticut's, vastly overestimated the imposts paid and did not understand that New York State paid virtually all of them. Taxes on New Jersey would not be lowered at all, which would cause aggravation when it time came to pay for the new national capital and the salaries of new federal officers. Eventually, William Paterson recognized this drawback and changed his approach to one that closely mirrored that of the Federalists. This change of heart was one reason that New Jersey was the first state to ratify the Bill of Rights.[6]

The unanimity expressed in New Jersey's approach to national politics quickly dissipated in the initial election in 1789 of New Jersey representatives to the U.S. Congress. After the state's quick passage of the new Constitution, conservative strategists, known as the "Junto," conspired in West Jersey to require that congressional representatives be chosen in general rather than district elections. Two men from East Jersey—Elias Boudinot of Elizabeth-town and James Schureman of New Brunswick—and two from West Jersey—Thomas Sinnickson of Salem and Lambert Cadwallader of Trenton—all destined to become prominent Federalists, made up the Junto. Their near unanimity and support for the new Constitution gave them considerable advantages compared with the local and Popular Whig candidates, who included such notables as Abraham Clark, a signer of the Declaration of Independence and a member of the Continental Congress, and Jonathan Dayton, a member of the Constitutional Convention. Dayton in particular was cast as an opponent of the new Constitution, though he had no more doubts about it than the Junto members (and later cast his lot with the Federalists). The electoral campaign was filled with vitriol, based often on family associations, and packed with ballot manipulation and fraud. Voting places were kept open late to ensure the success of the Junto, a process that turned the election into a farce and forced the House of Representatives to decide the results. After nearly four months, it declared the Junto members as victors, a result that, as Richard McCormick demonstrated, showed how democratic expression could be frustrated by the character of available electoral machinery.[7]

In the following years, the Popular Whigs evolved into Jeffersonian Republicans and eventually successfully challenged Federalist hegemony. From the early 1790s, there were clear differences between adherents of Federalism and their opponents. Federalists tended to be older, of old-stock New Jersey families, and very rarely were immigrants. Far more Federalists attended college and came from interrelated New Jersey political families or from political families in nearby New York, Pennsylvania, Maryland, and Delaware. Federalists and the future Republicans generally came from similar economic backgrounds and occupations, with important exceptions of artisans and printers, who were much more likely to be Republicans. Federalists accounted for more of the state's manufacturing and transportation businessmen. Religion was somewhat of a factor, with Episcopalians (former Anglicans) aligning with Federalism and Methodists and Baptists safely in the Republican camp. These characteristics remained true among top-echelon party leaders between 1796 and 1815.[8]

Washington's Reception by the Ladies, Trenton, April 1789. This print commemorates George Washington's welcome in Trenton on his way from Mount Vernon to New York City, where he was inaugurated as the first president of the United States. (Lithograph, 1845–1846. Library of Congress Prints and Photographs, LC-USZ62–34778.)

The influence of family power from the colonial period kept Federalists in office for more than a decade past the ratification of the Constitution. As in other states, Federalists regarded themselves as a natural aristocracy entitled to power. Once ensconced in office, Federalists benefited from patronage appointments as federal and circuit court judges, supervisors of the revenue, U.S. attorney, U.S. marshal, port collector, and postmaster. Qualifications included personal acquaintance with President George Washington and members of the existing Congress. Such a patronage chain locked national, state, and local Federalists together and served as a large target for Republican criticism and ambition.[9]

The lack of settled, old-stock families with wide connections at first hampered the nascent Republican Party. Opposition to Federalist rule in New Jersey remained weak for years after the 1789 election. Democratic-Republican societies formed in 1794 and 1795. These societies gained energy in the furor over the Jay Treaty of 1795, which resolved issues with Britain remaining since the end of the Revolution, but lapsed in its aftermath because of a lack of party organization. In the presidential election of 1796, the Newark *Centinel of Freedom* endorsed Thomas Jefferson over John Adams in a widely circulated pamphlet, yet Adams easily won the joint meeting of the legislature for New Jersey's presidential electors.[10] Even though Jeffersonian Republicans showed strength in the congressional elections in Essex and Morris Counties by attracting better and more connected candidates, Federalist nominees swept the delegation. Aware of the rising Republican appeal in Essex and Morris Counties, Federalists attempted to rearrange congressional districts to highlight their own strengths. Even with such tactics, the Republicans took three of five seats in the 1798 ballot, scoring their first victories.[11]

Republicans also benefited from Federalist mishandling of the Alien and Sedition Acts in the state. When President John Adams and his wife, Abigail, passed through Newark on their way to their summer home in Quincy, Massachusetts, on July 27, 1798, local residents honored him with a sixteen-gun salute. Luther Baldwin, a local fellow with too much to drink, shouted as the cannon fired: "There goes the President and they are firing at his a___." Federalists denounced Baldwin, who repeated his jest, amending it to "firing through his a___." Two months later a federal grand jury indicated Baldwin and two of this friends for "seditious words tending to defame the President and Government of the United States." Baldwin was convicted and jailed until $150 in fines plus court costs were paid. The Republicans flogged every facet of the case. The *Newark Chronicle* jeered, "Here's Liberty for you!"[12]

These triumphs foreshadowed a national Republican resurgence in the presidential election of 1800. Building on recent victories and national disenchantment with the Federalist Party and President Adams, the Republicans in New Jersey constructed county organizations early and rapidly cobbled together a statewide apparatus. There were stumbles as county and township organizations failed to nominate candidates or collapsed entirely. Mahlon Dickerson, a native New Jerseyan who practiced law in Philadelphia, spearheaded Republican efforts to win New Jersey, considered a key state in Jeffersonian hopes for victory. The *Sentinel of Freedom* and other presses put out assaults on Federalist candidates. The national party printed a number of pamphlets, which were distributed in New Jersey. Despite fervent appeals and massive campaigning, the state remained Federalist, with Adams wining its electoral votes by a wide margin (though he eventually lost to Jefferson). In contrast, Republican candidates swept all five congressional seats in 1800, a result made possible by the winner-take-all strategy imposed by Federalists eleven years earlier.[13]

The duel on July 11, 1804, between Alexander Hamilton, secretary of the Treasury under Washington, and Aaron Burr, the sitting vice president, took place in Weehawken, New Jersey, and was indicative of the tough, often insulting politics of the time. Although their confrontation stemmed from personal acrimony relating to politics in New York, the duelists chose to exchange shots in New Jersey because attitudes there were more lenient about this outlawed practice. Following Hamilton's death, Burr received vital assistance from Commodore Thomas Truxton of Perth Amboy. Senator Jonathan Dayton of New Jersey, a Federalist, also showed early support, but New Jersey became unsafe for Burr in October when a state grand jury indicted him for murder. Burr quipped to his daughter that the two states were vying for the honor of hanging the vice president. Friends in the U.S. Congress drafted a letter to Governor Joseph Bloomfield asking him to nullify the indictment, but that effort failed. New York State found Burr's seconds, William P. Van Ness and Nathaniel Pendleton, guilty of dueling and disenfranchised them for twenty years. Anxious, Burr hired attorney Aaron Ogden to push through appeals to higher courts in New Jersey. While Ogden labored, Dayton agreed to assist Burr financially in the latter's plan to secede the southwestern states and territories from the Union, an act for which Dayton would be indicted in 1807.

Despite Burr's troubles, Republicans, who now controlled the national office and issued patronage set by New Jersey's congressmen, were poised to create a powerful, successful state party machine. New Jersey was early in the development of the instruments of party, including partisan newspapers, party caucuses in the legislature, and conventions. Organization stemmed from the county level, and the earliest state leaders were county leaders. A uniform township committee system was used as a common blueprint for party organization in nearly all counties, and the party used either an open county meeting or a delegate convention. Party newspapers were critical to establish and energize party members, and sophisticated committee work was used to get out the vote. Still, Federalists sustained power in several counties, and factionalism in the county organizations plagued the Republicans after 1817.[14]

Digging out from defeat and the loss of patronage with Jefferson's election in 1800, the Federalists developed party newspapers that could match their Republican counterparts in vitriol. Major emphasis centered on the party's state newspaper, the *Federalist*. Although the Republicans dominated state offices for the next dozen years, several counties, including Bergen in the northeast, Middlesex and Somerset in the center, and Cape May in the south, remained dependably Federalist. The first three were largely Dutch, and the latter two were strongly Quaker. None of these counties had high demographic growth rates, which hampered Federalist comebacks. Even so, younger men, many from the same mold as their fathers, became party activists. Federalists served as a hostile opposition, slinging mud in the *Federalist* against their Republican peers, attacking their violation of the Constitution in the repeal of the Judiciary Act, which removed most Federalist judges, and denouncing the Louisiana Purchase as unconstitutional. Even as the Federalists sought to copy Republican organizing methods, they decried the Jeffersonian party machine as a tyrannical and undemocratic means of denying the popular vote. As in other states, the Federalists sought to divide Republicans by jumping into the least little personal skirmish. For example, when one Republican criticized Republican Governor Joseph Bloomfield, the Federalists staunchly defended the governor. Most of all, Federalists began to borrow from Republican Party organization and thereby claw their way back into political equality.[15]

New Jersey Federalists benefited from the unpopularity of the Embargo of 1807. All state residents rallied behind Thomas Jefferson's government in the initial dispute with England over the British navy's impressment of naturalized American merchant sailors and, particularly, its seizure of American ships trading with France. Governor Bloomfield prepared for war. Unity dissipated rapidly after the Embargo Act prohibited all American trade with foreign ports. Though New Jersey did not have major ports, its import/export trade was dependent on New York and Philadelphia. Smuggling out of Perth Amboy became rampant as farmers loaded produce for city markets and ferried during the night to avoid revenue agents. Federalists in New Jersey and other states used outrage over the Embargo to rally support in the 1808 presidential campaign. Ultimately, the Republicans and James Madison prevailed, but the Federalists cut deeply into the Republican majority in the state legislature.[16] In 1812, benefiting from anger over national Republican policies, New Jersey Federalists succeeded in electing Aaron Ogden governor.

The inability of American forces to conquer Canada in the War of 1812 and the return to the status quo marked by the terms of the Treaty of Ghent convinced Federalists in New Jersey that the war had been futile and demonstrated the bankruptcy of Republican military and foreign policy. The Federalists called for New Jersey voters to repudiate the Republicans. In turn, the Republicans contended that ultimately the war was successful because it enshrined the image of the American citizen-soldier again defeating the professional armies of a despotic Europe. Ancillary to that was the new belief that Americans had now won the respect of European nations. America, Republicans argued, was an exceptional nation, elevated by God and history as an example to the world. On the ground, the Republicans barely held sway over the legislative contests of 1814. A mere 150-person vote swing in the Monmouth and Hunterdon races would have ceded power to the Federalists.[17]

By the late 1810s, party methods and messages were so similar that Federalists extended their influence beyond their stalwart counties by aligning themselves with dissident Republicans. In addition, Federalists began to introduce socially liberal measures, such as funding free schools and abolishing imprisonment for debt. As the first American party system waned in the early 1820s, many former Federalists found themselves supporting Republican candidates, even to the extent of preferring Andrew Jackson over

John Quincy Adams for president in 1824, a choice that would have out-raged earlier Federalists. As with the Republicans, ideology had given way to party organization.[18]

WOMEN'S SUFFRAGE

One reform, female suffrage, was continually under scrutiny in the early years of the new Republic. In 1776 the new government of New Jersey en-acted a constitution under extraordinary duress. Alone among the first states, New Jersey defined qualified voters as adult inhabitants with at least £50 of property. Although this requirement effectively disenfranchised married women, whose property was controlled by their husbands, single women and widows with sufficient property participated in the state's elec-toral process until 1807. That year the state legislature passed a law that re-defined voters solely as adult, white, male, taxpaying citizens.

The anomaly of female suffrage between 1776 and 1807 has inspired a variety of interpretations among scholars. Some have contended that the original franchise clause was simply carelessly designed during a frighten-ing summer of war. Others have argued that it was thoroughly debated and purposefully written. Though no petitions in 1776 demanded women's suf-frage, another argument is that Quaker delegates, who were more accepting of women's rights, pushed the clause through. Still others have focused on women's acceptance of the 1807 law to demonstrate their ideological retreat into republican motherhood and the cult of domesticity. Women's right to own property remained unchanged. In 1790 the legislature specifically used the terms "he" and "she" in a voting act that applied to southern coun-ties and in 1797 extended the right to all qualified women throughout the state. Women were party activists, though at no point did they raise gender-specific issues or seek alteration in their legal status. Their eventual exclu-sion from voting stemmed from the Republican Party's desire to disenfran-chise elements of society, namely, blacks and women, whom party officials regarded, correctly, as pro-Federalist.[19]

Indeed, in the aftermath of the 1789 election, Federalist officials courted eligible female voters assiduously and in terms redolent of Revolutionary ideology. Although married women could not vote, single women were considered in the first U.S. census of 1790 to be "heads of households."

George Washington referred to women as "in the number of the best Patri-ots America can boast." Elias Boudinot, in a Fourth of July oration in 1793, asserted: "The rights of women are no longer strange sounds to an Ameri-can ear, and I devoutly hope the day is not far distant when we shall see them dignifying in a distinguishing code, the jurisprudence of several states of the Union."[20] In the hotly contested 1797 election, both Republicans and Federalists sought the female vote, though neither party was sure of wom-en's loyalty. Federalists were concerned that their only firm female support-ers were wealthy rural landholders, while Republicans could and did appeal to town women. Accordingly, Federalists began to rumble about the possi-ble need to disenfranchise women. Republicans appealed to women voters in the election of 1800 and strongly defended their right to vote. That sup-port proved temporary. In 1803 female voters helped elect Federalist Jona-than Dayton to the U.S. Senate. By 1807, New Jersey Republicans had split into a conservative rump and a moderate northern liberal one. In a com-promise that permitted construction of a new courthouse in heavily liberal Republican Essex County, moderates accepted conservative demands for the disenfranchisement of women. With a national election the following year and President Thomas Jefferson's unpopular Embargo Act alienating voters, party unity was essential. Federalists stood by the side and watched without great complaint as party politics trumped gender concerns.

AFRICAN AMERICANS AND GRADUAL EMANCIPATION

In 1804 New Jersey was the last of the northern states to pass a gradual emancipation act, five years after New York State. New Jersey's law required more than two decades of debate. In the aftermath of the American Rev-olution, enslaved blacks might have reasonably expected that the nation's new freedoms would be extended to them. But although most New Eng-land states had already put slavery on the road to extinction, New Jersey residents resisted, contending that blacks and their allies, the Society of Friends, had supported the British and therefore had not earned the right to freedom. The New Jersey legislature passed a weak ban on the importation of slaves in 1785, with very low fines for violators and no freedom for people imported illegally. The act also provided for easier emancipation, but only for enslaved people in the prime of their lives and capable of self-support.

Clauses limited travel outside of the county where the emancipation had occurred and mandated banishment from the state after conviction for any crime above petty larceny, making blacks second-class citizens. Frustrated by such acts, opponents of slavery, who came largely from the Society of Friends, pushed for a ban on the sale of slaves without their permission and a requirement that masters provide education to slaves. The legislature refused to act beyond these measures for a number of years. A gradual emancipation act failed in the assembly by a single vote in 1794, and lawmakers made emancipation more difficult in the aftermath of a number of successful suits freeing slaves.[21]

Such lawsuits were the efforts of the New Jersey Society for Promoting the Abolition of Slavery, formed in 1793, years after similar organizations started in New York and Pennsylvania. Headed by Joseph Bloomfield, later governor of the state, the society pursued emancipation in cases where the master's title was flawed and pushed legislators for further measures to chip away at the slave laws. Lawmakers resisted proposed abolition acts in 1797 and 1798 but passed measures in 1798 that allowed slaves to own property, gave free blacks permission to live anywhere, and increased penalties for abusing slaves. Still, the split between the two sections of the state continued. The abolition society decided not to hold annual orations because they were unnecessary in West Jersey and unacceptable in the eastern counties.[22] The Society of Friends, having eliminated slavery among its membership and generally shy of political engagement, likely contributed to the western counties' unwillingness to hold celebrations. In the eastern counties, abetted by rising racism, slavery was still sufficiently popular and vigorous that the society doubtless feared violent reprisals.

Blacks resisted their enslavement in New Jersey by bargaining with owners for reduced time of bondage and by suing for their freedom on the basis of loopholes in their property status or broken promises from masters. The New Jersey Manumission Society aided such suits in the early 1790s. But the most common method of resistance was flight. Enslaved black New Jerseyans ran away to New York City and Philadelphia or found work on ocean vessels or in the mines in northwestern New Jersey. By 1810 there were several well-established underground railroad routes running from southern states through Philadelphia to lower New Jersey and then on to Perth Amboy and New York City and beyond.[23]

The New Jersey legislature passed a gradual emancipation act in 1804,

Certificate of membership in the Society for Promoting the Abolition of Slavery, November 26, 1793. The society was organized to bring about the end of slavery in the state. (New Jersey Broadsides, 1793. Special Collections and University Archives, Rutgers University Libraries.)

which provided a legal formula by which newly born enslaved African Americans became apprentices to their mothers' masters for twenty-one years (for females) or twenty-five years (for males) and then were freed. In addition to owning the services of their black apprentices for the bulk of their productive years, masters could sell, bequeath, or trade time owed. As further compensation, the state allowed masters to "abandon the children of their slaves . . . and then to receive from the [state] Treasury for supporting these children *three dollars per month or thirty-six dollars per year,*" a subsidy that nearly bankrupted the state by 1807 and was repealed in 1811. Despite this generous compensation, slave masters from the northern part of the state petitioned the legislature to repeal the emancipation law for depriving individuals of their property without their consent and costing them the freedoms for which they had fought in the American Revolution. Scandalously, many masters "convinced" young enslaved blacks to allow sale of their time to slave dealers in southern states, where they would be held in slavery by local law and lacked any recourse to legal appeal. Critics were able to halt this nefarious practice in 1819, but resourceful masters then connived with kidnappers to continue the slave trade.[24]

Lack of opportunity for free blacks translated into a drop in their portion of the state's population. Overall, the state's black percentage hovered around 7.7 percent between 1790 and 1810 but dipped to just over 6 percent by 1830 and down to under 4 percent by 1860. More than 11,000 people were enslaved in 1790 in the state. Slavery in fact flourished in counties where blacks remained critical to the agricultural labor force. In Bergen County, the number of enslaved blacks rose between 1790 and 1800 and remained over 2,000 in 1810. Blacks then made up 20 percent of the population in Bergen County, the highest percentage in any New Jersey county, but dipped to 17 percent twenty years later as newly freed blacks left for better opportunities elsewhere. Slavery remained strong in all counties from Monmouth north, while rapidly declining in the southern counties, though 182 persons remained enslaved in those counties as late as 1820. Dutch and Huguenot masters, many of whom had small landholdings and could not retain their sons as labor, jealously guarded their enslaved property, correctly recognizing that once freed, former slaves would be unwilling to serve as cottage servants and would head for a new life in New York City and Philadelphia. Such masters ensured this prophecy by refusing to allot a fair share of wages or land to former slaves. Even so, some former slaves created towns in New

Jersey. Black settlers in Skunk Hollow in Bergen County eked out a living on tiny farms for several decades in the early nineteenth century.[25] Black entrepreneurs were far fewer in New Jersey than in the bordering states.

Itinerant ministers working out of New York City and Philadelphia proselytized to black congregations across the state. Richard Allen and Samuel Cornish were among black ministers preaching in New Jersey. Their efforts coalesced in the formation of the African Methodist Episcopal Zion (AMEZ) church conference in Philadelphia in 1816. Among those attending were congregants from the Mount Pisgah AME Church in Salem. Other churches soon followed in Monmouth and Essex Counties. These congregations provided the foundation for struggling black communities in New Jersey and offered resistance to the overbearing racism prevalent in the state.[26]

NEW JERSEY'S ECONOMY

Farming dominated New Jersey's economy well into the nineteenth century. An important exception was the rise of industrialism in Newark and a second halting effort in Acquackanonk (later Paterson). Formerly a farm community, Newark benefited from two groups of artisans: shoemakers and carriage makers. Shoemaking expanded after the War of 1812 with access via regular crossings by steam vessels to the voracious markets of New York City and beyond. Shoe masters enlisted nearby farmers to make shoes as a winter occupation. Entrepreneurs such as Seth Boyden started as leather masters and then shifted into iron production. By 1826, more than 35 percent of Newark's white male labor force worked as masters, journeymen, or apprentice shoemakers. Such development fostered other craft industries. That same year, only 81 of 1,700 adult white males in Newark were farmers. The rest toiled in thirty-four different crafts in workshops that rarely employed more than eight people. Except for shoemaking, Newark's crafts remained preindustrial.[27]

This slow passage into industrialism affected Newark's residents. Families remained large, with an average of eight people. Protestant values espoused in the churches of the city's four denominations (Presbyterians, Methodists, Episcopalians, and Baptists) created a code that frowned upon Sunday labor and drunkenness, though tippling was allowed. Problems endemic to larger cities, including prostitution and grog shops, were scarce in Newark. Local government created another source of stability and inclusion. The city was cohesive enough that nearby farmers apprenticed their sons to craftsmen in the city without fear of corruption. The artisanry remained the central structure of local society in Newark.[28]

Industrial development was not always smooth, even with the backing of one of the most powerful politicians in the nation, as demonstrated in Bergen County. The county had suffered greatly from marauding armies during the Revolutionary War. General postwar economic depression, a decline in demand for agricultural goods, and an influx of immigrants induced many of the county's farmers to seek other economic opportunities. Then Acquackanonk farmers heard rumors of plans to build a national cotton manufactory somewhere in New Jersey. Alexander Hamilton had visited the Great Falls of the Passaic during the New Jersey campaigns of the American Revolution, and later, as secretary of the Treasury, he urged Congress to support economic policies to encourage private industry, arguing that such policies would benefit all sectors of the economy and secure the nation's independence. The Society for Establishing Useful Manufactures (S.U.M.), a private group in which Hamilton was deeply invested, listed a series of criteria for its proposed site, including abundant waterpower, large, continuing supplies of wood, coal, or turf for fuel, and adequate provisions of wheat, corn, beef, and mutton for the workers. The S.U.M. also wanted ample supplies of building materials, access by water or land transportation to major markets, and a population that could become the labor force. Bergen County residents eagerly applied to the S.U.M. and in 1792 reached an agreement to facilitate sales of small lots in the area. Hamilton chose the name Paterson for the new town to flatter Governor William Paterson, who returned the favor by granting a charter to the society and giving it monopoly status and a ten-year tax exemption. Hamilton and his colleagues then created plans to make a brand-new town that would be the third largest in New Jersey.[29]

Opposition from local farmers to plans to incorporate Paterson forced a reduction in the size of the S.U.M.'s jurisdiction and ensured that Paterson would remain part of Acquackanonk Township for some time. Efforts to recruit a local labor force ran into fears that the S.U.M. would create a local version of England's "dark, satanic mills." Fever in September 1794 further winnowed the local employees. The S.U.M. sought Irish Catholic immigrants in New York City as laborers, thereby introducing a population unwelcome in Protestant Bergen County. The lack of churches serving the Irish and the new Protestant workers who faced language barriers in Dutch churches further convinced critics that the manufactories were ungodly places. The S.U.M. closed its factory in 1796, although it retained land rights.[30]

Paterson's population immediately declined, and industrialization slumbered there until the Embargo of 1807 awakened demand. By 1815, Paterson boasted thirteen cotton mills, a card and wire mill, a rolling mill, and a sawmill, primarily owned by local Dutch entrepreneurs. The S.U.M. retained its claims and profited from real estate and power development. By 1825, Paterson's mills employed a heterogeneous population of English and Irish immigrants and native-born New Jerseyans, particularly local Dutch. This group was able to secure a middle niche in small manufacturing and as supervisors and skilled workmen in the factories. Dutch women and children rarely worked in the large mills. The Dutch also were heavily represented in retailing. Significantly, few African Americans could find work in the mills, small shops, or stores in the town. Such absence of opportunity was a large contributing factor to the decline of the black population in Bergen County.[31]

Alexander Hamilton's industrial project in Paterson was not his last attempt to urbanize New Jersey. In 1804, after the Federalist Party lost control in New York City, he and fellow party members declared a grand plan to create a rival city across the Hudson River at a site then known as Powles Hook (today's Jersey City). Hamilton and his colleagues planned to divide the peninsula into one thousand lots and construct a metropolis based on the notion that most great cities arise on the west bank of an important river. Republican Mayor De Witt Clinton of New York City quickly challenged the plan, arguing that New York State had jurisdiction over all land below the low-water mark on the Jersey side and thus over any wharves and docks constructed there. The legal struggle lasted more than forty years. By the time the U.S. Supreme Court decided in favor of the Hamilton plan, there was no hope for a city to rival New York.[32]

Improvement of internal transportation was another major goal for the state government and populace. The terrible condition of New Jersey's roads at the turn of the nineteenth century mandated change. Henry Wansey, an English traveler, reported in 1796 that the road between New Brunswick and Trenton was "full of loose stones and deep holes, in going over which we were so violently shook, that when we got down, many of us could scarcely stand." Two broad rivers on either side of the state and many streams further hampered road travel, which prompted tavern keepers at key crossings to delay passage in order to secure business. Wooden bridges completed in 1795, financed by stock sales and lottery proceeds, helped Passaic and Hackensack river crossings, but their log construction still gave travelers back pains. A stone pillar bridge across the Raritan removed the need for three ferry crossings between New York and Philadelphia. The most elaborate span opened at Trenton across the Delaware River in 1806. More than 1,008 feet from end to end, with five massive arches resting on four tall stone pillars, the structure served the public until 1876.

To move goods faster, New Jersey's state legislature chartered fifty-one turnpikes between 1801 and 1829; although a number of these were never built, by 1825 there were nearly 550 miles of turnpikes, almost all north of Burlington. People on their way to church or work did not have to pay, but sheepherders, drovers, and stagecoaches did. The heavy demands of the War of 1812 wrecked the infrastructure. A prescient John Stevens of Hoboken applied for a charter in 1812 for a railroad using steam engines, but an incredulous legislature refused. Stevens had earlier secured a patent on an improved steam engine and boiler, and he built a steamboat at the Soho Works in Belleville in 1798. In 1804, he built the first steamboat using twin propellers, and in 1808 his masterpiece, the *Phoenix*, could move at more than five miles per hour. Deterred by Robert Fulton's monopoly over New York waters, he ordered the *Phoenix* around Cape May to Philadelphia, to become the first steamboat to cruise on ocean waters. After Stevens finally received his railroad charter in 1825, his model "Steam Waggon" achieved speeds of twelve miles per hour near Hoboken.[33]

In the countryside, George Rutgers of Belleville in Essex County cultivated a variety of crops, including tomatoes (though they were considered inedible for humans) and grains such as rye, oats, and corn. Unlike colonial-era farmers, Rutgers planted solely for the market in New York City, about ten miles away, and did little of the work himself. He also invested in merino sheep. His sales to New York were facilitated by neighbors who poured money into steamships and into land reclamation in the swamps. Other New Jersey farmers transformed their work into rural industrial production of firewood, charcoal, iron, and coal for the urban markets. Rutgers and his neighbors increasingly regarded themselves as rural businessmen. Such changes advanced with greater rapidity after the end of the war with Britain in 1815.[34]

EDUCATION

Educational opportunities for most residents of New Jersey were casual just after the American Revolution. Maintained with voluntary contributions, which kept budgets tight, schoolhouses were stuffy, comfortless, ill furnished, and staffed by poorly trained schoolmasters who used harsh discipline. Parental indifference also kept teachers' wages low.[35] Inspired by Thomas Jefferson's ideas on common schooling in his *Notes on the State of Virginia*, Federalist James Parker of Perth Amboy strove in the early nineteenth century to use an accumulating fund of $50,000, derived from the state's sale of bank stocks, to support free schools. Initially rebuffed, Parker found an ally in Governor Mahlon Dickerson in 1817 and succeeded in creating a permanent school fund; by 1829, it amounted to about $245,000. Even that sum was insufficient to establish schools across the state, and its existence allowed townships to evade school taxes. Nor did educational benefits extend to the state's black citizens. The American Colonization Society, organized to persuade free blacks to emigrate to Africa, operated a tiny free school near Newark; otherwise, church schools were the only answer for African Americans.[36]

There were several significant advances in education for white women in early nineteenth-century New Jersey. The Newark Academy had offered instruction to women since the late eighteenth century and operated as a coeducational institution for part of its history. Its successor, the Newark Institute for Young Ladies, referred to its curriculum as "collegiate" decades before women were admitted to colleges. In the early nineteenth century, several gentlemen affiliated with Queen's College (later Rutgers University) established a female academy in New Brunswick. These schools, which modeled themselves on male academies established during the same time period and were occasionally coeducational, were a significant intellectual improvement over the women's boarding schools operating in New Jersey after 1750. The new schools stressed academics and included instruction in reading, grammar, arithmetic, composition, geography, and natural philosophy. Some female academies also offered courses in Latin, botany, and chemistry. It was common, however, for many female academies to include "ornamental" offerings in music, drawing, painting, and embroidery. Despite such gendered courses, the overall curriculum generally matched the education found at young men's academies at the same time.[37]

For those men who could afford advanced education, collegiate life changed gradually in the first quarter of the nineteenth century. In the years after a 1802, when fire destroyed all but the outside walls of Nassau Hall, the College of New Jersey, under the leadership of Samuel Stanhope Smith, expanded dramatically. By the time Nassau Hall was repaired in 1804, a new building had opened with special rooms for literary societies and a divinity hall for theological students. The college created professorships of languages, theology, mathematics, and astronomy. The school's expansive spending attracted more students, and the number of undergraduates shot up to two hundred by 1806; the graduating class that year was fifty-four.

Growth created problems. The decline of clerical students at Princeton in favor of more generalized scholars, many of whom came from out of state, created a crisis in morality. The faculty strived to maintain a paternalist code and to check drinking, day trips to the city, billiards, and card playing, but found their charges increasingly unwilling to accept supervision. At Princeton and Rutgers, students demanded the right to live off campus, far from faculty supervision; strict rules sparked student pranks and even more raucous responses. One particular issue at Princeton was the presence of young southern gentlemen. Virginia Republicans chafed at the hierarchical order ordained by the Presbyterian and Federalist leadership at the college. The southern students placed high value on personal honor, with an emphasis on direct confrontation to perceived slights. During the winter of 1806–1807, several Virginians were cited for impertinence toward their professors. A decade later, student rioters used armed confrontation for four days. Seven were arrested and 24 members of the student body of 130 were either expelled or dismissed. As a result, the school's financial and physical presence declined, and the institution barely survived.[38]

RELIGION IN NEW JERSEY

New Jersey's Protestant denominations, which had always been an essential part of the social order, experienced new challenges in the 1790s. The

Presbyterian Church, for example, battled against infidelity (loss of faith) and the enthusiasm that many adherents felt for the French Revolution. Methodism also faced infidelity and suffered splintering despite general conferences aimed at fostering unity in 1802, 1804, and 1808. In Monmouth County a group calling itself the Independent Methodists broke off in 1803. Larger secessions occurred after 1813.[39]

Having rid their sect of slave owners and worked to end slavery in New Jersey, the Society of Friends became a mainstay of the gradualist, segregationist, and paternalist policies of early nineteenth-century antislavery politics. The contradictions of such an approach split the community between those who wished to continue in the path of gradualism and activist Quakers who, along with dissidents in other congregations, increasingly advocated black equality. The result was the Hicksite separation of 1829.[40]

In the aftermath of the American Revolution, the Reformed Dutch Church, one of the strongest congregations in the state, rapidly extinguished ties with the Netherlands and looked for association with other Protestant denominations, most notably the Presbyterians. By the late 1780s, the American Synod ordered churches to conduct services in English rather than Dutch. This action mirrored earlier Anglicization among the state's Huguenot, Swedish Reform, and German Moravian congregations. Dutch Reformed attitudes were doubtless affected by the pietism articulated by preachers alienated from the religious establishment.[41]

CONCLUSION

New Jersey in the decades after the American Revolution developed a nearly modern political system in advance of other states. The government was dominated initially by the Federalists, but the Republican Party rapidly developed as an effective counterforce. White male suffrage expanded. Although women had the vote for three decades, the national importance of that precedent is still debated. The state economy gradually shifted into industrialism, although its agricultural base remained potent well into the nineteenth century. Urbanization also lagged behind New York and Pennsylvania. Although New Jersey adopted gradual emancipation in 1804, few social or economic benefits accrued to its largest minority. Many blacks remained enslaved for the duration of the time owed their masters, and free blacks generally left the state. Educational opportunities for white males and females improved. New Jersey's religious denominations Americanized, though they were vulnerable to political and theological faction.

NOTES

1. To compare New Jersey with the nation in this period, see Gordon S. Wood, *Empire of Liberty: A History of the Early Republic, 1789–1815* (New York: Oxford University Press, 2009).

2. Susan B. Carter et al., *Historical Statistics of the United States . . . Earliest Times to the Present*, 5 vols., Millennial Edition (New York: Cambridge University Press, 2006), 1:298, 301.

3. Peter Wacker, *Land and People: A Cultural Geography of Preindustrial New Jersey Origins and Settlement Patterns* (New Brunswick: Rutgers University Press, 1975), 162–166; Graham Russell Hodges, *Slavery and Freedom in the Rural North: African Americans in Monmouth County, New Jersey, 1665–1865* (Madison, Wis.: Madison House Publishers, 1997), 147–171. See also Thomas L. Purvis, "The European Origins of New Jersey's Eighteenth Century Population," *NJH* 100 (Spring/Summer 1982): 15–31.

4. Richard Beeman, *Plain, Honest Men: The Making of the American Constitution* (New York: Random House, 2009), 160–163, 439. See also: Maxine N. Lurie, "Envisioning a Republic: New Jersey's 1776 Constitution and Oath of Office," *NJH* 119 (2001): 3–21; John E. O'Connor, *William Paterson, Lawyer and Statesman, 1745–1806* (New Brunswick: Rutgers University Press, 1979), 134.

5. Beeman, *Plain, Honest Men*, 180–183, 366.

6. Pauline Maier, *Ratification: The People Debate the Constitution, 1787–1788* (New York: Simon & Schuster, 2010), 122–123, 129, 340, 459; Richard P. McCormick, *Experiment in Independence: New Jersey in the Critical Period, 1781–1789* (New Brunswick: Rutgers University Press, 1950), 273–275; Eugene R. Sheridan, "A Study in Paradox: New Jersey and the Bill of Rights," in *The Bill of Rights and the States: The Colonial and Revolutionary Origins of American Liberties*, ed. Patrick T. Conley and John P. Kaminski (Madison, Wis.: Madison House, 1992), 247–273.

7. Richard P. McCormick, "New Jersey's First Congressional Election, 1789: A Case Study in Political Skullduggery," *W&MQ*, 3rd ser., 6 (1949): 237–250. For a recent update, see Liam Riordan, *Many Legacies, One Nation: The Revolution and Its Legacy in the Mid-Atlantic* (Philadelphia: University of Pennsylvania Press, 2007), 88–91.

8. Rudolph J. Pasler and Margaret C. Pasler, *The New Jersey Federalists* (Rutherford, N.J.: Fairleigh Dickinson University Press, 1975), 54.

9. Ibid., 56–57.

10. The newspaper was titled *Centinel of Freedom* from October 1796 to September 1797, and then *Sentinel of Freedom* from October 1797 to 1823.

11. Carl E. Prince, *New Jersey's Jeffersonian Republicans: The Genesis of an Early Party*

Machine (Chapel Hill: University of North Carolina Press for the Institute of Early American History and Culture, 1967), 20–29.

12. James Morton Smith, *Freedom's Fetters: The Alien and Sedition Laws and American Civil Liberties* (Ithaca: Cornell University Press, 1956), 270–274.

13. Prince, *New Jersey's Jeffersonian Republicans*, 56–61, 64–65.

14. Ibid., 69–73.

15. Pasler and Pasler, *New Jersey Federalists*, 113–129.

16. Harvey Strum, "New Jersey Politics & the War of 1812," *NJH* 105, nos. 3–4 (1987): 37–70, and Strum, "New Jersey and the Embargo, 1807–1809," *NJH* 116, nos. 3–4 (1998): 16–47.

17. Strum, "New Jersey Politics," 55, 59–61.

18. Pasler and Pasler, *New Jersey Federalists*,150–156.

19. Rosemary Zagarri, *Revolutionary Backlash: Women and Politics in the Early American Republic* (Philadelphia: University of Pennsylvania Press, 2007), 30–37. See 193n38 for a good summation of critical commentary.

20. Judith Apter Klinghoffer and Lois Elkis, "'The Petticoat Electors': Women's Suffrage in New Jersey, 1776–1807," *Journal of the Early Republic* 12 (1992): 159–193.

21. Arthur Zilversmit, *The First Emancipation: The Abolition of Slavery in the North* (Chicago: University of Chicago Press, 1967), 142, 159–162, 173.

22. Ibid., 188–189.

23. Charles A. Stansfield, *New Jersey: A Geography* (Boulder, Colo.: Westview Press, 1983), 84–86.

24. Graham Russell Hodges, *Root & Branch: African Americans in New York & East Jersey, 1613–1863* (Chapel Hill: University of North Carolina Press, 1999), 169, 172–173, 192; Hodges, *Slavery and Freedom*, 120–122, 129–130.

25. Hodges, *Root & Branch*, 175–176; Hodges, *Slavery and Freedom*, 163–164. On Skunk Hollow, see Joan H. Geismar, *The Archaeology of Social Disintegration in Skunk Hollow: A Nineteenth-Century Rural Black Community* (New York: Academic Press, 1982).

26. Giles Wright, "Moving Toward Breaking the Chains: Black New Jerseyans and the American Revolution," in *New Jersey in the American Revolution*, ed. Barbara Mitnick (New Brunswick: Rutgers University Press, 2005), 113–139; Graham Russell Hodges, ed., *Black Itinerants of the Gospel: The Narratives of John Jea and George White* (Madison, Wis.: Madison House, 1993).

27. Susan E. Hirsch, *Roots of the American Working Class: The Industrialization of Crafts in Newark, 1800–1860* (Philadelphia: University of Pennsylvania Press, 1978), 4; Brad R. Tuttle, *How Newark Became Newark: The Rise, Fall, and Rebirth of an American City* (New Brunswick: Rutgers University Press, 2009), 23–27. For a similar development, see Richard W. Hunter, Nadine Sergejeff, and Damon Tvaryanas, "On the Eagle's Wings: Textiles, Trenton, and a First Taste of the Industrial Revolution," *NJH* 124, no. 1 (2009): 57–98.

28. Hirsch, *Roots of the American Working Class*, 5–7.

29. Ron Chernow, *Alexander Hamilton* (New York: Penguin Press, 2004), 373–377.

30. Howard Harris, "'Towns-People and Country People': The Acquackanonk Dutch

and the Rise of Industry in Paterson, New Jersey, 1793–1831," *NJH* 106, nos. 3–4 (1988): 23–52; Chernow, *Hamilton*, 386.

31. Harris, "Towns-People and Country People," 36–38.

32. Thomas J. Fleming, *Duel: Alexander Hamilton, Aaron Burr, and the Future of America* (New York: Basic Books, 1999), 268–269.

33. John T. Cunningham, *New Jersey, America's Main Road* (Garden City, N.Y.: Doubleday, 1966), 131–135.

34. Kenryu Hashikawa, "Rural Entrepreneurship in New Jersey during the Early Republic" (Ph.D. diss., Columbia University, 2002), 30–36; Megan Michelle Giordano, "Artistry and Industry in Cast Iron: Batso Furnace, 1766–1840" (M.A. thesis, University of Delaware, 2005), 22–39.

35. Nelson R. Burr, *Education in New Jersey, 1630–1871* (Princeton: Princeton University Press, 1942), 247–250.

36. Hodges, *Root & Branch*, 229–230.

37. Lucia McMahon, " 'A More Accurate and Extensive Education than Is Customary': Educational Opportunities for Women in Early-Nineteenth-Century New Jersey," *NJH* 124, no. 1 (2009): 1–28.

38. Burr, *Education in New Jersey*, 136–139; Mark Lucas Langley, "The Origins of Student Life: A History of the Colonial College Extra-Curriculum at Rutgers and Princeton, 1800–1870" (Ph.D. diss., Rutgers University, 1996), 33, 40, 46–50, 84, 95; Mark A. Noll, *Princeton and the Republic, 1768–1822: The Search for a Christian Enlightenment in the Era of Samuel Stanhope Smith* (Princeton: Princeton University Press, 1989), 214–244, 280–281.

39. Barbara Christine Gray Wingo, "Politics, Society, and Religion: The Presbyterian Clergy of Pennsylvania, New Jersey, and New York and the Formation of the Nation, 1775–1808" (Ph.D. diss., Tulane University, 1976), 308–316, 321; Sarah D. Brooks Blair, "Reforming Methodism, 1800–1820" (Ph.D. diss., Drew University, 2008).

40. Jean Soderlund, *Quakers and Slavery: A Divided Spirit* (Princeton: Princeton University Press, 1985), 185–187.

41. Randall Balmer, *A Perfect Babel of Confusion: Dutch Religion and English Culture in the Middle Colonies* (New York: Oxford University Press, 1989), 151–154.

5 · NEW JERSEY IN THE JACKSONIAN ERA, 1820–1850

MICHAEL BIRKNER

In 1815, Hezekiah Niles, the editor of *Niles' Weekly Register*, the single most influential newspaper circulated at the time, remarked that the distinguishing feature of the American character was the desire to get ahead. Getting forward—the aspiration to improve one's lot in life—was at the core of the New Jersey experience in the decades before the Civil War. A new constitutional order, political democratization, and economic development in the early Republic had broadened the range of opportunities open to the white male population. Not all Jerseyans and their families prospered. But over time their initiative transformed the landscape of a state that at the close of the War of 1812 epitomized Thomas Jefferson's yeoman republic. The rolling, fertile farmland, dotted by villages in every region and nascent cities along important bodies of water, offered freedom, independence, and a decent livelihood to those who embraced hard work. Over time, this Jeffersonian ideal would erode, as industrialization and sustained new immigration contributed to a more stratified social order. But only inklings of this change were evident before 1850. For those who noticed, voluntary associations provided a vehicle to build an opportunity society by promoting free public education and improving the lot of the state's most vulnerable citizens. The increasingly vexing issue of chattel slavery in the land of the free remained peripheral to the everyday lives of most New Jerseyans and a puzzle to many. Who should care? The 1850s would bring answers to that question.

MOVING FORWARD

An agrarian world was a mixed blessing. A new political order deriving power from the people was liberating, but were traditional agricultural pursuits sufficiently in tune with an emergent capitalist ethos? In terms of its economic underpinnings and demographics, New Jersey was a backwater in 1815 compared with its larger neighbors, whose economies were driven in new directions by significant immigration and technological innovations. New Jersey's population in 1820—277,500, of which some 18,000 people were still enslaved—showed an increase of less than 100,000 over the three decades since the ratification of the Constitution. By contrast, New York's population rose by one million in those same years, and Pennsylvania's increased by some 600,000. Western states boomed—many of them populated by New Jersey farmers seeking more land and better opportunities. In his popular *Gazetteer of New Jersey*, published in 1834, Thomas Gordon described New Jersey as "a hive of nations, constantly sending out swarms, whose labours have contributed largely to build up the two greatest marts of the Union, and to subdue and fertilize the western wilds. Instead, therefore, of being distinguished for the growth of numbers within her borders, she is remarkable for the paucity of their increase."[1]

Gordon's version was hardly the whole story. New Jersey also was caught up in the major developments of the era, notably the transition to a more commercial-cosmopolitan society in which many citizens demanded better transport and more capital. The state fell in line with its larger neighbors in a growing embrace of the marketplace and technological innovation. Like their peers elsewhere in the Mid-Atlantic region, Jerseyans had, as one historian has observed, "one foot in manure and another in the telegraph office."[2] At the same time, they grew increasingly assertive in politics, moving from a deferential to a participant-oriented system by the 1830s, powered by an information revolution and the emergence of a highly competitive two-party system. Virtually every community boasted at least one local

newspaper, thanks to the patronage that editors enjoyed, along with frank-
ing privileges that allowed them to exchange information freely with their
peers. The rapid expansion of the postal system made it possible for yeoman and artisan alike to access news cheaply and to communicate more
readily, often about political prospects and economic opportunities. Banks
and insurance companies expanded their reach, even in rural counties.
Most important was the transportation revolution.[3]

From Rustic Turnpike to Iron Horse

Toll roads and bridges were a starting point for the revolution in transportation, which accelerated during the Federalist Era and kept up its mo-
mentum well beyond. Road construction advanced in the 1790s, mostly as
small-scale, localized enterprises. New Jersey's first toll road charter was
awarded in 1801 to build a Morris Turnpike, stretching ultimately from Elizabeth to the Pennsylvania border. The legislature chartered fifty-one roads
between 1801 and 1829, some of which did brisk business despite the rough
riding, not to mention lack of amenities.[4] Noticing the difficulties of moving people and goods during mud season, a Hoboken man, John Stevens,
began proselytizing for alternative transport, powered by steam. The time
was not yet ripe for the realization of Stevens's grand vision of a network
of railroads. All the same, Stevens turned his attention to steamboats and
challenged a long-lived New York–New Jersey steamboat monopoly associated with the interests of the aristocratic Livingston family. In the short
run Stevens was defeated, as was his compatriot, former Governor Aaron
Ogden. But over the longer run the monopoly was broken, thanks in part
to the labors of Thomas Gibbons. An outsized character in many respects,
including his physical girth, Gibbons grasped the potential of steamships,
became a partner with Ogden for a time, but fell out with him and ultimately aligned himself with the interests of a rising force in American transportation, Cornelius Vanderbilt. When Ogden sued Gibbons for operating
Vanderbilt's boat *Bellona* from New Jersey to Manhattan, tensions between
them intensified. The legal wrangle that ensued culminated in the famous
case of *Gibbons v. Ogden* (1824), in which the U.S. Supreme Court under
Chief Justice John Marshall ruled that only Congress could regulate interstate commerce. Consequently, the port of New York was open to all comers, and steamboat transport thrived, notably but not exclusively on the
Hudson River.[5]

Steamboats accelerated intercourse between New Jersey and New York City but had relatively little impact on the development of the state as a whole. The livelihoods of many more New Jerseyans were connected to the success of canal ventures, which were seen for a time as the key to economic prosperity. Among these ventures, none exceeded the Morris Canal in ambition. George P. Macculloch, a Morristown engineer, envisioned a means of connecting Pennsylvania coal to Morris County iron mills by raising the water level of Lake Hopatcong and constructing what were in effect ditches along his proposed route. Macculloch pressed his idea with investors and the state legislature. The former (mostly from New York) readily bought in once the legislature granted a charter in 1824 that included liberal banking privileges. Work commenced in 1825. By November 1831 the first boats passed from Phillipsburg to Newark. In 1832 the line was complete — 101 miles of towpath running from Easton, Pennsylvania, to Newark, with inclined planes to hoist the canal boats over the western mountains. To call the Morris Canal a major engineering feat is to say the obvious. Equally important, the canal helped transform its environs by carrying Pennsylvania coal, lime, and fertilizer eastward, reviving the state's dormant iron industry and thereby fueling the growth of industrial towns as markets for food and lumber.[6]

As the Morris Canal was constructed mile by mile by a workforce increasingly composed of newly arrived Irish immigrants, debate intensified in Trenton over a charter for other large projects, including a Delaware and Raritan (D&R) Canal and a new railroad, the Camden and Amboy (C&A). This second canal's backers faced a host of obstacles, from raising essential capital to gaining the right to divert Delaware River water, to protests from farmers whose lands would be flooded. Rival projects, including the proposed railroad, raised objections, as did representatives in the southern counties, whose constituents perceived that they would pay for a canal that would bypass them. For more than a year (1828–1829) the legislature found itself unable to reach agreement. Partisan lines were crossed as geographical proximity to the improvements affected responses to state sponsorship. Governor Peter D. Vroom, a former Federalist turned Jacksonian Democrat, favored both projects, but not until a deal was cut assuring passage of both projects did the improvements bills reach Vroom's desk.

The terms of each bill were remarkably (though not coincidentally) similar. Both companies were capitalized at $1 million. Neither would organize

Northeast view of New Brunswick. Behind the Raritan River (center) is the Delaware and Raritan Canal; to the right, a train crosses the railroad bridge. Several churches are shown, along with Rutgers College on a hill. (John W. Barber and Henry Howe, *Historical Collections of the State of New Jersey* [New York: S. Tuttle, 1845], facing page 312. Special Collections and University Archives, Rutgers University Libraries.)

until 5,000 shares had been subscribed. The state reserved the right to subscribe a quarter of the shares in each enterprise and to purchase the properties "at a fair value" thirty years after each commenced operation. Maximum toll rates were established, and, most important, each corporation was granted a monopoly. No canal or railroad could be constructed without permission within five miles of either the D&R or the C&A. In lieu of taxes, the companies were required to pay transit duties to the state on all goods and passengers conveyed. These duties would cover all costs of running what was admittedly a bare-bones government. The terms were soon adjusted, making the state a stockholder in the companies and guaranteeing a minimum dividend of $30,000 annually to the state treasury in exchange for the monopoly proviso.

Governor Vroom was no friend of monopolies or of Robert F. Stockton, the main investor (with his father-in-law's money) in the railroad. But for Vroom, the completion of essential transportation projects at no cost to the taxpayer was too good a deal to reject. By contrast, the fiery editor of the *Trenton True Emporium*, Stacy G. Potts, decried the monopoly grant for giving too much power to a few men. Gaining little traction with this point of attack, Potts backed off. The notion of letting corporations pay the state's bills was all too alluring.

Within a year, when a bill conjoining the two companies as the Joint Companies passed the legislature after extended debate, Potts found himself denying that any monopoly had been created. For his part, Vroom by 1832 was denouncing the near-monopoly powers of the Bank of the United States. And Robert F. Stockton, the fervent defender of the railroad monopoly, was in Vroom's (and Jackson's) camp in rallying faithful Democrats against the "monster" bank. Ideological leanings were relevant during the Jackson era, but among New Jersey's civic and public leaders a strong pragmatic streak predominated.[7]

Emerging Markets

Whether one favored the Joint Companies or despised them, there was no question that these improvements marked an important fault line between New Jersey's agricultural past and its urban-industrial future. Whatever a citizen's politics, republican simplicity increasingly gave way to a more entrepreneurial creed.

Infrastructure improvements near New York City and Philadelphia especially benefited fast-expanding cities and their rural hinterlands, including those in New Jersey. The sheer speed of transport and facility of commercial exchange were unprecedented and had obvious consequences. The value of farm goods produced by the market gardens in north Jersey increased noticeably during the antebellum era. Famed landscape architect and horticulturalist Andrew Jackson Downing observed in 1851 that fresh tomatoes had been scarce in New York markets in the mid-1830s but were no longer difficult to find. And the bounty included more than tomatoes. Asparagus, cabbages, cauliflower, peas, carrots, potatoes, strawberries, and melons were brought to the city by railroad, boat, and wagon from the gardens and farmers of New Jersey, Long Island, and Westchester County in New York. As many as six steamboats a day carried peaches from Middlesex County; at the same time, railroads were stimulating the planting and cultivation of orchards in northwestern New Jersey.

The potential for supplying New York City's teeming masses with agricultural produce encouraged visionary schemes, some of which bordered on the crackpot. In 1836 Robert Swartwout, an ethically challenged New York entrepreneur (and brother of the more famous swindler Samuel

Swartwout), proposed the transformation of the northern New Jersey Meadowlands into a giant dairy farm. Swartwout contemplated nothing less than the purchase and drainage of some 30,000 acres of marshland that could be divided into parcels and sold at great profit. Perhaps a mercantile commission house could be built on the property as well, he told a potential investor, that "would have the capacity to do a . . . better business than any one now on this continent." Swartwout's idea died for the lack of capital during the Panic of 1837, but it shows that a metropolitan mindset was already well developed even in the era of Andrew Jackson.[8]

Urbanization

If commercial agriculture was prospering and advancing thanks to transportation improvements, so too was the urban-industrial nexus. Even though it was still possible to talk of New Jersey as a "keg tapped at two ends," it was also true that New Jersey was taking full advantage of its location as a connector state in the Mid-Atlantic region. It may not have grown as quickly as its neighbors, but the pace of change was noteworthy all the same.

Hudson County's Jersey City, for example, grew because of its convenient location. At the time of Thomas Jefferson's inauguration in 1801, it could hardly claim status as a village, with a population not exceeding two dozen people. Jersey City's main selling point was that it lay directly opposite New York City. Growth was slow at first, because there was the matter of getting travelers conveniently and safely to New York and back. But as the distance between New York's residential and business districts increased, and once railroad and ferry service commenced in 1834, many New York entrepreneurs found it both convenient and cheap to live in Jersey City. New Jersey's leading Whig politician, Samuel L. Southard, long based in Trenton, moved with his family to Jersey City when he became president of the Morris Canal and Banking Company in 1837, seeking readier access to the company's New York offices. Southard found himself leading a wave of growth, as land values and building activity increased—especially as more immigrants began settling in Jersey City in the 1840s.

Passaic and Essex Counties experienced similar spurts, powered by the artisan-dominated industries of Paterson and Newark. Newark's population increased from 11,000 in 1830 ("barely enough to fill a single New York City ward") to more than 70,000 by 1860, thanks to the availability of decent-paying manufacturing jobs.[9] Many of the workers who obtained these jobs were new immigrants, notably Irishmen and Germans. Hoboken attracted so many Germans that by 1851 the *New York Evening Post* declared that this densely populated little city was "half-Germanized." For its part, Paterson reinvented itself first as a center for cotton and then silk textiles, and (more briefly) gun production; its superb water power provided the basis for impressive, albeit unsteady, growth. Samuel Colt, inventor of the repeating rifle, built a gun mill in Paterson in 1835, which complemented the textile mills already in operation under a revived Society for Useful Manufactures. Colt's revolver was popular with the military, and orders poured in during the Second Seminole War (1835–1842). But the end of that conflict, combined with the economic malaise of 1837–1843, forced Colt to close operations in Paterson. When the next major government orders arrived, during the Mexican War (1846–1848), Colt was making his revolvers in Connecticut. Nonetheless, Paterson continued to grow, as Colt's brothers Roswell and Christopher invested heavily in various enterprises there, including a silk mill. In Paterson and other urban centers, banking, insurance, and retail trades grew. Shopkeepers sold luxury imports as well as necessities and provided a market for local products, thereby enabling area residents, both urban and rural, to exchange goods and helping to raise the standard of living.[10]

Newark was the state's urban leader. Founded, like all New Jersey communities, as a farming village, Newark by the late eighteenth century was known for the manufacture of shoes for markets both in New York City and in the southern states. With the steamboat revolution, the shoe industry and others took off. By 1826, more than one-third of Newark's labor force worked at shoemaking, producing the whole range of footwear from cheap to top-of-the-line. Over time, Newark became a manufacturing center. By 1840, fully 80 percent of Newark's labor force was engaged in manufacturing. Access to raw materials from Pennsylvania, thanks to the opening of the Morris Canal, reinforced the trend. The completion of the railroad line to Jersey City in 1834 reduced travel time between Newark and New York to approximately an hour; it made Newark, like Jersey City and Hoboken, an important satellite to Gotham on the Hudson.

In addition to shoemaking, Newark artisans made hats, saddles, carriages, jewelry, trunks, and harnesses. In 1819 Massachusetts native Seth Boyden Jr. opened the nation's first patent leather factory, which prospered. Less than a decade later, Boyden disposed of his leather interests and opened a malleable iron foundry in Newark—again, the nation's first. This innovation aided the production of buckles, harnesses, and other parts used in the carriage industry.

The products of Newark workshops reached New York markets first and foremost, but over time increasingly found customers in Philadelphia and then the South. David Alling, a Newark chair-maker, shipped his first batch of 144 ornamented fancy chairs to New Orleans in 1819, on consignment. Sales were slow at first, but gradually built, to the point where by the early 1830s Alling was sending some three-quarters of his product to New Orleans, other southern port cities, and Latin America. Southern demand for Newark-made furniture continued strong through the 1850s, coming to a halt only with the outbreak of war.

Emphasis on artisanship, as in Alling's shop, rather than machinery was typical of the period. Artisans readily adapted to new techniques, including task differentiation, on what one scholar has labeled a "proto-industrial" model. Alling's chair-makers, however, were slow to exploit new woodworking technology (for example, steam-powered lathes and other woodworking machines) along English lines. Small shops with human-powered machinery continued to dominate chair-making and other Newark industries into and beyond the Civil War era. Industrialization on a larger scale under stringent work rules could not have been forecast in 1850, but its arrival was inexorable. Indeed, in Paterson's textile mills, increasing mechanization was evident as early as the 1830s. It contributed to the emergence of working-class consciousness (expressed in early walkouts) and the "struggle to maintain and expand" popular democracy, as one student of early Paterson has put it.[11]

Elsewhere, commerce and industry were less dominant, but the intimations of changing times were no less discernible. In Morris County, mines proved an important driver of employment, much as commercial fishing (and later tourism) would provide livelihoods for thousands living along the seacoast. Lumbering and shipbuilding were significant industries as well. Iron forges and furnaces dotted the state. But most of New Jersey was still agricultural—albeit branching out into new commercial activity, which in numerous instances became the economic dog rather than its tail.

Consider a community like Burlington County's Lumberton, which closely approximated the Jeffersonian ideal of farmers laboring on rich land and making a living at it, enjoying their birthright of citizenship in a

This painting of David Alling's house and shop in Newark (ca. 1840–1850) shows the location of his chair factory. (Attributed to Johan Jenny [1786–1854]. Oil on canvas. 20½ × 30 in. Collections of the Newark Museum. Purchase 1939 Thomas Raymond Bequest Fund, 39.265. Photo: Newark Museum/Art Resource, N.Y.)

yeoman republic. Lumberton was not even incorporated when Polish exile Julian Niemcewizc traveled through New Jersey in 1799, but it soon developed into a bustling community of cleared farmland, textile mills, and prospering retail markets. A steel furnace was launched early in the nineteenth century and proved exceedingly profitable for several decades. (It also polluted Lumberton substantially, though the smell of money seems to have overcome the odor of burning charcoal.) As the port closest to the Pine Barrens and Philadelphia, it was preeminent in transportation between the two until the opening of the Delaware and Raritan Canal. Lumberton was noteworthy for its balanced economy, with farming, mining, and trade all advancing, apparently without significant tension among them. A city-style grid served as the template for residential development, though no one imagined Lumberton as a major urban center—and none developed. Lumberton remained village-like, with a population through this era of fewer than 750 residents. Yet it reflected various aspects of modern life, including the erection of a public school and the opening of a coal yard, general stores, and a church, all in the 1840s. Better and cheaper transportation clearly undergirded Lumberton's development, as it did for small towns and cities throughout New Jersey in this era.[12]

Not all development was positive. Over time, poverty increased, according to the decennial census, with one-quarter of residents in Lumberton owning no personal property and two-thirds claiming property holdings equaling $200 or less. Merchants and professionals were comparatively better off. By the 1850s, social stratification had advanced and upward mobility diminished in Lumberton and larger communities across the state. At least young people had the option that made America distinctive: they could always move on and try their luck somewhere else. Many did. Such was the case with Sam Patch, a millworker in Pawtucket, Rhode Island, who took his skills to Paterson, where he prospered as a boss mule spinner, but ultimately gained fame by regularly leaping into the famous Passaic Falls. The celebrity earned for this distinctive talent encouraged Patch to jump from great heights in other communities, including Hoboken, Rochester, and Niagara Falls. Ultimately he made one jump too many.[13]

THE POLITICAL WHIRLIGIG

For those who set down roots in New Jersey, politics provided both something to jaw about with one's neighbors and the opportunity at election time to get caught up in the excitement of campaigns. Like most states after the War of 1812, New Jersey experienced an era of partisan confusion and local factionalism—the misnamed "Era of Good Feelings." Federalists, discredited by their opposition to the war, understandably sought new political outlets for their ambitions. For their part, the politically dominant Jeffersonians divided over whether to embrace the market or not. Gradually, new coalitions formed, based on personality conflicts and emerging issues, commencing with a multi-candidate presidential contest in 1824 and extending into what is often described as the Age of Jackson.

The so-called second party system took shape originally along pro– or anti–Andrew Jackson lines—a reminder of how powerfully polarizing the "Old Hero" was in his time. Divisions over Jackson's persona and military career gradually connected to debates over Henry Clay's "American system." Jacksonian voters remained wary of the emerging urban/industrial order, while most National Republicans (later Whigs) embraced the advent of banks, tariff protection, and nationally sponsored internal improvements, as advocated by such leaders as John Quincy Adams, Henry Clay, and Daniel Webster. By and large, New Jersey's Democrats shared Jackson's devotion to limited government and geographical expansion westward, while Whigs talked of economic development as a rising tide that would lift all citizens to a better life.

At the state level, the differences between Jacksonians and Whigs could be more difficult to discern. Prominent Jacksonians no less enthusiastically than Whigs embraced and invested in key transportation and banking ventures, thereby tempering some of the grass-roots emotionalism on these subjects. However, as Jackson increasingly advanced his argument for specie currency and against speculation in the latter years of his presidency, battle lines in New Jersey began to form over the question of corporate power. In these struggles Governor Peter Vroom took on the most prominent role for the Democrats, and U.S. Senator Samuel L. Southard spoke most influentially for Whig principles, backed by such rising Whig associates as William L. Dayton and Jacob Miller.

Like its more influential neighbors, New York and Pennsylvania, New Jersey was a battleground state during the Jackson period. Neither side could take statewide success for granted. For two decades Democrats and Whigs engaged in a series of hard-fought elections, with Democrats holding the upper hand during Jackson's presidency and Whigs usually enjoying a small but noticeable advantage from 1837 through 1848, whereupon the Democrats regained the ascendancy. The parties were remarkably well organized and competitive statewide, with a few thousand votes tipping the scale in any given election.

A close reading of election results during the Jacksonian Era reveals a remarkable consistency. Townships that embraced the "Old Hero" in his three runs for the White House—notably, the agriculturally minded northwestern and central areas—remained loyal to Jackson's party throughout the era. Urban and commercial centers—Newark, Trenton, and, to a lesser extent, Elizabeth, Burlington, and Jersey City—were consistently anti-Jacksonian, as was Burlington County, with its substantial Quaker population, and the far south. In Paterson, a strong cadre of pro-Jacksonian Irish voters made elections more competitive. Elsewhere in the state as well, support for the two parties was evenly matched and less predictable. Had the agricultural interest—some 80 percent of the state's population during the 1830s—been firmly in the Jacksonian camp, there would have been no viable Whig Party. But the Whigs had appeal beyond their urban base, particularly among Quakers and commercially oriented agriculturalists.

In light of its modest population and consequent paucity of electoral votes in presidential contests, New Jersey rarely played a decisive role in national campaigns, though that lack of influence seems not to have stifled the fervor of Democratic and Whig partisans. For most of the 1830s, the Bank War, which obsessed Andrew Jackson and many of his grass-roots partisans in rural New Jersey, endured as the defining issue in New Jersey politics. Whigs like Southard and his ally Theodore Frelinghuysen (who would later run for vice president on the Whig ticket with Henry Clay) hammered at Jackson for his alleged deficiency in understanding economics and, above all, for "executive tyranny" in his bold exertions of presidential power.

By contrast, Governor Vroom, a former Federalist drawn into the Jacksonian orbit, rallied behind Jackson and assumed the mantle of Democratic leadership in New Jersey. To Vroom, the bank issue was not simply a matter of economics, with one large bank having advantages over others. It was a matter of checks and balances. As he observed in a letter to a Democratic congressman during the campaign of 1832, "If the Bank, justly odious as it has become, can break down an administration supported by the sound head and strong popularity of Andrew Jackson—who or what set of men will dare to utter a breath against it, in future times?"[14]

At the conclusion of that lusty campaign, featuring innumerable newspaper editorials, rallies, and torchlight parades, New Jerseyans offered a mixed verdict, sending a majority of anti-Jacksonian legislators to Trenton but giving their support (by a relatively narrow margin) to Jackson in the presidential contest against a strong supporter of the National Bank, Kentuckian Henry Clay. Southard would shortly thereafter return to Washington to join Clay's fight against the Old Hero (in their view an old tyrant), but their cause was, on the whole, unsuccessful. Jackson killed the Bank of the United States. His policies generally—including rotation in office and Indian removal—enjoyed wide popularity. Whigs would savor their own moment of triumph in 1840, in the famous Log Cabin campaign that elected General William Henry Harrison. Interest in politics reached an almost fever pitch, with voter turnout of more than 80 percent in New Jersey, as virtually every Whig and Democrat in the state did his partisan duty, with

Harrison triumphing on the basis of new voters expressing a firm preference for the Whig ticket. Four years later, in a national election decided by
only a few thousand votes in the state of New York, the Whigs went down
to a bitter defeat at the hands of expansionist candidates James K. Polk and
George Mifflin Dallas. Voter interest in politics had reached its apogee.[15]

THE JOINT COMPANIES

Politics and internal improvements were closely linked from the canal era,
when lobbyists brazenly bought legislators' votes in Trenton, well into the
railroad era. No corporation was more powerful—or more reviled—in the
Garden State than the so-called Joint Companies, the combined Camden
and Amboy Railroad and Delaware and Raritan Canal, both of them crossing the "waist" of New Jersey. These two corporations, chartered separately
by the legislature in 1830, essentially controlled railroad and canal transport
between Philadelphia and New York. They were most closely associated
with the Jacksonians because of Robert F. Stockton's manifest direction of
their operations and his hardball politics. Yet it would be overly simplistic
to suggest that the Joint Companies were a true dividing line between the
major parties before the Civil War. Prominent Whigs invested in the corporation and in one instance came close to a full partnership with it. On the
other side of the coin, rising voices in the Democratic Party objected to the
monopoly conferred on the Joint Companies, arguing that in a democratic
polity there was no room for monopolies, whatever their economic stimu-
lus or infusions into the state treasury.

Peter Vroom, an outstanding Democratic attorney from Somerset
County who served six one-year terms as governor, represented the anti-
corporate wing of his party. Vroom and his allies resented what they called
the "Princeton Junta" and fought them with middling success through the
presidencies of Jackson, Martin Van Buren, and John Tyler. For their part,
Whig leaders, including U.S. Senators Samuel Southard and Theodore
Frelinghuysen, were so firmly in the camp of internal improvement that
they made their peace with the Companies. The fact that the Companies'
transit duties funded virtually the entire annual state budget made it easier
to defend their monopoly privilege. Towns along the railroad line, moreover, benefited from development. Passenger travel boomed. New Jersey's

economy enjoyed robust growth, even though it remained predominantly agricultural and did not absorb as many immigrants as surrounding states. Consequently, the major initiative of the anti-corporate caucus in Trenton was to eliminate special corporate charters in favor of general incorporation. This objective was achieved in stages, as thirteen different general incorporation laws were enacted between 1846 and the Civil War.[16]

STRESS AND STRUCTURE: BRINGING INSTITUTIONS INTO LINE WITH SOCIAL AND ECONOMIC EXIGENCIES

The year 1844 represented a pinnacle for Jacksonian democracy as well as Jackson's party, which narrowly prevailed in both state and national elections. Democratic currents remained strong and partisan turnout high throughout the era. A growing egalitarian ethos was reflected in the framing of New Jersey's 1844 constitution, the first revision since 1776. Under the revamped document, produced by popularly elected convention delegates, the governor, previously chosen annually by the legislature, would be elected by qualified voters for a single three-year term. Recognizing the incongruity of requiring a governor to engage also in judicial duties, via his role as state chancellor, the new constitutional arrangement relieved him of these duties and offered him, for the first time, limited veto power on legislation and enhanced, if still limited, authority to make appointments. The legislative assembly's membership was capped at sixty, and its members were still expected to face the voters annually. Senators, one per county, would serve three-year terms. As another sign of the times, suffrage was expanded, with privileges extended to all adult white male citizens who had resided for one year in the state and five months in a particular county. Missing from this democratic advance was any provision to restore female participation in the political process, which had been allowed by the constitution of 1776 but repealed by the legislature in 1807. New Jersey women had to wait until 1919 for the right to be counted at the ballot box.

Lame as the 1844 constitution was in affording legal and civil rights to women and minorities, it did much better in responding to the stresses of increased economic development and larger populations of the poor, criminal, and mentally ill. As Governor Daniel Haines argued before the Legislative Council, the 1776 constitution was "incompatible with the [needs of] the present age."[17] Some scholars have argued that the driving force behind the reforms of 1844 was popular democracy, first and foremost. Certainly the advent of a popularly elected governor reflected democratic impulses, as did extension of rights to non-Protestants and the decision to abolish imprisonment for debt. But for modern students of the period, including Richard P. McCormick and Frederick M. Herrmann, the main impetus for reform was the need to "reorganize political structures" to meet the demands of an industrializing society. Herrmann noted: "A growing population and a steadily increasing amount of activity in the business community pointed to the need for a better structured government that could process more legislation, regulate larger and more powerful commercial enterprises, and provide a decent system of public education and welfare."[18]

The state's response to population growth and the advance of capitalism is impossible to ignore. In an age of transition, some of it faster and broader than a person born in 1800 could possibly have anticipated, it was inevitable that enterprises would grow more complex, and so too the problems that society had to address. A capitalist culture, even a pre-industrial capitalist culture, spawns winners and losers. Lawyers, bankers, the politically well connected, most urban entrepreneurs, and farmers with easy access to transportation networks and markets were New Jersey's "winners" during the Jacksonian era. The many farmers whose properties were damaged or destroyed by canal or railroad construction were less fortunate. So were yeomen whose properties did not readily connect to canals or railroads, as well as low-paid workers in early mills. So was the increasing population of free blacks, whose journey from slavery to freedom was never a smooth ride.

The Status of African Americans

Discouraged by pro-slavery interests (notably in Bergen, Somerset, Gloucester, and Union Counties), New Jersey did not pass an act abolishing slavery until 1804. That act contained a noteworthy element, namely, the gradual emancipation of slave children born in the state after July 1804. It took more than a half century before the last of these individuals emerged from bondage. (The census of 1860 counts eighteen slaves still living in New Jersey.)

The number of slaves in the state, perhaps 12,500 in 1800, declined steadily after 1804, even as the court system offered continued support for heirs and creditors of slave owners. And as the number of free blacks in-

creased, inevitably there were frictions with whites in pursuit of employment. In these competitions, which increasingly included jostling in places
like Elizabethtown and Camden with freshly arrived Irish immigrants,
blacks were usually the losers. Some stayed and found what menial work
they could. Some launched businesses or worked as tradesmen. One such
person, Thomas Holmes, operated a ferry between Staten Island and Woodbridge, New Jersey. Several Bergen County African Americans owned their
own farms in the shadow of slave centers like Washington Township. Places
like Fair Haven were home to important free black communities, which
were involved in shipping oysters and farm produce to New York City. In
Monmouth County, characterized by historian Graham Hodges as "more
pluralistic" than Bergen, a tiny black middle class emerged by midcentury.
Most free blacks in Monmouth continued to do what they had done as
slaves—farm work, albeit for pay. A version of sharecropping also emerged
there. In cities like Newark, blacks primarily worked as laborers and domes-
tics. A Burlington County free black man, James Still, studied the healing
arts and successfully practiced medicine without any formal training or license, treating whites as well as blacks. In the money and respect he earned,
Still was doubtless an exception to a less inspiring rule of manifest racial
prejudice against New Jersey's African American population and its relegation to second-class citizenship.[19]

Thanks to the patronage and humanitarian interventions of local Quakers in Camden, which developed rapidly as a transportation hub during and
after the War of 1812, blacks prospered more noticeably than anywhere else
in the state. Historian Spencer Crew has documented a fascinating experiment in the communities of Fettersville and Kaighnville, on Camden's outskirts, where black churches thrived and a variety of programs evolved to
meet the "educational and fraternal needs" of the black community. Similar undertakings have been documented for other communities, notably in
Timbucktoo (Burlington County), New Brunswick, and Newark.

Considering the racial attitudes of the era, James Still's accomplishments and those of the community founders in Fettersville and Kaignville
are impressive. But they were uncommon. For most blacks, opportunities
for advancement in New Jersey, as in most northern states, were scarce.
Many New Jersey free blacks preferred to move west or emigrate, often to
the British colonies of Guiana and Trinidad, which recruited them. African
Americans' pessimism about acceptance, assimilation, and integration in

a white-dominated society was understandable. Slavery might be ending, but the notion of white supremacy retained its firm hold on the majority's sensibilities. Historian Frances Pingeon unearthed proposed legislation in 1837 that would have required all free blacks in New Jersey to register themselves and their families with county clerks or be liable to fines and arrests as fugitives. The measure never became law, but it overwhelmingly passed the state assembly, a sobering reminder that blacks were not seen as potential neighbors and positive contributors to the state's progress. "Ingrained racism," Pingeon concludes, was at the core of the 1837 measure. Ironically enough, it was at the core also of one of the leading "reform" efforts of the era: colonization.[20]

The False Promise of Colonization Schemes

For the political establishment in New Jersey, in the wake of northern states' gradual abolition of slavery, finding a way to deal with the problem of free blacks meant not embracing abolition but removing blacks to distant shores. Inspired initially by the writings of Basking Ridge clergyman Robert Finley, colonization quickly caught on with the religious and political elite. Even some prominent slaveholders, like Kentucky's Henry Clay, favored colonization. For Clay and others based in the upper South, the gradual elimination of slavery made sense, given changed economic circumstances, but a growing free black population made them anxious. In New Jersey, as elsewhere in the middle states and upper South, colonization was viewed as the best solution to avoid trouble once slavery died out. Organizers of the Colonization Society in New Jersey explicitly acknowledged their conviction that the black population of the state (estimated at 20,000 in the 1820s) represented "a moral and political pestilence." The best response was to remove the "enormous mass of revolting wretchedness and deadly pollution" from New Jersey. Colonization was one of the few public issues that generated little partisan heat in a hyper-partisan era. Jacksonian activists Peter Vroom, Robert Stockton, and James Green stood with anti-Jacksonian leaders like Samuel Southard, Theodore Frelinghuysen, and Lewis Condict. Not all would-be colonizers were equally hard-edged in their approach to colonization. Vroom, for example, offered sympathy for free blacks in New Jersey. But in the end, he concluded that colonization was essential because blacks "form a class with which we cannot commingle."[21]

In practical terms, colonization failed abysmally. Even if sending blacks to Africa could be interpreted in some quarters as "perfecting" America, the idea never attracted evangelical Protestants, who highlighted the sin of slavery. Although some abolitionists also favored the removal of blacks to Africa, the leaders of antislavery activism after 1830 viewed colonization as the product of an antiquated, gradualist mentality and, in any case, utterly impractical. Colonization generated ample attention in New Jersey and the support of the state's political elite, but it never attained much practical traction. Neither slave owners in the deep South, where slavery remained most profitable, nor free blacks themselves, who had no desire to leave the country of their birth, favored colonization. Lacking both patronage and clients, colonization schemes withered.

Utopian Reforms

On another reformist track were utopian experiments, both religious and secular, which represented both the anxieties and the hopefulness of millions of citizens. Among the more popular experiments were communes, intentional societies established on egalitarian precepts. New Jersey harbored its share, of which the longest-lived was the North American Phalanx, based near Red Bank in Monmouth County, which operated between 1843 and 1855 and attracted nearly two hundred people. The ideas of French philosopher Charles Fourier emphasized that society should be organized to tap the true potential of all individuals. His phalanxes (communities), which were spearheaded in the United States by Albert Brisbane and Charles Sears, varied in their organizing features, with some focused on light industry, others on agriculture. Individuals would labor where their talents and inclinations fit best.

For a time, the community in Red Bank seemed to work. With relatively open-minded members willing to talk out differences of values and opinion, the commune attracted idealists and nonconformists. (That attitude did not extend to blacks, who were not only denied membership but also promptly evicted from the property.) But even in this kind of community, the daily regimen of manual labor wore poorly on increasing numbers. When a fire burned down one of their key buildings in the 1850s, members decided to disband. One faction then organized the short-lived Raritan Bay Union.

Such communitarian reform movements as Fourierism and the better-known Owenite community of New Harmony, Indiana, were forerunners, according to historian Ronald Walters, of a new emphasis on quality of life. Above all, they "demanded a just measure of the good things of the earth for every human being."[22] In this respect, they embraced precepts utterly different from those of the colonizationists, but they also were disappointed. Utopians, all of them fallible humans, inevitably could not fulfill their own high ideals.

By contrast, reformers who set a more practical agenda—build more schools, erect a humane prison or asylum, reduce hours of work, and raise levels of pay—often had more success. They left ample room for further improvements, but their "can do" mentality inspired a rising generation.[23]

Winners, Losers, and Helpers

Although the economy expanded in tandem with substantial population growth after 1830 and new industries paid decent wages, the poor did not disappear in Jacksonian New Jersey. Rather, their numbers increased, most noticeably in the wake of the financial panic of 1837, which brought down many a high flier and increased the ranks of the indigent, both male and female. One example was an unnamed citizen encountered by the well-known reformer Dorothea Dix in the Salem County poorhouse in 1844. The man, "helpless, lonely, and yet conscious of surrounding circumstances," Dix noted, was a former judge and member of the state legislature. Business reverses had unhinged him. He had been committed to the county jail in chains "for greater security," according to authorities. Once the man calmed down, he was transferred to the poorhouse, with little hope of making his way out.[24]

Social reformers like Dix forced Jerseyans to confront the issue of what to do about those who were left behind in the age of go ahead. Whether the cause was disease, deviance, or social misfortune, a growing number of New Jerseyans found it impossible to function within or, in some cases, to abide by society's rules. There was, for example, a rising prison population. In this respect, New Jersey was little different from its counterparts across the nation. The state prison in Trenton, built in 1799 on traditional premises about incarceration (let convicted criminals rot), was filled to overflowing. A commission studying conditions there concluded in 1829 that it was little more than a "hatching ground for new crimes," with no serious program of moral or practical instruction that would facilitate a prisoner's return to society. A new prison was built in 1835 and a new prison regimen instituted, emphasizing solitary confinement as a means of encouraging reflection and rehabilitation. New Jersey was far from alone in embracing this prison reform—the implementation of which, in Auburn (New York State) and Philadelphia, respectively, inspired the Frenchmen Alexis de Tocqueville and Gustave Beaument to undertake their journey through America. Although prisoner separation proved to be a popular notion in this era, in the end it failed to produce the desired results.[25]

Reform efforts yielded a better outcome for the mentally ill population, at the very least in terms of humane treatment. As the state's population increased, both by births and immigration, and the move from farm to city accelerated, the incidence of mental illness kept pace, to the point where traditional institutions (family, church, and local government) could no longer manage the problem. State lawmakers understood that simply paying Pennsylvania or New York to handle emotionally disturbed citizens would not suffice. By 1840, Governor William Pennington, a Whig, was concerned enough to appoint a commission to explore the possibility of erecting a state asylum. Its members examined practices in other states and also produced a census, yielding a rough count of 700 insane persons living in New Jersey, most of them confined in jails either because they had violated social norms or because the local community believed them dangerous.

The state legislature, always tax averse, declined to act on a series of reports highlighting the ill treatment of the mentally ill, that is, until humanitarian reformer Dorothea Dix arrived on the scene. Conducting her own survey of conditions in 1844, Dix witnessed "scenes of almost incredible sufferings," as she described it, in jails and poorhouses across the state. In Salem County Dix encountered not only the former legislator, now a pauper, but a disoriented man who was regularly beaten by his keeper to "make him know I was his master."[26] In Burlington County's poorhouse near Pemberton, she counted twenty-two insane persons, ten of them occupants of a cellar pervaded by "foul air to an intolerable degree." Men and women in chains, treated like animals, could be found virtually everywhere Dix canvassed. There was, the director of a Somerset County poorhouse noted, "no fit place for crazy folks."[27]

Dix importuned New Jersey legislators to rectify the situation by constructing a large new state hospital where remedial care could occur and, at the very least, ill people would be treated more humanely. If legislators would not acknowledge the moral imperative to act, Dix was prepared to argue on another track, emphasizing that running an asylum was cheaper than supporting the insane in jails and poorhouses. In a well-run asylum, moreover, it would be possible to restore many supposed "incurables" to full function and productive membership in society.

Dix's arguments gained support from major state newspapers and ultimately prevailed with the legislature. A 200-bed facility, authorized in 1845, opened in May 1848 in Ewing Township near Trenton. New Jersey was the last state in the Northeast to construct an insane asylum.[28]

Not Just Wives and Mothers

It was no accident, perhaps, that a woman was at the forefront of reform efforts for the mentally ill. Despite their relegation to a "separate sphere" as wives and mothers charged with cultivating a happy and functional home life for their families, antebellum women had ways of breaking out of their expected roles. A good liberal education, something long viewed as superfluous for a future housewife, became increasingly possible for ambitious young women in New Jersey in the Jacksonian era. Academies (effectively, secondary schools) and seminaries (more or less the equivalent of colleges for men) sprang up in various urban environments in the first half of the nineteenth century. New Jerseyans followed the models established by better-known educators in New York, Massachusetts, and other states, but their work was no less meaningful. As Lucia McMahon notes, "New Jersey educators established numerous schools for women; wrote essays about the importance of women's education; and publicly celebrated women's intellectual achievements."[29] Among the New Jersey women who took a leading role in this advance was Hannah Hoyt, founder and principal of the New Brunswick Female Institute, also known as Miss Hoyt's Seminary. Following the example of more famous educators like Emma Willard of Troy, New York, Hoyt emphasized a classical education, including the study of geography, philosophy, astronomy, English, French, Latin, Greek, mathematics, and physiology. Her students received diplomas only after public examinations by Rutgers College professors.

To what end was this education used? For the most part, women were educated for the sake of improving their minds and their abilities to fulfill their domestic functions. But some, like Elizabeth Dodge Stedman Kinney, would push forward in the creative realm—in Kinney's case, as a widely published poet. Eventually, educated women would seek professional opportunities long believed exclusive to men and employ their skills in various public causes, much as Dorothea Dix had in the realm of better treatment for the insane.

Not yet did New Jersey women join the struggle for voting rights. But they were involved in almost every other reform movement of the antebellum period, most notably, the antislavery crusade. Louisa Sanderson Macculloch of Morristown for more than three decades (1830–1863) directed a "Female Charitable Society" designed to benefit "the aged, the lame, the sickly dependent on aged parents, the widow with children, the widow not able to work."[30] Rebecca Buffum Spring, best known for her leading role in establishing the North American Phalanx (in partnership with her husband, Marcus), was also an ardent abolitionist. Abigail Goodwin, a Salem County native and a Quaker educated at the local Friends' school, devoted much of her life to the abolitionist cause and took an active part in speeding slaves northward through the Underground Railroad. The more famous Grimkė sisters, Sarah and Angelina, periodically spent time in New Jersey. It was from Shrewsbury that Angelina wrote her famous 1835 letter to William Lloyd Garrison, commending his defiance of anti-abolition mobs. By one account, Angelina spoke to tens of thousands of people in the Mid-Atlantic region, including several New Jersey locations, between 1836 and 1838. The Grimkės and their peers were indeed trailblazers in a political culture still run by men for men.[31]

The Many Meanings of Reform

"Reform" in this era was a word with many meanings. For Dix, it meant changing the way a state treated its least functional citizens. For citizens impatient with a state government that did little beyond pass special incorporation laws and approve divorces, reform meant moving state governance beyond its *laissez-faire* attitudes, starting with giving the governor more effective authority. For a partisan newspaper editor like Stacy Potts, it meant throwing out incumbent officeholders when the voters demanded a change of men and measures. For Professor John McLean of the College of New Jersey, reform meant a common school system of free public education, funded by a combination of state aid and local taxes. On another plane were the secular utopian experiments that briefly flowered in New Jersey.

Reformers who set a more practical agenda enjoyed more success in the short and long term. The education reformers, for example, pointed to the disgraceful fact that more than 10,000 New Jersey children between the ages of five and fifteen received no schooling of any kind in the year 1828. Pleas for change were heeded. In 1829 the legislature passed, and the governor signed, the first comprehensive school law in New Jersey, with money promised to support local initiatives. The state's failure to provide adequate funding on a consistent basis could not gainsay the fact that it acknowledged the need for an educated citizenry and for substantive state commitments to that end. For the most part, localities responded constructively, though the elimination of tuition was slow in some jurisdictions, school buildings too often remained inferior, and attendance requirements were indifferently monitored.[32] Pragmatic idealists, the reformers of the 1830s and 1840s in New Jersey made real progress, notably in the push to secure school funding and the creation of the office of superintendent of schools. Ample opportunity nonetheless remained for a rising generation to build on the foundations laid in this era. "Reform" and "modernization" were not yet synonymous.

TOWARD SECTIONAL CONSCIOUSNESS

The "go-ahead" ethos in northern states like New Jersey did not in itself make a civil war between the sections inevitable. But the issue of slavery's expansion, for all practical purposes, forced the issue, beginning with the presidency of John Tyler (1841–1845) and accelerating during the Mexican War. Democrats and Whigs alike were comfortable running campaigns along the fault line of pro-market versus market restraint arguments well into the 1840s. But the pro-slavery policies of Tyler and his Democratic successor, James K. Polk, both ardent expansionists, forced the slavery issue to the front. During the Mexican War, New Jerseyans responded to patriotic appeals and for the most part supported the nation's warriors as they fought on foreign soil. As victory brought new territories into the Union, complications ensued. "America's manifest destiny to overspread the continent," historian Steven Woodworth has observed, "became its manifest destiny to face the issue of slavery."[33] Without question, the 1840s were, as Woodworth posits, a pivotal decade in American history, culminating in a great debate that threatened to explode into the secession of at least some southern states if their demands for protection of the peculiar institution were unmet. New Jersey Whig Senators William L. Dayton and Jacob Miller contributed to these debates, taking a strong antislavery stance. Both opposed the Compromise of 1850 and thereby earned the obloquy of New Jersey's business community and rural conservatives, who opposed any roiling of sectional sensibilities. Neither Miller nor Dayton was reelected. New Jersey was represented in the Senate by Democratic conservatives for much of the rest of the 1850s, even as new recruits joined the antislavery cause.[34]

For members of the Jacksonian generation, however, a sectional war was virtually unthinkable. Excited by technologies that made possible the movement of information practically by lightning and transportation advances that meant money in the pockets of many, the Jerseyan of 1850 was committed more than ever to "get forward," much as Hezekiah Niles had proclaimed at the close of the War of 1812. Population growth surged in the 1840s, approaching half a million by 1850, of whom more than 10 percent were foreign born, 31,000 of them Irish and thousands of others from Germany, Italy, Hungary, and Poland. That some would prosper and others would suffer as a result of changing times was widely acknowledged. By 1850, there was a growing awareness that New Jersey life could no longer be as homogeneous, self-sufficient, agrarian, decentralized, or Protestant as it traditionally had been. Some activists even suggested that attitudes about race and gender needed to change. Certainly the transformation to a more urban, industrial, and stratified society had affected sensibilities as well as social and environmental landscapes. There would be no turning back from a maturing capitalism, an evolving democracy, or the increasingly troubling and virulent debate over slavery.

NOTES

1. Thomas F. Gordon, *A Gazetteer of the State of New Jersey* (facsimile imprint; Westminster, Md.: Heritage Books, 1997), 29.

2. Walter A. McDougall, *Throes of Democracy: The American Civil War Era, 1829–1877* (New York: Harper Perennial Editions, 2008), as quoted in Daniel Howe, "Goodbye to the 'Age of Jackson'?" *New York Review of Books* (January 28, 2009): 37. Aspects of the transition to a capitalist economy are discussed in the essays collected in Joseph R. Frese and Jacob Judd, eds., *An Emerging Independent American Economy, 1815–1875* (Tarrytown, N.Y.: Sleepy Hollow Press, 1980).

3. There is a large literature on demographic, environmental, political, and social changes in the antebellum era. Leading works include John Lauritz Larson, *The Market*

Revolution in America: Liberty, Ambition, and the Eclipse of the Common Good (New York: Cambridge University Press, 2010); Scott C. Martin, ed., *Cultural Change and the Market Revolution in America, 1789–1860* (Lanham, Md.: Rowman and Littlefield, 2005); Daniel Walker Howe, *What Hath God Wrought: The Transformation of America, 1815–1848* (New York: Oxford University Press, 2007); and Sean Wilentz, *The Rise of American Democracy* (New York: Oxford University Press, 2007). Classic works on the transportation revolution include George Rogers Taylor, *The Transportation Revolution, 1815–1860* (New York: Rinehart, 1951), and John Lauritz Larson, *Internal Improvement: National Public Works and the Promise of Popular Government in the Early United States* (Chapel Hill: University of North Carolina Press, 2001), which offers a fresh and informative perspective. For a perceptive view of a rural community and the transport and economic changes in the age of go-ahead, see David C. Major and John S. Major, *A Huguenot on the Hackensack: David Demarest and His Legacy* (Madison, N.J.: Fairleigh Dickinson University Press, 2007).

4. On toll roads, the best account remains Wheaton J. Lane, *From Indian Trail to Iron Horse: Travel and Transportation in New Jersey, 1620–1860* (Princeton: Princeton University Press, 1939).

5. There are many accounts of *Gibbons v. Ogden*. For a pithy summary of the case at law, see Maurice G. Baxter, *The Steamboat Monopoly: Gibbons v. Ogden, 1824* (New York: Alfred A. Knopf, 1972). A more recent analysis, highlighting personalities, is T. J. Stiles, *The First Tycoon: The Epic Life of Cornelius Vanderbilt* (New York: Alfred A. Knopf, 2009), esp. 31–72.

6. For an excellent early account of canal building in New Jersey, see Gordon, *Gazetteer*, 23–28. Important scholarly sources include Robert T. Thompson, *Colonel James Neilson: A Businessman of the Early Machine Age in New Jersey, 1784–1862* (New Brunswick: Rutgers University Press, 1940); Lane, *From Indian Trail to Iron Horse*; and H. Jerome Cranmer, *The New Jersey Canals: State Policy and Private Enterprise, 1820–1832* (New York: Arno Press, 1978). For the national context, see the sources in note 2 above and the following: Carter Goodrich et al., *Canals and American Economic Development* (New York: Columbia University Press, 1961); John F. Stover, "Canals and Turnpikes: America's Early-Nineteenth-Century Transportation Network," in Frese and Judd, eds., *An Emerging Independent American Economy*, 60–98. For background on the importance of canals to the transport of Pennsylvania anthracite, Alfred D. Chandler, "Anthracite Coal and the Beginnings of the Industrial Revolution in the United States," *Business History Review* 46 (Summer 1972): 141–181, is the essential source.

7. Insights into political motivations and maneuvers on transportation issues may best be derived from the following works: Michael Birkner, *Samuel L. Southard: Jeffersonian Whig* (Rutherford, N.J.: Fairleigh Dickinson University Press, 1984); Walter R. Fallaw, "The Rise of the Whig Party in New Jersey" (Ph.D. diss., Princeton University, 1967); Herbert Ershkowitz, *The Origins of the Whig and Democratic Parties: New Jersey Politics, 1820–1837* (Washington, D.C.: University Press of America, 1982); and Robert R. Beckwith, "Mahlon Dickerson of New Jersey, 1770–1853" (Ed.D. thesis, Horace Mann Teachers College of Columbia University, 1964).

8. On Swartwout's scheme, see Birkner, *Samuel L. Southard*, 168–170 (quotation at 168).

9. Thomas Fleming, *New Jersey: A Bicentennial History* (New York: W. W. Norton, 1977), 109.

10. Urbanization is treated in John E. Bebout and Ronald J. Grele, *Where Cities Meet: The Urbanization of New Jersey* (Princeton: D. Van Nostrand, 1964); demographic change is discussed in Rudolph J. Vecoli, *The People of New Jersey* (Princeton: D. Van Nostrand, 1965). On a key immigrant cohort, see, among other sources, Dermot Quinn, *The Irish in New Jersey: Four Centuries of American Life* (New Brunswick: Rutgers University Press, 2004). See also Howard Harris, "'The Eagle to Watch and the Harp to Tune the Nation': Irish Immigrants, Politics, and Early Industrialization in Paterson, New Jersey, 1824–1838," *Journal of Social History* 23 (Spring 1990): 575–597; Howard Harris, "Towns-People and Country People': The Acquackanonk Dutch and the Rise of Industry in Paterson, New Jersey, 1793–1831," *NJH* 106 (1988): 22–51. For developments in Trenton, consult Jesse Rose Turk, "Trenton, New Jersey, in the Nineteenth Century: The Significance of Location in the Historical Geography of a City" (Ed.D. thesis, Horace Mann Teacher's College of Columbia University, 1964). Useful background on Jersey City's early development is provided in Douglas V. Shaw, *The Making of an Immigrant City: Ethnic and Cultural Conflict in Jersey City, New Jersey, 1850–1877* (New York: Arno Press, 1976). Among the most helpful of many sources on S.U.M. are Joseph S. Davis, *Essays in the Earlier History of American Corporations*, vol. 1 (Cambridge, Mass.: Harvard University Press, 1917), and James B. Kenyon, *Industrial Location and Metropolitan Growth: The Paterson-Passaic District* (Chicago: University of Chicago Press, 1960).

11. On craft industrialization, the best sources include Don C. Skemer, "David Alling's Chair Manufactory: Craft Industrialization in Newark, New Jersey, 1801–1854," *Winterthur Portfolio* 22 (Spring 1987): 1–21; Susan B. Hirsch, *Roots of the American Working Class: The Industrialization of Crafts in Newark, 1800–1860* (Philadelphia: University of Pennsylvania Press, 1978); and Susan B. Hirsch, "From Artisan to Manufacturer: Industrialization and the Small Producer in Newark," in *Small Business in American Life*, ed. Stuart W. Bruchey (New York: Columbia University Press, 1980), 80–99. For a focus on Seth Boyden's contribution to Newark's economic rise, see Brad R. Tuttle, *How Newark Became Newark: The Rise, Fall, and Rebirth of an American City* (New Brunswick: Rutgers University Press, 2009).

12. On Lumberton's development, I have leaned on Philip Yannella's manuscript, "Do These Bones Live: The Social History of a Small Town" (1977), available at Special Collections and University Archives. Rutgers University Libraries.

13. For more on Patch's background and daredevil activities, see Paul Johnson, *Sam Patch, the Famous Jumper* (New York: Hill and Wang, 2003).

14. Vroom is quoted in Michael J. Birkner, "Peter Vroom and the Politics of Democracy," in *Jacksonian New Jersey*, ed. Paul A. Stellhorn (Trenton: New Jersey Historical Commission, 1979), 18. On politics, see Harry L. Watson, *Liberty and Power: The Politics of Jacksonian America* (New York: Hill and Wang, 1990), Howe, *What Hath God Wrought*, and Wilentz, *Rise of American Democracy*, each of which offers a distinctive argument. For the New Jersey story, key sources include Richard P. McCormick, "Party

Formation in New Jersey in the Jackson Era," *Proc. NJHS* 83 (1965): 161–173; Birkner, *Samuel L. Southard*; Ershkowitz, *Origins of the Whig and Democratic Parties*; and Michael J. Birkner and Herbert Ershkowitz, "'Men and Measures': The Creation of the Second Party System in New Jersey," *NJH* 107 (1989): 41–60. On the nexus between politicians and newspaper editors in this partisan era, see Michael J. Birkner, "Journalism and Politics in Jacksonian New Jersey: The Career of Stacy G. Potts," *NJH* 97 (1979): 159–178.

15. On the campaign of 1840, see Birkner, *Samuel L. Southard*, chap. 8. For political developments in the 1840s, Wilentz, *Rise of American Democracy*, Howe, *What Hath God Wrought*, and McDougall, *Throes of Democracy*, are excellent.

16. Lane, *From Indian Trail to Iron Horse*, is reliable on these matters. For background on Stockton's maneuvers, consult Alfred Hoyt Bill, *A House Called Morven: Its Role in American History* (Princeton: Princeton University Press, 1954), and R. John Brockmann, *Commodore Robert F. Stockton, 1795–1866: Protean Man for a Protean Nation* (Amherst, Mass.: Cambria Press, 2009). On general incorporation, see Frederick M. Herrmann, "Stress and Structure: Political Change in Antebellum New Jersey" (Ph.D. diss., Rutgers University, 1976), chap.4.

17. Haines, quoted in Paul Stellhorn and Michael Birkner, eds., *The Governors of New Jersey* (Trenton: New Jersey Historical Commission, 1982), 114.

18. Frederick M. Herrmann, "The Constitution of 1844 and Political Change in New Jersey," *NJH* 101 (Spring–Summer 1983): 29–51. See also Maxine N. Lurie, "New Jersey's Three Constitutions: 1776, 1844, 1947," *Journal of the Rutgers University Libraries* (December 2000): 1–18. On women and the vote in New Jersey, see: Judith Apter Klinghoffer and Lois Elkis, "'The Petticoat Electors': Women's Suffrage in New Jersey, 1776–1807," *Journal of the Early Republic* 12 (Summer 1992): 159–193; and Graham Hodges, chapter 4 in this volume.

19. On slavery and free blacks, see especially Clement A. Price, ed., *Freedom Not Far Distant: A Documentary History of Afro-Americans in New Jersey* (Newark: New Jersey Historical Society, 1980); Arthur Zilversmit, "Liberty and Property: New Jersey and the Abolition of Slavery," *NJH* 88 (Winter 1970): 215–226; Peter O. Wacker, "The Changing Geography of the Black Population of New Jersey, 1810–1860: A Preliminary View," *Proceedings of the Association of American Geographers* 3 (1971): 174–178; Spencer Crew, "Black New Jersey Before the Civil War: Two Case Studies," *NJH* 99 (Spring–Summer 1981): 67–86. On James Still, see his memoir, *Early Recollections and Life of Dr. James Still* (New Brunswick: Rutgers University Press, 1973).

20. Frances D. Pingeon, "Dissenting Attitudes Toward the Negro in New Jersey—1837," *NJH* 89 (Winter 1971): 197–220. On racial issues in Camden County, see Jeffrey M. Dorwart, *Camden County, New Jersey: The Making of a Metropolitan Community, 1626–2000* (New Brunswick: Rutgers University Press, 2001). Graham Russell Hodges, *Slavery and Freedom in the Rural North: African Americans in Monmouth County, New Jersey, 1665–1865* (Madison, Wis.: Madison House, 1997), is a most valuable source; see Graham Hodges, *Root & Branch: African Americans in New York and East Jersey,*

1613–1863 (Chapel Hill: University of North Carolina Press, 1999), for developments in Bergen County.

21. P. J. Staudenbaus, *The African Colonization Movement, 1816–1865* (New York: Columbia University Press, 1961), is the standard source, but see also George M. Fredrickson, *The Black Image in the White Mind: The Debate on Afro-American Character and Destiny, 1817–1914* (New York: Harper and Row, 1971), and Lawrence J. Friedman, "Purifying the White Man's Country: The American Colonization Society Reconsidered, 1816–1840," *Societas* 6 (Winter 1976): 1–24. Quotes are in Douglas P. Seaton, "Colonizers and Reluctant Colonists: The New Jersey Colonization Society and the Black Community, 1815–1848," *NJH* 96 (1978): 7–22.

22. Quoted in Ronald G. Walters, *American Reformers, 1815–1860* (New York: Hill and Wang, 1978).

23. On the North American Phalanx, the best works are George Kirchmann, "Unsettled Utopias: The North American Phalanx and the Raritan Bay Union," *NJH* 97 (1979): 25–36, and George Kirchmann, "Why Did They Stay? Communal Life at the North American Phalanx," in *Planned and Utopian Experiments: Four New Jersey Towns*, ed. Paul A. Stellhorn (Trenton: New Jersey Historical Commission, 1980): 10–27. But see also Herman Belz, "The North American Phalanx: Experiment in Socialism," *Proc. NJHS* 81 (1963): 215–247. For broader context, see, among many works, Walters, *American Reformers*, and Daniel Feller, *The Jacksonian Promise: America 1815–1840* (Baltimore: Johns Hopkins University Press, 1995).

24. Frederick M. Herrmann, *Dorothea L. Dix and the Politics of Institutional Reform* (Trenton: New Jersey Historical Commission, 1981), 22.

25. See generally David J. Rothman, *The Discovery of the Asylum: Social Order and Disorder in the New Republic* (Boston: Little, Brown, 1971). On the physical environment in the newly designed prisons of the Jacksonian era, see Norman B. Johnston, "John Haviland, Jailor to the World," *Journal of the Society of Architectural Historians* 23 (May 1964): 101–105.

26. Quoted in Herrmann, *Dorothea L. Dix*, 19. For a more extended treatment, see Thomas J. Brown, *Dorothea Dix: New England Reformer* (Cambridge, Mass.: Harvard University Press, 1998). On responses to poverty, the best work remains Paul Tutt Stafford, *Government and the Needy: A Study of Public Assistance in New Jersey* (Princeton: Princeton University Press, 1941).

27. Dorothea Dix, *Memorial Soliciting a State Hospital for the Insane, Submitted to the Legislature of New Jersey, January 22, 1845* (Trenton: Legislature of New Jersey, 1845); Herrmann, *Dorothea L. Dix*, 24; Herrmann, "Stress and Structure." See also Frederick Herrmann, "The Political Origins of the New Jersey State Insane Asylum, 1837–1860," in Stellhorn, ed., *Jacksonian New Jersey*, 85–101.

28. Herrmann, *Dorothea L. Dix*, 28–29.

29. Lucia McMahon, "'A More Accurate and Extensive Education Than Is Customary': Educational Opportunities for Women in Early Nineteenth Century New Jersey," *NJH* 124, no. 1 (2009): 1–28.

30. Marie Marmo Mullaney, "Feminism, Utopianism, and Domesticity: The Career of Rebecca Buffum Spring, 1811–1911," *NJH* 104 (1986): 1–22. On New Jersey women activists, see the essays in *Past and Promise: Lives of New Jersey Women*, ed. Joan N. Burstyn (Metuchen, N.J.: Scarecrow Press, 1990). An interesting window onto a Quaker woman's experience in the 1840s is provided in Joyce S. Wagner, "A Nineteenth-Century Woman Diarist, or Rebecca of Green Brook Farm," *Journal of the Rutgers University Libraries* 46 (December 1984): 76–83. In key respects the woman, Rebecca Vail, lived a more representative life than women on the front lines of reform. For a broader perspective, consult Carmela Ascolese Karnoutos, *New Jersey Women: A History of Their Status, Roles, and Images* (Trenton: New Jersey Historical Commission, 1997).

31. On the Grimkès, see Burstyn, ed., *Past and Promise*, 66–68, and, more generally, Gerda Lerner, *The Grimkè Sisters of South Carolina: Rebels Against Slavery* (Boston: Houghton Mifflin, 1967).

32. Nelson T. Burr, *Education in New Jersey, 1630–1871* (Princeton: Princeton University Press, 1947).

33. Steven E. Woodworth, *Manifest Destinies: America's Westward Expansion and the Road to the Civil War* (New York: Alfred A. Knopf, 2010), as quoted in a review by Daniel Walker Howe, "How the West Was Won," *Wall Street Journal*, December 2, 2010, A17.

34. There is a serious lack of good scholarship on New Jersey politics from 1844 to the coming of the Civil War. Two exceptions, which chart the change from a functioning, ideologically meaningful two-party system in New Jersey to Democratic domination after 1848, include Lex Renda, "The Dysfunctional Party: The Collapse of the New Jersey Whigs, 1849–1853," *NJH* 116 (1998): 3–57, and the introduction to Hermann K. Platt, ed., *Charles Perrin Smith: New Jersey Political Reminiscences, 1828–1882* (New Brunswick: Rutgers University Press, 1965). On the Mexican War as a watershed, consult Howe, *What Hath God Wrought*, and Woodworth, *Manifest Destinies*.

6 · CIVIL WAR AND RECONSTRUCTION

State and Nation Divided

LARRY GREENE

The Civil War was one of the most cataclysmic events in American history, resulting in more than ten times the number of American casualties suffered in the Vietnam War. If the American Revolution created the American nation, then the Civil War preserved the nation and gave meaning to the phrase in the Pledge of Allegiance, "one nation, under God, indivisible, with liberty and justice for all." The depth of New Jersey's support for the northern cause and the preservation of the Union was questioned in the Civil War era by Republicans, defended by war Democrats, and debated by historians throughout much of the twentieth century.[1] There is no question, however, that significant numbers of New Jersey men donned the Union blue uniform and fought with valor in many regiments, especially the Army of the Potomac.

Abraham Lincoln lost the popular vote in New Jersey in 1860 but won four of the state's seven electoral votes. On his long pre-inaugural journey from Springfield, Illinois, to his swearing in as the sixteenth president of the United States in Washington, D.C., he made a number of stops in New Jersey, addressing citizens and the state legislature. In Jersey City, with his customary humility and humor, he made fun of his homely appearance and noted as he bowed to the gallery of ladies that he received the "best of the bargain, and in this matter I am for no compromises here,"[2] an obvious reference to his selection by the Republican Party as the moderate nominee who would be most likely to compromise with the South and thus avoid war.

Yet, a significant number of voters in New Jersey feared that Lincoln might be too unwilling to compromise and thus not capable of avoiding war between the states. Lincoln, appreciating the gravity of the times, told the citizens of Newark that in order to succeed at the task of the presidency he needed the "sustenance of Divine Providence" and the support of "this great, free, happy, and intelligent people."[3] On that whirlwind day of February 21, 1861, in which he made speeches in four New Jersey cities, he gave his most substantial speeches to the state senate and to the General Assembly. In the senate address, he paid homage to New Jersey's contribution to the "Revolutionary struggle," observing that "few of the States among the old Thirteen had more of the battle-fields of the country within their limits than old New Jersey." He noted how transfixed he was as a child reading about the Battle of Trenton, Washington crossing the Delaware, and "the contest with the Hessians." Lincoln acknowledged that he did not carry the popular vote in New Jersey, but he appreciated the turnout of those who greeted him as "the constitutional President of the United States."[4]

A little over three and one-half years later, Lincoln would again fail to carry the New Jersey popular vote by a slight margin, and he lost all of the state's electoral votes to General George McClellan, who then called New Jersey home. Lincoln's loss of the state in the 1860 and 1864 presidential elections contributed to the contemporary perception, particularly outside the state's borders, that New Jersey was a "Copperhead" state, one whose citizens were uninterested in fighting to maintain the Union, sympathized with southern secessionists, or even desired to join the Confederacy. The state legislature's initial refusal to ratify the Thirteenth Amendment ending slavery, the Fourteenth Amendment providing for citizenship for the former slaves, and the Fifteenth Amendment extending the vote to African Americans led to a view that New Jersey was out of step with other northern states and the Union cause during the Civil War and its aftermath. Governor Joel Parker's vigorous condemnation of the Emancipation Proclamation and its wholesale rejection by the Democratic Party of New Jersey also contributed to that view.[5]

The reality, however, is more complex. In fact, Lincoln's popularity in other northern states of the Midwest and the Mid-Atlantic region was not overwhelming. The Emancipation Proclamation was condemned by the Democratic Party in most northern states. And the Fifteenth Amendment was rejected in virtually all of the northern states in referendums on black voting. Within this ambivalent context, New Jersey was a state with a strong conservative element, which made its citizens highly suspicious of the centralizing necessities of a federal government engaged in a life-and-death struggle with the Confederacy. It was also a state with a weaker abolitionist movement than many other northern states, where the antislavery message and advocacy of legal racial equality were rigorously and consistently brought to the general population. Finally, New Jersey's economic trade ties to South, though not decisive, were important in shaping the views of many New Jersey residents toward the conflict. How New Jerseyans reacted to these conflicting messages, in part, was determined by their antebellum history and ideological beliefs.

EMANCIPATION AND COLONIZATION IN NEW JERSEY

If the roots of the secession are to be found in the sectional politics that preceded the firing on Fort Sumter and the southern states' internal discussions over the way to respond to what they saw as northern provocations like abolitionism and attempts to limit slavery's westward expansion, then an explanation of the myriad northern responses to the South must likewise examine internal debates over the legitimacy of slavery, its territorial expansion, the legal status of freed blacks, and the permanency of the Union. New Jersey's response reflected a higher degree of ambivalence than other northern states toward emancipation and the creation of a free black population from early colonial times to the highly partisan and heated sectional debates of the mid-nineteenth century.

Pennsylvania Quakers, motivated by humanitarian and religious beliefs about the immorality and incompatibility of slavery with Christianity, first raised objections to slavery in the famous Germantown Protest of 1688. John Woolman, a West Jersey tailor from Mount Holly, preached against the institution for thirty years in his travels as an itinerant preacher. His 1754 pamphlet, *Considerations on the Keeping of Negroes*, is a classic antislavery tract encapsulating the Christian case against slavery and employing arguments from Enlightenment natural law. In 1776 the Philadelphia yearly meeting began disowning coreligionists who refused to free their slaves, including members who lived in New Jersey. At the same time, however, the Dutch Reform and Presbyterians who dominated the East Jersey landscape, which contained the greatest concentration of slaves in Bergen, Somerset, Middlesex, and Monmouth Counties, were not as fervent in their antislavery beliefs. After the Revolution, in 1787, the Presbyterian synods of Philadelphia and New York indicated their approval of the abolition of slavery, but felt the need to urge moderation and caution.[6]

New Jersey's delegation to the 1787 Constitutional Convention in Philadelphia reflected this continuing ambivalence. In a debate over representation William Paterson stated that in 1783 Congress under the Articles of Confederation had considered an amendment, which did not pass, that would have changed its eighth article to count slaves when apportioning taxation among the states, but Congress had been ashamed to use the term "slave" and had substituted a description. Later, Jonathan Dayton of New Jersey told the House of Representatives that the purpose was to avoid any "stain" on the new government. Paterson, who owned slaves, was concerned that counting slaves for purposes of apportioning representatives in the national legislature would limit the influence of a small slaveholding state like New Jersey.[7]

Elements opposed to the continued presence of slaves in the state formed the New Jersey Society for Promoting the Abolition of Slavery in 1793. The society suffered setbacks when emancipation bills were defeated in 1792 and 1794. The abolition of slavery in New York in 1799 encouraged the New Jersey abolitionists, who successfully lobbied the state legislature to pass a gradual abolition law in 1804, making it the last northern state to do so. Contributing to New Jersey's willingness to pass such a gradual abolition law was the increase in the state's white population, which reduced the reliance on slave labor. The 1804 law reflected a belief in the sanctity of property rights over human rights that continued into the Civil War years, as well as a conviction that the federal government did not have the right to emancipate slaves.[8]

Gradual emancipation in the northern states following the end of the American Revolution created a free black population that began to fulfill the promise of democratic rhetoric but also generated fears concerning the new nation's capacity to assimilate former slaves, whom some Americans regarded as biologically inferior, incapable of assimilation, and a threat to the wages or job security of white workers. The size of New Jersey's free black population compounded these fears. On the eve of the Civil War, it had increased to 25,336 out of a total population of 646,699 and was proportionally twice the size of the black population in any other free state. New Jersey's legislature had passed a law in 1807 disenfranchising the state's black population and women, and the state would later reinforce this exclusion in the revised state constitution of 1844.[9]

Colonization of blacks in Africa or the Caribbean became an attractive solution to those envisioning a white republic free of both slavery and the presence of blacks as economic competitors. A New Jersey resident and distinguished educator, the Reverend Robert Finley of Basking Ridge, played a singularly important role in the founding of the American Colonization Society and the New Jersey auxiliary in the winter of 1816–1817. The founding meetings held in Washington, D.C., were attended by Daniel Webster, Henry Clay, Francis Scott Key, and John Randolph, among other important national figures. Finley died in October of 1817, leaving the colonization movement in New Jersey somewhat directionless. However, the expected increase in the state's free black population by 1825, due to the provisions of the 1804 gradual abolition law, sparked a renewed interest in colonization. The New Jersey Colonization Society was reorganized under the leadership of Robert Field Stockton, a Princeton graduate, distinguished naval officer, and future Democratic senator. Also involved were Theodore Frelinghuysen, a future senator and Whig candidate for vice president, Governor Isaac H. Williamson, and Charles Ewing, chief justice of the New Jersey Supreme Court.[10]

In October 1825 the New Jersey legislature endorsed a colonization resolution to achieve the emancipation of slaves in America and to encourage these freed blacks to establish a colony to Christianize Africa. Neither the state legislature nor the New Jersey Colonization Society favored the abolition of slavery by the national government, and it was unlikely that southern slaveholders would voluntarily manumit their valuable slaves. Nevertheless, colonization was the panacea for national divisions over slavery and the widespread belief that blacks could not be integrated into American society. Stockton maintained that emancipation without colonization would lead to "the letting loose upon the community of the United States such a body of men, who had not important interests at stake, nor any common concern in the permanency of our institutions."[11] The revived New Jersey Colonization Society purchased a ship named *Saluda* and 160,000 acres of land to be added to the Liberian colony founded by the national organization. However, only 8,204 blacks were colonized between 1820 and 1853, of which only 24 were from New Jersey, despite the pro-colonization sentiments and anti-abolition attitudes of a number of the Methodist churches in New Jersey.[12]

The inability of the New Jersey Colonization Society to make progress with its agenda derived from the hostility of the state's African American community, which mirrored the attitude nationally. In August 1817, a month after the founding of the American Colonization Society, approximately 3,000 blacks gathered in Philadelphia to condemn the colonization plan as a scheme to solidify slavery in America by removing its most vigorous critics, free blacks. Thomas D. Coxsin of Gloucester County helped prepare a report of the 1832 Convention of Free Persons of Colour condemning the American Colonization Society for coercing free blacks to emigrate to Canada. *The Colonization Scheme Considered*, a pamphlet written in 1840 by Samuel E. Cornish, pastor of the first Presbyterian Church in Newark, and Theodore S. Wright, a Presbyterian minister from New York City, received great support from blacks.[13] Although colonization as a viable solution to the problems surrounding slavery never materialized, the idea had a long life, advocated by politicians like Abraham Lincoln well into the 1850s and by others into the middle years of the Civil War.[14]

ANTEBELLUM NEW JERSEY

Colonization purported to solve the great dilemmas of slavery and race afflicting the American nation from its inception in the second half of the eighteenth century to the antebellum era (1830–1860). Its rejection by the two essential participants, free blacks and southern slave owners, paved the way for the Civil War. Southerners did not want to manumit their slaves and adopt the free labor system of the North. Free blacks distrusted the white-led colonization movement and did not want to turn their backs on their enslaved brethren. Furthermore, Africa was a distant memory for many, and others believed their labor had contributed to the building of America.

The failure of the colonization movement highlighted the differences between a modernizing and industrializing northern economy committed to a free labor economic system and a plantation-oriented southern economy that relied on a deeply entrenched slave labor system. At the same time, the northern-centered abolitionist movement had become far more aggressive in its opposition to an equally combative and inflexible southern ideology defending slavery. These economic, social, and political fault lines grew wider as each succeeding crisis eroded national unity and violently split any common ground.

The divisive issue of slavery in the western territories received national attention in 1819 and 1820 with the question of Missouri's admission to the Union. Thomas Jefferson perceived the threat to national unity and security posed by slavery and likened it to a "fire bell in the night." The final compromise provided for the admission of Missouri as a slave state and Maine as a free state (to maintain equal numbers of free and slave states in Congress), and allowed slavery below parallel 36°30' (the southern boundary of Missouri) across the entire Louisiana Purchase. New Jersey politicians, like their constituents, were ambivalent. Three of the state's delegation to the U.S. House of Representatives opposed placing restrictions on Missouri, including former governor and abolitionist Joseph Bloomfield. New Jersey' senators were split on the question, with former governor Mahlon Dickerson voting for the compromise and future governor Samuel Southard voting against it.[15]

If the Missouri Compromise of 1820 temporarily resolved the political controversy over the expansion of slavery into the western territories, it did not end the activities of individual partisans. Indeed, abolition in the 1830s became far more militant, impatient, and uncompromising. The Second Great Awakening, beginning in the 1820s, brought changes not only to northern and Midwestern Protestantism but also to the abolitionist movement. Earlier, abolitionism was characterized by the principles of gradual emancipation, compensation to slave owners, and colonization of freed slaves in Africa. The Second Great Awakening, with its emphasis on free will, the conversion experience, and eligibility of all persons for salvation, not simply a predetermined elect, rendered each individual accountable to collective judgment for society's sins. One became one's brother's keeper and therefore responsible for the sin of slavery whether one owned slaves or not. Thus a new antislavery movement emerged in the 1830s that rejected gradualism, compensation for slaveholders, and colonization. Many of its leading advocates were followers of the Second Great Awakening's preeminent evangelical preacher, Charles Grandison Finney. Among his early followers were some of the leading lights of the abolitionist movement, including Arthur and Lewis Tappan, Theodore Weld, and William Lloyd Garrison.[16]

New Jersey, unlike some northern states, never developed a strong abolitionist movement. In his support of the Wilmot Proviso of 1846, which would have banned slavery from any territory acquired from the current war with Mexico, U.S. Senator William Dayton of New Jersey, declared that neither he nor his constituents should be considered abolitionists. "I have to my knowledge," Dayton said, "never seen a genuine Jersey abolitionist."[17] Although well-known abolitionists Theodore Weld, Angelina Grimkė Weld, and Sara Grimkė first settled in Bellville and then were prominent in Perth Amboy's Raritan Bay Union, many of the state's prominent citizens supported colonization, and only a few of the state's reformers lent their voice or pen to the abolitionist cause. Militant abolitionism in the state appeared with the formation of the New Jersey State Anti-Slavery Society in 1840. Abolitionist activity in the state reached a pinnacle in the mid-1840s with the publication of the *New Jersey Freeman* from 1844 to 1850. Nevertheless, according to the American Anti-Slavery Society in 1838, of the 1,350 abolition societies in the country; only 14 were located in New Jersey (Ohio had 251).[18]

The *New Jersey Freeman*, published in Boonton and edited by John Grimes, consistently alerted readers to the failure of New Jersey's clergy, so active in the movement in other states, to take up the cause. In 1847 he counted only three ordained clergymen in the state who were abolitionists. He attributed this poor record to the insensitivity of ministers to the misery of the slave and their fear of losing status in a "corrupt church," which made them "unfit to stand as sentinels on the walls of Zion." Methodists tended to be supporters of colonization and opponents of the abolitionists. In 1848 Methodist clergy in Newark refused to announce that the itinerant lecturer and abolitionist William Larison would be making speeches in the city. Larison sent a scathing letter to the *New Jersey Freeman* in which he sarcastically identified himself as a "Jerseyman—and belong to the white-skinned aristocracy of this country; where kidnapping, plunder and butchery are lawful and respectable, if only prosecuted on a large scale."[19]

New Jersey's proximity to the border slave states of Delaware and Maryland made it a major passageway on the Underground Railroad, the network of safe houses ("stations") operated by sympathetic whites, religiously motivated Quakers, and free blacks that gave sanctuary to fugitive slaves fleeing from southern states. As the antislavery movement in many states became more active from the 1830s through the 1850s, the Underground Railroad helped hundreds, if not thousands, to escape to free states. New Jersey had three main routes: from Camden to Burlington following the Delaware River; from Salem through Woodbury, Mount Laurel, and Burlington to Princeton; and through Greenwich, with stations in Swedesboro, Mount Holly, and Burlington to the Camden route. One of the most famous Underground Railroad "conductors" or guides to freedom was Harriet Tubman, who escaped from bondage in Maryland in 1849. In the summer of 1852 she worked as a cook in a Cape May hotel, from which she probably continued to help slaves escape across Delaware Bay to Cape May.[20] Nearly as famous was William Still, born in New Jersey in 1821, who later joined the Philadelphia Anti-Slavery Society. He became a leader in the Philadelphia General Vigilance Committee, which gave financial and other assistance to fugitive slaves.[21] His brother, Dr. James Still, was a well-known doctor in New Jersey.[22]

Harriet Tubman and William Still, like other New Jersey conductors/agents, were in violation of the Fugitive Slave Act, a part of the Compromise of 1850 that, among other measures, increased penalties for aiding runaway slaves and allowed slaves to be returned south on evidence supplied by their masters. New Brunswick was considered one of the most dangerous branches on these freedom routes because slave hunters established a headquarters there and often stopped trains at the Raritan River bridge. Local conductors served as lookouts, alerting their colleagues when to transport the fugitive slaves in boats to Perth Amboy. Unlike many northern states, New Jersey never adopted a "personal liberty" law to hamper the return of captured fugitive slaves. Efforts to legalize a bonded person's freedom once on the soil of New Jersey also failed. Most New Jersey politicians, irrespective of their philosophical attitudes toward the morality or immorality of slavery, supported enforcement of the fugitive slave laws. During the 1850 debates over the compromise, when southern states claimed that northern states would never fulfill their duty to return southern property, Congressman John Van Dyke of New Brunswick said that he knew of only one case of a fugitive slave that came before a New Jersey court, and that case went against the fugitive in a jury trial.[23]

Ralph Waldo Emerson had prophetically noted the evils of Manifest Destiny when he asserted that "the United States will conquer Mexico, but it will be as the man swallows the arsenic, which brings him down in turn. Mexico will poison us."[24] The New Jersey congressional delegation split over the annexation of Texas in 1845, though most Democrats were in favor. Many of the Whig opponents also opposed the Mexican War in 1846. Although the state legislature passed resolutions supporting the Wilmot Proviso, Whig Party senators William Dayton and Jacob Miller argued that annexation of Mexican land was against the interests of small states. Dayton's opposition derived from his belief in the superiority of free labor economies over those based on slave labor and his fear that slave labor would preclude the development and opportunities for northern free white labor. New Jerseyans, however, gave little support to abolitionist or antislavery extension parties like the Liberty Party and the Free Soil Party, whose percentage of the vote was significantly less than in other states of the North.[25]

In 1854, in anticipation of further expansion west, Stephen A. Douglas proposed the Kansas-Nebraska Act, which obliterated the old Missouri Compromise line of 36°30' and introduced the possibility of the expansion of slavery through popular sovereignty. Even though it passed narrowly, Douglas's bill was ultimately so divisive that it sealed the doom of the declining Whig Party and provoked the formation of the modern Republican Party. The New Jersey Republican Party began with a meeting in New Brunswick in 1855, called by the editor of the *Newark Mercury*. This party, composed of ex-Whigs, some nativists, newly minted Republicans, and eventually a few anti-Nebraska Democrats, rarely used the term "Republican." Rather, they preferred "Opposition" to avoid the stigma of abolition that Democrats attached to the Republican Party. Their position, like that of the national Republican Party, called for a ban on slavery in the western territories and the admission of Kansas as a free state.[26] The Democrats smeared their new political opponents with racially charged messages. In 1854, the *Trenton (Daily True) American* proclaimed that only the Democratic Party supported the interests and "freedom of white men."[27] Robert Stockton, in an 1851 Fourth of July oration tinged with Anglo-Saxonist and Manifest Destiny justifications for expansionism, stated the position of the

Democratic Party most succinctly when he claimed that in "the North, a fanaticism . . . is at work . . . in the vain and delusive expectation of . . . the equality of the white and black races of men" that ignores the Constitution, which "nowhere gives authority to Congress to prescribe to an emigrant going to the public lands what kind of property he shall not take with him." In the event of secession, Stockton claimed that New Jersey would join Pennsylvania and other "northwestern states" (that is, the Midwest) in uniting with the South.[28]

The reaction of New Jersey residents is not so easily categorized by any one politician. Stephen Douglas was heckled at a stopover in Trenton in 1854 for his authorship of the Kansas-Nebraska Act. In the November 1854 election, voters reversed the composition of New Jersey's congressional delegation and sent four anti-Nebraska candidates and only one Democrat to Congress. Although Pennsylvania Democrat James Buchanan won New Jersey's electoral vote in 1856, he did not receive a majority of the popular vote (47 percent). The Opposition coalition succeeded in narrowly electing William A. Newell governor of the state. Nativist sentiment increased as the foreign-born population in the state doubled between 1850 and 1860. Nativist riots occurred in various cities across America, including Newark in 1854, when a Catholic church was attacked with guns and rocks.[29] The formation of the American Party gave political direction to this ethnically and religiously intolerant movement, whose ultimate target, immigrants, became a secondary story to issues of sectionalism, slavery, and race.

Politics in the latter half of the 1850s was dominated by two overriding events: the U.S. Supreme Court decision in the Dred Scott case in 1857 and John Brown's 1859 raid on the federal arsenal at Harper's Ferry, Virginia, as the first step in a plot to arm slaves. Abolitionists sued on behalf of Dred Scott, a slave who lived with his master in free states until the master died, claiming that by virtue of reaching a free state he was free. If the Court ruled in his favor, all northern fugitive slaves could claim freedom. The Court, in an opinion by Chief Justice Roger Taney, ruled that not only was Scott still a slave but that blacks were not citizens under the Constitution and that Congress could not deprive citizens of their property by prohibiting the expansion of slavery into the territories. The Court appeared to dismiss the doctrine of popular sovereignty so dear to the hearts of Douglas Democrats, who saw it as the logical way to resolve the intensifying sectional crisis over the western territories. The New Jersey reaction was divided along partisan lines: Republicans condemned it, and Democrats supported it. Democrats took control of the state legislature in 1857.[30]

John Brown's raid was widely condemned by both Democrats and Republicans in New Jersey. The Democratic press and politicians blamed the Republicans for the insurrection. The *Newark Journal* attributed the raid to the rhetoric of the leading Republican senator from New York, William H. Seward, and his 1858 speech about an "irrepressible conflict" looming on the horizon between the forces of slavery and freedom. Republicans denied Democratic charges and blamed the Democrats for repealing the Missouri Compromise.[31]

THE 1860 PRESIDENTIAL ELECTION AND SECESSION

The fortunes of the new Republican Party appeared on the rise in New Jersey in 1856 after a respectable showing in its first presidential election and the election of Dr. William A. Newell as governor under the banner of the "Opposition" coalition, which brought together both Republicans and anti-Nebraska Democrats. In a state so opposed to abolition, the Republican Party was burdened with all the negative imagery that the Democratic Party had placed upon the abolitionists, the Liberty Party, and the Free Soil Party. "Black Republicans" were accused of being a pro-black party, supporting miscegenation, encouraging slave uprisings, and acting against the interests of white working men. During the Civil War, New Jersey Republicans continued to shy away from that name and instead called themselves the "Union" party.

In 1859 the state again elected an Opposition Party candidate for governor, Charles Olden. A Quaker, but conservative on the questions of slavery and abolition, he articulated positions acceptable to a state never enthusiastic about abolitionists, emancipation, or equal rights for black residents. Olden held a conservative view of the Constitution and of the power of the federal government to regulate the domestic institutions of a state, thereby denying the legal tools used by abolitionists to emancipate slaves and aid runaway slaves. In his January 17, 1860, inaugural speech, Olden outlined his theory of government, which was not unlike that of many Democrats. He argued that each state "reserves to itself the exclusive independent control of its domestic policy; only the powers that are essential to the preservation of the body politic are conferred on the General Government." He acknowledged that a significant portion of American citizens are "unquestionably adverse to involuntary servitude," but added that "it is exclusively and eminently a matter of domestic policy, and controlled by each state for itself."[32] Fugitive slaves should be returned to their masters according to this conservative interpretation. Olden's conservatism is also revealed in his signing of the state legislature's "Joint Resolution in Relation to the State of the Union" on January 29, 1861, after South Carolina, Mississippi, Florida, Alabama, Georgia, and Louisiana had already seceded. The resolution supported the Crittenden Compromise of December 1860, which would have extended the Missouri Compromise line all the way west and protected slavery in all existing and acquired territories south of 36° 30'.[33]

Nationally, the Republican Party could not hide behind another name in the 1860 presidential election. At the Republican National Convention in Chicago, the front-runner, William Henry Seward, was considered too radical to win election. If Seward failed to gain the nomination on the first ballot, New Jersey's delegates, along with those from Pennsylvania and the border states, were prepared to support the more moderate Lincoln. The success of the strategy became evident when Lincoln won on the third ballot. The efforts of two members of the New Jersey delegation were especially appreciated: William Dayton became the American minister to France and Thomas Dudley was appointed consul at Liverpool, both in 1861.[34]

After Lincoln won the election, but lost New Jersey, Republican newspapers were eager to point out the lack of patriotism and Unionist sentiment in the state. The *New York Times* in exasperation proclaimed the election a "confused melee," and the *New York Tribune* declared that in no other non-slave state "are disloyal utterances so frequent and so bold as in New Jersey."[35] State Democratic Party supporters, for the most part, were not anti-Unionists, nor were they generally pro-southern or pro-Confederacy. They were, however, in favor of the antebellum status quo, which would keep the Union together and avoid emancipation, which, they feared, would result in an inundation of freed slaves, the collapse of white workers' wages, competition for jobs, and threats to racial purity. New Jersey Democrats often used the phrase, "the Constitution as it is, the Union as it was." Most Democrats did not perceive slavery as an institution capable of expanding into the West and thus were willing to compromise with the South and hold out the possibility of the extension of slavery through the principle of popular sovereignty. Commodore Robert F. Stockton told a Constitutional Union convention in Trenton in December 1860 that blacks were not worth fighting for and that the North should yield to the South.[36]

The Democratic Party had been playing on these racial, economic, and political fears for more than a decade. In many northeastern and upper Midwestern states the party intensified its campaign to cast opponents as "Black Republicans" who favored racial equality, and Republican Party events were referred to as "Republican miscegenationist balls."[37] Republicans were often pilloried in the Democratic Party press as a cabal of John Brown sympathizers and supporters. The virulent anti-abolitionist and anti-Republican *Trenton Daily True American* proclaimed that a Republican victory in 1860 would mean emancipation and urged northern men to contemplate the consequences: three million blacks "wild with their freedom, uneducated, unrestrained by any moral perceptions and ideas, led by their passions alone, lazy, vicious, and uncontrollable? —Have you thought of the horrors which this exodus from the South would entail upon you—of this mass of negroes perambulating your country, stealing and murdering as they go."[38] The threat to white womanhood and racial purity was self-evident in a picture carried in the Democratic parade held in Newark. Lincoln stands in the bow of a ship steered by Horace Greeley, the Republican editor of the *New York Tribune*. The white women on board sit in the laps of black men and embrace them, while Uncle Sam tries to prevent them from landing. The caption reads, "No Negro Equality."[39] Race was certainly not the only factor in the 1860 election, but it was a persistent theme in American life deepening American racial prejudice.

Lincoln did not win a majority of the 121,000 popular votes in New Jersey, but he did win four of the state's seven electoral votes. Still, the Republicans had doubled their support nationally since the 1856 presidential election. They were able to take advantage of the factionalism among their opponents, with northern Democrats supporting Stephen A. Douglas, southern Democrats supporting John C. Breckenridge, and John Bell of Tennessee (Constitutional Union Party) gathering support in some Midwestern and border states. Lincoln did better in the southern counties of New Jersey, where Quakers and antislavery Methodists were concentrated. His campaign fared poorly in the cities, capturing only 42 percent of the vote in Jersey City and Hoboken and 46 percent of the vote in Newark.[40] New Jersey residents backed Douglas because they thought he would be able to reach an accommodation with the South. In the final analysis, they supported Lincoln and Douglas rather than the other two candidates because they stood the strongest chance to negotiate a compromise to preserve the Union.

On April 4, 1861, just ten days before the surrender of Fort Sumter, former New Jersey Governor Rodman Price (1854–1857), who directed Douglas's presidential campaign, wrote a letter to the *Newark Journal* in answer to a letter writer who wondered what New Jersey's response should be if there were to be "two permanent confederacies." Price asserted that New Jersey should ally itself with the Confederacy because the South was an important market for New Jersey manufacturing. If New Jersey allied itself with the North, Europe would take the southern market, and New Jerseyans would be "compelled to seek employment elsewhere, our state becoming depopulated and impoverished." Price concluded, "We believe that slavery is no sin" and then quoted from the Confederacy's constitution: "Slavery —subordination to the superior race—is his [the black's] natural and normal condition."[41] Although many voters rejected a proposed alliance with the South in the event of armed conflict, Price's economic and racist attachment to the Confederacy explains the motives and outlook of a significant number of the "Peace Democrat" faction.

CIVIL WAR

Once the siege of Fort Sumter commenced from South Carolina shore batteries on April 12, 1861, New Jersey residents wholeheartedly supported the war to bring the South back into the Union. Probably greater unity and resolve was demonstrated in this early period of the war than at any other time. Most of the newspapers in the state, Republican and Democrat, rallied to the Union cause. Unity and loyalty were based on the assumption that the war would end in a quick and decisive victory.

According to the state adjutant general's figures, 88,305 New Jersey men served in the war, 10,057 more than called for by the federal government, and this number was achieved without the use of a draft.[42] Modern estimates, including those of William Wright, show these figures to be inflated. In fact, New Jersey failed to meet its quotas, and the federal government employed the draft to obtain troops for the Union Army.[43] New Jersey supplied 78,648 troops for the war, of which 77,346 actually served. The U.S. Provost Marshal General's report stated that 10,601 New Jersey men were drafted during four presidential calls for troops that led to conscriptions, the last three occurring in 1864, the final year of the war.[44]

Conscription was controversial and the drafts unpopular in New Jersey. The editors of the *Somerset Messenger*, *Bergen County Democrat*, and the *Newark Daily Journal* were arrested for denouncing the draft and urging men to evade it. Only Orson C. Cone of the *Newark Daily Journal* was indicted. Nevertheless, it should be remembered that the vast majority of New Jersey troops who fought in the Civil War were volunteers who believed the war to be necessary and even noble, as is made clear by Gary Gallagher in *The Union War* and by James McPherson in *For Cause and Comrades*.[45] Their ideals were tested in the carnage of numerous Civil War battles and in the suffering endured in many a battlefield military hospital. As the war dragged on, some soldiers experienced a sense of hopelessness or even despair. Private George B. Wright wrote to his friend James during the Peninsular Campaign (March–July 1862), urging him "not [to] enlist as a private in any Regiment just as present. You have no idea of the fatigue.... There are ten chances to one that your health would break down before you had been in service a month." Lieutenant Sebastian Duncan wrote to his brother Willie that "when you begin to see heads & arms & legs knocked off; see some fall dead by your side, & others bleeding and torn carried off on stretchers to the Rear, you would wish yourself playing doorkeeper with Josie Crosby again."[46] Yet, New Jersey soldiers continued to volunteer and serve with honor despite the physical and psychological hardships.

New Jersey men valiantly fought alongside their comrades from other states under various commanders of the Army of the Potomac. New Jersey's 33rd Regiment augmented the forces of General William T. Sherman on his famous "march to the sea" through Georgia. They suffered an astoundingly high casualty rate. New Jersey produced Medal of Honor winners like fifteen-year-old Willie Magee, the Newark drummer boy who led a charge on a Confederate battery in Tennessee in 1863. General Philip Kearny, commander of the 1st Brigade of New Jersey, was one of the state's outstanding officers, and Hugh Judson Kilpatrick was a daring cavalry officer.[47]

In a reaction against Lincoln's preliminary Emancipation Proclamation of September 22, 1862, and impatient with the war, New Jersey voters elected Democrat Joel Parker to the governorship. Parker's essential

Monument to the 13th New Jersey Volunteers who served at the Battle of Gettysburg, located in Gettysburg, Pennsylvania. (Courtesy of the New Jersey State Archives, Department of State.)

conservatism and racism is revealed in his January 20, 1863, inaugural address. While praising the courage of New Jersey troops and calling the doctrine of secession "political heresy," he suggested that the North provoked the war and held a long and deep-seated prejudice against the South. He acknowledged the existence of extremists on both sides, but saw the abolitionists as especially provocative because they believed in the necessity of ending slavery and in some semblance of racial equality. "Personal liberty is one of the absolute rights of man," Parker affirmed, but to give blacks freedom "without property, without homes, without education, industry or enterprise sufficient to provide for themselves" would benefit neither blacks nor whites. Rather, blacks would become an unproductive burden on the state. Parker rhetorically asked, "Does any sane man believe that two distinct races of men, of different color, who cannot by any means be brought into social equality, can long exist in the same locality, in equal numbers, without one race becoming subject to the other?" Parker suggested that all "energies should be devoted to the restoration of the Union, and the problem of emancipation is one to be solved here after by the people of the States where the institution of slavery exists."[48] He held up New Jersey as an example of a society where slavery was peacefully and gradually abolished. Parker's refusal to explore or at least acknowledge the differences between northern and southern abolition perhaps masked a belief in the attractiveness of southern slavery as a means of preventing black migration to New Jersey even after the restoration of the Union. His suggestion that emancipation was the prerogative of southern states would not have produced the gradual abolition of New Jersey and other northern states, but rather a continuation of slavery after the conclusion of the war.

Prior to Governor Parker's inaugural address, the New Jersey Democratic State Central Committee denounced the preliminary Emancipation Proclamation as a perversion of the congressionally authorized purpose of the war, which was the suppression of the rebellion. The committee referred to abolitionists as "fanatics" who had "become more bold and confident in their purposes" and had pressured the president to issue a "proclamation decreeing freedom to slaves after the 1st of January, 1863, unless the rebel states should before that time return to their allegiance." Emancipation would "destroy the private property of the innocent people of those states along with the guilty." Further, the Democrats deemed Lincoln's proclamation unconstitutional and not justified as a war power. They predicted all manner of catastrophes would befall the nation if "three or four millions of colored persons" were suddenly "let loose upon the country"; they would participate in "servile insurrection" in the South, and if "they escape to the North it would be ruinous to free labor and we should be loaded with intolerable burdens."[49]

Union failures on the battlefield, the Democratic Party's vigorous opposition to the Emancipation Proclamation, and Democratic exploitation of fears of black migration into northern states led to significant Democratic victories in New Jersey in the elections of 1862, which "turned narrow majorities in the legislature to solid ones—forty-five to seventeen in the assembly, and twelve to eight (and one Union Democrat) in the Senate."[50] In the U.S. House of Representatives, Democrats gained thirty-two seats, mainly in the lower north of New York, New Jersey, Pennsylvania, Ohio,

Indiana, and Illinois. Joel Parker easily won over Marcus Ward in the gubernatorial race by 14,597 votes out of 108,017 cast. In New York, Democratic gubernatorial candidate Horatio Seymour also succeeded by echoing themes similar to those of Parker.[51]

In March 1863, only two months after Governor Parker's inaugural address, the New Jersey legislature passed the infamous "Peace Resolutions" denying Lincoln's power to emancipate slaves and advocating a settlement with the South. State Senator Daniel Holsman introduced two sweeping resolutions condemning Republican war measures, like emancipation, and proposing an immediate unilateral armistice for six months, during which elected delegates from all the states, North and South, would attend a conference to negotiate an agreement. Republicans condemned the proposal, and war Democrats denounced Holsman for departing from their statements of unswerving loyalty to the Union cause. Prowar Democrats moved to block Holsman and his supporters by creating a joint committee on federal relations. Their proposals, unlike those of the peace faction, did not encourage resistance to paying taxes or defying conscription. Most importantly, the committee did not recommend an armistice or negotiations, stating that the Confederates had already rejected peace feelers. The state Democratic caucus supported the committee's majority report. However, to placate the peace faction, the caucus tacked on a provision urging Lincoln to dispatch emissaries to the Confederacy, provided he felt it "consistent with the honor and dignity of the national government."[52] Certainly, the "Peace Resolutions" were not a complete victory for the antiwar faction of the Democratic Party, but they did show the political power of the Peace Democrats since the election of 1862. Many New Jersey soldiers in the field were not happy with the legislature's actions. Officers of the 11th Regiment of New Jersey volunteers denounced those "we regard as traitors alike the foe in arms and the secret enemies of our government who at home foment disaffection and strive to destroy confidence in our legally chosen rulers." Suggestions that the Union Army was "demoralized and clamorous for peace on any terms are the lying utterances of traitorous tongues and do base injustice to our able comrades who have never faltered in the great work."[53]

Undeterred by Republican and soldier protests, the peace faction, or "Copperheads" as they were called by their opponents, continued their "Negrophobic" fear-mongering campaign into 1863, proclaiming dire consequences for northern white workingmen from the competition of emancipated slaves. Democratic Assemblyman John B. Perry introduced "An Act to prevent the immigration of negroes and to define the standing of the negro race in the State of New Jersey" on February 4, 1863. Anyone found harboring a black immigrant would be fined twenty dollars per day, and it would be a misdemeanor to entice a black person to enter the state. The bill defined a Negro as a person who possessed one-fourth Negro blood, and it made interracial marriage illegal in the state. Perry's bill died in the House Judiciary Committee chaired by Jacob Vanatta, a Morris County Democrat who soon introduced a Negro exclusion bill of his own.[54]

Vanatta's bill, "An Act to Prevent the Immigration of Negroes and Mulattoes," was introduced into the assembly on March 5, 1863. It revived the old colonization scheme by providing that blacks entering the state would be transported to Liberia or the West Indies. Although the assembly passed the bill on March 18, 1863, it died in the senate. The *Newark Daily Advertiser* attributed its demise to doubts about its constitutionality, even among some of its supporters. The *Trenton True American* attributed the failure to the expense of deportation. New Jersey's black population of 25,000 was nearly twice that of any other free state in 1860 and contributed to the fears of miscegenation and an impending black inundation. The demise of both bills left "Negrophobic" elements, at least in their own minds, feeling threatened by black inundation and subsequent miscegenation.[55]

Democrats believed that the Union army's inability to win a decisive battle to end the war and northern fears over the Emancipation Proclamation would enable them to defeat Lincoln and the Republicans in the presidential election of 1864. Lincoln staved off an attempt to replace him on the Republican national ticket and faced the Democratic nominee, George B. McClellan, the former commander of the Army of the Potomac, whom he had fired after the Battle of Antietam. McClellan was at his home in Orange, New Jersey, when he received news of his nomination. The Democratic platform, written by Peace Democrats, called for an immediate and unconditional armistice. McClellan, a War Democrat, later repudiated the platform, especially the unconditional armistice, and demanded reunion as a condition of peace. However, he was not willing to stand by the Emancipation Proclamation, which he had opposed from the outset of the war. Lincoln's reelection was in jeopardy after costly defeats with huge casualties in the first half of 1864 at the battles of the Wilderness, Spotsylvania, and Cold Harbor.[56]

The Democratic Party's fortunes in the election of 1864 were aided not only by Union battlefield reverses but also by its willingness to play upon the fears of racial "amalgamation" present in the northern electorate, which it had so actively cultivated over the last decade. As early as 1860, the Democratic National Executive Committee had circulated a pamphlet that accused Lincoln of advocating complete political and social equality between blacks and whites. The committee even rhetorically asked whether citizens wanted their daughters to marry blacks. The Democratic National Committee returned to these tactics in the 1864 presidential election, when it offered to send anyone in the country a copy of *Miscegenation: The Theory of the Blending of the Races* for thirty-five cents. The booklet had been written by two New York newspapermen who sought to obtain sympathetic responses from abolitionists and Republicans supporting its advocacy of racial amalgamation. Even though it failed to receive positive response, Democrats circulated the booklet as proof of Republican conspiracies. In March 1864 the New Jersey General Assembly unanimously passed "An Act to Prevent the Admixture of the Races." Thomas Dunn English introduced the bill, which died in the Senate, and another to introduce racial segregation into Trenton schools, which was also defeated. David Naar, editor of the fiercely anti-Lincoln *Trenton True American*, said: "Such is the last phase of abolitionism, for let it not be imagined that the author of this pamphlet is alone in his views."[57]

Despite the viciousness with which the Democrats played on racial fears and exploited passions over the draft, suspension of habeas corpus, and repression and imprisonment of dissenters, they failed to defeat Lincoln. McClellan lost every state except New Jersey, Delaware, and Kentucky. Lincoln carried the Mid-Atlantic states by only the slightest of margins (Pennsylvania, 52 percent; Connecticut, 51 percent; New York, 50 percent), and McClellan won New Jersey by only a little more than 7,000 out of almost 129,000 votes cast. If all the soldiers, including those on battlefields out of state, had been allowed to vote by absentee ballot, Lincoln might have won the state. As in 1860, Lincoln's strength was in the less populated southern counties, where antislavery sentiment had historically been stronger, while McClellan carried the more populous central and northern ones (except Essex and Passaic).[58]

Lincoln was finally saved by long-awaited Union victories just before the November 1864 election. In August, Admiral David Farragut seized

Mobile Bay; Sherman captured Atlanta on September 2, 1864; and Sheridan swept the Confederates from the militarily and economically strategic Shenandoah Valley in October. Lincoln's presidency and legacy were preserved.[59] The potency of race was diminished as a tactic in the election not by a decrease of racism itself, but rather by Union military victories. The negativity of racist political campaigns throughout the North lived on in northern attitudes and behavior and in the practices that African Americans had to endure.

RECONSTRUCTION

The end of the American Civil War brought with it the need to remake the defeated enemy into a more democratic society in the victorious Union image. Key political elements within the Union were split on the composition of a transformed South. How long were the defeated southern states to be under federal control and excluded from participation as equal partners in the Union? What was the plan for their readmission to the Union? What was to be the status of the four million freed slaves? How long were they to be in political and legal limbo, neither slave nor free person with citizenship rights? The answers appeared to come rather quickly with the passage of the Thirteenth Amendment (1865) abolishing slavery and reaffirming the Emancipation Proclamation, the ratification of the Fourteenth Amendment (1868) providing citizenship for African Americans, and the Fifteenth Amendment (1870) extending voting rights across the nation to male freedmen.

Yet the debates over these amendments reveal deep divisions concerning the nature of reconstruction and the future of a racially egalitarian society. The New Jersey legislature at various times rejected all three. It was not until the Thirteenth Amendment had already become part of the U.S. Constitution that New Jersey, under a newly elected Republican governor, Marcus Ward, and Republican-controlled legislature, finally ratified the amendment in January 1866.[60] Ward, apparently embarrassed over the state's initial rejection of emancipation, declared: "But for the honor of our State and people, we should avail ourselves of the occasion which is here afforded us of giving the right of our endorsement to the extinguishment forever of human slavery in our land."[61]

The new legislature proceeded to ratify the Fourteenth Amendment, which extended citizenship rights, but not voting rights, and "equal protection of the laws" to African Americans. In the 1866 election, Republicans attempted to make the Fourteenth Amendment the key to the election, while the Democrats sought to hang the albatross of "Negro suffrage" and "racial equality" around the necks of Republicans.[62] Democratic politicians and newspapers depicted them as purveyors of "racial equality," which would destabilize northern society. The *Daily True American* asserted that black suffrage would add nothing to the intelligence of government and that blacks were incapable of self-government. Playing the race card proved very successful, and the Democrats took control of both houses of the legislature in 1867. Republican support for black suffrage in the state, while laudable, was by no means entirely altruistic, as the party anticipated receiving the black vote. The *Newark Daily Advertiser* was concerned that Republicans held the state "by a very doubtful grasp and yet we do not dare to call seven thousand non-voting Republicans to our assistance."[63] Fears over black suffrage were so successfully heightened by Democrats that they were able to repeal the state's prior ratification of the Fourteenth Amendment (though the U.S. Congress refused to recognize the action).[64] A similar scenario played out when the Democrat-controlled legislature rejected the Fifteenth Amendment and a subsequent Republican legislature passed it in 1871 after the official national ratification in 1870. This tortuous road of rejection and ratification came to an end when Thomas Mundy Peterson of Perth Amboy became the first black man in the nation to exercise the vote under the Fifteenth Amendment on March 31, 1870. That historic day for constitutional equality was only the beginning of a new road of struggle for African American civil rights in New Jersey.

CONCLUSION

Although the ratification of the Civil War–era amendments to the Constitution can be seen as the close of one northern state's role in this crucial era, it foreshadows the struggle for the next 150 years over how the war and its aftermath were to be remembered. Joel Parker, the Democratic governor of New Jersey during the Civil War, was elected to another term during the Reconstruction era. In his 1872 inaugural address, he characterized the war as one provoked by abolitionist and secession extremists; during Reconstruction, the defeated South "acquiesced in constitutions extending suffrage."[65] Parker pleaded for amnesty for former Confederates excluded from participation in state governments by the Fourteenth Amendment.[66] Missing from his concerns were the "black codes" limiting black economic opportunity and mobility in the South, Ku Klux Klan assassination of black government officials, and intimidation of black voters.

Just seven years before, in his second inaugural address in March 1865, just a month before the final Confederate surrender, Abraham Lincoln described the origins, the great carnage, and the longevity of war as the nation's penance for the toleration of slavery, and he rejected any notion that moral equivalency existed on both sides: "Yet, if God wills that it continue, until all the wealth piled by the bond-man's two hundred and fifty years of unrequited toil shall be sunk, and until every drop of blood drawn with the lash, shall be paid by another drawn with the sword, as was said three thousand years ago, so still it must be said 'the judgments of the Lord, are

Meeting of the Grand Army of the Republic, veterans of the 7th Regiment, June 16, 1870, Long Branch, New Jersey. Union veterans who had served in the Civil War held reunions and played an active role in state affairs after the war. (Photograph by C. D. Frederick and Company. New Jersey Group Portraits, Oversized, Monmouth County–Long Branch. Special Collections and University Archives, Rutgers University Libraries.)

true and righteous altogether.' "[67] Lincoln, in his last public address before his assassination, anticipated the issues of citizenship and suffrage for the freedmen: "It is also unsatisfactory to some that the elective franchise is not given to the colored man. I would myself prefer that it were now conferred on the very intelligent, and on those who serve our cause as soldiers."[68]

The struggle over interpretation of the origins and consequences of the Civil War has been a continuous one, as historians and veterans organizations have demonstrated.[69] Following the war, organizations like the Grand Army of the Republic (GAR) were divided over Reconstruction, with some endorsing the rights of the freedmen and the exclusion of ex-Confederate leaders from political participation; others found these ideas abhorrent. While the GAR, nationally and locally, became less visibly political, its membership increased in the 1880s as memories of the war's carnage subsided and the public's celebratory interest in the war increased.[70] Patriotic education became the main focus, and the national need to reestablish sectional unity evolved into the depoliticizing of the Civil War and Reconstruction. As the New Jersey chapter of the GAR sought to educate New Jersey's schoolchildren about the Civil War, it could not point to a strong political legacy of championing the human rights of slaves or civil rights of the freedmen, but it could point to the strong contribution of New Jersey regiments upon the battlefield and to the preservation of the Union.

NOTES

1. Charles Merriam Knapp, *New Jersey Politics during the Period of the Civil War and Reconstruction* (Geneva, N.Y.: W. F. Humphrey, 1924); John T. Cunningham, *New Jersey, America's Main Road* (Garden City, N.Y.: Doubleday, 1966); Thomas Fleming, *New Jersey: A Bicentennial History* (New York: W. W. Norton, 1977); Maurice Tandler, "The Political Front in Civil War New Jersey," in *A New Jersey Anthology*, ed. Maxine N. Lurie (Newark: New Jersey Historical Society, 1994); William Gillette, *Jersey Blue: Civil War Politics in New Jersey, 1854–1865* (New Brunswick: Rutgers University Press, 1995); William J. Jackson, *New Jerseyans in the Civil War: For Union and Liberty* (New Brunswick: Rutgers University Press, 2000). Gillette's is the most thorough study.

2. "Remarks at Jersey City, New Jersey," in *The Collected Works of Abraham Lincoln*, ed. Roy Basler, 11 vols. (New Brunswick: Rutgers University Press, 1953–1990), 4:234.

3. "Remarks at Newark, New Jersey," *Collected Works Lincoln*, 4:234.

4. "Address to the New Jersey General Assembly at Trenton, New Jersey," February 21, 1861, *Collected Works of Lincoln*, 4:236.

5. Larry A. Greene, "The Emancipation Proclamation in New Jersey and the Paranoid

Style," *NJH* 91 (Summer 1973): 113; William C. Wright, "Joel Parker," in *The Governors of New Jersey, 1664–1774*, ed. Paul A. Stellhorn and Michael Birkner (Trenton: New Jersey Historical Commission, 1982), 132–135. For an excellent study of New Jersey's African American population, see Giles Wright, *Afro-Americans in New Jersey: A Short History* (Trenton: New Jersey Historical Commission, 1989).

6. John Woolman, *Some Considerations on the Keeping of Negroes* (Philadelphia, 1754); Jean R. Soderlund, "Quaker Abolitionism in Colonial New Jersey: The Shrewsbury and Chesterfield Monthly Meetings," in *Religion in New Jersey Life Before the Civil War*, ed. Mary R. Murrin (Trenton: New Jersey Historical Commission, 1985), 17–53; Cunningham, *New Jersey, America's Main Road*, 78; Jackson, *New Jerseyans in the Civil War*, 4–6; Arthur Zilversmit, *The First Emancipation: The Abolition of Slavery in the North* (Chicago: University of Chicago Press, 1967), 66. For a thorough discussion of Quakers and slavery, see Jean R. Soderlund, *Quakers and Slavery: A Divided Spirit* (Princeton: Princeton University Press, 1985).

7. Leonard B. Rosenberg, "William Paterson and Attitudes in New Jersey on Slavery," *NJH* 95 (1970): 201, 203–204; Staughton Lynd, *Class Conflict, Slavery, and the United States Constitution* (New York: Bobbs-Merrill, 1967), 159; Larry A. Greene, "A History of Afro-Americans in New Jersey," *Journal of the Rutgers University Libraries* 56 (June 1994): 19.

8. Clement Alexander Price, *Freedom Not Far Distant: A Documentary History of Afro-Americans in New Jersey* (Newark: New Jersey Historical Society, 1980), 53; Zilversmit, *First Emancipation*, 192–198, 215–230; Edgar J. McManus, *Black Bondage in the North* (Syracuse: Syracuse University Press, 1973), 178, 179; Frances D. Pingeon, *Blacks in the Revolutionary Era* (Trenton: New Jersey Historical Commission, 1975), 26, 27.

9. Jos. C. G. Kennedy, Superintendent, *Preliminary Report of the Eighth Census, 1860* (Washington, D.C., 1860), 271; Peter O. Wacker, "The Changing Geography of the Black Population of New Jersey: A Preliminary View," *Proceedings of the Association of American Geographers* 3 (1971): 174.

10. Douglas P. Seaton, "Colonizers and Reluctant Colonists: The New Jersey Colonization Society and the Black Community, 1813–1848," *NJH* 96 (1978): 7, 9–11. As early as 1777, Thomas Jefferson had proposed a black colony in the area later named the Northwest Territory. He believed this early colonization scheme was "the most desirable measure that could be adopted for gradually drawing off this part of our population." See Thomas Jefferson, *Notes on the State of Virginia*, ed . William Peden (Chapel Hill: University of North Carolina Press, 1955), 137–142.

11. New Jersey Colonization Society, *Proceedings of a Meeting Held at Princeton* (Princeton, N.J., 1824), 39–40.

12. Seaton, "Colonizers and Reluctant Colonists," 12; Robert J. Williams, "Blacks, Colonization, and Antislavery: The Views of Methodists in New Jersey, 1816–60," *NJH* 102 (1984): 62–64.

13. Benjamin Quarles, *Black Abolitionists* (New York: Oxford University Press, 1969), chap. 1; Seaton, "Colonizers and Reluctant Colonists," 13–15; Samuel Cornish and

Theodore S. Wright, *The Colonization Scheme Considered in Its Rejection by the Colored People* (Newark, 1840), 4–26.

14. Eric Foner, *The Fiery Trial: Abraham Lincoln and American Slavery* (New York: W. W. Norton, 2010), 51, 62, 127–129, 184–186, 239–240.

15. Jackson, *New Jerseyans in the Civil War*, 19; Michael Birkner, *Samuel L. Southard: Jeffrsonian Whig* (Rutherford, N.J.: Fairleigh Dickinson University Press, 1984), 50, 51; Paul A. Stellhorn and Michael J. Birkner, eds., *The Governors of New Jersey, 1664–1974* (Trenton: New Jersey Historical Commission, 1982), 85–88, 93–96, 101–105.

16. Gerald Sorin, *Abolitionism: A New Perspective* (New York: Praeger Publishers, 1972), 38–56; James McPherson, *Ordeal by Fire: The Civil War and Reconstruction* (New York: Alfred A. Knopf, 1982), 40, 41. For an excellent history of nineteenth-century evangelicalism, see Whitney R. Cross, *The Burned-Over District: The Social and Intellectual History of Enthusiastic Religion in Western New York, 1900–1950* (Ithaca: Cornell University Press 1965).

17. Quoted in Jackson, *New Jerseyans in the Civil War*, 22; see also John Y. Foster, *New Jersey and the Rebellion: A History of the Services of the Troops and People of New Jersey in Aid of the Union Cause* (Newark: Martin R. Dennis & Co., 1868), 815.

18. Williams, "Blacks, Colonization, and Antislavery," 62; Price, *Freedom Not Far Distant*, 89, 113–115.

19. Williams, "Blacks, Colonization, and Antislavery," 62, 63.

20. Greene, "Afro-Americans in New Jersey," 27; Walter Measdale, "Cape May and the Underground Railroad," *Cape May Magazine of History and Genealogy* 7 (1975): 140–142; Price, *Freedom Not Far Distant*, 92.

21. Greene, "Afro-Americans in New Jersey," 28.

22. William Still, *Underground Rail Road: A Record of Facts, Authentic Narratives, Letters, &c. . . .* (Philadelphia: Porter & Coates, 1872); James Still, *Early Recollections and Life of Dr. James Still* (1877; reprint, Medford, N.J.: Medford Historical Society, 1971); Giles Wright, *"Steel Away, Steal Away": A Guide to the Underground Railroad in New Jersey* (Trenton: New Jersey Historical Commission, 2002).

23. Jury trials were required under an 1846 New Jersey statute. See Charles L. Blockson, *The Underground Railroad* (New York: Berkley Books, 1987), 221; Jackson, *New Jerseyans in the Civil War*, 27.

24. James M. McPherson, *Battle Cry of Freedom: The Civil War Era* (New York: Oxford University Press, 1988), 51; *Journals of Ralph Waldo Emerson*, ed. Edward W. Emerson and Waldo E. Forbes, vol. 7 (Boston: Houghton Mifflin, 1909), 206.

25. Gillette, *Jersey Blue*, 5; Jackson, *New Jerseyans in the Civil War*, 22.

26. Gillette, *Jersey Blue*, 36. For the best study of the origins and development of the ideology of the pre–Civil War Republican Party, see Eric Foner, *Free Soil, Free Labor, Free Men: The Ideology of the Republican Party before the Civil War* (New York: Oxford University Press, 1970).

27. *Trenton (Daily) American*, April 15, 1854.

28. Robert F. Stockton, "The Union in Jeopardy: A Fourth of July Speech (1851)," in

Words That Make New Jersey History, ed. Howard Green (New Brunswick: Rutgers University Press, 1995), 125, 126.

29. Gillette, *Jersey Blue*, 28, 29, 34–36, 40–47.

30. Ibid., 49; Jackson, *New Jerseyans in the Civil War*, 29. For two excellent studies of the Dred Scott case, see Don E. Fehrenbacher, *The Dred Scott Case: Its Significance in Law and Politics* (New York: Oxford University Press, 1978), and Vincent C. Hopkins, *Dred Scott's Case* (New York: Atheneum, 1967).

31. Gillette, *Jersey Blue*, 64, 65; Jackson, *New Jerseyans in the Civil War*, 35.

32. *Proceedings Attending the Inauguration of Hon. Charles S. Olden, as Governor of New Jersey* (Trenton: Printed at the "True American" Office, 1860).

33. Gillette, *Jersey Blue*, 120; Jackson, *New Jerseyans in the Civil War*, 30–36.

34. Jackson, *New Jerseyans in the Civil War*, 30.

35. *New York Times*, November 16, 1860; *New York Tribune*, quoted in the *Sussex Register*, June 6, 1862, and cited in Maurice Tandler, "The Political Front in Civil War New Jersey," *Proc. NJHS* 83 (1965): 223n2.

36. Cunningham, *New Jersey, America's Main Road*, 175.

37. *New York World*, September 23, 1864; Forrest G. Wood, *Black Scare: The Racist Response to Emancipation and Reconstruction* (Berkeley: University of California Press, 1968), 40–80; Greene, "Emancipation Proclamation in New Jersey," 116–120; Sidney Kaplan, "The Miscegenation Issue in the Election of 1864," *Journal of Negro History* 34 (July 1949): 284–285.

38. *Trenton Daily True American*, October 10, 1860. For racial attitudes in the Midwest, see V. Jacque Voegeli, *Free But Not Equal: The Midwest and the Negro during the Civil War* (Chicago: University of Chicago Press, 1967).

39. *Trenton Daily True American*, September 8, 1860; *Newark Advertiser*, November 2, 1860; *Jersey City Standard*, September 6, 1860; Gillette, *Jersey Blue*, 93.

40. Gillette, *Jersey Blue*, 102–105; Jackson, *Jerseyans in the Civil War*, 31–32.

41. *Newark Journal*, April 4, 1861; Knapp, *New Jersey Politics*, 53, 54.

42. Foster, *New Jersey and the Rebellion*, 727; Earl S. Miers, *New Jersey and the Civil War: An Album of Contemporary Accounts* (Princeton: D. Van Nostrand, 1964), 36; William C. Wright, "New Jersey's Military Role in the Civil War Reconsidered," *NJH* 92 (1974): 197.

43. Wright, "New Jersey's Military Role," 197–205.

44. Ibid., 204–209.

45. Gary W. Gallagher, *The Union War* (Cambridge, Mass.: Harvard University Press, 2011), 1–7; James M. McPherson, *For Cause and Comrades: Why Men Fought in the Civil War* (New York: Oxford University Press, 1997), 3–13, 104–116.

46. Quoted in Leonard Bussanich, " 'To Reach Sweet Home Again': The Impact of Soldiering on New Jersey's Troops during the American Civil War," *NJH* 125 (2007): 48. This is an important study of the letters and memoirs of New Jersey's Civil War soldiers who saw combat.

47. Fleming, *New Jersey: A Bicentennial History*, 123; Jackson, *New Jerseyans in the Civil War*, 66–68, 88–91. For thorough studies of New Jersey soldiers during the Civil

War, see the works of Joseph G. Bilby, including: *"Remember You are Jerseymen": A Military History of New Jersey's Troops in the Civil War* (Hightstown, N.J.: Longstreet House, 1998); *New Jersey Goes to War: Biographies of 150 New Jerseyans* (Hightstown, N.J.: Longstreet House, 2010); *Forgotten Warriors: New Jersey's African American Soldiers in the Civil War* (Hightstown, N.J.: Longstreet House, 1993); "No Way to Raise an Army: Recruiting in New Jersey during the Civil War" (M.A. thesis, Seton Hall University, 1982).

48. *Inaugural Address of Joel Parker: Delivered at Trenton . . . January 20th, 1863* (Trenton: Printed by D. Naar, 1863), 11–13, 14.

49. *Address of the New Jersey Democratic State Central Committee to the Voters of the State* (October 1862), pamphlet in Special Collections and University Archives, Rutgers University Libraries.

50. Jackson, *New Jerseyans in the Civil War*, 109.

51. Ibid.; McPherson, *Ordeal by Fire*, 296.

52. Gillette, *Jersey Blue*, 219.

53. Quoted in "The Union Is the Only Guarantee: Soldiers Protest the Peace Resolutions (1863)," in Green, ed., *Words That Make New Jersey*, 147, 148.

54. New Jersey, "Petition," in *Minutes of . . . the Eighty-sixth General Assembly* (Trenton, 1862); New Jersey, "Petitions," in *Minutes of . . . the Eighty-seventh General Assembly* (Trenton, 1863); Carl Hatch, "Negro Migration and New Jersey—1863," *NJH* 87 (Winter 1969): 237–238.

55. New Jersey, *Minutes of . . . the Eighty-seventh General Assembly*, 277, 363–364; New Jersey, *Minutes of . . . the Eighty-eighth General Assembly* (Trenton, 1864), 379–380; Hatch, "Negro Migration and New Jersey," 241; Jos. C. G. Kennedy, Superintendent, *Preliminary Report of the Eighth Census, 1860* (Washington, D.C., 1862), 271; *Trenton Daily True American*, March 26, 1863; *Newark Daily Advertiser*, February 27, March 26, 1863. As Winthrop Jordan observed, "One of the most interesting and revealing aspects of American attitudes was the nearly universal belief that emancipation of Negroes from slavery would inevitably lead to increased racial intermixture." Winthrop Jordan, *White Over Black: American Attitudes Towards the Negro, 1550–1812* (Chapel Hill: University of North Carolina Press, 1968), 542.

56. Knapp, *New Jersey Politics*, 124. McPherson, *Battle Cry of Freedom*, 724–741; Gillette, *Jersey Blue*, 271–276.

57. Wood, *Black Scare*, 19, 51–54; *Trenton True American*, March 15, 1864. Naar repeatedly reprinted articles from the *New York World* labeling Republican social gatherings at which blacks were present as "miscegenation balls." See *Trenton True American*, September 24, 1864; Gillette, *Jersey Blue*, 257.

58. Gillette, *Jersey Blue*, 290–292; Jackson, *New Jerseyans during the Civil War*, 206; Cunningham, *New Jersey, America's Main Road*, 185.

59. Gillette, *Jersey Blue*, 272–275; McPherson, *Ordeal by Fire*, 442–456; McPherson, *Battle Cry of Freedom*, 718–750.

60. Greene, "Afro-Americans in New Jersey," 32. For a detailed study of the impact of Reconstruction in New Jersey, see Louis B. Moore, "Response to Reconstruction:

Change and Continuity in New Jersey Politics, 1866–1874" (Ph.D. diss., Rutgers University, 1999).

61. *Inauguration of His Excellency Marcus L. Ward, Governor of New Jersey, January 16, 1866* (Trenton: Printed at the "State Gazette" Office, 1866), 12.

62. Marion Thompson Wright, "New Jersey Laws and the Negro," *Journal of Negro History* 28 (April 1943): 189; Price, *Freedom Not Far Distant*, 131; David D. Furman, "Law and Morality Meet: The Thirteenth Amendment," in *Proceedings: Fourth Annual American History Workshop*, presented by the New Jersey Civil War Centennial Commission (New Brunswick: Rutgers University, 1964), 60–65.

63. Abner J. Gaines, "New Jersey and the Fourteenth Amendment," *Proc. NJHS* 70 (1952): 44–46; *Newark Daily Advertiser*, April 22, 1867; *Daily True American*, March 8, 1867.

64. Gaines, "New Jersey and the Fourteenth Amendment," 50–52.

65. *Inauguration of His Excellency, Joel Parker, Governor of New Jersey, January 16th, 1872* (Trenton: "State Gazette," 1872), 16.

66. *Inauguration of Parker*, 17.

67. Abraham Lincoln, "The Second Inaugural Address," March 4, 1865, in *Collected Works of Lincoln*, 8:333. See also Foner, *Fiery Trial*.

68. Abraham Lincoln, "Last Public Address," April 11, 1863, in *Collected Works of Lincoln* 8:403.

69. Charles F. Speierl, "Civil War Veterans and Patriotism in New Jersey Schools," *NJH* 110 (Fall/Winter 1992): 41–55.

70. An excellent study exploring the link between national memory and the re-creation of national unity following the Civil War is David Blight's *Race and Reunion: The Civil War in American Memory* (Cambridge, Mass.: Harvard University Press, 2001).

7 · THE GARDEN STATE BECOMES AN INDUSTRIAL POWER

New Jersey in the Late Nineteenth Century

PAUL ISRAEL

In 1870 a telegraph inventor named Thomas Edison opened his first manufacturing shop in Newark, New Jersey. Edison settled in the state's largest and most industrialized city because of its wealth of skilled machinists, many of whom had come to Newark as part of a large influx of German immigrants to the state in the post–Civil War era. Newark was also close to New York City, where the telegraph companies that financed Edison's inventive work were located. Within a decade Edison would become the most famous resident of the state.[1]

After finding his first success in Newark, Edison left the city in 1876 for Menlo Park, a failed suburban development in Middlesex County. Among the reasons Edison left Newark was the city's overcrowded and polluted environment, which gave it one of the highest mortality rates in the nation. Among those who fell to the many diseases that plagued Newark's citizens was Edison's first Newark partner, William Unger, who died of consumption in 1879, the same year his brother Frederick Unger was carried off by typhoid.[2]

In Menlo Park Edison built the nation's first industrial research-and-development (R&D) laboratory, which helped to transform the way invention took place. Menlo Park provided a model of research for the new electrical and chemical companies that increasingly found a home in the state between the 1870s and World War I during what historians commonly call the "second industrial revolution." The most visible feature of the new electrical system that Edison invented in his laboratory was the incandescent lamp, which he first manufactured in a factory at Menlo Park so that the laboratory could continue to improve the new technology needed to produce it. Within two years, however, he moved the factory into larger quarters in East Newark (now Harrison) so as to have access to the city's larger labor force in order to reduce his costs.

Edison built his first central power station in New York City, and he moved to Manhattan for several years in the early 1880s. But like many others who located in the region because of New York, he tired of city living and moved his family back to suburban New Jersey. Edison found a home in Llewellyn Park, the nation's first planned suburban community, and he built a new laboratory just down the road in present-day West Orange. While building this large new laboratory, Edison described his ambition: "to build up a great Industrial Works in the Orange Valley" that would produce the inventions developed by the laboratory. By World War I, firms in a variety of other industries followed Edison's lead and established R&D laboratories as part of growing industrial complexes. By 1900 these companies could draw on the state's growing population of immigrants from southern and eastern Europe, especially Italy, to lower the labor costs of their large factories. They also took advantage of New Jersey's liberal incorporation laws, which became the primary source of funding for state government.

Most of Edison's inventions served the growing cities of the United States. These included telecommunications (telegraphs and telephones), electric light and power, batteries for electric automobiles, cement for roads and commercial buildings, and copying technology and dictating machines for urban offices. Edison also was a leader in developing new forms of leisure entertainment—sound recording and motion pictures—that became popular among the growing urban populations that worked in large corporate offices and factories. Male middle-managers and female secretaries with higher incomes and greater leisure time than harried small-business owners or fatigued factory workers were among the first users of these new technologies, but even factory workers were beginning to experience a growth in real wages and a drop in working hours, which enabled them to take part in leisure activities.

Edison's exceptional career helped to influence the development of the state, and it also mirrored many of the changes that occurred in New Jersey and affected the lives of its residents. The sections that follow will explore in more detail how New Jersey changed in the thirty years after Edison moved there. The focus will be on three key forces of change: industrialization, urbanization, and immigration. But we will also see how New Jersey remained the Garden State by virtue of its agricultural and suburban communities.

INDUSTRIALIZATION

New Jersey's development following the Civil War was part of a general transformation in the American economy between 1870 and 1914, an era commonly referred to as the second industrial revolution. During these years industry became increasingly allied with science, leading to transformative new technologies in electricity, telecommunications, transportation, and materials and chemicals. Additional improvements occurred in older industries as steam power and mechanized production were applied more widely. The American system of production, with its emphasis on high-volume manufacturing with interchangeable parts, spread from the national armories into the production of new consumer goods, such as sewing machines, typewriters, bicycles, and eventually automobiles. These production techniques were part of a larger reorganization of the workplace as firms built new factories of unprecedented size and efficiency, designed to produce economies of scale that would enable them to take advantage of the growing national and international markets made possible by new communication and transportation systems. Agricultural activity and employment continued to grow during these years, aided in part by new machinery, but this growth was dwarfed by that of the manufacturing sector. Agriculture accounted for more than half of the nation's economic activity and employment in 1869, with manufacturing accounting for about one-third; by 1899, these figures had been reversed and the United States had been transformed into the world's leading industrial power. These changes

were especially notable in New Jersey, which rapidly became a major manufacturing center.

Even before the Civil War, New Jersey was becoming industrialized and
had a rail network that connected its factories to the cities of New York and
Philadelphia. Newark was by far its leading city and also one of the nation's
largest industrial centers, with a diverse manufacturing base that included
leather, shoes, hats, jewelry, beer, zinc, and paint. In the decades after the
war, Newark's industries remained highly diversified. In contrast, the
growth in the state's other cities was primarily spurred by a few major industries, although a variety of other manufacturing enterprises could be found
in them as well. In the north, bordering the Hudson River, Jersey City was
dominated by its rail terminals and docks as well as its sugar-refining and
tobacco-processing plant; Bayonne was the site of major oil refineries and
coal docks; and Elizabeth was dominated by the Singer sewing machine
factory. Paterson, the state's oldest industrial city because of the power provided by its falls for textile factories, was transformed into the center of the
silk industry but also had major locomotive manufacturing works. In the
middle of the state New Brunswick was known for its large rubber factories
and Trenton for its iron and pottery works. Camden, the only industrial city
in the southern part of the state and just across the Delaware River from
Philadelphia, became a center of shipbuilding but also had significant iron
and glass works.[3]

The differences between Newark and other cities in the state can be
seen by comparing it with Jersey City, the state's second-largest city. In 1860
Newark's population (71,941) was nearly three times that of Jersey City
(29,226). Over the next decade, Newark's grew to 105,131 while Jersey City's
exploded to 82,546. By 1880, Jersey City had grown to 120,728, aided in part
by the annexation of nearby towns, and was challenging Newark, which remained confined to its original boundaries even as its population grew to
136,400. While the populations of the two cities became less disparate, their
manufacturing bases remained very different. In 1880 Newark employed
41,510 workers in 1,291 manufacturing establishments; Jersey City employed
only 10,688 workers in 555 factories. Nonetheless, the value of the goods
produced in these two cities was much less unequal: Newark goods were
worth $66,985,766; those produced in Jersey City, $59,581,141. Unlike the
smaller-scale manufacturing enterprises of Newark, Jersey City's employers included sugar refineries producing five thousand barrels a day, tobacco

factories with three thousand workers who produced more than twenty million pounds of tobacco in a year, a factory manufacturing twenty-four million pencils annually, and another making six million cakes of stove polish. In addition, a million and half cattle were slaughtered in the city's abattoir, mainly for shops and restaurants in New York.[4]

The growth of New Jersey's industries in the years immediately following the Civil War was spurred by the ability to reach larger markets as the nation's telegraph and railroad systems expanded into national networks and trans-Atlantic shipping was speeded up by steamships and telegraph cables laid across the ocean floor. In New Jersey, the prewar rail system was dominated by the Camden and Amboy Railroad, which had lines running from Jersey City to Philadelphia and a charter that gave it a monopoly on rail traffic between these cities. The state had established this monopoly in exchange for stock ownership, with a minimum dividend of $30,000 per year, which provided most of the funding for the state's operations for thirty years. However, when New Jersey had to take on new debt to pay its share of the Union war effort, it had to reinstitute a property tax to make up the necessary funds. After the war, payment on that debt and other costs led to a continuation of the property tax and a resulting decline in the political influence of the railroad. The Camden and Amboy monopoly was finally up-ended when the out-of-state Pennsylvania Railroad leased the company's lines in 1871. The New Jersey legislature then passed a general railroad law in 1873 that opened up the state to more rapid rail development. The new openness also influenced the passage of a constitutional amendment in 1875 that outlawed special corporate charters; this was the first law of its kind in the nation.[5]

The extensive rail system that emerged helped to connect New Jersey industry and ports to markets throughout the country. Some sense of the growth of the rail system and its connections to both American and European markets can be seen in an 1882 description of Jersey City, which had become the terminus

of an immense railway system, which includes the Pennsylvania with all its Southern and Western Connections; the New York, Lake Erie and Western . . . now the short-line route to Niagara Falls and the Northwest; the Central Railroad of New Jersey, via its branches, which traverses the richest portions of the State and brings Jersey City within a few hours of the productive coal

and iron regions of New Jersey and Pennsylvania. Another important railroad
. . . is the Delaware, Lackawanna and Western, which also enters the coal and
iron section of the Keystone State. Beyond these trunk lines there are several
local lines running to Newark, Paterson, and other points near. Those railroads having their termini in New York and Brooklyn are nearly as convenient
to Jersey City and her business interests as those immediately within the city
limits. Many of the so-called New York lines of foreign steamships have their
docks in Jersey City and find that their business is greatly facilitated by the
conveniences here enjoyed over those secured in New York city. The immense
grain traffic from the West to Europe is shipped direct to its destination from
the steamship piers in Jersey City, and although accredited to the port of New
York, really should appear in the aggregate of this city's business.[6]

Even though Jersey City benefited from its position as the terminus of the
state's major rail lines, the city lost control over its waterfront to the railroads, whose significant property holdings could not be taxed by the city.[7]

One of the important examples of how the ability to reach national
and international markets affected industrial manufacturing is the establishment of the Singer Sewing Machine Company's factory in Elizabeth.
The Singer Company had grown rapidly after its incorporation in 1863 as
it established agencies in most large American and in a few foreign cities,
including Toronto, Montreal, London, and Hamburg. To meet an ever-
growing demand, the company moved its factory from New York to Elizabeth in 1873; the company also had another large factory in Glasgow and
later opened a small factory in Canada. In these factories Singer sought
to transform its production process by introducing the American system
of interchangeable parts based on specialized machinery and fine gauges.
True interchangeability was difficult to achieve, and for many years cheap
workmen were employed as fitters to assemble the machines. Yet the Singer
Company's production doubled in the first six years of the opening of the
Elizabeth plant. More than half of these sewing machines were produced
at the New Jersey factory. Production continued to increase over the next
six years, but it might have been even greater if the company had not also
introduced a new model in 1880. The new family machine had an oscillating
shuttle and was designed to sew faster, feed cloth more smoothly, produce
better stitching, use larger bobbins with more thread, and operate more
quietly. Publicity for the new machine created enormous demand, but con-

The Singer sewing machine factory in Elizabeth, New Jersey. (From *Genius Rewarded; or, The Story of the Sewing Machine* [New York: John J. Caulon, 1880], 13. Special Collections and University Archives, Rutgers University Libraries.)

verting the production process proved difficult, and it took several years before the factory regularized production and began to meet the demand. This new machine forced even greater attention on improved accuracy and efficiency of production methods and led to the creation of a blue book to specify all the operations, including those related to inspection and precision. By the mid-1880s, the plant, which was originally designed to produce 5,000 machines a week, was turning out 6,000–7,000 with a goal of 8,000 per week. By this time the factory at Elizabeth employed 3,000 workers. The scale of the Singer factory at Elizabeth represented the future of manufacturing, as did its use of specialized machinery and standardized interchangeable parts. Besides being one of the first truly multinational firms, Singer was also one of the first firms in New Jersey to be run by corporate managers who were not primary owners. At the time, most companies were still family-run firms.[8]

The precision manufacturing processes being introduced by Singer and other companies, as well as the rapid growth of rail lines, helped to spur expansion of the state's iron and steel industry. The new mills introduced innovations such as the Bessemer open-hearth and the Siemens-Martin process, which also placed a premium on high-quality ore from the mines of northern New Jersey and led to new or improved products, such as the fine tailor's shears and high-quality plows made in Newark. Another important New Jersey product was the wire rope developed by John A. Roebling, who had opened a factory in Trenton. Besides its application to suspension bridges, this rope was used widely in elevators, which helped make possible the development of the skyscraper. In 1882 a record 932,762 tons of iron was mined in New Jersey, but a decade later production had dropped to about 350,000 tons as mines became depleted of high-quality ores, forcing the state's iron and steel mills to import most of their ore.[9]

During the 1890s Thomas Edison attempted to revive the New Jersey iron mining industry by developing a system for processing low-grade iron ore. Edison used giant crushing rolls to break up the rock into fine sand, separated the iron ore from the sand with large electromagnets, and then combined these particles of iron into briquettes for use in steel mills. Edison sought to fully automate the plant so that he could process 20,000 tons of ore a day using only ten men in two shifts. However, by the end of the decade, after spending more than two million dollars, Edison still needed a staff of nearly 250 men working two ten-hour shifts because the complexity of the automatic machinery and the difficult conditions under which it operated caused frequent breakdowns. The cost of labor and repairs might have been acceptable if the price of ore had not dropped dramatically after the discovery of a large new iron range around Lake Superior. Facing competition from cheaper and higher-quality ore, Edison had to abandon his operation, and the New Jersey iron mining industry never recovered. However, the innovations in rock-crushing technology that Edison developed were later licensed to other mining companies, including New Jersey Zinc. Edison also used this technology in a plant he erected near Stewartsville to produce Portland cement; there he also developed a revolutionary long kiln that became an industry standard.[10]

Process innovations took place in other industries as well, especially the chemical industry. One of the most important took place in the marshlands of Bayonne in the last quarter of the century. In 1875 the first oil refineries were established there, and by 1880 Standard Oil had built a pipeline from the oil fields of Pennsylvania. The use of pipelines, which were later extended to Texas, significantly reduced the cost of transporting crude oil, which previously had been shipped in barrels by rail. At Bayonne the refineries could place refined oil directly into steam tankers, further reducing transportation costs. In the late nineteenth and early twentieth century these refineries primarily produced kerosene for lighting until the advent of the internal combustion automobile created a demand for gasoline. By the turn of the century, the extensive refineries of Bayonne employed 3,000 men and were refining 40,000 barrels of oil per day. Standard Oil of New Jersey coordinated 84 percent of the crude oil refined in the United States.[11]

Standard Oil of New Jersey was itself the product of another New Jersey innovation. In its efforts to find a new source of revenue to replace income from the Camden and Amboy Railroad, the New Jersey legislature adopted a series of liberal incorporation laws between 1888 and 1896 that allowed in-state corporations to merge horizontally and to hold stock in corporations outside of the state. New Jersey also protected the interests of its state-chartered corporations that operated in other states by imposing on companies chartered in other states but doing business in New Jersey the same obligations and taxes as those states imposed on New Jersey corporations. By establishing such liberal incorporation laws, New Jersey ran counter to the tide of anti-monopoly sentiment in the country. It also created a major revenue generator. By 1890 corporate charters produced enough revenue to put the state's budget in the black, and by 1902 New Jersey had retired its bonded debt and ended the state property tax. In the process, New Jersey played a major role in the merger wave that took place in American industry between 1896 and 1904, as half of the country's trusts found a home in the state, including almost all of the largest trusts. New Jersey's liberal corporation laws enabled the creation of new large firms that took advantage of economies of scale by integrating each stage of production, from processing of raw materials through production to distribution and sales. Among these was Standard Oil, reincorporated in New Jersey as a holding company in 1899 following an unfavorable decision in an antitrust suit in Ohio, where it was originally chartered as an operating company. By incorporating in New Jersey, Standard Oil was able to maintain the dominant position in the oil industry that it had gained by taking over smaller competitors, which also gave it sufficient economic power to demand and receive rebates from shippers and to control the price of refined oil. In industry after industry, mergers produced industrial giants that took advantage of New Jersey corporate charters. Other holding companies, such as Edison's Motion Picture Patents Company, used New Jersey incorporation law to bring together the holders of key patents as a means of controlling competition in their industries.[12]

A NEW MODEL FOR INNOVATION

Innovations in business organization and manufacturing were essential to the emerging industrial power of New Jersey and the United States. Just as important were changes in how technological innovation itself took place. The development of the improved machines, such as the New Family model introduced by Singer in 1880, was largely mechanical in nature and was created by skilled operatives, machinists, and manufacturers who drew on practical experience to design, build, and refine new technology and who worked in manufacturing and experimental machine shops. This process can be seen in the early career of Thomas Edison, who subsequently became one of the key figures who transformed the process of invention.[13]

Edison's first significant invention was the improved stock ticker he developed under his contract with the Gold & Stock Telegraph Company. Known as the Universal stock printer, this instrument required less battery power and incorporated a device that kept all the machines on a line in unison so that they printed out the same stock quotations. Another improvement was its adjustable shaft mountings, which enabled its parts to be readily fitted and thus made interchangeable. In developing his early telegraph inventions, Edison was involved in manipulating electromechanical apparatus, and mechanical skill was at least as important as an understanding of electricity. Recognizing the value of having a machine shop in which he had skilled machinists who could assist him with his inventions, Edison opened a telegraph manufacturing shop rather than just an experimental shop in order to provide not only additional income for himself but also steady work for these machinists. Between 1871 and 1874, for example, Edison manufactured nearly 3,600 of the printers, which became a fixture on the New York and London stock exchanges. At this time Edison was probably the largest electrical manufacturer in New Jersey.

As Edison worked on new telegraph systems designed to increase line capacity and transmission speeds for long-distance telegraphy, he encountered more complex electrical problems than presented by the stock ticker. A trip to England in 1873 and experience with the performance of underground lines and undersea cables gave him a growing appreciation of how much he did not know about the electrical and chemical phenomena he observed in tests of his high-speed automatic telegraph system. As a result, Edison began to develop a new experimental approach and to establish a fully equipped electrical and chemical laboratory to carry out his experiments. Within a few months of his return, Edison established his first laboratory in a corner of his Newark telegraph works, with "every conceivable variety of Electrical Apparatus, and any quantity of Chemicals for experimentation."[14]

In his new laboratory, Edison began to focus his experiments on electrical and electrochemical phenomena rather than on the electromechanical designs that had made his early reputation. At times Edison's research verged into the scientific as he explored little-understood phenomena and even proposed more general theories to account for his results. Indeed, for nearly a year following his return from England, Edison's experiments produced few patents. Nonetheless, he continued his experiments in order to produce a more general understanding of the electrical or chemical action of the devices with which he worked, with the goal of using the knowledge he gained to develop new inventions. Among these was his quadruplex telegraph, which could transmit four messages on one wire and was adopted by Western Union.

By the spring of 1875, Edison's income from his telegraph inventions enabled him to expand his laboratory and make it entirely independent of the manufacturing shop. Edison took half the building for his laboratory, as well as some of the machine tools and two of his key machinists. In addition, he had two experimental assistants, both of whom were self-taught in electricity and experimentation. Charles Batchelor, who became Edison's long-time chief assistant, had been foreman of the telegraph factory and had originally come from England to install machinery in the Clark Thread Mills in Newark, which became one of the largest factories in the city, employing more than a thousand workers.

By making his experimental machine shop entirely independent of manufacturing and by incorporating it into the research laboratory, Edison completed the process he had started nearly two years earlier following his return from England. With the skilled workmen and tools from his Newark telegraph shops adapted solely to inventive work, Edison could rapidly construct, test, and alter experimental devices, significantly increasing the rate at which he could develop new inventions. At the end of 1875, Edison decided to further expand his laboratory by building his now famous facility in Menlo Park, New Jersey, which was designed to be an "invention factory" where Edison planned to produce "a minor invention every ten days and a big thing every six months or so."[15] Menlo Park did not mark a sharp

Thomas Edison's Menlo Park laboratory. Detail from *Frank Leslie's Illustrated Newspaper*, January 10, 1880. The full illustration, titled "New Jersey.—The Wizard of Electricity—Thomas A. Edison's System of Electrical Illumination," shows a cluster of snow-covered buildings in Menlo Park, the inside of Edison's laboratory, and some of his equipment.

break with the shop tradition of invention. Instead, it represented Edison's continuing efforts to amplify rather than replace that tradition.

Nonetheless, Menlo Park looked forward to a new model of research as Edison continued to merge the shop tradition with increasingly sophisticated chemical and electrical laboratory research. Edison was not alone in these efforts. Electrical and, to a more limited extent, chemical laboratories could be found in a number of American telegraph shops. What set Edison's effort apart from those of his contemporaries was its scale and scope. The laboratory he built in Menlo Park was probably the best-equipped private laboratory in the United States and certainly the largest devoted to invention.

It was during the work on electric lighting that Menlo Park became a true research and development facility. Funding for Edison's work on electric lighting came primarily from Western Union investors, including several individuals connected with the banking firm of Drexel Morgan & Company. After forming the Edison Electric Light Company in October 1878, they provided nearly $130,000 for research and development of his electric lighting system over the next two and a half years. This support enabled Edison to increase his staff to more than fifty at the height of work and to expand his laboratory resources greatly. He built a separate and larger brick machine shop, which enabled him to spread out his electrical laboratory on the ground floor as well as add a photometric laboratory. In addition, he built a two-story brick office and library building and stocked it with an impressive collection of technical and scientific books and journals. He also had augmented teams of researchers who could work simultaneously on all elements of the electric lighting system. These new resources enabled him to leapfrog past his competitors and to develop not just a laboratory prototype of a lamp or generator but a complete commercial system of electric lighting.

Edison's great success at the Menlo Park laboratory made it a model for other inventors. Alexander Graham Bell was influenced by what he called Edison's "celebrated laboratory at Menlo Park" when he set up his own Volta Laboratory in Washington, D.C., in 1881.[16] The Bell Telephone Company likewise drew on the example of Edison's laboratory when it established an experimental shop in 1883. Another electrical inventor influenced by Menlo Park was Edward Weston, who built what he considered to be "the most complete private lab in the country" in 1886.[17] It contained a well-equipped machine shop, chemical laboratory, and physical laboratory, as well as an office and library with 10,000 volumes. Weston's laboratory, with its staff of five men, resembled Edison's early Menlo Park laboratory and probably provided Edison with an incentive to build an even larger laboratory in West Orange in 1887, which he planned to be the "best equipped & largest Laboratory extant, and the facilities incomparably superior to any other for rapid & cheap development of an invention, & working it up into commercial shape with models patterns special machinery."[18] As he anticipated, by 1903 Edison had built up "a great Industrial Works in the Orange Valley" as factory building sprung up around the laboratory to manufacture phonographs, sound recordings, motion picture equipment, electrical appliances, batteries, and other inventions.

The most lasting influence of Edison's laboratories in Menlo Park and West Orange was on American industry. The creation of these laboratories had been made possible by the growing interest of large-scale, technology-based companies like Western Union in acquiring greater control over the research process by supporting the work of key inventors. The investors who formed the Edison Electric Light Company understood that Edison's approach to invention gave him an advantage over his competitors, and they continued to invest large sums in the research over a period of more than two years. Edison's success in developing an improved telephone transmitter, the phonograph, and an entire system of electric lighting in the five years he was at Menlo Park, along with his further innovations at West Orange, helped lay the groundwork for modern industrial research and development by showing how invention itself could be an industrial process and how corporate support for it could produce large benefits. Edison's facilities served as models for laboratories established by other companies during the first decades of the twentieth century, especially in the electrical and chemical industries. By 1920, New Jersey was second only to New York as the home of nearly thirty industrial research laboratories.[19]

While Thomas Edison was demonstrating how scientific research in corporate laboratories could create new and improved products, George Hammell Cook, another important figure in New Jersey history, helped to demonstrate the value of scientific agriculture. Cook was the professor of chemistry and natural philosophy at Rutgers College when he became head of the new Rutgers Scientific School in 1864 after the Morrill Act of 1862 created land grant colleges in each state to teach agriculture and the mechanic arts. Cook quickly established scientific and engineering courses as well as a college farm for teaching agriculture. Cook expected the farm to serve as a site for experimentation to advance the state of agricultural science; as a chemist, he was especially interested in fertilizer experiments and analysis. Cook was also the state geologist, and his reports included extensive information on what was known as applied or economic geology that could be of use to various industries, including agriculture. Following a European trip in 1870, Cook also began to lobby for the creation of a state agricultural experiment station. In 1880 New Jersey became the third state in the nation to fund a station, and Cook played a major role in the national effort to pass the Hatch Act of 1887, which provided federal funding for stations at land grant colleges in each state. These units later give rise to state cooperative extension services under the Smith-Lever Act of 1914.

New Jersey's first station, in New Brunswick, initially had a small staff that included Cook and another chemist, an assistant, and a clerk. By 1888, with funding from the Hatch Act, a second station was established and located at the Rutgers agricultural college. Work was divided between the stations: the original one focused on chemical research, and the college station undertook research on biology, botany, horticulture, entomology, and chemical geology, especially soil science. Under Cook, the New Jersey Agricultural Station became well known for its extensive studies of fertilizers in cooperation with farmers around the state, as well as its analyses of all commercial fertilizers sold in New Jersey. The station also conducted trials of new field crops, studied the best methods for growing fruits and vegetables, and sought to develop better methods for dealing with pests and plant diseases. Dairy science was another area of intensive research at the college, especially in regard to the best breeds of cows and the relationship between feeds and fodder and the amount and quality of milk they produced. At the request of the state legislature, the station also conducted an extensive study of the growing of sorghum cane and its use in sugar refining in Cape May County. The station's chief chemist, Arthur Neale, conducted experiments to increase the yield of sugar from sorghum plants and also worked with Harvey Wiley of the U.S. Department of Agriculture to perfect a sorghum milling process. Although these efforts produced significant innovations, sorghum production was largely abandoned in New Jersey after 1889, when adverse weather led to a reduced crop and Neale decided to leave the station following Cook's death the same year.

Under Cook's successors both the New Jersey agricultural experiment station and the college agricultural station continued to produce important research to advance agricultural science and to increase farm productivity as the average size of farms in the state dropped from 108 acres in 1860 to only 82 by 1900, even as the number increased from 30,200 in 1870 to 34,500 by 1900. During this period, New Jersey farmers turned to the production of fresh produce and milk for urban markets on small truck and dairy farms in the face of competition from large farms in the Midwest and West that could grow grain and cattle in vast quantities.[20]

URBANIZATION AND IMMIGRATION

During the last three decades of the nineteenth century the American population became increasingly urbanized. Between 1870 and 1900 the percentage of the population living in cities increased from a little over one-quarter to nearly 40 percent. In New Jersey, which was already one of the most urbanized places in the United States before the Civil War, urban growth was even more dramatic. By 1860, when the urban population of the entire country was only about 20 percent, nearly 33 percent of New Jerseyans lived in cities or towns of at least 2,500 people, nearly double the number of a decade earlier. Only a decade later the state's urban population was 44 percent, and by 1890 over 50 percent of New Jerseyans lived in cities of 10,000. By then, nearly a third of the population could be found in its three largest cities—Newark, Jersey City, and Paterson. The percentage in these three cities held steady in 1900, by which time New Jersey had become the third most densely populated state in the nation and ranked fifth in the percentage of urban residents, with 70 percent of its people living in urban areas of at least 2,500.[21]

The growing urban population of New Jersey came primarily from two sources: migration from rural America and immigration from other countries. In general, these newcomers were younger than the rest of the population, with most between the ages of fourteen and forty. As a result, the median age in New Jersey's urban areas was seven years younger than in the state's rural regions. The cities also contained many more single men and women and most of the state's immigrant population. By 1870, over half of the state's population was foreign born or had a parent who was, and this demographic continued into the 1930s. Nearly two-thirds of this immigrant population lived in six counties. Over half could be found in Essex, Hudson, and Passaic; most of the rest resided in Bergen, Middlesex, and Union. Elsewhere in the state, only Atlantic, Camden, and Monmouth Counties had any sizeable number of foreign minorities. The demographic disparities between New Jersey's rural and urban populations produced major cultural differences within the state. Rural New Jersey was dominated by native-born Americans, most of whom were Protestant, while the cities came to have a lively mix of religious and ethnic cultures.

The immigrant populations that came to New Jersey changed over time. Following the Civil War, most came from Ireland and Germany, with a significant number from England. The Irish were largely unskilled workers who found employment as laborers or domestic servants; the Germans and English flourished as skilled workers and entrepreneurs in the state's growing industries. Some of the skilled German and English machinists who came to New Jersey found employment in Thomas Edison's Newark shops and at his laboratories in Menlo Park and West Orange, where they played a crucial role in developing his inventions. By the 1890s, Italians and Eastern Europeans were increasingly able to take advantage of the low steerage fares offered by the trans-Atlantic steamship companies to seek opportunity in the booming American economy. Most of these new immigrants came from rural areas, but only a few were able to continue to farm. Notable exceptions were the Italian farmers who settled in a large colony near Vineland in Cumberland County and the Jewish settlers who founded agricultural colonies in Cumberland and Salem. Most immigrants settled in the cities and found employment as laborers and semi-skilled machinery operators in New Jersey's rapidly expanding factories. By 1900, two-thirds of those employed in the state's manufacturing and mechanical industries were first- or second-generation immigrants.[22]

A much smaller though significant group of people who came to New Jersey to find new opportunity were African Americans from the South. Emancipation started a movement north that would culminate in the Great Migration from 1910 to 1930, when some 2 million blacks left the southern United States to settle in other regions of the country. In the first wave of black migration to New Jersey between 1870 and 1900 the number of African Americans in the state increased from 30,658 to 68,444, and during the last decade their population increased at a much faster rate than the white population. Like European immigrants, the blacks who came to New Jersey settled in the cities. There they primarily worked as unskilled laborers, deliverymen, teamsters, janitors, maids, and laundresses, although a few found employment in more skilled occupations.

There was one notable exception to the primarily industrial cities where most of New Jersey's African Americans lived. Between 1870 and 1885, the black population of the resort town of Atlantic City increased dramatically, from 15 to 1,220, which was 15 percent of the population. The black population would more than double to 3,893 over the next decade, rising to 21 percent of the city's population, and by 1905 Atlantic City's 8,846 African Americans represented 23.5 percent of the population. As the state's leading resort town, Atlantic City provided a significant number of jobs in the hotel-recreation service industry, and by the turn of the century blacks made up 95 percent of this labor force, working as cooks, waiters, bellmen, porters, and chambermaids.[23]

Atlantic City became the premier Shore resort in New Jersey as railroads made it readily accessible to the urban masses. Unlike the more elite and genteel resort of Long Branch or the sedate Methodist camp meeting of Ocean Grove, Atlantic City was always envisioned as a place where the "work-worn artisan shut up in the close and debilitating shops of the city, whose limited means prevent a long absence from his calling, will find . . . the rest and recreation he cannot now obtain."[24] The artisan of the 1850s was replaced by semi-skilled factory workers, and, increasingly, the state's cities attracted a new population of white-collar workers. These included office clerks, secretaries, and accountants who coordinated the production and shipment of factory goods and maintained sales and accounting records, salesmen and shop girls who sold the mass-produced products of New Jersey's factories, and the teachers who taught in the state's public and private schools. The growing factories also increasingly relied on companies that provided financing and insurance, and employees in these industries were almost entirely white-collar. Especially notable was the Prudential Insurance Company, which was founded at Newark in 1875 and grew rapidly by offering the first life insurance policies to industrial workers. By 1900, Prudential had a national workforce of more than 10,000 and was issuing more than one million of these policies per year. Throughout the economy, the numbers of white-collar workers increased at a faster rate during the 1890s than their blue-collar counterparts who manned the factory floors.[25] Unlike the working class, they had sufficient income and leisure time to vacation at the Jersey Shore. But the railroads also made the Shore accessible to working-class families who would come for the day to experience not only the healthful climate of the seaside but also the excitement of the new amusement parks found on the boardwalks.

During the last decade of the century mechanical rides and other entertainments gave rise to a new amusement industry along the Shore. On the boardwalks at Atlantic City and its smaller counterpart, Asbury Park, new mechanical entertainments began to join older pleasures, such as bandstands, dancehalls, and vaudeville theaters. The first of these new amusements was built by Isaac Forrester about 1872 on the Atlantic City beach in front of the Seaview Excursion House, which already ran a carousel. Forrester's "Epicycloidal Wheel" was one of the first devices to provide an experience similar to the later Ferris wheel. By 1889, the Excursion House had added a toboggan ride that was an ancestor of the modern roller coaster. Other mechanical rides and amusements soon followed. Asbury Park had been founded in 1871 by Methodist layman James Bradley as a health resort with middle-class Christian sensibilities akin to its neighbor, Ocean Grove, which served as a combination seaside resort and Methodist camp meeting community. By the late 1880s, Asbury Park was being transformed into a site of amusement that attracted working-class as well as middle-class vacationers. In 1887 a carousel could be found on the boardwalk, and within five years a Ferris wheel was built. As in Atlantic City, these innovations were followed by a roller toboggan and then other mechanical rides. Early in the new century other amusement parks appeared, promoted by trolley lines outside of the larger cities and by railroad lines in places like Wildwood on the shore, Bertrand Island on Lake Hopatcong, and on the Palisades above the Hudson River.[26]

The urban masses could only occasionally escape the crowded cities by taking a day excursion to these amusement parks or to more healthful environs like the Shore or the northern New Jersey lakes. For the upper and some of the middle classes, the rail lines enabled a daily escape to new suburban homes. In the decades after the Civil War the expansion of the state's rail lines made possible the rise of suburban communities as rural towns and newly built communities attracted those who could afford to live outside the city. A few towns, such as Morristown, Llewellyn Park, Plainfield, and Short Hills, became enclaves for the wealthy, but many like Montclair, Englewood, and Ridgewood attracted middle-class commuters. A similar pattern took place on the outskirts of Camden as new suburbs such as Merchantville, Collingswood, and Haddon Heights became home to Philadelphia commuters. The proliferation of suburban enclaves was further encouraged by the passage of a state law in 1878 that enabled property owners who controlled at least 10 percent of the taxable real estate in a township to petition the county freeholders to hold a special election and create a new borough.[27]

Suburban growth was also spurred by the environmental crisis in the cities, where rapid industrial growth fouled water supplies, dirtied the air, and strained the housing market, leading to crowded and unhealthy living conditions for workers and their families. Although households added to this pollution, industrial production was the largest contributor. Maintaining clean water supplies and removing waste through proper sewage presented especially significant problems for city leaders. These projects, as well as the building of better roads and the installation of street lights, involved a mix of public and private enterprise that helped give rise to political machines and political corruption even as it improved the urban environment. The distribution of public works was also affected by disparities of class and

wealth as certain improvements, especially for roads and sewers, often depended on special assessments that wealthier property owners, who could
also pay for maintenance, were more likely to approve.

We can see these forces at work in Jersey City, which led the way in infrastructure development in New Jersey. Even before the Civil War, city leaders had established a water commission that constructed a comprehensive
water and sewage system. The Jersey City waterworks also supplied many
other towns in Hudson County, and after the war city officials sought to
annex them to create a large metropolis that would rival New York. Their
ambition was only partially realized: residents in many of the surrounding
suburban communities rejected consolidation in 1869. Only the cities of
Hudson, Bergen, and Union, along with Union Township, voted in favor,
although Greenville later agreed to annexation in 1873 because excessive
taxation for street paving made consolidation more palatable. The annexation vote was driven by concerns over debt, taxation, corruption, and suburbanization. Bergen and Hudson were burdened by debt and saw consolidation as a way to relieve residents of heavy taxes. Citizens of Hoboken, by
contrast, viewed their community as a commuter suburb of New York with
an identity separate from Jersey City. They believed annexation would bring
political corruption and higher taxes. They also had a viable alternative, because the city purchased its water from Jersey City, which threatened to but
did not stop supplying it after the vote. Later, as Hoboken grew into a city,
it was able to remain separate by contracting with the Hackensack Water
Company, which had a system that was initially designed by a professor at
the Stevens Institute of Technology in Hoboken and subsequently enlarged
and improved by a firm of Jersey City engineers. Bayonne, too, was dominated by New York suburbanites, who took the lead in promoting road and
sewer improvements. In addition, Bayonne had a good supply of water
from wells, which sufficed until 1881, when the city finally found it necessary to buy water from Jersey City.

The fear of political corruption growing out of consolidation was a real
one. A new city charter passed by the state legislature in 1871 was designed
to reduce the power of the Irish Catholics who dominated Democratic
politics in Jersey City. It replaced elected officials with commissioners appointed by the legislature. As a consequence, William H. Bumsted, who
was well connected to city's Republicans, not only won election to the Jersey City council but also became president of the Board of Public Works,

one of the three state-appointed commissions created under the new charter. A contractor for street and sewer work in Bergen before consolidation, which he strongly advocated, Bumsted seized the opportunity to expand public projects in Jersey City. These projects, including a new water reservoir, resulted in rising tax rates and city debt, an investigation into Bumsted's activities by Democrats on the county grand jury, and the indictment of Bumsted and other public officials. He was subsequently convicted of colluding with a real estate speculator in connection with the land for the new reservoir. Overspending on infrastructure threatened to bankrupt Jersey City, and, especially following the Panic of 1873, the city greatly reduced its spending on infrastructure and sought to professionalize its development by creating a bureau of civil engineering and surveying. Infrastructure spending and corruption did bankrupt Elizabeth and Rahway by the early 1880s. In response, Leon Abbett of Jersey City, the state's first governor from a major urban area, signed legislation to tax the railroads in order to provide more revenue for cities and to improve the system of municipal bonding for the construction of urban water systems. Nonetheless, it took Jersey City until 1895 to join Newark in seeking new water supplies from the Pequannock watershed to replace the polluted waters of the Passaic that brought death and disease to the city's citizens.[28]

In contrast to Jersey City, Newark adopted a program of public improvement only slowly. Although Newark grew rapidly before the Civil War, it was dominated by an elite that emerged from the city's manufacturing shops and subscribed to a "mechanics' ideology" that preferred low taxes, little public debt, and minimal local government. A public waterworks project was not completed until 1870, just when the Passaic River that supplied it was becoming badly polluted from the factories that used it to dispose of waste. As the river became polluted, it still supported a flourishing fishing industry and was a site for recreation. But even though polluted water became one of the principal reasons for Newark's high mortality rate during the 1870s, the city did not turn to the Pequannock watershed for an alternative source of water until the 1880s, after Joseph E. Haynes, a strong promoter of public works, became mayor. During his ten years in office Haynes developed a more comprehensive sewer plan that relied on funding from bonds rather than special assessments, and he contracted with Edward Weston's Newark Electric Light and Power Company for the first electric street lights in the city. Haynes also created a Board of Works, appointed by the mayor, to oversee sewer and street construction, though there were charges that it was also a vehicle for graft. But it was in connection with his most important public works project—the acquisition of water from the Pequannock watershed—that Haynes himself was accused of corruption. Because of the city's long delay in obtaining water from this source, speculators had bought up most of the land and had formed the East Jersey Water Company, which became the contractor that supplied water to Newark. Although the charges were never proved and Haynes won a narrow reelection bid in 1891, he did not run again in 1893. The next year the Board of Works was made elective. Haynes's successor, Julius Lebkuecher, sought to streamline the city's public works operations to reduce costs. In order to fund necessary new infrastructure, especially sewers, he also sought new funds by plotting to annex surrounding communities into a Greater Newark. This effort was the first of several unsuccessful plans over the next fifteen years to expand the city. Even without annexation, Newark greatly enlarged its infrastructure during the 1890s, building a more extensive sewer system to complement its safer water supply, increasing the number of paved roads, and creating a modern electric trolley system that helped to transform Newark's downtown into a vibrant place for suburbanites to visit for shopping and entertainment by the turn of the century.[29]

Improvements in urban infrastructure helped to reduce mortality rates. In Newark, for example, deaths from typhoid fever and diarrheal diseases in young children dropped dramatically after polluted Passaic River water was replaced by clean water from the Pequannock watershed. But further problems arising from crowded housing conditions and industrial workplaces persisted in Newark and other New Jersey cities, particularly for working-class and poor families. Adequate housing was a serious problem and led to the creation of the Tenement House Commission in 1903. Prior to this commission, Newark had many large tenement houses and frame dwellings with windowless rooms or rooms that were inadequately lighted and ventilated, contributing to high rates of tuberculosis. The same was true of many one- and two-family houses in working-class neighborhoods. Tenements were a problem in all of the state's industrial cities, but only in Jersey City did they occur on a scale like that found in New York City; in fact, only Boston, Hartford, and Cincinnati had similarly large tenement problems.[30]

Labor conditions were another pressing problem for New Jersey workers. Like most other states, New Jersey offered few protections for workers, and state laws and the courts generally favored owners over labor. Labor strife was particularly frequent during the late nineteenth century throughout the United States. In New Jersey, Paterson industries alone experienced 137 strikes between 1881 and 1900. The most frequent reason for strikes was low pay. But strikes were expensive for workers, who lost income that might not be readily recovered even if the strike was successful in gaining higher pay. Workers also faced significant health problems caused by industrial processes and injuries from machinery.[31]

New Jersey factories also made extensive use of cheap child labor, one of the reasons that Edison moved his lamp factory from Menlo Park to Harrison in 1882. At the time, about 13,000 children, some as young as nine, were employed in New Jersey's factories. The state did seek to deal with the problem by creating the position of inspector of child labor, setting the minimum age at which children could be employed to twelve for boys and fourteen for girls, and requiring that children had attended school during the year prior to their employment. The state also restricted the hours of those under fourteen to no more than ten hours a day, but many older children worked longer hours, leading the state's inspector of factories to observe that "there are thousands of children in the State who know no change but from the workshop to the bed and from the bed to the workshop."[32]

By the end of the nineteenth century, New Jersey was an industrial powerhouse, but one that faced enormous problems created by its rapid industrialization and urbanization as well as by an influx of new immigrants. The state and private organizations, spurred by reformers committed to social justice and politicians like Governor Leon Abbett, drew on a growing body of professional experts to deal with these problems by creating boards and commissions focused on such problems as labor, health, and housing. But political corruption often thwarted reform as municipal governments were beset by graft and state government was dominated by lobbyists working for railroads and trusts. As the new century arrived so, too, did a vigorous progressive reform movement that stirred American society, including the citizens of New Jersey, as it sought to transform political and social institutions in order to spread the benefits of economic growth fueled by new technology and industrialization.

NOTES

1. On Edison, see Paul Israel, *Edison: A Life of Invention* (New York: John Wiley and Sons, 1998).

2. Stuart Galishoff, *Newark: The Nation's Unhealthiest City, 1832–1895* (New Brunswick: Rutgers University Press, 1988); U.S. Federal Census Mortality Schedules, 1850–1885, 64 (http://ancestry.com).

3. Richard Edwards, ed., *Industries of New Jersey*, 6 vols. (New York: Historical Publishing Co., 1882); *Industries of New Jersey and Quarter-Century's Progress of New Jersey's Leading Manufacturing Centers* (New York: International Publishing Co., 1887).

4. Edwards, ed., *Industries of New Jersey*, 5:620–623, 6:802.

5. John T. Cunningham, *New Jersey, America's Main Road*, rev. ed. (Garden City, N.Y.: Doubleday, 1976), 194–195; Christopher Grandy, *New Jersey and the Fiscal Origins of American Corporation Law* (New York: Garland Publishing, 1993), 22–26.

6. Edwards, ed., *Industries of New Jersey*, 6:804.

7. Hermann K. Platt, "Railroad Rights and Tideland Policy: A Tug of War in Nineteenth-Century New Jersey," *NJH* 108 (1990): 35–57; Hermann K. Platt, "Jersey City and the United Railroad Companies, 1868: A Case of Municipal Weakness," *NJH* 91 (1973): 249–265; Eugene M. Tobin, "In Pursuit of Equal Taxation: Jersey City's Struggle Against Corporate Arrogance and Tax-Dodging by the Railroad Trust," *American Journal of Economics and Sociology* 34 (1975): 213–224.

8. David Hounshell, *From the American System to Mass Production, 1800–1932: The Development of Manufacturing Technology in the United States* (Baltimore: Johns Hopkins University Press, 1984), chap. 2; *Genius Rewarded; or, The Story of the Sewing Machine* (New York: John J. Caulon, Printer, 1880); *The City of Elizabeth, New Jersey, Illustrated: Showing Its Leading Characteristic* (Elizabeth: Elizabeth Daily Journal, 1889), 114–116.

9. Irving S. Kull, *New Jersey: A History*, 4 vols. (New York: American Historical Society, 1930), 3:900–901; John T. Cunningham, *Made in New Jersey: The Industrial Story of a State* (New Brunswick: Rutgers University Press, 1954), 12–13.

10. Israel, *Edison*, 348–362, 403–410

11. Cunningham, *Made in New Jersey*, 162–163; Kathleen M. Middleton, *Bayonne* (Dover, N.H.: Arcadia, 1995), 31; Testimony of Harry H. Willock, in *United States of America, Petitioner, v. Standard Oil Company of New Jersey et al., Defendants* (Washington, D.C.: GPO, 1908), 5:2562.

12. Charles M. Yablon, "The Historical Race: Competition for Corporate Charters and the Rise and Decline of New Jersey: 1880–1910," *Journal of Corporation Law* 32 (2007): 323–380; Grandy, *New Jersey and Modern American Corporation Law*; Christopher Grandy, "New Jersey Corporate Chartermongering, 1875–1929," *Journal of Economic History* 49 (1989): 677–692; Robert Jack Anderson, "The Motion Picture Patents Company" (Ph.D. diss., University of Wisconsin, Madison, 1983).

13. The following account of Edison's career is taken from these sources: Israel, *Edison*; Robert Friedel and Paul Israel, *Edison's Electric Light: The Art of Invention* (Baltimore and London: Johns Hopkins University Press, 2010); William Pretzer, ed., *Working at*

Inventing: Thomas A. Edison and the Menlo Park Experience (Baltimore and London: Johns Hopkins University Press, 2002).

14. Edison to Charles Buell, December 1, 1873, in Reese V. Jenkins et al., eds., *The Papers of Thomas A. Edison*, vol. 2, *From Workshop to Laboratory* (*June 1873–March 1876*) (Baltimore and London: Johns Hopkins University Press, 1991), 379.

15. The term "invention factory" first appears in "A Visit to Edison," April 29, 1878, Thomas A. Edison Papers Digital Edition (http://edison.rutgers.edu/digital.htm; hereafter cited as TAED), SM029054a; the rest is quoted in Matthew Josephson, *Edison: A Biography* (New York: McGraw-Hill, 1959), 133–134.

16. Bell to Edison, May 25, 1879, TAED, D7903ZEC.

17. *Newark Call*, November 7, 1886, quoted in Andre Millard, *Edison and the Business of Innovation* (Baltimore: Johns Hopkins University Press, 1990), 330n12.

18. Draft of Edison to James Hood Wright, ca. August 1887, N-87-11-15 (TAED, NA011005).

19. Some New Jersey companies had their laboratories in New York, including New Jersey Zinc and Standard Oil, which were among the forty laboratories that could be found just in the city of New York. Alfred D. Flinn, Ruth Cobb, Clarence J. West, and Callie Hull, *Industrial Research Laboratories of the United States, Including Consulting Research Laboratories* (Washington, D.C.: National Research Council, National Academy of Sciences, 1920), 105–110.

20. Jean Wilson Sidar, *George Hammell Cook: A Life in Agriculture and Geology* (New Brunswick: Rutgers University Press, 1976); U.S. Office of Experiment Stations, *Report: Volume 180* (Washington, D.C.: GPO, 1900), 316–325; U.S. Census Bureau, *Bulletins of the Twelfth Census of the United States: Issued from October 6, 1900 to [October 20, 1902]*, no. 133; New Jersey History Committee, *Outline History of New Jersey* (New Brunswick: Rutgers University Press, 1950), 128–130.

21. These percentages are rounded to the nearest whole number. Don Dodd, *Historical Statistics of the States of the United States: Two Centuries of the Census, 1790–1990* (Westport, Conn.: Greenwood Press, 1993), 1–104, 451–456; Adna Ferrin Weber, *The Growth of Cities in the Nineteenth Century: A Study in Statistics* (New York: Macmillan, 1899), 31–32, 153; John E. Bebout and Ronald J. Grele, *Where Cities Meet: The Urbanization of New Jersey* (Princeton: D. Van Nostrand, 1964) .

22. Bebout and Grele, *Where Cities Meet*, 31–35; Rudolph J. Vecoli, *The People of New Jersey* (Princeton: D. Van Nostrand, 1965), chaps. 3–6, appendix B; William Paul Dillingham, *Reports of the Immigration Commission* (Washington, D.C.: GPO, 1911), 47–52; Ellen Eisenberg, *Jewish Agricultural Colonies in New Jersey: 1882–1920* (Syracuse: Syracuse University Press, 1995).

23. Giles R. Wright, *Afro-Americans in New Jersey: A Short History* (Trenton: New Jersey Historical Commission, 1989), 45–46; "The Negro in Manufacturing and Mechanical Industries," in New Jersey, Bureau of Statistics of Labor and Industries, *Annual Report* (1904): 163–168, 183–191; Charles E. Funnell, *By the Beautiful Sea: The Rise and High Times of That Great American Resort, Atlantic City* (New Brunswick: Rutgers University Press, 1983), 14–15.

24. Quoted in Funnell, *By the Beautiful Sea*, 4.

25. Most Prudential employees were agents in local offices throughout the country, but the main office in Newark employed several hundred clerks and other white-collar workers. Frederick L. Hoffman, *History of the Prudential Insurance Company of America* (*industrial insurance*) *1875–1900* (Newark, N.J.: Prudential Press, 1900). On the rapid increase of white-collar workers, see Margo J. Anderson, *The United States Census and the New Jersey Urban Occupational Structure, 1870–1940* (Ann Arbor, Mich.: UMI Research Press, 1980), 108–112.

26. Funnel, *By the Beautiful Sea*; Bill Brown, *The Material Unconscious: American Amusement, Stephen Crane, and the Economies of Play* (Cambridge, Mass.: Harvard University Press, 1996), 34–69; Glenn Uminowicz, "Recreation in Christian America: Ocean Grove and Asbury Park, New Jersey," in *Hard at Play: Leisure in America, 1840–1940*, ed. Kathryn Grover (Amherst: University of Massachusetts Press, 1992), 8–38; Jim Futrell, *Amusement Parks of New Jersey* (Mechanicsburg, Pa.: Stack Pole Books, 2004).

27. Ann Marie T. Cammarota, *Pavements in the Garden: The Suburbanization of Southern New Jersey, Adjacent to the City of Philadelphia, 1769 to the Present* (Madison, N.J.: Fairleigh Dickinson University Press, 2001); Susan A. Nowicki, "Montclair, New Jersey: The Development of a Suburban Town and Its Architecture" (Ph.D. diss., City University of New York, 2008); Carol A. Benenson, "Merchantville, New Jersey: The Development, Architecture, and Preservation of a Victorian Commuter Suburb" (M.S. thesis, University of Pennsylvania, 1984); Alan J. Karcher, *New Jersey's Multiple Municipal Madness* (New Brunswick: Rutgers University Press, 1998), 85, 105–106.

28. Thomas J. Fleming, *New Jersey: A History* (New York: W. W. Norton, 1984), 130–136; Richardson Dilworth, *The Urban Origins of Suburban Authority* (Cambridge, Mass.: Harvard University Press, 2005), chap. 4; Richard A. Hogarty, *Leon Abbett's New Jersey: The Emergence of the Modern Governor* (Philadelphia: American Philosophical Society, 2001), chaps. 4, 7–8.

29. Dilworth, *Urban Origins*, chap. 5; Galishoff, *Newark*, chap. 9; Brad R. Tuttle, *How Newark Became Newark: The Rise, Fall, and Rebirth of an American City* (New Brunswick: Rutgers University Press, 2009), chap. 3.

30. Galishoff, *Newark*, 186–187; James Ford, Ernest P. Goodrich, and George B. Ford, *Housing Report to the City Plan Commission of Newark, N.J.* (Newark: Matthias Plum, 1913), 7–14; Mary Buell Sayles, "Housing Conditions in Jersey City," *Annals of the American Academy of Political and Social Science* 21 (1903); "Tenement-House Conditions," *The Survey* 5 (December 15, 1900): 10; Charles J. Allen, "Tenement House Commission," in New Jersey Commission for the Panama-Pacific International Exposition, *The State of New Jersey: Brief Articles, Descriptive of Its History, Industries, State Departments and Resorts* (New Jersey: The Commission, 1915), 51.

31. Kim Voss, *The Making of American Exceptionalism: The Knights of Labor and Class Formation in the Nineteenth Century* (Ithaca: Cornell University Press, 1993), 117–122; Maxine N. Lurie, "Introduction," in *A New Jersey Anthology*, ed. Maxine N. Lurie (New Brunswick: Rutgers University Press, 1994), 18–19; R. R. Bowker, "Plain Talks on Economics," *The Million* 2 (1885): 306.

32. "Report of the Inspector of Factories and Workshops," in *Documents of the 110th Legislature of the State of New Jersey* 3 (1886): 3–4, 9, 100–103; William Franklin Willoughby and Mary Clare de Graffenried, *Child Labor* (Baltimore: American Economic Association, 1890), 27n1; Hogarty, *Leon Abbett's New Jersey*, 241–244.

8 · THE PROGRESSIVE ERA

BRIAN GREENBERG

Looking back over the three decades since she had founded Whittier House in Jersey City in 1893, Cornelia Bradford eulogized New Jersey's first social settlement house as an agency of democracy, "This was the basic stone." Yet allied to that institution's unceasing commitment to democracy was the paternalistic conviction "that as all are simply human, the strong should bear the infirmities of the weak."[1] To fulfill the at times discordant objectives of democracy and paternalism, Whittier House had established Jersey City's first kindergarten, its only playground, a free dental clinic, a mothers' club, evening clubs and classes for working women, and even a pawnshop.[2] Bradford's reminiscence provides an unwitting example of the complexities and tensions that historians have associated with the Progressive Era. For example, to free Jersey City's immigrant population from the predatory practices of loan sharks, the settlement's pawnshop offered to loan money to immigrants "without the obligation to pay high rates of interest." But the pawnshop would make no loan without an investigation of the personal habits of each applicant, and it rejected solicitations from "persons under the influence of spirituous liquors."[3] The social services that Whittier House offered to improve the lives of and to empower Jersey City's impoverished immigrants were often accompanied by an effort to impose middle-class standards on them and reshape their behavior.

The term "progressive" came into common usage in the United States around 1910, after first being employed to describe a wide-ranging and loosely defined political movement.[4] Since then, historians have framed the broad reform movements of the early twentieth century as the Progressive Era. The lack of a generally accepted definition led some historians in the 1970s to recommend abandoning the term. Yet "progressive" was what many politicians and socially conscious activists earlier in the century had called themselves and their movement.

Daniel Rodgers suggests that historians take a more pluralistic approach, one that identifies the rhetoric of anti-monopolism, an emphasis on social bonds, and a focus on efficiency as the three languages that fueled the efforts of politically active progressives. In contrast, Richard L. McCormick highlights the transformation of American politics and government that took place during the Progressive Era.[5] In New Jersey, progressivism, political change, and economic and social reform often followed complementary trajectories in the decades before World War I.

PROGRESSIVE POLITICS

As the nation's most urban, industrial, and ethnically diverse state, New Jersey has been called the "prototype" for the progressives' political, economic, social, and cultural agenda during the first decades of the twentieth century. The economic dislocation and social problems associated with the growth of big business, large-scale factories, immense cities, and mass immigration dominated New Jersey politics and reform in the decades immediately before and after the beginning of the twentieth century.[6] Often combining the antagonistic purposes of social justice and social control, progressivism in New Jersey encompassed a variety of constituents: a business elite who sought to turn government into an ally of the modern corporate order; female reformers who attempted to protect women and children from exploitation; social scientists and other professionals who believed that the disorderly forces of modern society could be controlled through investigation, agitation, and legislation; and an optimistic group of political reformers who challenged the corruption of the traditional political order, insisting, even as they frequently questioned the people's worthiness as voters, that citizens should take charge of the political process.[7]

Over the last third of the nineteenth century, the population of New Jersey more than doubled to exceed 1.8 million residents by 1900.[8] New Jersey ranked third in population density in the United States in 1910, and much of this population explosion took place in the Garden State's cities, both large and small.[9] Extensive increases in manufacturing fueled New Jersey's population growth in these years. In the four decades before the end of World War I, New Jersey experienced the second highest growth rate in manufacturing of any state in the United States. Most of that growth was concentrated in the center and north: potteries in Trenton, the silk and locomotive works of Paterson, Camden's canneries, and massive rail and shipping networks in Hoboken and Jersey City. Newark harbored widely diverse industries, including leather, jewelry, chemicals, and clothing, as well as a vibrant commercial center.[10] In Middlesex County huge brickworks could be found in Sayreville, and Perth Amboy was considered the national center of the terra-cotta industry. Moreover, job growth came not only to the industrial sector. By the second decade of the twentieth century, there were even higher increases in the number of typists, teachers, clerks, and persons in the retail trade in the Garden State.[11] The state's large-scale businesses employed a growing immigrant population. By 1920, six of every ten of the state's urban residents were either foreign born or the children of foreign-born parents.[12] Beginning in the 1880s, New Jersey, like the rest of the nation, experienced a shift in the origins of its immigrant population. "New" immigrants from Italy began to outnumber the "old" immigrant groups from Germany, Ireland, and England. Prior to World War I, Italians became the largest ethnic group in the state, followed by Russians and various Slavic groups. In Jersey City, the Italian population more than tripled in the first decade of the twentieth century. Likewise, Passaic became a Slovakian city, and Hungarians flocked to Perth Amboy and New Brunswick.[13]

The physical transformation of New Jersey in the decades before and after the beginning of the twentieth century, especially as a result of the expanding industrial and transportation sectors, notably the railroads, produced a politico-business alliance that corrupted the state's political process.[14] New Jersey in the 1880s and 1890s passed incorporation laws that provided big trusts like Standard Oil, U.S. Steel, and American Sugar Refining with the means to escape the legal barriers to multi-state operation imposed by federal courts. A New Jersey law of 1889 was one of the first state laws that allowed one corporation to own stock in another, thus legalizing the formation of holding companies.[15] The liberalization of the state's incorporation laws in 1896 made New Jersey the only state where corporate directors could hold office and conduct business outside the state so long as they maintained a corporate office within the state and paid the state's chartering fees. By 1901, 2,347 corporate charters had been granted under the new law.[16] The Corporation Trust Company, located in Jersey City, served as "home office" for more than twelve hundred corporations, including the seven largest companies in the nation. By 1904, 150 of the top 298 companies in America were chartered in the Garden State.[17] What has been called "corporate chartermongering" paid off for New Jersey in the form of increased state revenues. After 1896, corporation fees covered almost all state expenses, and by 1905 New Jersey had eliminated its bonded debt and had abolished the state property tax.[18]

New Jersey's longstanding favoritism toward railroads, going back to the chartering of the Camden and Amboy in 1830, meant that the rail lines could absorb ever-larger amounts of property, especially in the state's bigger cities, and that much of this land was exempt from local taxes. In 1903 the Interstate Commerce Commission revealed that since the late 1880s the gross earnings of railroads in New Jersey had risen 46 percent, whereas taxes paid by the rail companies had increased by only 16 percent. In Jersey City, which served as the terminus for major trunk lines in the Northeast, the Board of Assessors in 1901 determined that railroads, which owned one-third of the city's assessable property, had paid just $236,000 on their real estate holdings, whereas non-railroad corporations had paid $2 million on the remaining two-thirds of assessable city property.[19]

During the "Gilded Age," the Democratic and Republican parties in New Jersey were commanded by impressively organized cliques. Led by a series of corrupt party bosses, both parties proved to be dependable allies for the state's growing corporate interests. The "selling out of the interests of the city, state, and nation to the business leaders" made New Jersey, in the words of muckraker Lincoln Steffens, "a traitor state."[20] From 1869 to the mid-1890s, an unbroken line of Democratic governors held power in the Garden State, until a particularly notorious racetrack scandal in the early 1890s led to John W. Griggs's election as New Jersey's first Republican governor in the post–Civil War era. The scandal revealed the extent to which the state's legislature was under the sway of corrupt racetrack gamblers and operators. Despite the change in political parties, a younger generation of Republican leaders demonstrated a willingness equal to that of their Democratic predecessors to preserve the interests of the state's railroads and other powerful corporations, which continued to escape an equitable taxa-tion of their property. They included Griggs, who was the director of many corporations; Franklin Murphy, a varnish manufacturer; John F. Dryden, president of the Prudential Insurance Company; and Thomas N. Carter of the Public Service Corporation, which dominated public utilities in the state.[21] Powerful Republican bosses like William J. Sewell, who had risen through the ranks as a railroad track laborer to become president of the West Jersey and Seashore Railroad Company, made certain that the "right" men—that is, corporation men—were selected to serve on state commis-sions or nominated as candidates for office by the Republican county and state conventions.[22]

During the period of Republican ascendancy, which lasted until the election of Woodrow Wilson as governor in 1910, the Democratic Party in New Jersey dissolved into a number of factions. Leadership was provided by James Smith Jr. of Newark and Robert Davis of Jersey City. Smith, the owner of manufacturing, banking, newspaper, and utility interests, ran Essex County, and Davis, who had the backing of E.F.C. Young, a financier and influential board member of four utility concerns, dominated politics in Hudson County.[23] The Democratic Party bosses, much like their Repub-lican counterparts, sought to use their control of the state's political ma-chinery to advance and protect the valuable privileges enjoyed by special interests in New Jersey.[24]

As historian Eugene Tobin notes, the "monopolization of the state's political and economic life by an alliance of political bosses and corporate magnates" and the grossly unequal tax system kindled an extensive reform movement in New Jersey in the early twentieth century.[25] Widespread rec-ognition of the evils of concentrated wealth and calls for the restoration of economic democracy led many citizens to denounce the monopoly of the state's political and industrial sectors by an alliance of political bosses and corporate magnates.[26] Beginning in the 1880s, reform in New Jersey moved in many directions. The earliest efforts sought to change the conduct of elections, including the adoption of an official secret ballot in 1890, the nomination of candidates through direct primaries, the direct election of senators to replace a legislative appointment process that was usually con-trolled by the bosses of the party in power, and the introduction of strict voter registration requirements.[27] This process would culminate in a series of reform acts passed just after Wilson became governor.

The assault on unequal taxes and on the extensive power of chartered corporations surfaced first in Jersey City during the mayoral administration of Mark M. Fagan, a Republican progressive elected in 1901 at the age of thirty-one. Fagan and his corporate counsel, George L. Record, who were followers of the radical political economist Henry George, devised a platform consisting of economic and political demands: equal taxation; limits on utility and transportation franchises, including the taxation of franchises at local rates; and direct election of senators. Working with State Senator Everett Colby, Fagan and Record launched a campaign in 1905 among the "New Idea" progressives to demolish the political machines of the Old Guard Republicans and Democrats in New Jersey.[28]

Both Fagan and Record subscribed to the single-tax program advanced by George in *Progress and Poverty*, one of the most widely read economic reform tracts in American history and a significant influence on the thinking of many social progressives. George targeted private ownership of land as the main cause of inequality and corruption. All privilege based on monopoly had to be eradicated if the economic ills of society were to be cured.[29]

Fagan adapted George's single-tax principles to the political and economic realities he found in Jersey City. For his part, Record, although convinced of the basic soundness of the competitive capitalistic system, nevertheless advocated the public ownership of utilities and transportation facilities. He also favored government support for competition through the use of taxation to offset the privileges of the steel, oil, and coal trusts. Both Fagan and Record agreed that economic privilege was the basis of industrial monopoly. They were deeply suspicious of corporate economic and political power in New Jersey and, according to Tobin, "urged the stringent use of taxation both to break up the trusts and to regulate the railroads."[30] Record's lifelong commitment to making the political machinery more democratic originated in his firm belief that fundamental reform was not possible until the people controlled their government.[31] Tobin concludes, "Both men were mavericks in terms of Jersey City's political and cultural traditions."[32]

Fagan had been elected as a "good government" or "businessmen's" candidate who pledged to end municipal extravagance and reduce the tax rate. Yet he also had an ambitious civic betterment agenda that sought to expand such basic services as education, housing, parks, public concerts, and public health, including construction of a new hospital, free medical clinics, public baths, and better sewers.[33] The new mayor quickly discovered, how-ever, that his administration would be unable to lower the tax rate or cut government spending unless the city's tax base was significantly broadened. The first area for tax reform was the tax dodging practiced by several local corporations, especially the railroads. Fagan sought to equalize the munici-pal tax burden by reassessing the property of the trusts that operated in Jer-sey City and then taxing them on the actual value of their property. In Janu-ary 1903 the state Board of Assessors increased the valuations on railroad property in Jersey City by more than $1 million and transferred to the city rolls, to be taxed at full local rates, more than fifty acres of property that had previously been taxed by the state.[34]

Fagan easily won reelection in 1903. But in challenging the utility com-panies in Jersey City, Fagan found himself facing the organized opposition of the Public Service Corporation (PSC), which was headed by Thomas N. Carter and backed by the Republican boss Samuel Dickinson.[35] Function-ing under the PSC umbrella, the Prudential Insurance Company, Fidelity Trust Company, and United Gas Improvement Company controlled Jersey City's gas, electric light, and trolley service. Fagan charged Dickinson with demanding a perpetual franchise for the PSC and blocking the passage of an equal tax bill. He pledged that he would "fight the boss system itself, by which unscrupulous men get between the people and the public official by control of party machinery ... and attempt to drive out of public life all who will not take orders from the boss and his real masters, the corporations."[36]

In 1905 the New Jersey Tax Commission submitted the results of its year-long investigation into the charges and countercharges leveled by the util-ity companies and the Fagan administration. Endorsing the goal of equal tax, the commission recommended raising the tax on main-stem (primary) property, taxing second-class property at full local rates, creating a new state tax tribunal, and establishing maximum rates for municipal taxation. In response, the Republican-led legislature passed the Duffield Railroad Tax Act, which provided for the taxation of second-class railroad property at local rates. In practical terms, as applied to Jersey City, the act increased the tax that railroads paid the city from $15 per thousand ratables to $28 per thousand ratables on property worth $22 million. However, the impact of this legislation was largely negated by the state senate's passage of the Hillery Maximum Tax Act, which reinstated the 1.5 percent rate on second-class railroad property. The act's mandated cuts in local tax rates meant that the Fagan administration had to impose higher tax rates on property owners in Jersey City or end some of the social programs that it had initiated.[37]

Fagan and Record found an ally in Everett Colby, a state assemblyman from nearby Essex County. A wealthy young lawyer, Colby had entered politics under the sponsorship of the local Republican Party boss. But in 1905 he declared his independence from the political machine and offered a concurrent resolution announcing that the senate and general assembly's acceptance of all public utility franchises granted in perpetuity to public utility corporations was wrong in principle. Apprised by a party leader that "our friends" (the Prudential–Public Service group) opposed his resolution, Colby refused to accept their proposed amendments. He then introduced a bill to limit the grant of public utility franchises to a period of no longer than twenty-five years. When the Republican machine refused to endorse Colby for reelection to the assembly, George Record suggested that he run for the state senate and make an independent appeal to progressive sentiment in the county. In June 1905 Colby announced his candidacy and pledged himself to work for equal taxation, limited franchises, taxation of franchises at local rates, and greater popular participation in the selection of each party's choice for U.S. senator. The principles announced by Colby's Essex declaration became the agenda adopted by the "New Idea" men, a progressive group of state legislators.[38]

New Idea progressives dedicated themselves to the principle that all political activity should be conducted openly and that every voter should have an equal voice in the activities of his party.[39] Strongest in the state's urban northeastern corridor—the counties of Hudson, Essex, and Passaic, where railroad and utility development was most pronounced—the New Idea initiative served very much like a third party, agitating, lobbying, and prodding the Democrats and Republicans to adopt more progressive positions on railroad taxation, franchise reform, and utility regulation. Yet, even though they achieved some success when the state legislature enacted a measure designed to limit the term of utility franchises and another law that increased municipal taxes on trolley company franchises, the New Idea progressives too often degenerated into quarrelsome factions. In September 1906 the regular Republican organization routed New Idea progressives in the primaries.[40]

In his 1907 bid for reelection to a third term as Jersey City mayor, Fagan found himself facing not only a revitalized regular Republican organization but also opposition from the Catholic Church, which supported his Democratic opponent, H. Otto Whittpenn. Fagan had already been excommunicated by the Catholic Church because of his support for Henry George when he lived in New York in the 1880s. Now he found himself facing the church's censure for "flirting with the liquor traffic."[41] This charge referred to Fagan's reluctance to enforce the "Bishop's Act," a law that imposed harsh penalties, including license revocation, for selling liquor on Sunday and banned backrooms in saloons. Although he agreed with Fagan on the law, John Franklin Fort, a fellow New Idea Republican who was running for governor that year, pledged to enforce it if he was elected. Afterward, Fort attributed his narrow victory to having made that pledge.[42]

Declaring that "you cannot serve the church and saloon, " Monsignor John A. Sheppard of the Archdiocese of Newark and Father John J. Ryan of Fagan's own parish church, Saint Bridget's, denounced Fagan for violating his oath of office. Although the Catholic Church did not openly campaign against Fagan, it did praise his Democratic opponent, even though the local Democratic Party was the leading anti-temperance voice in the city. Also working against Fagan's reelection was the failure of equal taxation to produce the economic benefits that local homeowners had expected. Faced with disgruntled taxpayers, opposition from the city's religious community and regular Republican Party, and the wholesale identification of Jersey's City's German American community with his Democratic opponent, Fagan and the New Idea went down to overwhelming defeat. Nevertheless, the statewide reform effort would soon be revived by Wittpenn and other Democratic recruits to the progressive cause.[43]

Outside of some changes in civil service rules and in primary election machinery, the insurgents' scorecard showed few victories for political democracy in the years 1907–1910. Progressives found themselves unable to counter the entrenched corporate interests in both political parties, whose strategy was to make small concessions in order to resist more fundamental reforms. Yet the political lay of the land in New Jersey was changing. In 1909 the Essex New Idea changed its name to the Progressive Republican League for Limited Franchises and Equal Taxation, and members began referring to themselves as Progressive Republicans. Democrats too felt progressivism's pull. Among Democrats who joined the movement for reform were liberals like Joseph Tumulty of Hudson County, Harry V. Osborne, Colby's successor in the Senate, Julian A. Gregory, who was active in the

Citizens Union, and Whittpenn. Late in 1905 the Essex Democratic League was formed, calling for the elimination of boss and corporate control and for a long list of progressive reforms. The progressives of both parties committed themselves to a campaign to democratize government and to ensure that it served as an instrument for social and economic betterment.[44]

By 1910, James Smith Jr., who had risen from modest beginnings to become a prominent manufacturer, banker, and newspaper publisher, had become the leader of the Democratic political machine in Newark and Essex County. Among Smith's allies were his nephew James R. Nugent, chair of the state Democratic committee, and Robert Davis of Jersey City, who sometimes fought Smith and Nugent for control of the state party. Early in 1910 these three men became convinced that the president of Princeton University, Woodrow Wilson, would be an excellent candidate for governor in the 1910 election. When first approached, Wilson expressed reluctance; he would be willing to run only if he did not have to campaign actively for the nomination. However, by 1910 Wilson appears to have been ready to consider a change in careers. After considerable early success in reshaping undergraduate education at Princeton through the reorganization of the curriculum, Wilson had recently suffered bitter defeats in his attempt to replace the elite eating clubs with more egalitarian and communal residential quads and in his efforts to integrate the graduate school into the life of the campus.[45]

When Smith approached Wilson to ascertain his willingness to cooperate with the Democratic machine if elected, Wilson sought to reassure him: he would not "'set about fighting and breaking down the existing Democratic organization and replacing it with one of . . . [his] own.'" Still, he insisted, he must be "'absolutely free in the matter of measures and men.'" Working in Wilson's favor was the growing sentiment that he would make an excellent candidate for president of the United States in 1912. Smith also expected to gain Wilson's support for his own selection as U.S. senator. Democratic progressives attacked the Smith-Davis machine's endorsement of Wilson as representing the manipulations of the "corrupt State House ring." Nevertheless, Wilson won the nomination. Moreover, in his acceptance speech he issued a straightforward declaration of independence from machine control and an unequivocal promise to stand by the platform that had been framed by the progressive delegates. George Record and many other leading New Idea Republicans responded favorably to Wilson's nomination.[46]

WITH APOLOGIES TO "THE SPIRIT OF '76"

Woodrow Wilson marches uncomfortably with Democratic political bosses during the gubernatorial election campaign of 1910. (*Paterson Daily Press*, October 3, 1910.)

During the campaign, Wilson sought to distance himself from Smith and Nugent and the regular Democratic organization. Record, who was running as a Republican candidate for Congress, challenged Wilson to meet in a public debate. Rather than engage in open debate, Wilson agreed to respond to "a series of searching questions" that would cover every aspect of progressive reform in New Jersey. To some questions, such as whether he favored establishing a public utilities commission with the power to set "just and reasonable rates," Wilson responded with a simple "yes." To the question of what his relations would be with the Democratic Party leaders, Wilson announced, "I shall not, either in the matter of appointments to office or assent to legislation, or in the shaping [of] any part of the policy of my administration, submit to the dictation of any person or persons, special interest or organization." Record complained that this letter "would elect Wilson governor."[47] Wilson's personal appeal in the election seems to have transcended partisanship: one-third of the Republican voters from 1908 crossed party lines to vote for him in 1910. Summing up the results, the *Jersey Journal* concluded that Wilson's election represented less a Democratic victory than "a victory of the progressive and independent voter."[48]

Governor Wilson quickly established his credentials as an independent by refusing to endorse Smith in his bid to be a U.S. senator, supporting instead the victor of the recent nonbinding primary, James E. Martine, an inexperienced follower of the national Democratic leader William Jennings Bryan. To plan his legislative agenda, Wilson met with progressive legislators the day before his inauguration. They agreed to propose legislation forbidding corrupt practices, calling for the direct primary and for election reform, regulating public utilities, and mandating employer liability for workmen's accident compensation. Wilson assigned to Record the responsibility for writing both the corrupt practices and direct primary bills.[49] The new governor then turned to one of his former Princeton students, Assemblyman Elmer Geran of Monmouth County, to introduce Record's bills in the assembly.

The Geran bill and the Corrupt Practices Act sought to restrict the activities of party organizations in the conduct of elections by shifting responsibility for running elections to either the state or the electorate. The legislation replaced the practice of having roving canvassers register voters and required that registration be renewed any time a voter missed an election. Other changes disallowed registration less than four days before an election, required foreign-born voters to show their citizenship papers, prohibited payment to party workers, and forbade parties to offer voters a drink or even a ride to the polls. The direct primary was extended to cover all elective offices in the state, including, for the first time, president, governor, and congressman. Progressives like Wilson "equated greater public administration of the elections with greater democracy."[50] Democratic legislators from cities with large numbers of immigrant voters were able to amend the legislation to eliminate the requirement that foreign-born voters show their naturalization papers at the polls and to prevent voting hours from being shortened. To progressives, the proposed legislation would, by removing illiterate, ignorant, or uneducated voters, upgrade the quality of the electorate. Although supporters denied having an explicit nativist intent, their measures did fall most heavily on immigrants and nonwhites. The effect of the new legislation, which in the end further complicated the voting process, appears to have been an increase in voter apathy and a diminished turnout.

Public utility regulation had long been a touchstone for both Republican and Democratic progressives in New Jersey. With the support of Governor Wilson, Harry V. Osborne, the Democratic minority leader in the senate, and Charles M. Egan, a Democratic assemblyman from Jersey City, introduced utility regulation legislation in their respective houses. The Osborne-Egan bill, modeled on a 1906 New York statute, created a three-person commission that, subject to possible review by the state supreme court, could fix rates for and regulate many of the business practices of public utility companies.[51]

A final piece of progressive legislation, which Wilson initiated during his first year in office, concerned employer and employee liability for accidents in the workplace. As in most states, New Jersey's liability laws accepted the legal principle of "assumption of risk," the idea that an individual assumes the ordinary risks connected to his work when he takes a job. In practice, the burden of industrial accidents fell entirely on the injured employees. After consultation with Wilson, Senator Walter E. Edge of Atlantic City introduced legislation that became New Jersey's first workers' compensation law.[52]

Wilson soon found himself in a fight with the bosses over a municipal reform law that would enable the cities and towns of New Jersey to adopt a commission form of government. Having been told that the commission form of government was popular in the West, Wilson, perhaps thinking of his presidential ambitions, urged the state senate's adoption of legislation introduced in the assembly by Allan B Walsh and by Harry D. Leavitt. Commission government reformers, usually led by the business community and by Chamber of Commerce groups, contended that a small number of commissioners elected on a nonpartisan, citywide ballot could provide the efficient and "scientific" administration required by a modern city. The Walsh-Leavitt bill provided that once voters passed a local municipal referendum, the usual mayor-council system of government would be replaced with a five-member board of commissioners.[53]

Progressives viewed the innovation of commission government as a panacea that would liberate American cities from corrupt boss rule. Known as the Galveston Plan because it was first successfully introduced in that Texas city after a devastating flood, commission government replaces an elected mayor with a small group of commissioners who take charge of specific municipal functions, including one who performs the largely ceremonial responsibilities of mayor. Despite the enthusiastic support of Mark Fagan and the endorsement of the incumbent mayor, H. Otto Wittpenn, Jersey City voters rejected the proposed commission reform in 1911. But two years later a second referendum was more successful. Jersey City adopted the commission form of government in April 1913, and the new commissioners appointed Fagan as mayor.[54] What followed in Jersey City reveals not only the limitations of the commission form of government but also the narrowness of the progressives' idea of "the people," which encompassed educated, upper-class Americans but not working-class, immigrant, or nonwhite city residents. Moreover, Frank Hague, the Democratic leader of the Second Ward and a vigorous opponent of commission government, had become convinced that the reform could be adapted to serve his own political purposes.

Known as the "Horseshoe," Jersey City's Second Ward was home to many immigrants, especially Irish Americans. In 1913 the new commissioners appointed Hague to be the city's director of public safety. The boss repackaged himself as a reformer and led campaigns to protect the welfare of children, a prototypical progressive reform. Deploying an elite and secret squad of plainclothesmen, called the "Zeppelins," Hague also transformed an undisciplined and corrupt police department into an effective law enforcement agency. Moreover, the greater efficiency of the city's fire department under Hague resulted in reduced fire insurance rates for residents, which made Hague popular with homeowners and businessmen. At the same time, by ignoring violations of Sunday saloon-closing laws, Hague remained faithful to his immigrant constituents in the Horseshoe.[55] He also used his powers as director of public safety to harass his Democratic rivals and other political opponents. The machine politician who "reinvented himself as a Progressive" was unrelenting "in his use of political power, political spectacle, and when necessary physical violence" to advance his personal agenda.[56] As head of the police and fire departments, Hague controlled appointments to both of these vital services and by 1916 had built a patronage base that would serve him throughout his career. Hague's ticket carried the city's preferential election in 1917 by a wide margin, and Hague was named mayor of Jersey City. Once in power as a "new boss," he remained a county, state, and national political force for the next thirty years.[57]

In his inaugural address as governor in 1911, Wilson had signaled a radical shift in New Jersey's corporate policy: "If I may speak very plainly we are much too free with grants of charters to corporations in New Jersey." Although he called for new laws to "prevent the abuse of the privilege of incorporation," it was not until he had won the presidential nomination two years later that he proposed the antitrust legislation that became known as the "Seven Sisters" acts. This legislation outlawed the "corporate charter-mongering" policies of the 1880s and 1890s that had made the merger wave of those years possible. As the economist Christopher Grandy observes, the Seven Sisters statutes "proscribed monopolistic practices generally and price fixing, price discrimination, and the issuance of watered stock in particular." The laws also limited the extent to which New Jersey corporations could hold stock in other firms and regulated the terms on which corporations could merge. Despite the clear anti-monopoly intent of the Seven Sisters laws, minimal funding made enforcement very difficult. Of greater consequence, the precipitous decline in state revenue by 1917, which Governor Walter Edge attributed to the "drastic provisions of the [Seven Sisters] laws," led state leaders to come "to their senses" and substantially weaken or repeal the incorporation reforms.[58]

The quick demise of incorporation reforms reveals the limitations of the progressives' assault on the politico-business alliance in New Jersey. Alongside the progressives' anti-business and pro-people approach to addressing the problems brought on by the concentration of wealth and power that had developed in the United States since the end of the Civil War, a counterbalancing tendency toward an acceptance of big business and large-scale organization of society proved to be equally strong.[59] Although often expressed in highly moralistic terms, the progressives' defense of individualism and democracy against political and business corruption embraced economic and political reforms that were more palliative than curative. To be sure, progressive reforms moved the United States beyond a reflexive acceptance of the laissez-faire attitudes that had left corporate enterprise and party bosses largely unregulated. In later years progressives understood that they had achieved at most only a partial victory. Primary and ballot reforms had made elections more orderly, but large corporations and party organizations had been able to adapt to reform, and they still dominated the electoral process.[60]

SOCIAL PROGRESSIVISM

Working sometimes independently and at other times cooperatively with political reformers, social progressives actively sought, in the words of Jane Addams, who personified their movement, "to aid in the solution of the social and industrial problems which are engendered by the modern conditions of life in the great city."[61] As mayor of Jersey City, Mark Fagan attempted to merge political reform and economic justice with social justice. Soon after becoming mayor in 1901, Fagan pledged to initiate measures "which shall operate to make the condition of life easier for the masses." Yet he recognized that administering the city on sound business principles would not be enough to ensure the financial resources required to meet the needs of the poor immigrant neighborhoods. Only by creating new sources of revenue through the equalization of the tax burden could his administration produce the necessary financing to improve such basic social services as education, housing, and public health.[62] Between 1902 and 1908, the Fagan administration developed programs to improve prenatal care in the city, curtail infant mortality by ensuring the purity of the city's milk supply, organize the city's juvenile court and probation systems, and build parks and playgrounds. Fagan hoped to make saving children, that is, "the preservation of family, community, and society," the hallmark of his administration.[63]

Social justice goals were also deeply imprinted in the reform programs embraced by Jersey City's voluntary humanitarian activists, such as Cornelia Bradford, head resident of the Whittier Settlement House. Bradford, whose father was a minister active in abolition and women's rights, was born in 1847 in the northern Finger Lakes region of New York. After college, Bradford moved to Chester, New Jersey, where she experienced firsthand the changing industrial conditions in America. Her search to find a meaningful purpose in life led Bradford, as it had Addams, to the slums of East London, where she visited Toynbee Hall and resided as a settlement house worker in Mansfield House. After returning to the United States in 1893, and following a brief stay at Addams's Hull House in Chicago, Bradford established Whittier House (named after the poet John Greenleaf Whittier, whose sentiment, "He serves Thee best who loveth most / His brothers and Thy own," became the settlement's motto) to serve the poor and immigrant communities of Jersey City.[64] Like the other American adaptations of England's settlement movement that were established in numerous cities throughout the United States, Whittier House became a social and cultural center for the neighborhood and a locus for diverse reform activities.

Bradford located Whittier House in the First Ward in Jersey City, a neighborhood that became home to many old and new immigrant groups soon after they were processed at Ellis Island. Traditionally known as Paulus Hook, the area had become an industrial center where Irish, Polish, Russian, Scottish, and Swedish immigrants worked in the factories of Colgate, Lorillard Tobacco, and Dixon Crucible (a local pencil company). Whittier House aimed "through friendship, neighborliness and personal influence to promote in the community such a relation of fellowship and mutual helpfulness between people of different occupations and different opportunities, as shall improve the physical, intellectual and moral welfare of the neighborhood." By developing basic social service programs in education, housing, and public health—often the first of their kind in Jersey City—its middle-class residents sought to make Whittier House "the common meeting ground for the development and expression of the social, civic and moral spirit of the community."[65]

Whittier House was an immediate success. Among the earliest programs established there were a sewing school, a milk dispensary, a gymnasium for boys and girls, a mothers' club (the first women's group in Jersey City), a lending library, and the city's first free kindergarten. Many area professionals, both men and women, became residents of Whittier House, volunteering to teach courses, lead clubs, and provide such services as legal aid. Like Bradford (and Addams), the social progressives active in Whittier House shared a common background. The "typical" humanitarian reformer was a middle-class, native-born, college-educated, Protestant, and professional young man or woman. Although they were a distinct minority within the city, the men and women active in Jersey City's social justice movement were motivated by an "awareness of the gravity of their community's problems" and informed by a sense that they had a "vital stake in the preservation of that community."[66]

In the two decades prior to World War I, settlement houses were founded in some eighteen communities throughout the Garden State. The settlements in New Jersey, unlike those established elsewhere, did not necessarily operate solely in the most impoverished urban areas of the state. Even so, the settlement house movement in New Jersey, like that in other states,

Whittier Settlement House cooking class, ca. 1929. This class for girls, held in Jersey City, is representative of Progressive Era efforts to ensure safe food and to help educate immigrant and poor families in urban areas. (Jersey City Free Public Library, the New Jersey Room.)

pursued the often contradictory goals of social justice and social control. Bradford asserted that in its programs to "better" the lives of the poor and immigrant members of the surrounding community, the settlement's "mental attitude" was "an open one. . . . [We] have ever tried to bear in mind that our way is not the only way, neither need it necessarily be the best way."[67] Yet Whittier House also supported programs that sought to restrict what its middle-class residents viewed as the urban immigrant's deviant behavior.[68]

Celebrating the many accomplishments of Whittier House, Bradford revealed that she saw the settlement as a shaper of young men's and women's habits and values. Visiting the settlement's smoking room and pool room, which she did every night, Bradford observed the young men "playing pool, reading the papers, smoking and having a generally social time. . . . [Were] it not for Whittier House and its simple attractions" these same young men would be "out in the streets [where] saloons are open every evening."[69] Looking back over Whittier House's first fifteen years, Bradford also expressed admiration for the Vigilance League, on which many residents served, which worked "for the suppression of disorderly places of amusement in what is known as Little Coney. . . . This place is given over to vile amusements, drinking, carousing, and [the] general ruination of young girls." Bradford lauded these efforts to encourage the acceptance of a middle-class standard of behavior among the settlement house's immigrant neighbors.[70]

Bradford proudly affirmed Whittier House's role as an incubator for social services that eventually were replaced by similar public programs established by the city or the state. Its free kindergarten was discontinued when the public school in the neighborhood opened one, and because Whittier House was the first agency to hire a district nurse, Bradford also took credit for the organization of a municipal nursing service in Jersey City. Moreover, the public playground at Whittier House was the only one in Jersey City until similar recreation facilities were built throughout the city by 1912. This pattern of pioneering social programs can be applied as well to Whittier House's health dispensary and its legal aid department, both of which would be replaced by statewide agencies. Bradford believed that "better work" could be done in the public dispensaries, "not only because they are better equipped" but also because local physicians take a more "active interest in work conducted by the city."[71] She considered her appointment to the city Board of Education in 1912 by Mayor Whittpenn (Bradford was the first woman to serve in this capacity) to be recognition of Whittier House's spirit of "cooperation."[72]

As with many Progressive Era activities, the line between private initiative and public action often proved to be highly porous at Whittier House. Investigations undertaken by settlement house residents frequently resulted in the passage of social reform legislation. In 1903, while living in Whittier House, Mary B. Sayles, a recent graduate of Smith College, received a fellowship from the College Settlements Association to conduct a survey of housing conditions in Jersey City. Her published report, described as the first "scientific" investigation of the conditions of tenements in the city, noted the dangerous conditions endured by foreign-born immigrant factory workers: "'the stagnant air wells,' windowless bedrooms, locked fire exits or nonexistent fire escapes, lack of privacy, unsanitary conditions, and damp and 'unwholesome' cellars and yards with 'nauseating odors.'"[73]

Sayles's research provoked a public response. Whittier House organized a public meeting in March 1903 that led to the formation of the Tenement House Protective League, headquartered at the settlement, and to the formation by Mayor Fagan of a blue ribbon committee on housing. Soon afterward, Governor Franklin Murphy created a state tenement house commission, to which he appointed two residents of Whittier House. The commission's report led to the enactment of the first statewide tenement code in 1904,[74] which set minimum standards for construction, maintenance, and regulation. But actual enforcement was left to local officials, and they were often reluctant to antagonize influential property owners through rigorous application of the new codes. Of even greater concern was the probability that strict enforcement would lead to condemnation of "bad" tenements without providing any alternative "good" housing.[75]

In the public health movement in New Jersey, as in housing reform, the initiatives of private individuals were soon taken up by elected officials who developed local and statewide programs. A notable health reform effort in New Jersey in these years was the certified milk movement, which began in Newark and was led by a pediatrician, Dr. Henry Leber Coit, "the Father of Clean Milk." His own difficulty in finding unadulterated milk to feed his deathly ill young son prompted Dr. Coit to launch a crusade to upgrade the state's standards for milk purity. In 1890 the New Jersey State Medical Society sponsored committees of two physicians in each county to study the connection between the local infant mortality rate and the milk supply. After the failure of an initial attempt to pass a law controlling milk production, Coit successfully lobbied for the formation among private physicians of a certified milk commission in Essex County. Representing less than one percent of the total milk supply of large cities nationwide, certified milk was used mainly by physicians in their research and in their work with sick children and was not available for general sale. Still, by 1906 there were thirty-six medical milk commissions throughout the United States, and a year later the American Association of Medical Milk Commissions was organized.[76] But in Newark, the focus of Coit's efforts, the Board of Health did not pass a comprehensive milk reform ordinance providing for proper controls—daily inspections, pasteurization, sanitary bottling, milk grading, and the tuberculin testing of cows—until 1918.[77]

Child welfare was foremost among the reform initiatives advanced by social progressives. In 1917, after Jersey City had adopted the commission form of government and Mark Fagan had become director of the Department of Public Affairs, the former mayor observed that, as he grew older, "I found myself realizing that one sure and permanent way to reform the cities of America is through children."[78] Especially prominent in New Jersey were efforts to regulate child labor and to develop a juvenile court system.[79] The state's initial foray into regulating child labor dated back to an ineffective 1883 law that attempted to set the minimum age for boys at twelve and for girls at fourteen. In 1904 New Jersey strengthened relatively weak child labor restrictions that the legislature had passed a year earlier. The 1904 legislation emerged after Cornelia Bradford, working with the New Jersey Consumers' League and the New Jersey State Federation of Labor, examined child labor conditions in the glass-blowing region of southern New Jersey. This investigation led to the formation of the Child Protective League, which lobbied for a comprehensive child labor bill.[80] The law prohibited the employment of children up to the age of fourteen in manufacturing in New Jersey and required school attendance to that age. Enforcement was also improved, and for children under the age of sixteen the workday was limited to ten hours and the work week to fifty-five hours. Intense lobbying by the glass manufacturers meant that these protections were not extended to children working in the Garden State's glass factories. A new law in 1907 prohibited children under sixteen from working in mercantile establishments for more than fifty-eight hours per week or at night. Backed by labor unions, civic groups, and religious organizations, and supported in the legislature by both New Idea Republicans and progressive Democrats, this law was extended in 1910 to all factories in New Jersey.[81]

The prevention of juvenile delinquency was another goal of child welfare advocates. Outside of the activities at the settlement houses, child-based institutions such as juvenile courts and homes were absent in the state's urban areas. While awaiting trial, young and old mixed in jails. Protests by the State Charities Aid Association over these conditions led the legislature in 1903 to authorize county judges to create temporary courts for juvenile offenders. In December 1904, Police Judge Frank J. Higgins, a Fagan appointee, organized Jersey City's first juvenile court to try and confine juvenile offenders separately from adult prisoners. Also, those children who could not be safely returned to their own homes served their probation at the Society for the Prevention of Cruelty to Children.[82] Working as an unpaid assistant to the Essex County probation officer (who happened to be the mayor's brother), Mary Philbrook, New Jersey's first female attorney, lobbied hard for the establishment of a juvenile court in Newark. She was successful, and by 1904 that city too boasted a separate juvenile court.[83]

Progressives like Fagan, Record, and Bradford became directly engaged in trying to solve the problems that they believed were created by modern life in America. Others who were searching for solutions experimented by creating utopian communities. Two examples of such communities in New Jersey in the early twentieth century were Helicon Hall (also known as Home Colony) and Free Acres. In 1906, Upton Sinclair used the proceeds generated by his popular novel *The Jungle* to found Helicon Hall. Although Sinclair himself was a socialist, he planned Helicon Hall less as an experiment in socialism than as one in communal living. The community, which was located near Englewood, appears to have been built in a manner suggested by the feminist Charlotte Perkins Gilman, whose major work, *Women and Economics* (1898), had impressed Sinclair.[84]

In a July 1906 letter to the *New York Times*, Sinclair announced that a meeting was to be held at the Berkeley Lyceum in New York City for persons interested in establishing "a cooperative home in the vicinity of New York."[85] Sinclair claimed that the "purpose of the Home Colony was to simplify the domestic problem," that is, the desire of middle-class intellectuals and professionals, especially women, to be liberated from the tedious burdens of domestic labor but in a way that did not exploit the poor.[86] Thus, each person could build a home however he or she desired; but, in accord with Gilman's precepts, the homes would not have kitchens or nurseries. Cooking would take place in a central kitchen and childcare in a cooperative children's area. Also in accord with Gilman's tenets, housework in the utopian community was to be carried out on the principles of scientific management. Because applicants for membership in Helicon Hall were screened for their "congeniality"—by which Sinclair meant "whites only" —there was racial and social homogeneity among those who lived in the community. Helicon Hall flourished after its opening on November 1, 1906, only to be destroyed by fire some five months later. Busy with other projects and with his writing, Sinclair never rebuilt the community.[87]

A more sustained experimental community, Free Acres, was established in the spring of 1910 by Bolton Hall, a New York attorney and real-estate developer and a visitor to Helicon Hall. A protégé of Henry George and a correspondent with the Russian novelist and moral thinker Leo Tolstoy, Hall believed that living a simple life in a small cooperative community provided the best opportunity to realize George's single-tax principles. Located on Murphy's Farm, a 160-acre site near a rail station just outside Berkeley Heights, Free Acres originally consisted of a bungalow and campsites, tents, and platforms to which the founders hoped to attract travelers coming to the area from urban centers. According to its constitution, the Free Acres Association was founded "for the study and demonstration of problems of self-government, social progress, and taxation where all shall be mutually helpful and free from all forms of monopoly of natural resources."[88] In furtherance of these principles, Hall mandated that the land be held in trust by the community rather than by individuals.[89]

Through its first decade, Free Acres remained a pioneer settlement where some fifty families lived during the summer months. Their homes were mainly tents or lean-tos, although some structures had fireplaces and indoor plumbing. Classes in arts and crafts, dance, sewing, singing, and drama were taught by residents, who received payment by services in kind. As one of the residents recalled, the community consisted of "free thinkers," most of whom were "unashamedly radicals."[90] Liberation from conventional roles especially attracted women to Free Acres. One female resident, who had previously lived at Helicon Hall, observed in a letter to a friend, "We have so much freedom in the matter of dress and then, everybody lets everybody alone . . . all do as they please."[91] With the onset of the Great Depression, residents began to winterize their modest homes and to live in them year round. But by then, under pressure from new settlers and from the surrounding communities, Free Acres had begun to modify its founding principles.[92]

Like their fellow reformers elsewhere, early twentieth-century social progressives in New Jersey shared a faith in the possibility of ameliorating the worst consequences of modernization. Believing that people are products of their environment, social progressives developed a range of targeted reform programs to improve the lives of immigrants and workers who resided in the Garden State's urban enclaves. Committed to the ideal of cooperation among all members of society, Cornelia Bradford dedicated the settlement house she founded to cooperation with all local agencies on behalf of the "development and expression of the social, civic and moral spirit of the community." [93] Yet, too often the reforms embraced by the social progressives also sought to "uplift" the poorest city dwellers by imposing uniform standards of behavior on a very diverse population. Further, even though the relief and welfare programs run by Whittier House and other settlement houses in New Jersey did make life better for their poor and immigrant neighbors, they did not confront the economic and political system that produced such disparities in the first place. Like the measures advocated by political progressives, the well-intended reforms pursued by the social progressives emanated from mixed motives and produced mixed results. As a result, the progressive program in New Jersey, as elsewhere, proved to be insufficient to address the extensive disparities caused by the economic, political, social, and cultural changes that had been accumulating through the later decades of the nineteenth century.

POST-PROGRESSIVISM

Speaking before the state legislature on January 14, 1913, Woodrow Wilson, now president-elect of the United States, laid out an ambitious reform agenda for New Jersey. In addition to endorsing ratification of the Sixteenth (income tax) and Seventeenth (direct election of senators) Amendments to the U.S. Constitution, Wilson called for a constitutional convention in New Jersey to recommend measures to streamline and democratize the state's government, to make changes in the jury system to reduce political manipulation, and to reform securities trading to discourage fraud and monopoly. Two months later, Wilson's successor, the Democratic president of the state senate, James F. Fielder, was sworn in as acting governor. As the first candidate to be chosen under new primary laws, Fielder was elected in his own right in November 1913. Except for ratification of the federal amendments, few of Wilson's legislative initiatives survived the resurgence of Garden State machine politics and the growing political power of a now conservative-led Republican Party. For his part, once he was settled in the White House, Wilson distanced himself from direct involvement in New Jersey politics.[94]

In New Jersey's 1916 election for governor, Walter E. Edge, the Republican candidate who had been a leader of the New Idea progressives, ran against H. Otto Wittpenn, the former mayor of Jersey City who had been Frank Hague's chief opponent for control of Democratic Party politics in the state. Wittpenn, who lost, might have won the election had he received the level of support usually provided Democratic candidates by the Hudson County machine.[95] During the campaign, Edge promised to lead a more "efficient government with the governor as 'the business manager, the legislature as the board of directors, and the people as the stockholders.'"

But even though he eviscerated the Seven Sisters laws, Edge was no reactionary. In his two years as governor, before being elected to the U.S. Senate, Edge established commissions that led to notable improvements in state institutions, especially the prisons, and successfully guided the New Jersey legislature through such reforms as a franchise tax on public utility corporations.[96]

Edge's 1916 election as governor presaged a pattern that came to dominate New Jersey politics into and beyond the 1920s. The Democratic governors who followed the Republican Edge owed their victories to the political maneuverings of Frank Hague. The Jersey boss was instrumental in securing the governorship in 1919 for his friend and close political ally, Edward I. Edwards, a businessman and bank president. To appeal to traditional Democratic urban ethnic voters in the Garden State, Edwards ran what was called "The Applejack Campaign" based on his opposition to Prohibition. Nevertheless, Edwards was confronted by large Republican majorities in the state legislature, and his initiatives, such as a proposal to reduce trolley fares for urban residents, were rejected.[97]

Frustrated during his one term as governor, Edwards ran for election to the U.S. Senate in 1921 under the slogan "Wine, Women, and Song," and his large margin of victory helped carry Judge George S. Silzer, the Democratic gubernatorial candidate, to victory. In the forefront of New Jersey progressivism early in his political career, Silzer also owed his election to the machinations of Hague. In his inaugural address, Silzer promised "to put government back into the hands of the people" and proposed new protections for labor and stringent regulation of public utilities. However, the Republicans had retained their majorities in the legislature, and Silzer, much like his Democratic predecessor, became known as a "veto governor." In 1925, Silzer was followed into the governor's office by another Hague protégé, A. Harry Moore. Although a long-time friend of Wittpenn, Moore had formed an alliance with Hague during Wittpenn's unsuccessful run for governor in 1916. Because he was able to work more cooperatively than his predecessors with the Republican legislative majorities, Moore helped to secure state jobs for Hague's patronage machine. Hague's string of victories finally came to an end in 1928, when a national Republican landslide propelled Morgan F. Lawson into the governor's chair. But even more than Herbert Hoover's presidency, Lawson's tenure as governor was overwhelmed by the economic crisis of the Great Depression. For his part,

Hague, despite the defeat of his candidates in 1928, continued to control Democratic politics in New Jersey into the late 1940s.[98]

Even as political progressivism began to fade in New Jersey after Wilson's departure in 1913, the reform activism of socially progressive women, both in the state and nationally, persisted into the World War I era and the 1920s as a natural corollary to the women's suffrage movement. Throughout the history of their movement, suffragists insisted that securing the vote was at once an issue of natural rights, a matter of equality for all, and a means by which women, who were by nature more virtuous, compassionate, and nurturing than men, would elevate the moral and political standards of America. Indeed, women in New Jersey who controlled property worth at least £50 had been entitled to vote until the state legislature passed a law in 1807 that restricted voting to "free, white, male" citizens. The movement for universal suffrage quickened in the aftermath of the ratification in 1868 of the Fifteenth Amendment, which enfranchised African American men. The year before, woman suffrage activists met in Vineland to found the New Jersey Woman Suffrage Association (NJWSA). With little progress toward passage of a women's suffrage law through the end of the nineteenth century, women's rights activists in the state joined forces with the state women's club movement to recruit public opinion for suffrage. Among their other goals were to advance women's participation on municipal boards and in such public agencies as state hospitals, to build a state reformatory for women, and to improve women's and children's working conditions.[99]

Two strategies dominated the women's suffrage movement in the early twentieth century. First, under the leadership of Anna Howard Shaw, who had succeeded Susan B. Anthony, the National American Woman Suffrage Association (NAWSA) concentrated on winning suffrage rights on a state-by-state basis. In New Jersey, Lillian Feickert, who had been active in a number of woman's associations, led the NJWSA's state campaign, which resulted in a 1915 public referendum on the vote for women. It was opposed by urban political bosses such as James R. Nugent, the leader of the Essex County Democrats; the brewing industry (many suffragists were also members of the Woman's Christian Temperance Union); and anti-suffrage groups that viewed a woman's direct involvement in politics as "inconsistent with the [domestic] duties of most women." The suffrage amendment was defeated.[100]

The second suffragist strategy concentrated on securing a federal constitutional amendment. Its chief proponent was Alice Paul, who was born in Moorestown in 1885. After personally participating in the more radical and confrontational British suffragist movement, Paul returned to the United States in 1912 and in 1916 founded the National Woman's Party (NWP) to direct the effort for a federal amendment. Two years later, after militant struggles that included mass arrests outside the White House and hunger strikes, President Wilson endorsed a federal suffrage amendment as a necessary war measure. Although opposed to the extreme tactics employed by the NWP, the NJWSA under Feickert worked cooperatively with Paul and, unlike the NAWSA, prioritized suffrage work over war work during World War I. Finally, in 1919, both houses of Congress passed the Nineteenth Amendment, which declared that the right of citizens of the United States to vote could not be abridged on account of sex. Feickert then spearheaded an intense grass-roots effort to win the amendment's ratification in New Jersey. Hague, who was battling Nugent for control of the Democratic Party, became an unlikely ally for ratification, and the state's Democratic Party endorsed the amendment. The NJWSA also secured a pledge of support from the Republican assembly speaker. After the vote on ratification in the New Jersey Assembly was announced, thirty-four in favor, twenty-four against, "silence followed for long seconds, and then the wild, almost hysterical cheers of women reverberated through the halls." New Jersey became the twenty-ninth state to ratify the Nineteenth Amendment.[101]

Lillian Feickert viewed ratification of the Nineteenth Amendment as marking the beginning of a new era in which women voted to elect both men and women candidates who supported passage of favored legislation. In 1920 the New Jersey Republican State Committee selected Feickert to be its vice chairman in charge of organizing Republican women throughout the state. Rejecting the nonpartisan stance of the League of Women Voters (LWV), Feickert, in her letter of resignation as state league treasurer, wrote that with the vote "we should become political workers. . . . I want to see the women well organized in both parties, so that we can work for the measures we believe in by direct methods instead of indirect methods." During the twenties, Feickert also worked with the New Jersey Consumers' League for passage of a night work bill. This legislation would prohibit women from working between the hours of 10:00 PM and 6:00 AM in manufacturing and other businesses.[102]

Founded in 1920 by Carrie Chapman Catt, former president of the NAWSA, the League of Women Voters sought to educate women as voters and to lobby for passage of favored legislation. In New Jersey, the league was led by Agnes Anne Schermerhorn, a former head of the State Federation of Woman's Clubs. In contrast to the equal rights stance taken by women like Feickert, the NJLWV insisted that women would be most effective when working in cooperation with other women to influence male politicians on such "women's issues" as child labor and minimum wage and hours laws. Celebrating the special capacities of women, especially their family consciousness, the league looked to safeguard the rights of working women without jeopardizing a woman's primary role as wife and mother.[103]

In 1923 (and for the next forty-nine years), Alice Paul and the National Woman's Party submitted to the U.S. Congress a "Lucretia Mott" amendment that declared that "Men and women shall have equal rights throughout the United States and every place subject to its jurisdiction."[104] In New Jersey, Mary Philbrook, the attorney who had successfully lobbied for a juvenile court in Newark, led the effort for such an amendment to the state constitution. Insisting that the benefits of industrial reform laws should be shared equally by men and women, the NWP opposed special women's protective legislation like the Night Work Act, which the organization viewed as impeding women from earning a livelihood.[105] Yet most advocates of special industrial legislation were unwilling to risk the hard-won protections that these laws offered working women, and as a result, they opposed equal rights amendments.

Some four-fifths of New Jersey suffragists, most of whom were white, native born, middle or upper class, and Protestant, supported the Republican Party in the 1920s. By 1922 the New Jersey Women's Republican Club (NJWRC), which had been founded by Feickert, had some 60,000 members. But Feickert's outspoken lobbying for protective legislation for women and for the strict enforcement of Prohibition led to her falling out with Republican leaders, who worked for her defeat when she ran for reelection in 1925 to the party's state committee. Unlike the Republicans, the Democratic Party in New Jersey did not create any special local or state organizations for women. Instead, they recruited women to work for the party through regular party clubs or women's auxiliaries. In 1924, supported by her patron Frank Hague, Mary T. Norton became the first New Jersey woman elected to the U.S. Congress and the first woman Democrat in the

House of Representatives. Still, by the mid-1920s, many female political activists had become disenchanted. Male politicians gave at best grudging support to their special legislation, and women found themselves largely isolated from the political power establishment of either party. As a clear measure of her disaffection, Feickert, while still president of the NJWRC, called for the defeat of any Republican legislator who did not vote to pass women's bills.[106]

For progressivism, the 1920s proved to be a time of retrenchment in the nation and state. Controlled by the Hague machine, the Democratic Party seemed most interested in assuring that a steady flow of patronage jobs would keep the machinery well oiled. Republicans, taking their cues from national party leaders, celebrated their ties to big business. Despite some successes, such as the Night Work Act (and reformers were divided over this law), progressive reform faded as an active political force. Yet Whittier House continued to serve the needs of Jersey City's community, and both the New Jersey League of Women Voters and the State Federation of Women's Clubs grew in membership over the decade. After the economy crashed in 1929 and the New Deal arrived four years later, reformers, many of whom had roots in the Progressive Era, again actively sought the means to reconcile the needs of Americans with the problems that resulted from modern society.

ACKNOWLEDGMENTS

I would like to acknowledge the generous support of Jules Plangere and to recognize him for his contributions to the history of New Jersey.

NOTES

1. Ella Handen, "Cornelia Foster Bradford," in *Past and Promise: Lives of New Jersey Women*, ed. Joan N. Burstyn et al. (Metuchen, N.J.: Scarecrow Press, 1990), 111.

2. Carmela Ascolese Karnoutsos, *New Jersey Women: A History of Their Status, Roles, and Images* (Trenton: New Jersey Historical Commission, 1997), 72.

3. *New York Times*, January 26, 1894.

4. Eric Foner, *Give Me Liberty! An American History*, 2nd ed., vol. 2 (New York: W. W. Norton, 2009), 638.

5. Daniel T. Rodgers, "In Search of Progressivism," *Reviews in American History* 10 (December 1982): 113–132; Richard L. McCormick, *The Party Period and Public Policy:*

American Politics from the Age of Jackson to the Progressive Era (New York: Oxford University Press, 1986), 263–288.

6. John F. Reynolds, *Testing Democracy: Electoral Behavior and Progressive Reform in New Jersey, 1880–1920* (Chapel Hill: University of North Carolina Press, 1988), 6.

7. Foner, *Give Me Liberty!* 638–639; Reynolds, *Testing Democracy*, 125; McCormick, *The Party Period and Public Policy*, 281.

8. Thomas Fleming, *New Jersey: A History* (New York: W. W. Norton, 1984), 126.

9. Paul A. Stellhorn and Michael J. Birkner, eds., *The Governors of New Jersey, 1664–1974* (Trenton: New Jersey Historical Commission, 1982), 175; John E. Bebout and Ronald J. Grele, *Where Cities Meet: The Urbanization of New Jersey* (Princeton: D. Van Nostrand, 1964), 43; *New Jersey Population Trends, 1790 to 2000*, New Jersey State Data Center Publications, http://lwd.dol.state.nj.us/labor/lpa/census/2kpub/njsdcp3.pdf: 23 (accessed 9/4/2011).

10. Reynolds, *Testing Democracy*, 8, 10–11.

11. Bebout and Grele, *Where Cities Meet*, 42.

12. Reynolds, *Testing Democracy*, 7.

13. Bebout and Grele, *Where Cities Meet*, 32–33, 45.

14. McCormick, *The Party Period and Public Policy*, 247.

15. Morton J. Horwitz, *The Transformation of American Law, 1870–1960: The Crisis of Legal Orthodoxy* (New York: Oxford University Press, 1992), 83–85.

16. Theodore H. Davis Jr., "Corporate Privileges for the Public Benefit: The Progressive Federal Incorporation Movement and the Modern Regulatory State," *Virginia Law Review* 77 (April 1991): 603, 616, 618.

17. Ransom E. Noble Jr., *New Jersey Progressivism Before Wilson* (Princeton: Princeton University Press, 1946): 5; Maxine N. Lurie, ed., *A New Jersey Anthology* (New Brunswick: Rutgers University Press, 2002), 23.

18. Christopher Grandy, "New Jersey Chartermongering, 1875–1929," *Journal of Economic History* 49 (September 1989): 677.

19. Eugene M. Tobin, "In Pursuit of Equal Taxation: Jersey City's Struggle Against Corporate Arrogance and Tax-Dodging by the Railroad Trust," *American Journal of Economics and Sociology* 34 (April 1975): 214.

20. Lincoln Steffens, "New Jersey: A Traitor State," Part 1, *McClure's Magazine* 24 (November 1904–April 1905): 649–664; Part 2, 25 (May 1905–October 1905): 41–55.

21. Arthur S. Link, *Wilson: The Road to the White House* (Princeton: Princeton University Press, 1947), 133–134; Bebout and Grele, *Where Cities Meet*, 41.

22. Fleming, *New Jersey*, 149.

23. Bebout and Grele, *Where Cities Meet*, 41–42; Link, *Wilson*, 140.

24. Noble, *New Jersey Progressivism before Wilson*, 4–11.

25. Eugene M. Tobin, " 'Engines of Salvation' or 'Smoking Black Devils': Jersey City Reformers and the Railroads, 1902–1908," in *The Age of Urban Reform: New Perspectives on the Progressive Era*, ed. Michael H. Ebner and Eugene M. Tobin (Port Washington, N.Y.: Kennikat Press, 1977), 144.

26. Stellhorn and Birkner, eds., *Governors of New Jersey*, 175.

27. Reynolds, *Testing Democracy*, 170.

28. Eugene M. Tobin, "The Progressive as Politician: Jersey City, 1896–1907," *NJH* 91 (Spring 1973): 18–19; Link, *Wilson*, 134–135, Noble, *New Jersey Progressivism before Wilson*, 65–83.

29. Noble, *New Jersey Progressivism before Wilson*, 15–16.

30. Tobin, "In Pursuit of Equal Taxation," 214–215.

31. Ransom E. Noble Jr., "George L. Record's Struggle for Economic Democracy," *American Journal of Economics and Sociology* 10 (October 1950): 73.

32. Eugene Tobin, quoted in Carmela Karnoutsos, "Jersey City Past and Present: Mark M. Fagan 1869–1955," http://www.njcu.edu/programs/jchistory/pages/F_Pages/Fagan_Mark.htm : 1–3 (accessed 1/12/2011).

33. Noble, *New Jersey Progressivism before Wilson*, 19.

34. Tobin, "In Pursuit of Equal Taxation," 215.

35. Karnoutsos, "Jersey City Past and Present," 4.

36. Tobin, "The Progressive as Politician," 17.

37. Tobin, "In Pursuit of Equal Taxation," 218.

38. Noble, *New Jersey Progressivism before Wilson*, 48–64.

39. Tobin, "The Progressive as Politician," 18.

40. Link, *Wilson*, 137; Tobin, "The Progressive as Politician," 19.

41. Tobin, "The Progressive as Politician," 21.

42. Martin Paulsson, *The Social Anxieties of Progressive Reform: Atlantic City, 1854–1920* (New York: New York University Press, 1994), 74.

43. Tobin, "The Progressive as Politician," 18–23.

44. Noble, *New Jersey Progressivism before Wilson*, 130–153; Link, *Wilson*, 130–140.

45. Link, *Wilson*, 140–143; W. Barksdale Maynard, *Woodrow Wilson: Princeton to the Presidency* (New Haven: Yale University Press, 2008); Robert Dallek, "Woodrow Wilson, Politician," *Wilson Quarterly* 15 (1991): 109–110.

46. Link, *Wilson*, 143; see also 140–172.

47. Ibid., 189–195.

48. Reynolds, *Testing Democracy*, 138–141.

49. Link, *Wilson*, 239–240.

50. Reynolds, *Testing Democracy*, 142–159.

51. Link, *Wilson*, 261–263.

52. Leonard W. Levy, *The Law of the Commonwealth and Chief Justice Shaw* (New York: Oxford University Press, 1957), 169; Link, *Wilson*, 263–265.

53. Eugene. M. Tobin, "The Commission Plan in Jersey City, 1911–1917: The Ambiguity of Municipal Reform in the Progressive Era," in *Cities of the Garden State: Essays in the Urban and Suburban History of New Jersey*, ed. Joel Schwartz and Daniel Prosser (Dubuque, Iowa: Kendall/Hunt Publishing Company, 1977), 72–84.

54. Tobin, "Commission Plan in Jersey City," 75–81; Link, *Wilson*, 265–267; Fleming, *New Jersey*, 173–174.

55. Tobin, "Commission Plan in Jersey City," 72–84; Carmela Karnoutsos, "Jersey

City Past and Present: Frank Hague, 1876–1956," http://www.njcu.edu/Programs/jchistory/Pages/H_Pages/Hague_Frank.htm.

56. Matthew Taylor Rafferty, "Political Ethics and Public Style in the Early Career of Jersey City's Frank Hague," *NJH* 124 (2009): 29.

57. Tobin, "Commission Plan in Jersey City," 72–84; Karnoutsos, "Jersey City Past and Present: Frank Hague," 1–9.

58. Grandy, "New Jersey Chartermongering," 687–689; Stellhorn and Birkner, eds., *Governors*, 187.

59. Richard L. McCormick, "The Discovery that Business Corrupts Politics: A Reappraisal of the Origins of Progressivism," *American Historical Review* 86 (April 1981): 247–248.

60. Reynolds, *Testing Democracy*, 173.

61. Jane Addams, *Twenty Years at Hull-House*, ed. Victoria Bissell Brown (Boston: Bedford/St. Martin's, 1999), 95.

62. Karnoutsos, "Jersey City Past and Present: Mark Fagan," 3; Tobin, "The Progressive as Politician," 12.

63. Eugene M. Tobin, "The Progressive as Humanitarian: Jersey City's Search for Social Justice, 1890–1917," *NJH* 93 (1975): 83–84.

64. Handen, "Cornelia Foster Bradford," 120.

65. Cornelia F. Bradford, "The Settlement Movement in New Jersey," *New Jersey Review of Charities and Corrections* 10 (April 1912): 23–24; Tobin, "The Progressive as Humanitarian," 79.

66. Tobin, "The Progressive as Humanitarian," 97–98.

67. Cornelia F. Bradford, "For Jersey City's Social Uplift: Life at Whittier House," *The Commons* 10 (February 1905): 102.

68. McCormick, *The Party Period and Public Policy*, 280–282.

69. New Jersey History Partnerships, "Cornelia Bradford's Report on Whittier House Activities in 1907," http://www.njhistorypartnership.org/proRef/munRef/pdf/mun RefDoc1.pdf (accessed 8/29/2011).

70. Ibid., 2.

71. Bradford, "Settlement Movement in New Jersey," 24.

72. Ibid.

73. Jeannette D. Kahlenberg, "Mary Buell Sayles," in Burstyn, ed., *Past and Promise*, 190.

74. Ella Handen, "In Liberty's Shadow: Cornelia Bradford and Whittier House," *NJH* 100 (1982): 57.

75. Tobin, "The Progressive as Humanitarian," 83.

76. Manfred J. Waserman, "Henry L. Coit and the Certified Milk Movement in the Development of Modern Pediatrics," *Bulletin of the History of Medicine* 46 (1972): 359–367, 375.

77. Stuart Galishoff, *Safeguarding the Public Health: Newark, 1895–1918* (Westport, Conn.: Greenwood Press, 1975), 100–101.

78. Tobin, "The Progressive as Humanitarian," 95.

79. *New York Times,* August 11, 1903.

80. Handen, "In Liberty's Shadow," 58; Arthur Sargent Field, "The Child Labor Policy of New Jersey," *American Economic Association Quarterly* 11 (1910): 415.

81. Noble, *New Jersey Progressivism before Wilson,* 122–124.

82. Tobin, "The Progressive as Humanitarian," 85–87.

83. Barbara Petrick, *Mary Philbrook: The Radical Feminist in New Jersey* (Trenton: New Jersey Historical Commission, 1981), 18–19.

84. Lawrence Kaplan, "A Utopia during the Progressive Era: The Helicon Home Colony, 1906–1907," *American Studies* 25 (1984): 59–64; Linda Simon, "Socialism at Home: The Case of Upton Sinclair," *NJH* 107 (1989): 49–57; Perdita Buchan, *"Utopia," New Jersey: Travels in the Nearest Eden* (New Brunswick: Rutgers University Press, 2007), 5–11.

85. Buchan, *Utopia,* 8.

86. Simon, "Socialism at Home," 52.

87. Kaplan, "A Utopia during the Progressive Era," 60–63, 70–71; Buchan, *Utopia,* 20–25.

88. Martin A. Biebaum, "Free Acres: Bolton Hall's Single-Tax Experimental Community," *NJH* 102 (1984): 44–45.

89. Biebaum, "Free Acres," 37–46; Buchan, *Utopia,* 28–34.

90. Biebaum, "Free Acres," 51.

91. Buchan, *Utopia,* 38.

92. Biebaum, "Free Acres," 46–63.

93. Bradford, "Settlement Movement in New Jersey," 23.

94. John Milton Cooper Jr., *Woodrow Wilson: A Biography* (New York: Vintage Books, 2009), 188–189; Benjamin R. Bede, "Fielder, James Fairman," in *Encyclopedia of New Jersey,* ed. Maxine N. Lurie and Marc Mappen (New Brunswick: Rutgers University Press, 2004), 272–273; Stellhorn and Birkner, eds., *Governors,* 184.

95. Fleming, *New Jersey,* 175.

96. Stellhorn and Birkner, eds., *Governors,* 187–189.

97. Ibid., 190–193; Fleming, *New Jersey,* 173–175.

98. Stellhorn and Birkner, eds., *Governors,* 194–201; Fleming, *New Jersey,* 178–182.

99. Delight Wing Dodyk, "Woman Suffrage," in Lurie and Mappen, eds., *Encyclopedia of New Jersey,* 881–882.

100. New Jersey Women's History, "Women Opposed to Suffrage" (http://www.nj womenshistory.org/Period_4/antisuffrage.htm); Sylvia Strauss, "The Passage of Woman Suffrage in New Jersey, 1911–1920," *NJH* (1993): 20–30.

101. Strauss, "The Passage of Woman Suffrage," 30–35.

102. Felice D. Gordon, "Lillian Ford Feickert, 1877–1945," in Burstyn et al., eds., *Past and Promise,* 136–137.

103. Karnoutsos, *New Jersey Women,* 87–88.

104. Amelia Fry and Sheila Cowing, "Alice Stokes Paul, 1885–1977," in Burstyn et al., eds., *Past and Promise,* 179; Alice Kessler-Harris, *Out to Work: A History of Wage-Earning Women in the United States* (New York: Oxford University Press, 1982), 206.

105. Kessler-Harris, *Out to Work,* 206.

106. Felice D. Gordon, *After Winning: The Legacy of the New Jersey Suffragists, 1920–1947* (New Brunswick: Rutgers University Press, 1986); Felice D. Gordon, "After Winning: The New Jersey Suffragists in the Political Parties, 1920–30," *NJH* 101 (1983): 20–21; Karnoutsos, *New Jersey Women*, 90; Gordon, "Lillian Ford Feickert," 137.

9 · DEPRESSION AND WAR

G. KURT PIEHLER

The Great Depression and World War II played a pivotal role in transforming New Jersey's political, economic, and social contours. With the state incapable of coping with the impact of the Great Depression alone, the federal government became increasingly involved in the affairs of New Jersey residents. During the war effort, New Jersey's industrial and agricultural sectors played a crucial role. World War II brought the state full employment, but also propelled a movement to restructure the state government through a new constitution in the immediate postwar era.[1]

THE DEPRESSION

Although historians generally acknowledge a number of structural causes, the collapse of stock market prices on the New York Stock Exchange in October 1929 precipitated this unprecedented economic decline. As capital dried up and consumer demand faltered, industrial expansion ground to a halt and factories started to close throughout the state and nation. Farmers suffered, too, as the prices of agricultural products plummeted. For local governments heavily dependent on property taxes to fund municipal services, unemployment and declining home prices led to a steep drop in revenue at the very time demands for relief soared.

New Jersey's government was ill prepared to cope with the magnitude of the Great Depression. Under the constitution of 1844, the governor had limited powers and served for only three years. In 1929, the state government levied neither income nor sales taxes and relied primarily on corporate taxes and a range of excise taxes and fees for revenue. Expenditures for services were modest and largely confined to supporting the criminal justice system, maintaining state highways, operating state institutions for the mentally ill and disabled, and providing a network of state parks and forests. Local governments bore most of the burden for education and social welfare spending, with the state providing only modest support. Rutgers University received minimal state funds and remained largely autonomous; the state's most significant support for higher education centered on maintaining teacher's colleges in Jersey City, Montclair, Paterson, Trenton, Newark, and Glassboro.

Throughout the Depression New Jersey remained fractured politically and culturally. The largest rifts separated the interests of its ethnically diverse industrial urban centers and its rural counties. The single most powerful figure in New Jersey was Frank Hague, the long-term mayor of Jersey City and Hudson County political boss. The Great Depression and the New Deal served to strengthen Hague's iron grip over Hudson County and the statewide Democratic Party. His power in state politics however was often checked by Republicans, who dominated the state senate and statewide races for governor and United States senator. To maintain political power and the graft that followed, Hague often struck deals with Republicans in the state senate and with other GOP officeholders, most notably Governor Harold G. Hoffman. Moreover, Hague had little compunction about turning against Democrats who threatened his interests, including Governor Charles Edison.

Republicans benefited from the economic prosperity of the 1920s. Herbert Hoover had little difficulty capturing the state's Electoral College votes in 1928. The following year Republican Morgan Larson, an engineer and former state senate majority leader, won election as governor, and his party controlled both houses of the legislature. In his campaign, Larson argued for modernizing New Jersey's transportation network and protecting the state's supplies of drinking water. During his term in office, Larson faced enormous divisions within his own party and had few notable achievements, except for negotiating an agreement with New York Governor Franklin D. Roosevelt to begin construction of the Lincoln Tunnel, the second trans-Hudson vehicular tunnel linking New Jersey with Manhattan.

It would be Larson's misfortune to preside over a deteriorating economic situation that caused widespread misery throughout the state .

Initially, the stock market crash affected only overleveraged sectors of the economy. With the decline of business confidence, banks and investors proved less willing to extend new loans or refinance existing ones. Construction was one of the first industries to struggle; investors who had purchased tracts of land for future development in places such as Delaware (Cherry Hill) and Voorhees in Camden County lost them for nonpayment of property taxes.[2] Scores of municipalities in Bergen County had borrowed heavily to fund sewers, schools, and roads during the building boom of the 1920s. By March 1933, when real estate prices collapsed and delinquency rates on taxes soared, even well-healed communities such as Dumont had to default on tax obligations to the Bergen County government and drastically cut municipal spending.[3]

Fear and the lack of an adequate safety net accelerated the steady economic deterioration. People who had jobs cut back on their discretionary spending, leading businesses to reduce production and wages. For instance, wages for silk workers in Paterson fell 40 percent from 1929 to 1933, and employment remained erratic as mills constantly closed during slack periods. Private charities and local governments provided relief for the unemployed, but by 1931 they were overwhelmed. As conditions worsened, scores of people became homeless and struggled to find food. When asked by a social worker how she fed her family, one Newark mother in early 1931 confessed that she relied on the kindness of neighbors: "I used to sit and wonder if the people next door would send in something after they'd finished eating. Sometimes they would and other times they would have nothing left and we wouldn't eat. I'd tell the kid to drink lots of water and we'd wait for the next meal."[4] Roy Reisert, who grew up in Highland Park during the 1930s, remembered how his father lost his home and endured declining wages and bouts of unemployment. Sixty years later, reflecting on his family's struggles, he recalled the mental toll that the worsening economy took on the families he knew:

> [A] lot of my friends' fathers committed suicide. I know one very prominent fellow, who I went around with, his father was a banker in New York and he went down in the cellar and blew his head off with a shotgun. . . . Then, there were other young boys that I went to school with, my age, whose fathers lost

everything. . . . This one kid hanged himself in his garage on Abbot Street there in Highland Park, a young boy who was depressed because he couldn't go to the seashore that summer. His father lost his business and . . . his summer cottage down at the shore. He was just distraught and hanged himself.[5]

One clear sign of the worsening impact was the collapse in milk prices due to diminishing demand; economists had previously thought demand for milk was inelastic. In major cities, the homeless and unemployed slept in public parks and erected shantytowns on public land and abandoned industrial sites, which soon earned the derisive nickname of Hoovervilles. In the harsh winters, the floors of police stations served as a shelter of last resort.

Scores of businesses and more than 140 New Jersey banks failed, leaving in their wake unpaid bills and depositors who lost their life savings in an era before the Federal Deposit Insurance Corporation guaranteed individual deposits. Municipalities and county governments saw their revenues plunge as demand for social services soared: 28 percent of Newark and Camden homeowners could not pay their taxes in 1931; in Paterson, the figure was 38 percent in 1932. Municipalities laid off public workers, cut the pay of their remaining employees, and even resorted to paying their workers scrip (essentially an IOU); at the same time, they begged investors to continue purchasing bonds to cover their deficits.[6] The staggering rate of unemployment prodded city officials in Newark to abandon mechanized equipment and have the unemployed dig tunnels by hand for the planned subway line. To cope with this unprecedented misery, Governor Larson established and won legislative approval in 1931 for the State Emergency Relief Administration, which provided assistance to local and county governments to meet the needs of more than 300,000 unemployed New Jerseyans. This program, funded by diverting monies from highway construction and selling the bridges over the Delaware River, made matching grants to municipalities for both work and direct relief. Although the Relief Administration preserved local autonomy, it had the authority to assume complete control of relief efforts where a municipality failed to raise sufficient matching funds. By June 1932, the Relief Administration had taken charge of providing relief in 128 municipalities.

As the party in power, Republicans were blamed for the Great Depression. In the 1931 gubernatorial race, A. Harry Moore, a protégé of the Hague machine, handily beat Camden County Republican leader and U.S. Senator David Baird Jr. As governor, Moore embraced the expansion of public relief and sought to channel more government aid to struggling municipalities. Although Moore was unsuccessful in his efforts to enact a state sales or income tax, he remained fiscally conservative and pruned state spending in response to falling tax receipts. When he took office in 1931, state expenditures stood at $34.5 million; by the time he left in 1934, they had fallen to $20.7 million.[7]

At the Democratic National Convention in 1932, Hague served as Al Smith's floor manager and did all he could do to deprive New York Governor Franklin D. Roosevelt of the party's nomination. Once FDR secured the nomination, however, Hague quickly mended fences with James Farley, FDR's campaign manager, and promised to host an enormous rally for the governor. In August 1932 more than 100,000 spectators converged on Sea Girt, where FDR promised to end Prohibition. Although Hague would rise to become vice chairman of the Democratic National Committee his relationship with FDR was never close. Ideologically, the two differed on a wide range of issues, most notably over the influence of organized labor in the Democratic Party. At the same time, FDR treaded carefully with Hague because any chance of carrying New Jersey required winning Hudson County by a large margin.[8]

Despite Hoover's growing unpopularity, many rural New Jersey counties and suburban towns stayed loyal to the GOP. FDR's statewide margin of victory was narrow, and Republicans continued to hold a majority of New Jersey's seats in the U.S. House of Representatives. Although Roosevelt's vote totals improved in 1936, many rural and suburban counties did not change their allegiance, and the Democrats never captured the rural-controlled state senate. Frank Hague continued to dominate the state Democratic Party; even when Democrats gained control of Newark's city government in the 1930s, the city and Essex County Democratic leaders remained in Hague's shadow. In Atlantic City and County, Republicans dominated under the leadership of Enoch L. Johnson, who made a fortune from kickbacks from brothels, gambling joints, and, during Prohibition, speakeasies.[9]

When Franklin D. Roosevelt assumed office on March 4, 1933, fears of total economic collapse were so pervasive that some states, including New Jersey, had already declared a bank holiday effective that day. Roosevelt suspended all banking transactions nationwide on March 6, and Congress passed the Emergency Banking Act on March 9. New Jersey banks remained closed until federal officials determined which ones could be saved and which had to be liquidated. The depth of the collapse meant that even many traditional opponents of government intervention in the economy favored a more activist role for the federal and state governments.

Through wide-ranging legislation, termed the "New Deal," President Roosevelt and the Congress fundamentally reordered the role of the federal government and its relationship with state and local governments as well as with individual citizens. In addition to emergency legislation to stabilize the banking system, FDR sought a partnership between business and government to regulate various sectors of the economy. Under the National Recovery Administration (NRA), industries were allowed to write codes that established prices, wages, and a host of other matters to promote fair competition. Businesses complying with the NRA were entitled to display a poster with the logo of the "Blue Eagle" and the motto, "We Do Our Part." New Jersey followed the federal government and established a state version of NRA.[10]

Because a significant portion of New Jersey's agricultural sector was devoted to truck farming for nearby urban centers, its farmers fared better than those in states dependent upon the production of cotton, wheat, and hogs. Nevertheless, dairy farmers faced a dramatic fall-off in milk prices as the Depression worsened. In 1932 the state legislature enacted a system of regulations that promoted higher safety standards and established minimum prices for milk. Although these state measures enjoyed bipartisan support, New Jersey's two Republican U.S. senators in 1933 opposed the Roosevelt administration's Agricultural Adjustment Acts, which attempted to balance supply and demand for certain commodities, including milk. New Jersey state officials and dairy farmers objected to federal efforts to regulate the interstate sale of milk, which limited the ability of the New Jersey Milk Control Board to set milk prices.[11]

The New Deal saved many of New Jersey's residents from starvation and homelessness. In 1933 Congress established the Federal Emergency Relief Administration (FERA) and provided substantial support for relief until the enactment of the Social Security Act of 1935. In 1935 the state received $33 million from FERA, which covered 75 percent of the costs of emergency relief. Moreover, FERA grants encouraged local and county relief offices to employ social workers and take other measures to professionalize the delivery of welfare services.[12] For the able-bodied, the Public Works Administration (PWA) and the Civil Works Administration (CWA), both established in 1933, represented the first federal programs to put large numbers of the unemployed to work. Federal public works spending, though generous, required matching grants from local and state governments. In the case of the PWA, administered by Secretary of the Interior Harold Ickes, projects were generally contracted out to private firms and focused on permanent infrastructure projects. The CWA, administered by FDR's close advisor Harry Hopkins, was designed to get America through the winter of 1933–1934 and employed scores of New Jersey residents on a range of temporary projects.

One of the Roosevelt administration's earliest achievements was the successful repeal of Prohibition. Although many rural areas in New Jersey with strong Protestant populations supported temperance, urban residents, especially the large German and Irish communities, had never supported the ban on alcohol. Moreover, Prohibition had fostered the rise of organized crime, and the Jersey Shore offered an ideal haven for smugglers. Most localities quickly permitted the sale of alcoholic beverages, with bars and taverns springing up throughout the state, though holdouts like Ocean Grove refused to sanction the sale of liquor within municipal boundaries. Legalization of alcohol sales did not deter major crime organizations, which simply redoubled their efforts in gambling, prostitution, loan sharking, and labor racketeering.

As the economy stabilized and fears of total collapse eased, conservatives in both parties increasingly challenged many aspects of the New Deal. In the 1934 midterm elections, Democrats did exceedingly well nationally, but not necessarily in New Jersey. Although Democratic Governor H. Harry Moore was elected to the U.S. Senate, his successor in the statehouse was Republican Harold Hoffman. In 1935 the U.S. Supreme Court declared the National Recovery Administration and the Agricultural Adjustment Acts unconstitutional and forced the Roosevelt administration to develop alternative initiatives to combat the lingering Depression. Unemployment remained high, and pressure from the left demanded greater action on behalf of unemployed workers and the dispossessed.

In 1935 the New Deal took a new direction with significant implications for New Jersey. Bowing to the need for greater efforts to aid the unemployed, FDR created a permanent public works agency, the Works Progress Administration (WPA, renamed in 1939 as the Works Project Administration), overseen by Harry Hopkins. By 1936, 120,000 New Jersey residents were working for this agency. In contrast to their reaction to other New Deal initiatives, Hague and many conservative Democrats in the state embraced this program. In order to court favor with Hague, Hopkins even appointed one of his allies, William H. J. Ely, as state director of this agency, which opened up endless opportunities for the Hudson County boss to bestow patronage on supporters throughout the state. Moreover, Hudson County received funding for scores of construction projects, including Roosevelt Stadium and a massive medical center in Jersey City that Hague used to bolster his support among poor and working-class constituencies.[13]

As governor, Harold Hoffman alienated many members of his own party by allying with Hague on a number of issues, the most important of which was the state's first broad-based tax, a sales tax. Enactment of the tax produced a storm of public condemnation that led Hoffman to support its repeal after only a few months in operation. Without the tax, the state government continued to struggle to assist municipalities and individuals impoverished by the Depression.

In 1936, lacking adequate funds, Hoffman and the state legislature ended the Emergency Relief Administration and returned principal responsibility for relief to municipal governments. Hoffman's actions received considerable support from conservative leaders in both parties, including Hague. Although the state established a new agency, the State Financial Assistance Program, set minimum standards for relief payments, and supplied state funds to pay for them, municipalities took full responsibility for administering the program and had the option of offering more generous benefits. Social workers condemned the return of relief administration to local politicians and feared many towns would trim benefits. To protest these actions, workers belonging to a number of leftist organizations seized control of the state assembly chambers in Trenton for nine days before disbursing peacefully. Nationally, New Jersey's actions received widespread condemnation in the liberal press and among social work organizations.

While serving in the U.S. Senate, A. Harry Moore broke with FDR on a number of key elements of the New Deal. He was the only Democrat to vote against the Social Security Act, declaring that old-age pensions would "take all the romance out of life" and essentially create a nanny state. Although he voted for the National Labor Relations Act, he opposed the Public Utilities Act and Roosevelt's plan to expand the U.S. Supreme Court. In 1937 Moore, at Hague's behest, ran for a third term as New Jersey's governor in an election that was widely seen as a repudiation of Hoffman's tenure. The Reverend Lester Clee of Essex County won the Republican Party nomination with the support of Arthur Vanderbilt's Clean Government Republicans. In a hotly contested election, Clee and his supporters challenged Moore's narrow victory and charged the Hague organization with massive vote fraud in Hudson County. In response to a series of investigations by state legislative leaders and federal officials, Hudson County officials ignored subpoenas to turn over election board records and eventually destroyed key evidence.

Although the state government reduced its role in providing and administering relief, in other areas it increased its power over municipal affairs. As revenues collapsed during the 1930s, business interests pressured many communities to rein in spending by refusing to purchase municipal bonds. Business interests working in conjunction with Arthur Vanderbilt's Clean Government Republicans commissioned a team of Princeton University professors to examine and make recommendations regarding municipal finances and oversight. In their report, the Princeton panel of experts called for greater statewide supervision of municipal spending through a new Department of Municipal Affairs, and Vanderbilt managed to push the bulk of these recommendations through the state legislature.

Hague's grip on state power was strengthened during the 1930s. Controlling all levels of local government in Hudson County, he routinely harassed and marginalized his local opponents, but he did not rely solely on strong-arm tactics. Rhetorically, Hague gave voice to the urban ethnic communities concentrated in New Jersey's cities, especially in Hudson County. Even before the New Deal, the Hague regime had a reputation for aiding poorer residents, especially at election time. A large city and county payroll rewarded supporters, and employees were expected to contribute to the organization. To pay for the patronage that sustained the organization, Jersey City and Hudson County had one of the highest property taxes in the nation.

One of the most significant breaks between Hague and the Roosevelt administration concerned the government's attitude toward organized labor. Increased labor strife had been a hallmark of the decade both in New Jersey and nationally. Workers became emboldened by the guarantee in the

NRA statute that trade unions had the right to organize and bargain collectively. Many New Jersey businesses resisted by encouraging the formation of company or local unions that remained unaffiliated with national organizations. When workers did strike, businesses generally sought to counter union pressure by refusing to bargain and by replacing picketing workers with "scab" workers. Businesses spent significant sums infiltrating labor organizations and protecting strikebreakers, often hiring private detective agencies. They could count on New Jersey's Chancery Court to issue injunctions against striking workers as well.

The increased militancy produced a fissure in the labor movement nationally and in New Jersey. The American Federation of Labor (AFL) traditionally focused on organizing skilled craftsmen, especially in the construction business; with the exception of the garment industry, it largely ignored mass production workers in steel, chemicals, automobiles, and rubber. At the 1935 national convention of the AFL, held at Atlantic City, United Mine Worker President John L. Lewis defiantly quit the labor organization, though not before engaging in a fistfight with a major opponent. Lewis formed the Committee (later Congress) of Industrial Organizations (CIO), which made a number of gains in organizing large factories, most notably in Michigan, where the United Auto Workers succeeded in winning contracts by employing sit-down strikes.

In 1935 the Roosevelt administration supported the passage of the National Labor Relations Act, which offered new protections for the right of workers to organize and establish unions through federally supervised elections. This act also stated that workers could not be fired for exercising their right to join a union. By this time, Hague had turned against organized labor in an effort to lure big business to Hudson County with the promise of a docile labor force. During his early years in power, Hague had permitted AFL-affiliated unions a presence in the construction industry and on the docks. In the late 1930s he declared open war on the CIO and attracted national attention for his efforts to crush organizing efforts in Hudson County with his willingness to use the police to suppress free speech.

Hague also wanted to ensure that the CIO would not challenge his control over the state's Democratic Party. Within Hudson County, Hague virtually crushed organized labor in the 1930s, even the more conservative AFL unions. During the construction of the Pulaski Skyway, Hague used local police to thwart efforts to disrupt recruitment of non-unionized labor.[14]

When Harry Bridges sought to bring longshoremen into his International Longshore and Warehouse Union (ILWU), Hague drove him out of the city. In 1937, CIO organizers in Hudson County were arrested when they tried to assemble or distribute literature. Hague and state Democrats even dropped their traditional demand to deprive the Chancery Court of the power to issue injunctions against striking workers and joined Republicans in embracing the use of the courts to rein in the power of organized labor.

Allies of organized labor and advocates of free speech, most notably Socialist Party leader Norman Thomas, descended on Jersey City to challenge Hague, only to find themselves harassed and deported. On May Day 1938, while attempting to speak at Journal Square in Jersey City, Thomas was quickly taken into custody by local police and sent back to Manhattan on a ferry. He returned to Jersey City by Trans-Hudson Railway later the same day and gave a statement to the *Jersey Observer* at its offices, after which he was again deported to Manhattan. Hague even enlisted the help of a reputed crime boss to disrupt a rally Thomas organized in nearby Newark. As he attempted to speak, Thomas faced a barrage of eggs and physical assaults on his supporters while the Newark police sat idly by. Hague's actions generated a wave of protests in editorial pages across the nation, letters poured into the White House,[15] and the U.S. Justice Department and Congress pressed for action. But FDR remained undecided on how to proceed.

Subsequently, the American Civil Liberties Union challenged Hague's actions in federal court, claiming they represented an abridgement of the constitutional rights of speech and assembly. In 1939, in *Hague v. CIO*, the U.S. Supreme Court affirmed the right of union members to gather and distribute literature in public streets and parks. This case set an important legal precedent for strengthening the application of the First Amendment to individual citizens and groups. In response, Jersey City passed a free speech ordinance and allowed a CIO rally to proceed without attack in July 1939.

Hague was not alone in his attempts to squash organized labor. The Radio Corporation of America (RCA) relied on local police in Camden to harass and arrest strikers and on judges to meet out harsh punishments. In a struggle that lasted two years, RCA in 1937 refused to sign a contract with the United Electrical Workers and sought to break the strike by relying upon replacement workers. Ultimately, the support of organized labor from outside the state and the protections afforded by the National Labor Relations Act forced the company to negotiate. Even as RCA bowed to pressure to sign a contract, it began to shift jobs to areas of the country that it perceived to be less receptive to unionization.[16]

Sit-down strikes proved to be a potent tactic for the CIO and a widely used one in the 1930s. Its success depended not only upon the dedication of workers but also upon the willingness of government officials to forgo force to dislodge strikers. In the case of New Jersey, Republican Governor Hoffman publicly proclaimed that he would not tolerate such strikes. In spring 1937 Hoffman sent in the state police to quash a CIO-led strike against Thermoid Company in Trenton, even though workers were not sitting down on the job. In the end, divisions within the labor movement, the fierce resistance of the business community, and the hostility of many state and local officials meant that organized workers in New Jersey made few gains. In 1939 most major industrial states, including New York and Pennsylvania, had a higher percentage of workers unionized.[17]

Despite Frank Hague's conservatism and virulent opposition to much of the New Deal, Hudson County sent the first female member to the U.S. House of Representatives who was elected in her own right and not succeeding her husband. Over the course of her career, from 1929 to 1951, Mary Teresa Norton chaired three congressional committees and played a pivotal role in advancing FDR's New Deal agenda. While Hague sought to suppress the CIO, Norton was shepherding the Fair Labor Standards Act of 1938 through Congress. One of the last major pieces of New Deal legislation, this act established a minimum wage and the forty-hour work week with a provision for overtime pay.

New Deal programs played an important role in modernizing New Jersey's infrastructure and institutions. Projects supported by the PWA and WPA improved virtually every form of transportation, contributing huge sums for roads, bridges, harbors, mass transit, and airport facilities. Many municipalities gained new schools, town halls, sidewalks, playgrounds, and parks, as well as water and sewer systems. These improvements were not imposed on local governments: the PWA and WPA required local governments to share part of the costs of improvement projects.

The Civilian Conservation Corps (CCC) enlisted 91,500 recruits in New Jersey, provided countless young men and veterans the chance to find gainful employment in the outdoors, and provided a total of $18 million of badly needed financial support to their families. CCC participants lived in a series of camps administered by the U.S. Army, and 200,000 workers from throughout the country were trained at Fort Dix during the program's existence (1933–1942). CCC accomplishments left an enduring mark on the landscape of New Jersey: 199 bridges constructed, 47 dams built, and 21.8 million trees planted. In the New Deal's first year, grants from the Federal Emergency Relief Administration enabled the establishment of six junior colleges housed in New Jersey high schools. In an era when only a small percentage of high school graduates could afford to attend college, FERA and local officials created valuable new opportunities for many working-class sons and daughters. Although several of these institutions were short-lived, Union College became a permanent community college, and another evolved into privately run Monmouth University.[18] The National Youth Agency provided scholarships to high school and college students, as well as funds for student employment.

Culturally, the New Deal played an important role in fostering music and the arts in New Jersey. A whole generation of artists, writers, musicians, and thespians received employment through the WPA. Many public buildings are still graced by artwork commissioned by this agency and by the Treasury Department.[19] Writers working for the WPA produced what remains one of the most comprehensive guides of the state's history and geography, conducted oral history projects documenting different ethnic communities, and compiled bibliographies of manuscript collections held by private and public institutions. The CCC, CWA, and the WPA played an instrumental role in the development of the nation's first designated historical park at Morristown, including the construction of a museum next to the Ford Mansion and significant restoration of nearby Jockey Hollow.

Perhaps one of the most innovative programs of the New Deal was a series of planned cooperative communities across the country to resettle displaced farmers and urban workers. Benjamin Brown, a Jewish immigrant from Russia, received funding from the Resettlement Administration (later the Farm Security Administration) to establish Jersey Homesteads in rural Monmouth County, with a cooperatively owned garment factory, farm, housing, and grocery store. Formally incorporated as a borough in 1937 and later renamed Roosevelt in memory of FDR, Jersey Homesteads was intended to offer a haven for working-class Jews from New York and to promote Jewish culture. Although the cooperative factory and farm ran into problems even before the end of the 1930s, Jersey Homesteads attracted the interest of a number of Jewish intellectuals and artists. Soon after the artist

The WPA's Federal Theater Project. Actors rehearing scenes from the production *Brother Mose* in Newark, New Jersey, April 8, 1936. (Franklin D. Roosevelt Presidential Library and Museum, Hyde Park, New York, 72115.)

Ben Shahn painted a mural in the community's school, he made Jersey Homesteads his permanent home.[20]

African Americans also benefited from New Deal programs. Widespread housing discrimination forced most black urban residents to pay disproportionately high rents for substandard housing. The expansion of relief initiatives spared many from starvation and destitution. Moreover, African Americans found employment on many public works programs, although they often had to endure segregation in such agencies as the CCC. In New Jersey, black voters increasingly abandoned the party of Lincoln for the Democratic Party. In 1921, Essex County had sent the physician Walter G. Alexander to Trenton as the state's first black assemblyman, and in 1936 Walter Moorhead from this same county was elected the first black Democrat to the assembly.

To ensure New Jersey's electoral votes in the 1936 election, Roosevelt formed an alliance with Hague that strengthened the latter's stranglehold on Hudson County and gave him a pivotal role in shaping state policy. Although FDR did little to challenge Hague's power directly, he encouraged Charles Edison, the son of the inventor Thomas A. Edison, to leave his post as secretary of the Navy and return to New Jersey to run for governor in 1940. Hague, who had placed a series of governors under his thumb, assumed he could do the same with Edison. Once in office, however, Edison broke with Hague and exercised considerable independence, although his call for the passage of a new state constitution was unsuccessful.

By the end of the 1930s, public spending remained too low to revive the economy fully, and unemployment levels continued to be depressingly high. Many New Jerseyans feared that the state and nation would have to live with a permanent class of unemployed. Only the massive spending required during World War II, which led to an unprecedented mobilization of the economy, lifted the United States out of the Great Depression. But war was not an answer many Americans in New Jersey welcomed or sought in the 1930s. Instead, they retreated inward. When running for the presidency in 1932, Roosevelt had distanced himself from his earlier support of internationalism and American membership in the League of Nations. Few observers questioned the Roosevelt administration's focus on combating the Great Depression, and until 1939 most foreign policy initiatives focused on Latin America.

WORLD WAR II

Adolf Hitler came into power as chancellor of Germany just weeks before Franklin D. Roosevelt assumed the presidency. A vocal minority within the German American community greeted the ascendance of Hitler and the Nazi Party with favor and formed the Friends of New Germany. This organization never gained the allegiance of the majority of German Americans, but it did host meetings in a number of urban and suburban communities in New Jersey, including Newark, Irvington, and Trenton. In 1936, Nazi Germany instructed its supporters to leave the Friends of New Germany and join a new organization, the German American Bund, which remained active until 1941. This organization maintained chapters in a number of counties, including Essex, Hudson, Passaic, Bergen, and Mercer, held numerous public meetings and rallies, and built a large camp in Andover.

Camp Nordland served as a youth summer camp as well as a gathering place for rallies and recreational outings on weekends.[21]

The Friends of New Germany and later the German American Bund sparked enormous public controversy. Meetings were regularly picketed by protesters, who often vastly outnumbered the Nazi sympathizers, which resulted in several violent clashes. In Newark, Jewish mobsters supported the elusive Minutemen organization, which physically disrupted meetings of the Friends and later the Bund. The violence that resulted from these confrontations often provided an excuse for local officials to ban meetings in advance. State and federal legislators throughout the 1930s held hearings to examine the threat posed by these organizations and their potential to undermine American society. With little dissent, except from the American Civil Liberties Union, the state legislature passed a series of laws in the 1930s that restricted the rights of pro-Nazi organizations. In what became commonly known as the Anti-Nazi Law of 1935, state legislators banned speech that promoted "hatred, violence, or hostility against any group . . . by reasons of race, color, religion, or manner of worship." In 1939 the state legislature went further and banned the use of the Nazi salute and quasi-military uniforms. Even before the United States entered the war against Germany, state and local authorities took decisive action to shut down the German American Bund.[22]

The Nazi threat divided both the Jewish community and Americans in general. The Jewish War Veterans and the American Jewish Congress (led by Rabbi Stephen Wise) organized a boycott of German goods in 1933. Non-Jewish allies joined these groups in protesting Nazi racial policies, and an active chapter of the national Non-Sectarian Anti-Nazi League emerged in New Jersey in the 1930s. Other Jewish organizations, most notably the Manhattan-based American Jewish Committee, argued for a more conservative approach to avoid a public backlash and heightened anti-Semitism.

Many New Jersey Jews feared for the fate of their relatives in Europe, especially after Hitler began his aggressive expansion. New Jersey offered refuge to some immigrants who fled Nazi-controlled Europe. Most famously, Albert Einstein, settled in Princeton and accepted a position at the Institute for Advanced Study. Joachim Prinz, one of Berlin's leading rabbis, managed to emigrate to the United States in 1937 and, after struggling to earn a living as a lecturer, assumed the rabbinate of Temple B'nai Abraham in Newark.[23] Despite the worsening fate of Jews living in Germany and in German-annexed Austria and Czechoslovakia, there was little support for liberalization of the 1920s American immigration laws that had established national quotas limiting the number of immigrants from eastern and southern Europe. Moreover, Jews and other refugees seeking to emigrate to the United States had to demonstrate that they had sufficient economic resources and that they would not be a public burden. An alternative was to find a qualified American sponsor, which for many meant convincing a distant relative to take on this responsibility.

Although the virulent nativist sentiment that had predominated in the 1920s faded during the Great Depression, it did not disappear. Roman Catholics continued to endure discrimination in employment and exclusion from many elite private clubs. Prejudice and discrimination also remained pervasive for Jews: Princeton University and a number of private colleges, medical schools, and law schools continued to enforce quotas to limit the number of Jewish students, and anti-Semitic vandalism often plagued Jewish farmers in Monmouth County.[24] Some voices did condemn religious intolerance, and New Jersey had several active chapters of the National Council of Christians and Jews. Under state law, there were few legal remedies against religious, ethnic, and racial discrimination until 1945.

The dominant consensus in New Jersey was to avoid engaging in another foreign war. New Jersey's congressional delegations voted for a series of Neutrality Acts in the 1930s that severely restricted the sales of arms to belligerents and banned American citizens from traveling on belligerents' passenger ships. Students at many New Jersey colleges expressed opposition to war and held strikes for peace that called for an end to hosting Reserve Officers' Training Corps (ROTC) on college campuses. In 1936 two students at Princeton University formed the Veterans of Future Wars and demanded early payment of veterans' bonuses to every male citizen, the country's inevitable future combatants.[25] Overnight chapters of this satiric organization sprang up around campuses across New Jersey and the nation. Drew University's chapter created a fabricated cemetery bearing the names of students who would fall in future conflicts and called for a Tomb for the Future Unknown Soldier.[26] Although interest in this organization quickly dissipated, the generation that came of age in the late 1930s expressed great misgivings about fighting another overseas war.

One small group of leftists proved willing to engage in an armed struggle against fascism in the 1930s. In 1937 several thousand Communists and other leftists volunteered to serve in the Abraham Lincoln Brigade and fight against Francisco Franco's efforts to overthrow the Republican government of Spain. Franco, supported by both Nazi Germany and Fascist Italy, prevailed over Republican forces in part because Britain, France, and the United States maintained an arms embargo. The only aid that Republican Spain received from these nations, aside from volunteers fighters, was privately raised humanitarian relief. The North Stelton community in Piscataway, home to the socialist Ferrer Colony and the Modern School, engaged in a fund-raising campaign to purchase an ambulance for Republican forces. This community also sent Valentin Kenner to fight with the Abraham Lincoln Brigade.[27]

President Franklin D. Roosevelt proclaimed neutrality when war finally broke out in Europe in August 1939 with Hitler's invasion of Poland, and few thought the United States should enter the conflict. After France fell in June 1940, the Roosevelt administration embarked on a massive military and naval build-up and began a controversial policy of providing aid to Great Britain and, later, to the Soviet Union. The British defense orders, combined with the re-arming of American forces, had a dramatic impact on New Jersey's economy. New York Shipbuilding in Camden, Hercules Powder Company in Roxbury, Curtiss-Wright aircraft in Paterson, and a host of other industrial enterprises dramatically increased production and payrolls. In 1940 Congress enacted the first peace-time draft in the nation's history, which led to the reactivation of Fort Dix as a major training base for the region. New Jersey National Guard units were also federalized, and Governor Charles Edison set up an extensive civil defense structure to prepare for a possible enemy attack.

Like the rest of the nation's citizens, New Jersey residents were divided over FDR's efforts to ally the country with Britain and the Soviet Union after it was invaded by Hitler in June 1941. Chapters of the non-interventionist America First organization dotted the state, and in 1941 the Jersey City chapter protested the showing of such war films as *Sergeant York*, *The Great Dictator*, and *I Married a Nazi*. Charles Lindbergh, who had lived in New Jersey in the early 1930s until the tragic death of his son during a botched kidnapping, was among the most prominent opponents of America's entry into the war. However, his mother-in-law, Mrs. Dwight Morrow, remained a committed internationalist and served as chair of the Englewood chapter of the Committee to Defend America by Aiding the Allies.

Despite America's worsening relations with Germany and Japan, New Jersey residents were stunned when the Japanese attacked Pearl Harbor on December 7, 1941. Fears of sabotage led state and federal authorities to take measures to protect key facilities and transportation centers throughout New Jersey. Army soldiers, members of the recently organized state guard, and state police troopers guarded key bridges, tunnels, and other vital facilities. An elaborate civil defense network staffed by thousands of volunteer air raid wardens prepared for possible attack from enemy bombers. Residents were urged to cover windows and municipalities initiated blackout drills. To prevent the landing of saboteurs, the United States Coast Guard instituted foot patrols of the Jersey coastline.

Although neither Germany nor Japan possessed long-range aircraft capable of reaching the Atlantic coast, German submarines brought the conflict to New Jersey's shores in early 1942. Disregarding the advice of British naval commanders, the U.S. Navy did not require tankers and other merchant ships to travel in convoys along the coast, and German U-boats were able to attack them with impunity. Sadly, too, cooperation with the war effort faltered in several shore towns as residents resisted blackout restrictions for fear of dampening the tourist trade.

The military and naval presence in New Jersey expanded drastically during the war.[28] At Fort Hancock on Sandy Hook and farther down the coast in Cape May County, artillery batteries stood guard against a possible enemy attack on New York and Philadelphia. Camp Kilmer in Piscataway served as the final staging point for more than 2.3 million soldiers before boarding troop ships en route to war. Atlantic City and Asbury Park hotels were converted into barracks and later served as hospitals and recuperation centers for wounded GIs. The Overseas Air Technical Command took over Newark Airport and transported scores of critical supplies to overseas installations. Fort Monmouth housed several research laboratories for the U.S. Army Signal Corps and served as a major training facility for men in this branch of the service. The Naval Air Station in Wildwood and the Millville Army Airfield in South Jersey trained pilots.

More than 560,500 men and women from New Jersey served in all branches of the armed forces and virtually every corner of the world. Of those who served, 13,000 were killed and an even higher number wounded. Navy Admiral William F. Halsey was perhaps the most prominent senior commander with ties to New Jersey, and he scored an impressive number

An aircraft on its nose in front of Hangar 1 at Naval Air Station Wildwood in 1944–1945. Designed and built by the North American Aircraft Company, the plane was used as an advanced trainer for dive bomber pilots during World War II. Some of the trainees were not as lucky as this one; there were forty-two fatalities at this facility. (Photograph courtesy of Dr. Joseph E. Salvatore and the Naval Air Station Wildwood Aviation Museum.)

of victories in the Pacific against Japanese naval forces. Seventeen residents won the Medal of Honor. The most famous was Marine Sergeant John Basilone of Raritan, who earned the award for gallantry while fighting the Japanese at the Battle of Guadalcanal in 1942. Like other war heroes, Basilone was brought home to aid the war effort by touring the country and urging Americans to buy war bonds. More than 30,000 people turned out for one rally at Doris Duke's estate in Somerville. At his own request, Basoline was reassigned to the combat ranks and later killed during costly assaults against the Japanese-held island of Iwo Jima in February 1945.

In contrast to earlier wars, women served in the armed services in unprecedented numbers—more than 10,000 enlisted from New Jersey. Ruth Cheney Streeter of Morristown served as head of the U.S. Marine Corps Women Reserves, and Joy Bright Hancock of Wildwood rose to the rank of commander in the U.S. Navy WAVES (Women Accepted for Volunteer Emergency Service) and played an instrumental role in convincing the Navy to train women in aircraft maintenance and other technical positions.[29]

The war also touched the lives of residents who remained at home. Shortages of rubber, food, clothing, and other products forced New Jersey civilians to sign up for ration books. To dampen inflation, the federal government established price ceilings on retail items and rents. Armies of citizen volunteers monitored consumer prices on behalf of the Office of Price Administration (OPA).[30] To fund the war, residents purchased millions of dollars of war bonds, but even this was not enough. For the first time, the average American wage earner paid federal income taxes—taxes that until the war years had been imposed only on the wealthy. Although there was considerable support for the war effort, grumbling could be heard about the war's cost, the burden of taxation, and rationing. A black market thrived throughout the war, with unscrupulous businessmen and consumers unwilling to abide by government restrictions.

Nevertheless, New Jersey's economy boomed during the war years, and unemployment vanished. State businesses received over $12 billion worth of contracts, and the industrial workforce, which in 1939 numbered approximately 433,000, doubled to nearly a million workers. The output of New Jersey factories was staggering. New York Ship Building in Camden built twenty-nine major capital ships for the Navy, including aircraft carriers, battleships, and cruisers. Campbell Soup, also in Camden, produced millions of ready-to-eat meals for combat. Curtiss-Wright Corporation of Paterson manufactured more than 139,000 airplane engines. Merck and Company in Rahway was given top priority by the federal government to produce the new synthetic pesticide DDT (banned decades later for environmental damage) to be used to control typhus and malaria by killing pests. Ralph Schmidt, who became a manufacturing chemist after graduating from Rutgers University in 1942, recalled his first job with Merck during the war. His account illustrates the dangerous working conditions in plants that ran full-time:

> We used to vaporize the stuff and reacted it with ethanol and all that sort of thing to make the DDT. Well, . . . we had so many chlorine leaks in this old equipment that we were using, we used to look through the building and see this green haze and we were working in that green haze. I was in charge of a

shift of operators producing this DDT and we would work seven days on and one off, seven days on and one off, etc. . . . . One week would be four to twelve, another one would be twelve to eight, another would be eight to four, so it kept constantly going around the clock. . . . And we used to get complaints from some of our operators during a course of a shift, "Hey, I'm having trouble breathing."[31]

In contrast to the contentious 1930s, labor peace reigned during much of the war, aided by the decision of most unions to abide by "no strike pledges" made shortly after the attack on Pearl Harbor. Membership in labor unions soared during the war, reflecting the struggles businesses had in coping with increasing labor shortages and their willingness to call a truce between capital and labor. By 1942, New Jersey businesses and government agencies had to look hard for workers to replace the increasing number of men drafted into military service. Women already in the workforce gravitated from lower paying jobs as secretaries, food service workers, and other traditional jobs to better paying ones at defense factories and shipyards. Often reluctantly, many employers began to hire African American workers, although job discrimination on the basis of race lingered.[32] But there were some clear gains in employment; for instance, 25 percent of the staff of the U.S. Office of Dependency Benefits were African Americans in 1945. This federal agency, headquartered in one of the Prudential company's office buildings in Newark, employed African Americans in a diverse range of positions, including supervisors, payroll clerks, secretaries, interviewers, and adjudicators.[33] Demographically, the war inspired a massive migration to the state, especially by southern black workers seeking better opportunities in northern states.

The war also produced a host of new problems at home. Large military bases, especially Camp Kilmer and Fort Dix, brought an influx of GIs who often sought alcohol, gambling, and prostitutes when on leave. The military stepped up the presence of its police in the state, and scores of United Service Organization (USO) clubs, staffed by a mix of professionals and volunteers, sprang up to meet the recreational needs of military personnel and war workers. The USO club in Dover made it a point to serve both war workers from the nearby Picatinny Arsenal and also soldiers stationed in the area.[34] In Newark's Pennsylvania Station, the USO provided a lounge for GIs traveling through the city. Unfortunately, the USO often permitted local clubs to discriminate against black servicemen and women, even though official policies called for equal access. The Newark USO lounge remained proud of the services it offered to African American GIs. Lounge supervisor Marion N. Echols reported to national headquarters in June 1942:

> We have one Negro volunteer worker who represents the YMCA. Because of her presence in the program the Red Caps in the station are cooperating wholeheartedly in referring Negro service men to the Lounge. The initial incredulity of these soldiers at being completely accepted, and their later almost inarticulate appreciation for whatever service is given seems one of the strengthening forces of the program.[35]

The migration of both white and black workers from southern states led to a significant housing shortage in New Jersey's urban areas and around military bases. During the Great Depression, little new residential housing had been built, and the federal government sharply restricted the supplies allocated to builders in wartime. To fill part of the gap, public housing units for war workers were constructed in Camden and Newark, and also in rural counties like Cape May. Not all communities welcomed war workers. Clark residents successfully lobbied the New Jersey legislature in 1941 to transform the federally sponsored Winfield Park Defense Housing Project into a self-governing municipality over the objections of labor union leaders and Governor Edison. Intended to house Kearny Shipyard workers, the project attracted national attention for delays in construction, shoddy work, and cost overruns. In Audubon, residents sought to enact a series of building codes and ordinances in an effort to derail another federally sponsored housing project. In 1947, the Audubon Park community became one of New Jersey's smallest municipalities (0.2 square miles) when it was split off from Audubon. In Randolph, the federal government built 250 cinderblock homes for war workers as a planned community that in 1951 became the independent municipality of Victory Gardens. Public housing construction remained insufficient for wartime needs, however, and war workers resorted to boarding with families, creating living quarters in garages, and in some cases sleeping in cars or camping in tents.

Like its industries, New Jersey's colleges and universities were mobilized in service of the war effort. Research contracts flowed to Princeton and Rutgers, and faculty members working on a range of projects to aid the war effort. Students also tried to do their part. In the case of the all-female New Jersey College for Women (Douglass College), first-year students gravitated toward courses in the sciences, with chemistry replacing home economics as the most popular major by 1944.[36] Several institutions housed military training programs. Princeton and Drew served as sites for the Navy V-12 program, which trained naval officers, and Rutgers housed a unit of the Army Specialized Training Program. Even though civilian men almost disappeared from the undergraduate student bodies of Rutgers and Princeton, both institutions failed to adopt coeducation until the 1970s. In the case of the smaller Drew University, the war prodded it to begin admitting women as undergraduate students.

Ideologically, the war fostered important shifts in attitudes toward race and ethnicity. Supporters of American intervention prior to Pearl Harbor argued that the United States must enter the conflict in order to preserve fundamental human rights. In his State of the Union Address in January 1941, FDR argued that the United States must oppose Nazi tyranny in order to preserve the "four freedoms": religion, speech, want, and fear. African American leaders and many advocates on the left noted the contradiction between these ideals and the continued pattern of discrimination that existed within New Jersey and American society. In 1941 the African American labor leader A. Philip Randolph threatened to organize a march on Washington, D.C., to protest racial discrimination. He backed down only after the Roosevelt administration issued an executive order banning discrimination on the basis of race, religion, or national origin. Even so, discrimination remained rampant throughout New Jersey, with many industries employing black workers only reluctantly and limiting them to custodial positions. Although most communities in northern New Jersey did not segregate public schools, many public and commercial establishments continued to enforce a color bar. Moreover, segregation remained the norm in the armed forces, and most black GIs were sent to service units in the army or served as ship's stewards in the navy.[37]

The nation's largest black organization, the National Association for the Advancement of Colored People (NAACP), while proclaiming support of the war, advocated a "Double V" campaign that sought to secure victory against the Axis overseas and against segregation at home. Pressure on the Roosevelt administration forced the Marine Corps to accept African Americans in its ranks for the first time, pushed the Navy to commission the first group of black officers, and led to the eventual desegregation of officer training in all branches of the armed forces. The latter reform had important implications for Princeton University. During the war years there emerged an intense debate among students, faculty, and administrators over the wisdom of continuing to bar African Americans from the undergraduate student body. In 1945 the Navy forced Princeton to admit four black students sent there under the Navy V-12 Program, and one of them became the first African American to earn a B.A from this Ivy League institution.[38] In 1945 New Jersey was the second state, after New York, to pass a statewide fair employment act barring discrimination by employers on the basis of race, ethnicity, and religion. Grass-roots protests from black and interracial organizations had some success in challenging entrenched institutional discrimination. In 1946, after years of protest, the Newark City Hospital finally opened its doors to African American physicians and nurses.[39]

Prosperity dampened support for the New Deal, and Republicans made significant electoral gains during the war years. In New Jersey, Walter Edge, who had served as governor during World War I, was elected to another term in 1943 and continued his predecessor's efforts to check the power of Frank Hague. Although Edge failed to garner support at the polls for a new constitution, he laid the groundwork for a successful effort in 1947. Moreover, Edge devoted significant attention to planning the postwar transition and reintegration of veterans into civilian life. Looking back to the failures of 1918, in 1944 the U.S. Congress enacted the G.I. Bill of Rights, which played a pivotal role in ensuring a smoother return of servicemen and women to civilian life. Veterans unable to find work were entitled to fifty-two weeks of unemployment and other benefits, along with services for those who were disabled.

Veterans widely embraced the G.I. Bill, and enrollment at colleges across the state soared. Veterans also used the opportunity to attend prestigious law schools, go on to medical schools, and even pursue advanced degrees at foreign universities. Still others returned to high school to complete the coursework necessary for a diploma. John Ragone, a physical education teacher in the New Brunswick High School in the 1940s, remembered years later how veterans were clustered into his homeroom in order to allow them to smoke cigarettes each morning.[40] Even more veterans took advantage of the opportunity to attend vocational school. For others, low-interest loans allowed them to purchase homes in suburban communities across New Jersey.

There were rough spots in the transition. Although the postwar depression many expected did not materialize, a severe housing shortage endured for several years until homebuilders could catch up with demand. New Jersey, like much of the nation, was gripped by a series of strikes as labor organizations, no longer bound to no-strike pledges, sought to build on the gains made during the war years. Corporations fought hard against labor, and many industrial firms began their exodus to regions of the country promising a more docile and cheaper labor force. When price controls ended, inflation soared. Moreover, the sense of an enduring peace faded as international tensions increased during the Cold War.

The postwar era brought New Jersey unprecedented prosperity and a vastly expanded middle class. The social innovations of the war years provided tremendous impetus for a major transformation of the state government under a new constitution. When written and adopted in 1947, it strengthened the governor's executive power, mandated an end to discrimination in public schools and the militia, and guaranteed the right of labor to organize and bargain collectively. The fundamental re-ordering of the relationship of the government and individuals in American society as a result of the New Deal and the war years continued to be built upon by both the state and the federal government through the 1970s, especially in the areas of education, social welfare, and economic development.

ACKNOWLEDGMENTS

I want to express my appreciation to Susan G. Contente and M. Houston Johnson for reviewing earlier drafts of this chapter and making a number of helpful suggestions. I also thank John W. Chambers for sharing a portion of the manuscript of his history of Cranbury, New Jersey (Rutgers University Press, 2012).

NOTES

1. For a broad overview of this period see David M. Kennedy, *Freedom from Fear: The American People in Depression and War, 1929–1945* (New York: Oxford University Press, 1999).
2. Jeffrey M. Dorwart and Philip E. Mackey, *Camden County, New Jersey, 1616–1976:*

A Narrative History (Camden: Camden County Cultural and Heritage Commission, 1976), 261.

3. Michael J. Birkner, *A Country Place No More: The Transformation of Bergenfield, New Jersey, 1894–1994* (Rutherford, N.J.: Fairleigh Dickinson University Press, 1994), 94.

4. Paul A. Stellhorn, "Depression and Decline: Newark, New Jersey: 1929–1941" (Ph.D. diss., Rutgers University, 1982), 82.

5. Roy William Reisert, interview with Kurt Piehler and Jan Pattanayak, October 17, 1996, Somerset, N.J., transcript, 6, Rutgers Oral History Archives, Rutgers University, New Brunswick, New Jersey (http://oralhistory.rutgers.edu).

6. Joel Schwartz and Daniel Prosser, eds., *Cities of the Garden State: Essays in the Urban and Suburban History of New Jersey* (Dubuque, Iowa: Kendall/Hunt Publishing Company, 1977), x; Richard A. Noble, "Paterson's Response to the Great Depression," *NJH* 96 (1978): 87–98.

7. Richard J, Connors, "A. Harry Moore," in *The Governors of New Jersey, 1664–1974*, ed. Paul A. Stellhorn and Michael J. Birkner (Trenton: New Jersey Historical Commission, 1982), 199.

8. Lyle W. Dorsett, "Frank Hague, Franklin Roosevelt, and the Politics of the New Deal," *NJH* 94 (1975–1976): 21–35.

9. Nelson Johnson, *Boardwalk Empire: The Birth, High Times, and Corruption of Atlantic City* (Medford, N.J.: Plexus Books, 2010), 79–124.

10. Edward H. Michels Jr., "New Jersey and the New Deal" (Ph.D. diss., New York University, 1986), 10–87.

11. Ibid., 89–177.

12. Ibid., 196.

13. Ibid., 333–347.

14. Steven Hart, *The Last Three Miles: Politics, Murder, and the Construction of America's First Superhighway* (New York: New Press, 2007).

15. W. A. Swanberg, *Norman Thomas: The Last Idealist* (New York: Charles Scribner's Sons, 1976), 221–224.

16. Jefferson Cowie, *Capital Moves: RCA's Seventy-Year Quest for Cheap Labor* (New York: New Press, 2001), 12–40.

17. Leo Troy, *Organized Labor in New Jersey* (Princeton: D. Van Nostrand, 1965), 99–121.

18. Donald R. Raichle, *New Jersey's Union College: A History* (Rutherford, N.J.: Fairleigh Dickinson University Press, 1983), 20–26.

19. Hildreth York, "The New Deal Art Projects in New Jersey" *NJH* 99 (1981): 132–159.

20. Edwin Rosskam, *Roosevelt, New Jersey: Big Dreams in a Small Town and What Time Did to Them* (New York: Grossman, 1972).

21. Warren Grover, *Nazis in Newark* (New Brunswick: Transaction Publishers, 2003).

22. Martha Glaser, "The German-American Bund in New Jersey," *NJH* 92 (1974): 33–49.

23. Joachim Prinz, *Joachim Prinz, Rebellious Rabbi: An Autobiography—The German and Early American Years*, ed. Michael A. Meyer (Bloomington: Indiana University Press, 2008).

24. Gertrude W. Dubrovsky, *The Land Was Theirs: Jewish Farmers in the Garden State* (Tuscaloosa: University of Alabama Press, 1992), 49–50, 159.

25. Lewis J. Gorin Jr., *Patriotism Prepaid* (Philadelphia: J. B. Lippincott Company, 1936).

26. John T. Cunningham, *University in the Forest: The Story of Drew University* (Florham Park, N.J.: Afton Publishing Company, 1990), 214.

27. Samuel Blum, interview with G. Kurt Piehler, July 8, 1994, New Brunswick, Rutgers Oral History Archives.

28. New Jersey's main role in both World War I and World War II was to provide manufactured material for the war effort, as well as to train troops transported to Europe.

29. Mark Lender, *One State in Arms: A Short Military History of New Jersey* (Trenton: New Jersey Historical Commission, 1991), 93–94.

30. Lizabeth Cohen, *A Consumer's Republic: The Politics of Mass Consumption in Postwar America* (New York: Random House/Vintage Books, 2003), 79–82.

31. Ralph Schmidt, interview with G. Kurt Piehler, June 22, 1994, New Brunswick, Rutgers Oral History Archives.

32. Daniel Sidorick, *Condensed Capitalism: Campbell Soup and the Pursuit of Cheap Production in the Twentieth Century* (Ithaca: Cornell University Press, 2009), 68–109.

33. State of New Jersey, Urban Colored Population Commission, *New Jersey Negro in World War II: Contributions and Activities* (Trenton, 1945).

34. Sherwood A. Messner, Assistant Director of Field Operations, United Service Organizations, Inc., to Frank L. Weil, December 2, 1942, folder 20/6, box 26, Frank L. Weil Papers, Jacob Rader Marcus Center of the American Jewish Archives, Cincinnati Campus, Hebrew Union College Jewish Institute of Religion (hereafter Weil Papers).

35. Marrion N. Echols, "Report on USO Lounge for Service Men, Pennsylvania Station, Newark, N.J., April 20th—June 1st, 1942," file, 20, box 20, Weil Papers.

36. Laura M. Michelitti, "'Carrying On': Students at New Jersey College for Women and World War II" (B.A. thesis, Rutgers University, 1999), 87–88.

37. Kevin Mumford, *Newark: A History of Race, Rights, and Riots in America* (New York: New York University Press, 2007), 32–75.

38. Mark F. Bernstein, "Princeton's Black Student Pioneer," *Journal of Blacks in Higher Education* 52 (2006): 75–77.

39. Clement A. Price, "The Struggle to Desegregate Newark: Black Middle Class Militancy in New Jersey, 1932–1947," *NJH* 99 (1981): 215–228.

40. John C. Ragone, interview with G. Kurt Piehler and Jennifer Grigas, November 2, 1994, New Brunswick, Rutgers Oral History Archives.

10 · SUBURBANIZATION AND THE DECLINE OF THE CITIES

Toward an Uncertain Future

HOWARD GILLETTE JR.

With 1,200 persons per square mile, New Jersey is the nation's most densely populated state. Not surprisingly, it has been described as the most urban state in the United States, but it also has been described as the nation's most suburban state. This apparent contradiction is resolved through the realization that the state's division into 566 distinct communities has facilitated the creation of low-density suburbs apart from historically high-concentration cities, leaving relatively little land for development that is not already designated for open space.[1] The stark juxtaposition of cities and their suburbs took a long time to develop, but the pattern accelerated and solidified in the half century following the end of World War II. "The economic structure of New Jersey and the metropolitan regions of its neighboring urban centers—New York City and Philadelphia," a 1993 report asserted," has been reinvented by nearly one-half century of large-scale residential suburbanization, by over a quarter century of large-scale retail decentralization, and by more than a decade of large-scale office and service industry deconcentration."[2] In the process, patterns of work as well as residence have been scrambled to create entirely new rhythms of day-to-day life. Moreover, because these changes affected residents differently, depending on race and class, New Jersey's communities became even more sharply differentiated over time. Visionary efforts to counter such practices as disinvestment in cities and exclusionary zoning in suburbs have yet to bridge those divides, leaving New Jersey's promise as the second-richest state in the nation largely unfulfilled for a large segment of its residents.

From the Civil War to the mid-twentieth century, cities represented the state's primary engines of growth. The concentration of jobs at historically favored sites for the transportation of goods by water or by rail made New Jersey's six major cities—Newark, Trenton, Paterson, Elizabeth, Jersey City, and Camden—magnets for human settlement and capital investment. Banks, retail facilities, and entertainment venues joined factories to create bustling centers of opportunity, drawing settlers, including large numbers of immigrants, within city boundaries to live as well as to work. Marvels of production and associated means of distribution created considerable wealth. A leader in the production of rubber, pottery, and primary metals, Trenton proudly promoted itself through the phrase "Trenton makes, the world takes." As late as 1950, 38 percent of the city's residents found employment in manufacturing. New Jersey's other cites similarly employed large portions of the regional work force in a range of manual occupations, from skilled leatherworkers in Newark and electronics specialists in Camden to rail workers in Jersey City and oil refiners in Elizabeth. Historically, holders of these blue-collar jobs lived close to their places of occupation, forming dense, often ethnically distinct neighborhoods anchored by parish churches, which served to bind neighbors through social as well as religious affiliation. New York and Philadelphia offered special employment opportunities for New Jersey residents, as well as shopping and entertainment, but the state's urban areas maintained their primacy.

To be sure, there were some workers who took advantage of electric rail lines radiating outward to the countryside to assure their families a cleaner and more exclusive environment in surrounding suburbs while still commuting to the city. Around Newark, in the late nineteenth century, these pioneer suburbanites worked successfully to keep the influence of the city at bay.[3] Until the 1950s, however, such contests represented a side story, one neither typically celebrated by boosters nor widely commented upon. For

convenience and cost, cities remained the preferred location for a large segment of state residents. Then the situation changed dramatically.

CITIES LEFT BEHIND

Fears that the nation would suffer an economic setback following the close
of World War II, when demand for manufactured goods was at its peak,
prompted business, government, and labor to enter an unwritten compact
to assure growth by encouraging high levels of individual consumption,
a goal later realized by higher wages and easy credit. The motivation for
this "consumer's republic," as historian Lizabeth Cohen identifies the new
ethos, "would not be a personal indulgence, but rather a civic responsibility designed to provide 'full employment and improved living standards
for the rest of the nation.'"[4] Targeted especially was the home-building
industry, deemed capable of boosting employment and stimulating secondary spending for home appliances and furnishings, to say nothing of
the family automobile. Because the best opportunities for new construction lay outside city boundaries, where land was cheaper and open space
made larger projects feasible, suburbs attracted the bulk of new investment.
Federal guarantees for home loans helped spur development, even as they
assured that these communities were overwhelmingly white and middle
class through appraisers' guidelines that directed loans away from racially
mixed or changing areas. In the meantime, government appraisers discouraged loans in cites whose populations were becoming more racially mixed,
a practice known as "red-lining" for the colored maps used to discourage
investments in areas considered risky. Not surprisingly, suburbs boomed
across the country, and New Jersey, helped in part by its proximity to two of
the nation's largest cities, provided an especially inviting target for growth.

Differences between suburbs were in part a product of geography, but
not entirely. Once established, race and class differentiations were institu-
tionalized by local land use decisions. Most important was the power of
each community to pass zoning regulations that prohibited undesirable
practices, including the introduction of lower-cost residential properties
that might attract lower-income residents. By requiring minimum lot sizes
in order to keep prices high or prohibiting more affordable structures, such
as trailers and even multi-unit buildings, communities could maximize

property values while minimizing social costs. Such exclusionary zoning, as it came to be called, helped some suburbs, if not all, maintain their distance from urban influences. Moreover, prohibitions against multiple-unit developments and ordinances restricting new housing to single-family use were initially upheld in the courts.[5]

For a while, cities held their predominant place in the state economy. Although their relative share of employment dropped in the first part of the twentieth century, they continued largely, even beyond World War II, to hold their own. Camden, for instance, employed even more industrial workers in 1960 (39,000) than it had in 1948. Over the next decade, however, the city lost almost half of those jobs; the biggest loss came in 1967, when New York Ship, which at its height had employed more than 40,000 workers, closed entirely. The city's population dropped accordingly, by 15,000 in the 1960s and another 30,000 in the 1970s. From a height of 125,000 in the mid-1920s, Camden's population fell to only 84,910, and its industries supplied just over 10,000 jobs.[6] Similarly, manufacturing drained away from Trenton with the sale and ultimate abandonment of its Roebling steel mill and the almost total departure of its rubber and pottery industries. Although Trenton gained some economic growth through state jobs, the city also experienced a decline in population, from a high of 128,009 in 1950 to 92,124 in 1980.[7] Between 1952 and 1962, Newark lost nearly 20,000 jobs, and no new industry located in the city after the Anheuser-Busch brewery in the late 1940s.[8]

The new pattern of decentralized development extended throughout New Jersey. Even though the state's population increased by 50 percent between 1940 and 1960, every major city except Paterson lost population. Newark, the largest city in the state, fell in national rankings from twenty-first in 1950 to fifty-sixth in 1990, as both jobs and residents flowed out of the city (see table 10.1). Soon 70 percent of New Jersey land could be classified as suburban. "The 'garden state,'" Lizabeth Cohen asserts, "was fast becoming the 'backyard garden' state, as housing subdivision became the New Jersey farmer's final crop."[9]

Both the loss of jobs and the powerful pull of the suburbs idealized as the preferred places of residence after World War II sharply altered New Jersey's geography. Camden, which was once the anchor of the entire south Jersey region, underwent a rapid change of status. In the mid-1950s, as developers offered attractive new suburban housing at affordable prices, residents

TABLE 10.1   The Big Six: Population in New Jersey's Historically Major
Cities, 1950–2000

City	1950	1960	1970	1980	1990	2000
Newark	438,776	405,220	381,930	329,248	275,221	273,546
Jersey City	299,017	276,101	260,350	223,532	228,537	240,055
Paterson	139,336	143,663	144,824	137,970	140,891	149,222
Elizabeth	112,817	107,698	112,654	106,201	110,002	120,568
Trenton	128,009	114,167	104,638	92,124	88,675	85,403
Camden	124,555	117,159	102,551	84,910	87,492	79,318

SOURCE: U.S. Census.

starting moving out of the city. Institutions followed, beginning with the
Jewish Community Center, which relocated from Kaighn Avenue in the
heart of the city to still largely undeveloped Delaware Township just across
the city border. The process of decentralization accelerated with completion of the Cherry Hill Mall in 1961, the first enclosed regional shopping
facility on the East Coast, also in Delaware Township. Within only a few
years, the town had not only adopted the name Cherry Hill, but residential
development, boosted by the mall, returned property taxes that exceeded
those for all of Camden, despite Cherry Hill's smaller population. Employers left the city, too, some for nearby suburbs like Pennsauken, which developed an attractive office park near accessible transportation routes, and
others, most notably RCA-Victor, to Cherry Hill and to Moorestown in
adjacent Burlington County. By the late 1960s, white-collar employers that
had typically located near county offices in Camden—most notably law
and engineering firms—also relocated to the suburbs. Major "anchor institutions"—educational and medical facilities—remained in the city, but
Camden by 1970 no longer served as the region's hub.[10]
   Initially, dispersion followed established routes: Haddon Avenue out of
Camden; Bloomfield, Park, Central, South Orange, and Frelinghuysen Av-
enues out of Newark. Immediate growth appeared along these corridors.
In Newark, which had been losing population gradually since the 1930s, the
process accelerated after the war. The earliest beneficiaries were the communities of Irvington, Orange, and East Orange, each of which grew considerably during the period. This first wave of settlement from city to suburb captured the attention of novelist Philip Roth, whose family could not

afford to leave Newark's lower-middle-class Jewish neighborhood of Wee-quahic for the emerging and more affluent suburbs. Starting with *Goodbye, Columbus*, published in 1959, and continuing through a good deal of his writing since, Roth has both charted the outward migration of Jews to suburbs like West Orange and the effects of this change on his native city.[11]

Where whites once dominated the old industrial neighborhoods, their places were taken by minorities, predominantly African Americans, with the exception of Paterson, which drew a larger number of Hispanics to its older neighborhoods. Both African Americans and Hispanics were initially drawn to the cities during World War II, when manpower shortages opened employment opportunities, but adequate housing was difficult to find in still racially restricted markets. Only when the suburbs proved more attractive to returning servicemen who wanted to start their families did urban housing open up. In some neighborhoods, including the one where Philip Roth grew up, the change in residential composition was startling. In only five years between 1961 and 1966, Weequahic shifted from 19 to 70 percent African American.[12] Moreover, as urban neighborhoods changed, newcomers faced two major obstacles: a shrinking market for nearby employment and demands from city officials that many of the homes they had moved into give way to redevelopment.

As one of only three states in the nation without a state income tax or a general sales tax, New Jersey in the mid-1950s placed the burden of paying for services on its localities. Given the high demand for land within their boundaries, cities did well enough into the early 1960s, but as investment went elsewhere and land values dropped, the tax burden fell on smaller numbers of people, even as social costs rose. To attract businesses as well as residents, cities looked to the federal government for funding for "urban renewal" under programs made available by the national housing acts of 1949 and 1954. Typically, federal subsidies were used to replace older housing stock located near now abandoned industrial sites in the hopes of attracting new businesses and higher-income residents, whose tax payments could compensate for declining revenues. Inevitably, clashes occurred as minorities, spurred by an increasingly militant civil rights movement, fought back, describing ambitious redevelopment plans as "black removal." In some places, publicly funded lawyers aided court challenges to these plans; in others, protests erupted, some of them resulting in physical clashes with police.

Tensions reached their height in the latter part of the 1960s as civil disturbances wracked Newark and Plainfield in 1967, Trenton in 1968, Asbury Park in 1970, and Camden in 1971. The destruction over six days of riots in Newark was especially devastating, with 26 people killed, 750 injured, some 1,500 arrested, and millions in property damage. The immediate response from state and local officials to social unrest included greater sensitivity to concerns about relocation and some modest programs for housing reinvestment and job training. But the damage had been done. The psychological and physical damage was more than any particular program could overcome. The flight of population following each of these riots was accompanied as well by further loss of employment, as businesses closed and regional patrons found other locations at which to shop, eat, and be entertained. Badly stigmatized by signs of decline everywhere, New Jersey's cities increasingly struggled to be self-sustaining. The cycle of decline that had started slowly in the postwar years accelerated and deepened in the last third of the twentieth century.[13]

NEW SUBURBAN DOMINANCE

The first postwar generation of suburban development was largely accomplished by the mid-1970s, as communities close to urban centers filled up. Cherry Hill in Camden County, for example, which had fewer than 11,000 residents in 1950, peaked just below 70,000 persons. New growth moved to the open land of outer suburbs. The next generation of development was exemplified by Vorhees, a town of just 1,823 people in 1950 and 12,919 in 1980, which reached 24,559 a decade later. In line with the outward migration of more affluent residents, Vorhees became the preferred location of new upscale shopping centers and office parks. Not insignificantly, the Jewish Community Center moved once again, from the border with Camden to the eastern part of Cherry Hill, immediately adjacent to Vorhees.

At the same time, development spread well beyond the immediate influence of cities to less developed portions of the state. Here, boosted by massive investments in highways made possible by the National Highway Act of 1956, an entirely different world of ex-urban development arose, closely tied to the new post-industrial economy. A number of these communities emerged at major highway interchanges. In the Camden area the opening of the New Jersey Turnpike's Exit 4 at Mount Laurel in 1952 boosted the development of office parks and hastened the conversion of farmland to commercial and residential development. From a hamlet of only 2,800 people in 1950, the town doubled its population every decade thereafter, exceeding 40,000 residents by 2000. Farther north, where the New Jersey Turnpike intersected with the Garden State Parkway, once rural Woodbridge Township boomed, aided by the completion of an enclosed regional mall in 1971 as well as construction of single-family homes marketed to new homeowners benefiting from government programs for veterans after the war. By 2010, the town had almost 100,000 residents and ranked sixth in the state, well ahead of both Camden and Trenton.[14] Impelled initially by the completion of the Garden State Parkway in 1955 and subsequently by construction of the Ocean County Mall, Tom's River (known until 2006 as the Township of Dover) in Ocean County grew from only 7,000 people in 1950 to 43,000 in 1980.[15] Its 2010 population of 91,239 made it New Jersey's eighth-largest jurisdiction (see table 10.2).

The introduction of Interstates 80 and 287 through the state's central and northeastern counties helped to create a new suburban "wealth belt" characterized by all the elements of the new post-industrial economy. With some 1,000 housing units built per week, the state added one million units in the period 1950–1970, primarily located in this new region. Increased reliance on trucking and single-story manufacturing structures in growth industries—electronics, oil, petrochemicals, and aviation—undercut the dense physical structure and functions of the state's older cities. The pharmaceutical industry favored the new suburban settings and attracted other development. Merck & Company, for example, moved its world headquarters from Rahway in the northeastern part of the state to Readington Township in Hunterdon County at the shoulder of I-78. Eighty percent of the state's total office space by the 1980s was located in the state's freeway-oriented suburban growth corridor. During the 1980s alone, the area added 173 million square feet of office space, more than the entire standing office inventory of the Chicago metropolitan area. Route 1 through "Greater Princeton" proved another magnet for development.[16]

Suburban growth also promoted new regional retail facilities, following the lead of Cherry Hill, which in turn sharply altered traditional shopping patterns. Shopping malls in Paramus, seven miles from the George Washington Bridge, for instance, had the effect of curtailing shopping trips to nearby towns and cities as well as New York City. Per capita retail sales in Paramus lagged behind Hackensack in 1954, but surged with the opening in 1957 of the Bergen and Garden State malls. By 1963 Paramus's return was more than twice the level in Hackensack. As these and similar malls added facilities for dining and other services, including movie theaters and children's play activities, they fast became the new regional downtowns.[17]

The dispersion of residential and commercial facilities away from cities was matched by job creation. At the conclusion of World War II, most state jobs were highly centralized, especially in portions of Essex and Hudson counties nearest New York, where Newark and Jersey City were located, respectively. As late as 1960, these areas accounted for 700,000 positions, 33.2 percent of the state's 2.1 million jobs. But a suburban ring composed of Bergen, Passaic, Morris, Somerset, Union, Middlesex, and Monmouth counties offered even more employment in 1960: 900,000, or 43 percent of the state total. In the following decade, employment in Bergen County alone jumped from 225,000 to 350,000 jobs, overtaking Hudson County as the state's second most populous workplace. Overall, north suburban counties listed 1.3 million jobs, nearly 50 percent of the statewide total. These changes fulfilled a 1974 report's predictions:

> As interstate 287 thrusts past Morristown and into Bergen County it will reach the final stage of its evolution into the New Jersey equivalent of the Boston Route 128 beltway, where a tremendous complex of industries has spawned. As has been the experience nationally, developers have followed the freeways with their commercial emporiums and industrial shells, while major employers quickly flee their less than fashionable core locations. It appears that freeways will have emerged fully victorious in the seemingly Darwinian struggle over commuter rail lines, busses, and traffic lights—they will have completely molded and shaped the life of New Jersey. Broad and Market Streets in Newark have long given way to the major highway intersections as the crossroads of New Jersey.[18]

The pace of development in once rural areas put pressure on poorer residents, who often struggled to meet costs as housing prices rose. In Mount Laurel, African Americans with deep historic ties to the area sought the town's support for the introduction of multi-unit garden apartments not authorized by the town's zoning law. Their plea for access to more affordable

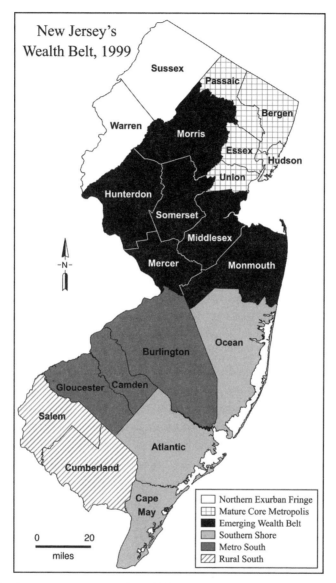

New Jersey's
Wealth Belt, 1999

Sussex

Passaic

Bergen

Warren

Morris

Essex

Hudson

Union

Hunterdon

Somerset

Middlesex

-N-

Mercer

Monmouth

Ocean

Burlington

Gloucester Camden

Salem

Atlantic

Cumberland

Cape
May

Northern Exurban Fringe
Mature Core Metropolis
Emerging Wealth Belt
Southern Shore
Metro South
Rural South

0   20
miles

Wealth Belt Map, 1999. New Jersey's wealth belt was the product of rapid mid-twentieth-century growth and a marked trend away from concentrated to dispersed development. (Map drawn by Michael Siegel, Rutgers University Cartography Lab, based on the original provided courtesy of Joseph J. Seneca and James W. Hughes from *The Emerging Wealth Belt: New Jersey's New Millennium Geography*, Rutgers Regional Report no. 17 [September 1999]. Copyright Rutgers, The State University of New Jersey, Edward J. Bloustein School of Planning and Public Policy.)

housing options was summarily rejected by the mayor, who told a gathering of petitioners, "If you people can't afford to live in our town, you'll just have to leave." Not deterred, long-time resident Ethel Lawrence sought to over-turn the mayor's decision through the courts. In decisions rendered in 1975 and 1978 the state supreme court ruled in her favor, declaring that the general welfare provision of the 1947 New Jersey Constitution required every town in the state to modify its own preferred land use to provide its "fair share" of affordable housing options. Affirming the state's primary control of land use, Chief Justice Robert Wilentz declared: "In exercising that control it cannot favor rich over poor. It cannot legislatively set aside dilapidated housing in urban ghettos for the poor and decent housing elsewhere for everyone else. . . . While the state may not have the ability to eliminate poverty, it cannot use that condition as the basis for imposing further disadvantages."[19]

Despite the force of court rulings and the institution of a Council on Af-fordable Housing under the Fair Housing Act of 1985 to assure compliance under state law, affordable options remained limited in many of the state's fastest-growing suburban areas. According to a comprehensive regional as-sessment issued in 1996, "The American dream of single-family home own-ership has driven national and regional development patterns and financial policy for nearly half a century. But now, as the housing stock of the region becomes increasingly unaffordable, the dream has become little more than a myth." A subsequent 1997 analysis of affordable housing across the state confirmed that the people least likely to have benefited from the court rul-ings were minorities concentrated in cities, where housing prices had de-clined but employment opportunities were sharply limited.[20]

URBAN REVITALIZATION

With suburban housing relatively inaccessible to them, the state's poorest residents concentrated in urban areas, where not just jobs but also tax rev-enues continued to decline. Although mayors explored a number of one-time fixes to their budget woes, including payments for accepting unwanted service industries such as waste and trash processing plants, inevitably they had to raise property taxes even higher. The combination of lowered rev-enues and higher needs proved devastating. Cities struggled to balance their budgets, often at a cost to their residents in the form of higher taxes

The Camden waterfront, early twenty-first century. This overview of the Camden waterfront shows the result of efforts to convert former industrial sites to tourist destinations, including an entertainment center, the battleship *New Jersey*, an aquarium, and a minor league baseball stadium. (Courtesy Cooper's Ferry Partnership, Camden.)

or reduced services. When federal funding for urban renewal terminated in the mid-1970s, cities looked increasingly to the state to provide incentives for private investment to help meet revenue shortfalls. Camden took the lead, following Baltimore's example, in an effort to convert its working waterfront to a tourist destination. The city succeeded in securing state support for an aquarium, which opened in 1992 with the promise of attracting paying visitors to the downtown. However, when Campbell Soup dropped its commitment to build a new international headquarters nearby, further development lagged. Other investments followed—for a regional entertainment center, some office buildings, and a minor league stadium—all located on land once occupied by departed industries. But because the process evolved slowly, the impact was limited. Tax abatements offered to induce investment crimped revenue return to the city, and employment opportunities for local residents were limited.[21] Nonetheless, the lure of tourist revenues continued to influence urban policy across the state.

In Newark, the city built not only a minor league baseball stadium, following the leads of Camden and Trenton, but also a new arena to lure the

National Hockey League Devils from the Meadowlands Sports Complex to the heart of the city. Most significantly, it secured state support to open a $180 million performing arts center in 1997, just blocks from the city's historic downtown core along Broadway. This investment, more than the others, had a positive effect on the surrounding area, spurring renovation of the Robert Treat Hotel and assisting other commercial activities nearby. But the facility was no more able than Camden's aquarium to act as the city's savior. Well after the first praise for the center had been recorded, the city continued to struggle with the high costs of concentrated poverty and inadequate tax revenues.[22]

Although Paterson did better than New Jersey's other cities in holding its population, it too struggled with the loss of industry after World War II and ranked seventh among the state's most distressed communities in 1990. Between 1990 and 2000, despite modest growth overall, the city lost an additional 20 percent of its employment base. Hoping to gain new revenue, the city created a historic district near the Great Falls that had assured its early reputation as a center of silk manufacturing After a long campaign, supporters secured approval to make the area a national park, though how many benefits that action would bring to the city remained to be seen. Continued immigration to the area, which by 2010 was almost 58 percent Hispanic, helped sustain small businesses, but the city remained poor, especially in relationship to its more affluent suburban neighbors.[23]

The failure of major cities to improve resources sufficiently to provide adequate services—schools, public safety, and maintenance of streets, sewers, and parks—continued to be a burden on their residents, even those who remained fiercely committed to their home towns. Inevitably, a significant number of those who could afford to do so moved, following a pattern of outward migration a generation earlier along primary transportation corridors to nearby suburbs. These older areas—often referred to as the inner ring or first-generation suburbs—began to change socially and demographically in the 1990s and into the twenty-first century. The proportion of minorities in public schools rose, and with that trend also the number of students eligible for free lunches. Diversification of New Jersey's suburbs did not advance across the board, however. Newer areas, developed with larger homes and lots and few affordable housing opportunities, remained nearly all white.

The pattern was well illustrated in Essex County. Three suburbs attracted the bulk of black out-migration from Newark, and as a consequence by 2000 the proportion of African American residents had soared to 89 percent in East Orange, 82 percent in Irvington, and 75 percent in Orange. Although the median income of these communities—ranging from $35,000 to $45,000—was higher than Newark's $26,913, they looked and felt very much like extensions of the black sections of Newark, which was itself 53 percent African American in 2000. According to an assessment of the state's most distressed areas issued in 1990, these communities ranked closely with Newark, which was second; East Orange, Orange, and Irvington ranked seventeen, twenty-one, and thirty, respectively. Clearly, this inner suburban ring could be closely identified with patterns of racial concentration and poverty associated with Newark.[24] Alternatively, Essex County suburbs farther from the city, notably West Orange, South Orange, and Millburn, though affected by growth, maintained a predominantly white population. Their median incomes—$69,254, $83,611, and $130,869, respectively—set them apart from other less affluent suburban areas.

The real estate boom that spread across the state from the late 1990s into 2008 helped to moderate some differences among communities. Higher housing and gasoline prices had the effect of attracting new investment to older suburbs, which remained close in many instances to employment centers. "A drive through any of New Jersey's older post-1950 tract-house suburbs shows considerable evidence of an upsurge in revitalization and reinvestment," James Hughes and Joseph Seneca reported in 2004. New construction on transit lines to regional job opportunities and state incentives to direct investment away from open space to centers of population combined to improve the prospects of these areas, even as they diversified their populations. In Collingswood, immediately adjacent to Camden, for instance, a process of decline was reversed along Haddon Avenue through the intervention of an aggressive merchants' association. By improving amenities along the avenue, introducing a hugely successful farmer's market and other public events, and investing in new housing at the PATCO High Speed Line, the town staved off what appeared to be an inevitable extension of Camden's blight. In 2006 the town had the lowest percentage of households living in poverty in the state, 6 percent. By contrast, Camden's poverty rate was the state's highest, at 36 percent.[25]

The boom benefited some of New Jersey's aging cities as well. By the end of the century, a few cities appeared to be making progress at revitalization, most notably in the northern part of the state. Soaring land costs in New York City encouraged investors to seek less costly options for development in New Jersey. "In a real estate boom taking place up and down New Jersey's industrial coast, developers are building as fast as they can, and reshaping the skyline from Bayonne to the George Washington Bridge," the *New York Times* reported in 1999. "For decades, developers have struggled to build a post-industrial frontier along what many wishfully call New Jersey's 'gold coast.' And for many, these wishes are finally coming true: white-collar office parks are going up where factories once stood; luxury apartments are replacing gantry cranes on the piers, and stylish shops are being carved out of railroad warehouses."[26] As one consequence of the region's changing fortunes, the populations of Newark, Elizabeth, and Jersey City increased for the first time in decades. No city benefited more than Jersey City.

As early as the 1980s, Jersey City began to attract capital to remake a waterfront once occupied by rail yards and factories. The location of banking facilities, including Goldman Sachs, UBS, and Merrill Lynch, earned the area the moniker "Wall Street West." Fears generated by the 2001 attacks on the World Trade Center only accelerated the pattern. Towering structures, for residences as well as employment, filled in the waterfront development, prompting one developer to declare, "We did it! June 2006 marks the 20th anniversary of Newport, the largest and most successful mixed-use development in the United States." Such new investments put Jersey City in the lead among the state's larger cities in job growth, new construction, and median income. Nevertheless, not all areas of the city benefited. Two reports, also in 2006, noted a 10 percent rise in violent crime and an income decline from 71 to 69 percent of the statewide median between 1990 and 2000. Such uneven development remained a challenge for all New Jersey cities, as demonstrated particularly in Atlantic City.[27]

Known for generations as a prime location for combining the best of resort living with urban amenities, Atlantic City's luster faded in the 1950s, when the ease of air travel provided middle-class tourists with more destinations; at the same time, the city's decline compromised the visitor experience. By 1970, the city's poverty rate was the highest in New Jersey. The decision to introduce gambling, approved by a statewide referendum in 1976, gave new life to the entertainment venues clustered at the Boardwalk and considerable returns to the state. Funds collected through a Casino Redevelopment Association went some way toward helping to rebuild select neighborhoods in Atlantic City, but poverty on the whole remained high. "If visitors somehow break free or stray from the landscaped corridor and underground tunnel, they find themselves in a city of bleak projects, painted-over storefronts, blocks with more holes than houses, and packs of African American and, increasingly, Asian and Latino teenagers on street corners," Bryant Simon reports. "Most middle-class visitors see this city— as they do most real cities without theme park markers—as a place to be avoided at all costs."[28]

The state attempted to learn from Atlantic City's mistakes when it assumed full oversight of Camden in 2001. A $175 million fund intended to leverage new investment for the city included $25 million to expand the aquarium, even as it was turned over to private ownership. Another $75 million was designated to revitalize the city's downtown "anchor institutions," that is, education and hospital facilities that were committed to staying in the city and were expected to increase employment prospects for area residents as they grew. Most of the remaining funds were targeted for neighborhoods, with the intent of building on existing community development efforts. By the time the legislature lifted control seven years later, the money directed downtown had succeeded in bringing new investment. Neighborhood revitalization floundered, however, due to the failure to work effectively with existing organizations and initiatives. Repeating the mistakes of the 1960s, the Camden Redevelopment Agency tried to force large-scale clearance projects on neighborhoods in order to create high-end retail and residential facilities set apart from prevailing areas of poverty. These efforts were blocked in court and were not in place by the time funds ran out. Moreover, what was supposed to be a complementary effort to help Camden residents improve their job prospects, through training and through access to better housing, educational, and employment opportunities in the surrounding suburbs, failed for lack of will on the part of the political establishment. As a result, as in Jersey City and Atlantic City, there were pockets of well-being downtown largely surrounded by poor neighborhoods.[29]

NEW JERSEY: A STATE DIVIDED

However much differences between jurisdictions narrowed in the early twenty-first century, underlying patterns of settlement served to underscore

TABLE 10.2   Population of New Jersey's Ten Largest Communities,
             1950 and 2010

Jurisdiction	Population 1950	Population 2010	Percentage change
Newark	438,776	277,140	−36.8
Jersey City	299,017	247,597	−17.1
Paterson	139,336	146,199	+4.9
Elizabeth	112,817	124,969	+10.7
Edison	16,348	99,967	+511.4
Woodbridge	35,758	99,585	+178.49
Lakewood	10,809	92,843	+758.9
Toms River	7,707	91,239	+1202.1
Hamilton Township	41,146	88,464	+115
Trenton	128,009	84,913	−33.6

SOURCE: U.S. Census.

the structural gulf between affluent suburbs and less affluent cities and
older suburbs. Such disparities appeared in growth patterns, which resulted
in five once suburban areas ranking among the ten largest jurisdictions in
the state. Although five of the state's historic big cities remained on the list,
their overall population pattern was decline, while the once suburban newcomers to the list all grew exponentially in the postwar era. Although Trenton remained on the list, it had dropped from fifth to tenth, surpassed by its
own suburb, Hamilton Township. Lakewood joined Tom's River in Ocean
County as a newcomer to the list; its population soared more than 50 percent between 2000 and 2010 alone (see table 10.2).

Behind these statistics stands a revealing story of immigration, which
was responsible for most of the growth in the state in the new century. According to the 2010 federal census, Asians represented the fastest-growing
immigrant sector, increasing from 5 to 8 percent of state population. Hispanics remained the largest immigrant group in New Jersey, increasing
from 13 to 18 percent over the decade. Yet the two streams of immigration
could not have been more different. The great majority of Hispanic immigrants followed an earlier generation by settling in urban staging areas,
where housing was cheap and patterns of settlement were established. In
addition to areas already known for concentrating Hispanic population—
Union City at 84.7 percent and Perth Amboy at 78 percent—the areas of
greatest growth came in the state's older cities: Passaic, which reached 71

percent Hispanic, Elizabeth, 59.5 percent, Paterson, 57.6 percent, and New Brunswick, 49.9.percent. Even Camden's population, majority African American since 1980, approached 50 percent Hispanic. Asians, on the other hand, bypassed cities almost entirely for suburban locations, most notably in the state's wealth belt, especially Middlesex and Bergen counties. Edison, for example, added some 10,000 new Asian residents in the century's first decade, helping to enlarge the town toward a population of 100,000. While many Hispanics scrambled for work in resource-poor cities, more affluent Asian and especially Indian immigrants took advantage of superior schools and housing choices to climb the economic ladder.[30]

This latest chapter in New Jersey's settlement history is yet another example of the long and largely unbroken trend of migration of people and resources away from cities and toward the state's suburban periphery. In the years after World War II, such a pattern might not have been fully predicted. A new constitution, finalized in 1947, ostensibly strengthened local jurisdictions by assuring their right to a liberal interpretation of their municipal responsibilities.[31] By also sharply strengthening the powers of both the governor and the courts, the constitution helped break the power rural areas had wielded for generations through control of the state senate. Not incidentally, the state's most powerful and astute urban politician, Jersey City Mayor Frank Hague, joined rural interests in opposing the changes. Whether Hague foresaw the consequences fully or not, Barbara and Stephen Salmore argue persuasively that the long-term effect of constitutional reform was to shift power to the burgeoning suburbs. Henceforth, the importance of traditional party organizations was weakened, and a new ethos that focused not just on economic opportunity but also quality-of-life issues took hold, driving policy away from traditional class interests and toward the demands of a growing middle class.[32]

At a crucial point in this process, the New Jersey Supreme Court stepped in, ruling both that the state had an obligation to provide adequate funding to poor school districts (*Abbott v. Burke*)[33] and, through the *Mount Laurel* decisions, that every community must offer adequate housing opportunities for people of lower incomes. In such ways the court lived up to the expectations in the constitution that it protect and promote "the general welfare." When it came to implementing these directives, however, neither the governor nor a majority of the legislature have had the will to advance the fortunes of those left behind, especially in the state's hollowed-out cities.

When fiscal emergency added further weight to community complaints about the costs of providing affordable housing, both the governor and the legislature agreed in 2011 to eliminate the Council on Affordable Housing as part of a larger move to lighten the regulatory burden. They did so at the same time that a definitive report appeared, documenting the state's continued failure to overcome suburban sprawl and the affordable housing gap it helped create.[34]

Even when the immediate fiscal crisis ends, the state will still face deep divisions among its constituent communities. Its major cities continue to struggle. Older suburbs, despite organizing their own association to seek a larger share of state resources, continue to fight to sustain the hopes that once were invested in them. If sprawl has slowed as the last available open land is filled, newer growth areas still face issues of traffic congestion and increased costs for schools and other facilities. The 1992 New Jersey State Plan for development garnered considerable praise for encouraging investment in older areas, but because its recommended measures were voluntary, it has had only limited effect in promoting "smart growth." As cities and suburbs continue to compete for scarce resources, chances for greater equality across all of New Jersey's communities remains remote. Place matters greatly in New Jersey, and the legacy of a half century of uneven development leaves the state as divided as it has ever been and the fate of its cities and suburbs very much in question.

NOTES

1. This will become 565 when Princeton Township and Borough merge.
2. James W. Hughes and Joseph H. Seneca, "The Tidal Wave of Income Suburbanization: New Jersey, New York and Philadelphia Metropolitan Dynamics," Rutgers Regional Report Issue Paper Number 8 (October 1993), 3.
3. Joel Schwartz, "Suburban Progressivism in the 1890s: The Policy of Containment in Orange, East Orange, and Montclair," in Cities of the Garden State: Essays in the Urban and Suburban History of New Jersey, ed. Joel Schwartz and Daniel Prosser (Dubuque, Iowa: Kendall/Hunt Publishing Company, 1977), 53–70.
4. Lizabeth Cohen, A Consumer's Republic: The Politics of Mass Consumption in Postwar America (New York: Knopf, 2003), 113.
5. Ibid., 206.
6. Howard Gillette Jr., Camden after the Fall: Decline and Redevelopment in a Post-Industrial City (Philadelphia: University of Pennsylvania Press, 2005), 42.

7. John T. Cumbler, *A Social History of Economic Decline: Business, Politics, and Work in Trenton* (New Brunswick: Rutgers University Press, 1989), 139–144.

8. Leo Adde, "Newark," in Adde, *Nine Cities: The Anatomy of Downtown Renewal* (Washington, D.C.: Urban Land Institute, 1969), 53.

9. Cohen, *Consumer's Republic,* 197, 199.

10. Gillette, *Camden after the Fall,* 44–51.

11. Cohen, *Consumer's Republic,* 223–224.

12. Brad R. Tuttle, *How Newark Became Newark: The Rise, Fall, and Rebirth of an American City* (New Brunswick: Rutgers University Press, 2009), 140.

13. For reports on the riots in these cities and their devastating effects, see Kevin Mumford, *Newark: A History of Race, Rights, and Riots in America* (New York: New York University Press, 2008); Tuttle, *How Newark Became Newark,* 142–170; www.67riots .rutgers.edu/index.htm; Cumbler, *Social History of Economic Decline,* 174–176; Gillette, *Camden after the Fall,* 84–86. In describing four of New Jersey's cities—Newark, Camden, Trenton, and Atlantic City—as "past the point of no return," urban critic David Rusk significantly pointed to loss of population, the decline in wealth relative to adjacent suburbs, and the concentrations of minorities as chief indicators of disadvantage, all elements that plagued New Jersey's post-industrial and post-riot cities. David Rusk, *Cities Without Suburbs* (Washington, D.C.: Woodrow Wilson Center Press), 76–77.

14. Bill Glovin, "Woodbridge," in *Encyclopedia of New Jersey,* ed. Maxine N. Lurie and Marc Mappen (New Brunswick: Rutgers University Press, 2004), 883.

15. Barbara G. Salmore and Stephen A. Salmore, *New Jersey Politics and Government: The Suburbs Come of Age,* 3rd ed. (New Brunswick: Rutgers University Press, 2008), 2.

16. James W. Hughes and Joseph J. Seneca, "The Emerging Wealth Belt: New Jersey's New Millennium Geography," Rutgers University Bloustein School of Planning and Public Policy Issue Paper Number 17, September 1999; Laura Mansnerus, "Where the Money Is," *New York Times,* March 12, 2000; Hughes and Seneca, "Tidal Wave of Income Suburbanization," 16; Michael H. Ebner, "The Megapolitan Transformation: Princeton, the 'Brains Town,'" in *Mapping New Jersey: An Evolving Landscape,* ed. Maxine N. Lurie and Peter O. Wacker (New Brunswick: Rutgers University Press, 2009), 53–54.

17. Cohen, *Consumer's Republic,* 259–269.

18. Thomas P. Norman, ed., *New Jersey Trends* (New Brunswick: Rutgers University Institute for Environmental Studies, 1974), 73–75.

19. David L. Kirp, John P. Dwyer, and Larry A. Rosenthal, *Our Town: Race, Housing, and the Soul of Suburbia* (New Brunswick: Rutgers University Press, 1995), 2; Gillette, *Camden after the Fall,* 177–178. In "The Paradox of Progress: Three Decades of the *Mount Laurel* Doctrine," *Journal of Planning History* 5 (May 2006): 129, John A. Payne points out that the state constitution permitted delegation of zoning power to local governments, but only to serve "the general welfare." "Reasoning from this inherently ambiguous phrase," Payne writes, Justice Frederick Hall of the New Jersey Supreme Court "held that an exclusionary local zoning ordinance was invalid if it disregarded *general* needs of the state or region in favor of serving parochial local needs only."

20. Robert D. Yaro and Tony Hiss, *A Region at Risk: The Third Regional Plan for the New York–New Jersey–Connecticut Metropolitan Area* (Washington, D.C.: Island Press, 1996), 54; Naomi Bailin Wish and Stephen Eisdorfer, "The Impact of *Mount Laurel* Initiatives: An Analysis of the Characteristics of Applicants and Occupants," *Seton Hall Law Review* 77, no. 4 (1997): 1268–1337.

21. Gillette, *Camden after the Fall*, 123–144.

22. Ralph Blumenthal, "Newark Hopes for Revival Far Beyond Arts Center," *New York Times*, October 15, 1997; Andrew Jacobs, "A Newly Cool Newark Says, 'C'mon Over!' " *New York Times*, November 24, 2000; Dennis E. Gale, *Greater New Jersey: Living in the Shadow of Gotham* (Philadelphia: University of Pennsylvania Press, 2006), 95–104.

23. Clifford J. Levy, "Paterson, Used to Struggling, Struggles for Control," *New York Times*, February 26, 1995; Maxine N. Lurie, "Paterson," in Lurie and Mappen, eds., *Encyclopedia of New Jersey*, 618–619.

24. *Municipal Distress—New Jersey* (New Jersey Department of the Treasury, Office of Management and Budget, 1990). These inner ring suburbs not only drew poorer, minority populations, they did so as new highways facilitated the departure of existing residents. Orange suffered especially from the construction of Interstate 280, which sliced the town in half and propelled many residents to emerging suburban areas in Essex and Morris Counties. Shoppers who had once patronized Main Street shifted their business to suburban malls. Andrew Jacobs, "Knocked Down, Yes. Knocked Out, Never," *New York Times*, April 24, 1999; Kevin Coyne, "Avenue that Used to Be Awaits a Rebirth," *New York Times*, November 4, 2007.

25. James W. Hughes and Joseph J. Seneca, "Controlling Sprawl," *New York Times*, January 18, 2004; "Cities in Transition: New Jersey's Urban Paradox," Housing and Community Development Network of New Jersey, September 2006, 12.

26. Charles V. Bagli, "Robust Economy Feeds Builders' Frenzy to Transform New Jersey Riverfront," *New York Times*, August 2, 1999.

27. Advertisement, *New York Times*, June 14, 2006; Jonathan Miller, "Amid the Glitter, Jersey City's Growing Pains," *New York Times*, March 5, 2006; "Cities in Transition," 12.

28. Bryant Simon, *Boardwalk of Dreams: Atlantic City and the Fate of Urban America* (New York: Oxford University Press, 2004), 211, 214; Lee Eisenberg and Vicki Gold Levi, "Atlantic City," in Lurie and Mappen, eds., *Encyclopedia of New Jersey*, 43.

29. Gillette, *Camden After the Fall*, 191–215.

30. Rohan Mascarenhas, "Census Data Shows Hispanics as the Largest Minority in N.J.," *Star-Ledger*, February 3, 2011; Brad Parks, "Census Shows Spike in N.J. Asian Population," *Star-Ledger*, August 7, 2008; Brent Johnson, "Edison on Brink of Reaching 100,000 residents," *Star-Ledger*, July 25, 2010.

31. The wording referring to these powers reads, "The provisions of this Constitution and of any law concerning municipal corporations formed for local government, or concerning counties, shall be liberally construed in their favor. The powers of counties and such municipal corporations shall include not only those granted in express terms, but also those of necessary or fair implication, or incident to the powers expressly conferred, or essential thereto, and not inconsistent with or prohibited by this Constitution

or by law." Robert F. Williams, *The New Jersey State Constitution: A Reference Guide*, updated edition (New Brunswick: Rutgers University Press, 1997), 79.

32. Salmore and Salmore, *New Jersey Politics and Government*, 130–149, 372.

33. For a summary of this case, see Cohen, *Consumer's Republic*, 245–248.

34. Maya Rao, "Affordable-Housing Impasse," *Philadelphia Inquirer*, February 8, 2011; Beth DeFalco, "New Jersey Court to Rule on Affordable Housing," *Philadelphia Inquirer*, April 1, 2011; John Hasse, John Reiser, and Alexander Pichacz, "Evidence of Persistent Exclusionary Effects of Land Use Policy within Historic and Projected Development Patterns in New Jersey: A Case Study of Monmouth and Somerset Counties," paper issued by the Geospatial Research Laboratory, Rowan University, June, 2011, and reported by Megan DeMarco, "Report Blames Zoning Laws for Lack of Affordable Housing in New Jersey," *Star-Ledger*, July 7, 2011.

LIST OF CONTRIBUTORS

MICHAEL BIRKNER, a professor of history at Gettysburg College, is an expert on the Jacksonian Era and has published articles on New Jersey in this period. He has written *McCormick of Rutgers* (2001); *James Buchanan and the Political Crisis of 1850* (1996); *A Country Place No More: A History of Bergenfield, New Jersey* (1994); and *Samuel L. Southard: Jeffersonian Whig* (1984). He also edited, with Paul Stellhorn, *The Governors of New Jersey* (1982) and is currently updating it.

JOHN FEA, an associate professor at Messiah College in Pennsylvania, is the author of *The Way of Improvement Leads Home: Philip Vickers Fithian and the Rural Enlightenment in Early America* (2008). His articles have appeared in a host of scholarly and popular journals, including *The Journal of American History*, *Common-Place*, and *New Jersey History*. He teaches courses on the American Revolution and has been working on the connection of religion to the Revolution in the Mid-Atlantic region for a book tentatively entitled, "A Presbyterian Rebellion: The American Revolution in the Mid-Atlantic."

HOWARD GILLETTE JR., professor emeritus at Rutgers University–Camden and a former director of the Mid-Atlantic Regional Center for the Humanities, works in modern U.S. history with an emphasis on urban and regional planning. His most recent works are *Camden After the Fall: Decline and Renewal in a Post-Industrial City* (2006) and *Civitas by Design: Building Better Cities from the Garden City to the New Urbanism* (2010). He is one of three editors of the online *Encyclopedia of Greater Philadelphia*.

BRIAN GREENBERG, a professor and the Jules Plangere Jr. Chair in American Social History at Monmouth University, is an expert on labor history and the Progressive period. His most recent publications include (with Linda S. Watts) *Social History of the United States: The 1900s* and (with Leon Fink) *Upheaval in the Quiet Zone: 1199SEIU and the Politics of Health Care Unionism* (2nd ed., 2009). He has also published works on industrialization in Albany, New York, and on other labor and social history topics.

LARRY GREENE, a professor of history at Seton Hall University, has most recently co-edited (with Anke Ortlepp of the University of Munich) *Germans and African Americans: Two Centuries of Exchange* (2011) and is working on a book about the Harlem Renaissance. He is the author of a history of African Americans in New Jersey and an article in *New Jersey History* on the Civil War and Reconstruction period, as well as (with Lenworth Gunther) *The New Jersey Afro-American Curriculum Guide* (1997). He has long taught courses and given public lectures on the Civil War and Reconstruction.

GRAHAM RUSSELL GAO HODGES, a professor at Colgate University, has written about slavery in New Jersey in two books: *Root & Branch: African Americans in New York and East Jersey 1613–1863* (1999) and *Slavery and Freedom in the Rural North, Monmouth County, New Jersey* (1997). He has also written on numerous other topics in reviews and essays in historical journals and taught a variety of courses on American history.

PAUL ISRAEL is the director and editor of the Thomas Edison Papers Project at Rutgers University, which is producing electronic and print volumes of Edison's work. He has written *Edison: A Life of Invention* (1998), *From Machine Shop to Industrial Laboratory: Telegraphy and the Changing Context of American Invention, 1830-1920* (1992), and, with Robert Friedel, *Edison's Electric Light* (1986).

MAXINE N. LURIE, professor emerita of history at Seton Hall University, has co-edited *Mapping New Jersey: An Evolving Landscape* (2009) with Peter Wacker; the *Encyclopedia of New Jersey* (2004) with Marc Mappen; as well as the *Minutes of the East Jersey Proprietors*, vol. 4 (1985), with Joanne Walroth. She edited *A New Jersey Anthology* (2nd ed., 2010) and is the author of numerous book chapters and journal articles on New Jersey, most dealing with its early colonial history.

MARC MAPPEN, the former director of the New Jersey Historical Commission, has written numerous articles on New Jersey, including a series for the *New York Times*. He is the author of *There Is More to New Jersey than the Sopranos* (2009) and *Jerseyana: The Underside of New Jersey History* (1992), and the co-editor of the *Encyclopedia of New Jersey* (2004).

G. KURT PIEHLER, who taught at the University of Tennessee, is now an associate professor at Florida State University, and was the founding director of the Rutgers World War II Oral History Project. He has written on military history and World War II, including *Remembering War the American Way* (1995) and *World War II* (2007).

RICHARD VEIT, a professor at Monmouth University, specializes in the historical archaeology of New Jersey and has written on the archaeology of colonial New Jersey, Native Americans, grave markers, and the state's ceramics industry. He has published two books with Rutgers University Press: *New Jersey Cemeteries and Tombstones* (2008) and *Digging New Jersey's Past* (2002). He is also the author of numerous articles on the history and archaeology of New Jersey published in *New Jersey History, Historical Archaeology, Northeast Historical Archaeology,* and other journals.

INDEX

Page numbers in italics refer to illustrations and tables.